The desert – simultaneously alluring and repellent – has a hypnotic presence in Australian culture. The 'Centre' is distant and unknown to most Australians, yet has become a symbol of the country, most recently being promoted as a site for eco-tourism, new age enlightenment, environmental renewal and racial reconciliation. This exciting book reveals the singular impact that the desert, both geographical and metaphorical, has had on Australian identity. While it concentrates on the period from white settlement to the present, it also examines prehistory, touching on the geological significance of the Australian desert. At the heart of the book is the contrast between the European-driven notion of an empty, monotonous wilderness, and the profound spiritual relationship that Aboriginal Australians have with the desert.

Roslynn Haynes is Associate Professor of English at the University of New South Wales. Her previous books include *H. G. Wells: Discoverer of the Future* (1980), *High Tech, High Co$t?: Technology, Society and the Environment* (1990) and *From Faust to Strangelove: Representations of the Scientist in Western Literature* (1994).

Seeking the

Centre

THE AUSTRALIAN DESERT IN LITERATURE, ART AND FILM

Roslynn D. Haynes

CAMBRIDGE
UNIVERSITY PRESS

PUBLISHED BY THE PRESS SYNDICATE OF THE UNIVERSITY OF CAMBRIDGE
The Pitt Building, Trumpington Street, Cambridge, United Kingdom

CAMBRIDGE UNIVERSITY PRESS
The Edinburgh Building, Cambridge CB2 2RU, UK   http://www.cup.cam.ac.uk
40 West 20th Street, New York, NY 10011–4211, USA   http://www.cup.org
10 Stamford Road, Oakleigh, Melbourne 3166, Australia

First published 1998

Printed in Australia by Brown Prior Anderson

Typeset in New Baskerville 10.5/12 pt

Designed by Guy Mirabella

A catalogue record for this book is available from the British Library

National Library of Australia Cataloguing in Publication data

Haynes, R. D. (Roslynn D.).
   Seeking the Centre: the Australian desert in literature, art and film.

   Bibliography.
   Includes index.
   ISBN 0 521 57111 1 (hbk.).

   1. Deserts – Australia, Central. 2. Deserts in literature. 3. Deserts in art.
   4. Australia, Central, in literature. 5. Australia, Central, in art.
   6. Australian, Aborigines – Australia, Central. I. Title.

820.8

ISBN 0 521 57111 1 hardback

Publication of this book was assisted by a grant from the Humanities Research
Program, University of New South Wales.

Australia Foundation
for Culture & the Humanities

Illustrations

COLOUR

BLACK AND WHITE

viii

It is a great pleasure to acknowledge the many and diverse kinds of assistance I have had in writing this book.

A period of Special Studies Project leave from the University of New South Wales, and a grant from the Australian Research Council enabled me to travel to the desert and to spend essential and illuminating hours in art galleries with their collections of desert paintings and drawings. Financial assistance from the Australia Foundation and a subvention from the Humanities Research Program of the University of New South Wales have made it possible to include the fifty colour reproductions that are an integral part of this book.

I have been privileged to receive assistance from experts in many fields who generously provided information, interest and enthusiasm for the project. In particular I would like to thank Richard Kimber of Alice Springs for sharing his wealth of experience about the desert and Aboriginal art; David Boyd, Mandy Martin and Jörg Schmeisser for allowing me to see works in progress at their respective studios and taking precious time from their creative endeavours to talk to me about their work; Mary Eagle, Curator of Australian Art, Wally Caruana, Curator of Aboriginal Art, and other members of staff at the National Gallery of Australia who allowed me access to the collections; Jane Hylton, Curator of Australian Art, and staff at the Art Gallery of South Australia who welcomed me and made time to show me relevant examples of the gallery's collection of works on paper; Peter Haynes, Director of the Nolan Gallery, who advised and assisted with the reproductions of the Nolan paintings; John Masterson whose photography is truly great art; the many people with whom I checked specific details of this book; Frances Parsons who read and criticised the almost-final typescript; Sally Moss who copy-edited the final typescript; and the many good friends and colleagues who continued to ask how the book was progressing and listened gallantly to the latest saga.

Most of all I would like to thank my family. My husband Raymond has shared with me the unforgettable experience of driving and camping in Central Australia; my daughter Rowena took time off from her Science Honours year researching lizards in the Simpson Desert to write 'Some Facts about Australian Deserts' and to key in the Bibliography, not to mention reading and constructively criticising the final draft. Together with my daughter Nicky they gave me endless encouragement and support, at many levels and in many forms, ranging from perfectly timed mugs of coffee, through hours of impromptu discussions, to stunning desert photos placed on my computer as inspiration. Above all they made it fun.

ix

My clearest memory of primary school history lessons is that they concentrated almost exclusively on the explorers of the Australian inland. In the back of our Bartholomew and Cramp school atlas was the classic series of exploration maps, showing an all-black Australia becoming increasingly yellow and written upon with European names. 'Why were there no names when it was black?' I asked once, and gullibly accepted the teacher's weary explanation that there were no names before the explorers and settlers brought them from England. After a token gesture towards Cook, Bass and Flinders, and having despatched Mitchell, Hume and Hovell with some ant tracks wobbling down the right side of our own smudgy maps, we trudged, year after year, through the sandy wastes with Eyre, Sturt and Stuart, and with Leichhardt, Burke and Wills, wishing fervently that they, and especially the records of their journeys, had not survived to plague us. We were running out of colours and kinds of dots in which to record their separate journeys. What did they achieve anyway? I would seditiously wonder. No one appeared to live in this place with virtually no names on it, and certainly none of us ever wanted to go there. At high school Australian history gave way to apparently more important things – European history and the causes of World War I. I rejoiced; it seemed that I would never again have to think about the Australian explorers.

Australian literature, as represented in school anthologies, was depressingly similar. Paterson's drovers and the down-and-out swagmen of Lawson's poems inhabited the same hostile territory where only men ventured, all too often leaving their bones as testimony to blinding sandstorms and death from thirst. Australian landscape painting seemed similarly preoccupied with the presentation of a drought-ridden land where no one went and nothing happened.

Decades later the sandy blur of Australian literature snapped into focus for me when I read novels and poetry by contemporary Australian women writers and was subsequently lured to reconsider their predecessors, viewed through post-colonial and feminist lenses. Freed from the primary school obligation of nationalist admiration, I found the writing and art intriguing and provocative. The desert, in particular, emerged as a continuing preoccupation, but one with ever-changing innuendoes and resonances. I wanted to investigate this extraordinary gamut of emotional responses to the desert, from execration to rapture.

When I set out to write this book I intended to concentrate almost exclusively on the literature and art of desert landscape – literature being defined as poetry, drama and novel – with a gesture towards the more notable critics. Had it occurred to me in advance that I would have to engage again with those explorers, I would possibly have abandoned the project. But I quickly realised that I could not escape them: the literary and artistic perceptions of the landscape remained haunted by them. And I, too, became absorbed in the journals of those same explorers, fascinated by the way successive versions of their journeys changed over time and for different audiences; the psychology of their motivation and self-justification; the heroic public face of exploration versus the private anguish and self-doubt; the Gothic fears; the construction of a gendered land that seemed to explain so much about the social attitudes of twentieth-century Australia. We cannot see the desert landscape without their influence.

The attitudes they generated are deeply embedded in two of the most notorious news stories about the Centre in recent times.

In 1980 the Chamberlain family – Michael, Lindy and their children – were on a camping holiday near Uluru (then known almost exclusively as Ayers Rock). While the parents were cooking an evening meal at the communal barbecue, and the two boys and the baby, Azaria, were in their tent a few metres away, the baby was dragged from the tent allegedly by a dingo. Azaria was never seen again. With amazing swiftness this individual tragedy was appropriated by the nation and slotted into the 200-year-old construct of the innocent white child killed by malevolent Nature. In this version of the Lost Child motif, a favourite subject in literature and art, the Bush was replaced by a wild animal (since the extinction of the Tasmanian tiger, the dingo is Australia's only carnivorous mammal of any size) and a mysterious monolith, Ayers Rock. Formerly regarded chiefly as an intriguing geological oddity, Ayers Rock was suddenly recast as a sinister place, site of macabre Aboriginal religious rituals. The exact nature of these was never spelled out, but suggestions of bloodletting ceremonies were made. The name change to Uluru, already proposed by Aboriginal groups, was accelerated by the bad press Ayers Rock received internationally after the Azaria Chamberlain disaster. The failure of police or rangers to find any remains of the baby was a powerful addition to the mystery, invoking comparisons with both the actual disappearance of the explorer Ludwig Leichhardt and the fictional disappearance of three school girls and a teacher from Hanging Rock in Joan Lindsay's novel *Picnic at Hanging Rock*.[1] The disappearance and death of a child in the desert is fair game for any horror stories, any mysterious cult happenings that can be invented. The name Azaria was discovered to mean 'sacrifice in the wilderness', sparking rumours that the child's parents were involved in a cult of devil worship and ritual murder and had travelled to Uluru specifically to sacrifice her. Only the accumulated Gothic fears associated with the desert could have nurtured such bizarre hysteria.

In December 1986 two teenage boys, Simon Amos from Adelaide and James Annetts from Sydney, died of thirst and dehydration in the Great Sandy Desert, 400 kilometres from the station where they had been employed as jackaroos. Disenchanted with the harsh life they were expected to endure, and virtually imprisoned on the station, they had been trying to escape to the nearest town, Kununurra, when they ran out of petrol and water. The desert is a harsh environment; mistakes are often fatal. Mistakes made while crossing a road or swimming can, of course, be equally fatal – but that is not the cultural perception. Dying of thirst is a spectre that haunts our culture, the legacy of the explorers: Eyre struggling on, parched and desperate for water on his trek along the Great Australian Bight; Sturt and his party marooned at Depôt Glen by drought which ultimately forced them to retreat; Leichhardt lost for reasons unknown, but assumed to have died of thirst; Lasseter dying, according to rumour, within a short distance of his alleged gold reef.

Notorious modern disasters notwithstanding, at the end of the twentieth century the desert has, more often than not, been embraced by tourists and Australians alike. Today the once-dreaded Birdsville Track is thick with traffic as four-wheel drivers race north from Marree to leave their business cards and messages of triumph tacked to the ceiling of the Birdsville pub. Even the Simpson Desert, last of the Australian deserts to be crossed, seems to offer little challenge to the many retirees, the 'grey nomads', who swarm across its parallel dunes, tea towels fluttering from their well-equipped vehicles. There is a brisk market in caps and tee-shirts proclaiming 'I conquered the Simpson'.

This book examines the changing reaction of white Australians to the desert – from fear to delight – and the contrast between these responses and the relationship that indigenous Australians have with their land. Writing it has been a fascinating experience, involving a steep learning curve. With a background in science and literature, I found myself now engaging with history, geography, art history and criticism, and especially with Aboriginal understandings of the desert that continually called into question the assumptions of European-derived culture. In each area I was fortunate to meet experts who were extremely generous with their knowledge and time.

Most of all, I enjoyed being in the desert and having my preconceptions shattered, preconceptions that had been shaped largely by writers and artists and, before them, those ever-present patriarchal figures, the explorers. My clearest memories are of the amazing variety of the desert – not just the diversity of the well-known scenic spots on every tourist's itinerary, but the differences between two places as little as five kilometres – or even perhaps a metre – apart: different ripple patterns made by the winds in the sand, different tracks made by birds, lizards, desert spiders, thorny dragons, or tiny marsupials. The birds, especially, are beautiful and varied: ubiquitous crested pigeons with the garter-stitch pattern of grey and iridescent pink along their wings and brilliant orange eyes; white cockatoos, corellas and galahs shrieking joyfully at the artificial wetland created by Purni Bore; pelicans gliding majestically along the Cooper at Innamincka.

However much you have seen in pictures, nothing prepares you for the desert landscape. The vastness, the sense of space, the silence and most of all the colours: the deep rust red of iron-oxide sand outlining the silver trunks of ghost gums; the brilliant white of crusted salt against a cobalt blue sky. Yet most Europeans of last century, obsessed with their search for green, saw only monotony in such a scene. It is the artists, writers and photographers of the last hundred years who have taught us to see the desert differently. The absence of conventional European markers of perspective and the clear, dry atmosphere allow us the rare sensation of seeing both an immense distance and minute detail, so that the concluding lines of Les Murray's poem 'Equanimity' seem extraordinarily appropriate:

> a field all foreground, and equally all background,
> like a painting of equality. Of infinite detailed extent
> like God's attention. Where nothing is diminished by perspective.[2]

ROSLYNN D. HAYNES

For Raymond, Rowena, Nicky and Damien

We would like to thank the following for permission to reproduce copyright material:

HarperCollins Publishers for extracts from: 'The Birdsville Track' by Douglas Stewart from his *Selected Poems*; extracts from 'Australia' by A.D. Hope from his *Collected Poems*; extracts from 'Envoi' by James McAuley from his *Collected Poems*; and extracts from 'Poet, Leichardt in Theatre' and 'Eyre All Alone' by Francis Webb from his *Collected Poems*.

ETT Imprint for extracts from Ernestine Hill, *The Great Australian Loneliness*.

Johns Hopkins University Press for extract from *Nature Pictorialized* by Gina Crandell.

Sheil Land Associates Ltd. for extracts from *A Counterfeit Silence* © Randolph Stow 1969, first published by Angus & Robertson.

Gerald Murnane for extract from 'The Plains' reprinted by permission of the author.

Les Murray for extracts from 'Equanimity'.

George Seddon for extract from *Landprints: Reflections on Place and Landscape*.

Wakefield Press for 'I do not Climb the Rock' by Kevin Roberts.

Every effort has been made to obtain permission to use copyright material reproduced in this book. The publishers would be pleased to hear from copyright holders they have not been able to contact.

Deserts form a major terrestrial environment, occupying over one-third of the Earth's land surfaces. They are characterised by evapo-transpiration that exceeds rainfall and by consequent aridity. In general, temperate deserts usually have less than 200 millimetres of rainfall per year. The clarity of the atmosphere above most deserts allows high penetration of solar radiation. Daytime temperatures are therefore often very high (over 60 or 70 degrees Celsius)and night-time cooling is rapid, yielding huge diurnal (daily) as well as annual temperature ranges.

Australia is often described as the driest of the continents outside the polar region. This results from two characteristics: firstly the extent of Australia's arid zone, which covers more than seventy per cent of the country; and secondly the low mean precipitation and runoff across the continent. Australian deserts are varied, containing a wide range of landscapes – from sand dunes, open stony gibbers, claypans and breakaway rocks ('residuals') left after erosion to broad heavily vegetated river channels.

Six major deserts are found in Australia's interior: the Great Sandy, the Tanami, the Gibson, the Great Victoria, the Simpson and Sturt's Stony Desert. However, the arid zone does not contain distinct boundaries; rather, the different types of arid zone merge.

Australian deserts are not considered to be hyper-arid deserts, like Africa's Namib or Sahara deserts which have a reasonable ground cover of vegetation. Nevertheless they experience the highest variability in, and lowest predictability of, rainfall and temperature regimes of anywhere in the world. This means that the array of native flora and fauna is adapted to cope not only with the harsh aridity of the desert but also the unpredictability and large variation in timing and quantity of rainfall. Scientists have marvelled at the adaptation of taxa to the poor environment, which enables endurance through periods with diminished productivity and unpredictable droughts. Frugality in energy use is of utmost importance. Animals deal with particularly harsh periods by migration, by producing eggs and then dying, or by changes in activity.

Among the features of Australian deserts that reduce the productivity of the environment are the extremely poor soils. Due to their age, they are markedly deficient in nutrients such as nitrogen and phosphorus.

Deserts, although superficially simple, often exhibit great spatial and

temporal complexity of ecological structure. Australian deserts are characterised further by exceptional richness in the number of species that co-occur.
For example, Australian deserts have the highest diversity of reptiles in the
world, with up to forty species discovered to coexist per square kilometre. The
continent's arid-zone vegetation is largely dominated by spinifex grasses
(*Triodia* species) which are endemic to Australia, and comprise up to half of
the ground cover, and approximately ninety-six per cent of the plant biomass
in local areas. Many scientists have noted the importance of spinifex in shaping arid-zone faunal communities. The plant, with its hemispherical growth
form and closely packed leaves, provides a food resource for a wide array of
insects, which in turn support the many reptiles, mammals and birds found
there. As well, spinifex hummocks provide stability in the face of shifting sand
dunes and, importantly, provide an area of compacted sand around the roots.
This allows animals to burrow without the sand collapsing on them. Also, by
holding air within its folded, outwardly projecting leaves, the plant minimises
its own diurnal temperature fluctuations, providing internal shade in the heat
of the day and holding warm air in the spaces at night when the general
temperature drops significantly.

An interesting ecological feature of the Australian arid zone is the importance of fire in regulating the diversity and abundance of species that are
present in particular areas at any given stage of the fire cycle. Some species are
adapted to have seeds survive fire and germinate afterwards, while other plants
survive as roots or just trunks. Animals survive fire just as they do harsh
periods – by migration, or some by hibernation.

Deserts are particularly vulnerable to ecological disturbance, owing to
their fragile ecosystems, low population numbers of the resident species and
refined adaptations to very detailed micro-environments. Australian deserts
have been placed under threat by the introduction of exotic species, pollution,
extensive clearing of vegetation, modification to the structure of plant communities, altered fire regimes and the change in the range of feral animals.
These all put this fragile ecosystem at high risk. An affirmation of the importance of the Australian desert and an ability to see the beauty and treasure at
the heart of Australia are integral to its preservation.

ROWENA HAYNES

A note to the reader

While recognising that there are six separately named deserts scattered west
of the Great Dividing Range and encompassing an immense diversity of landforms, vegetation and fauna, I have referred throughout this book to 'desert'
as a single, homogeneous entity because I am primarily concerned here with a
cultural concept, the *notion* of 'desert'.[3] Again, while the desert and the Bush
are not divided by fences, I have endeavoured to treat them as separate entities, excluding from my consideration any art or literature, such as *Capricornia*

Australia, showing relevant desert regions and places.

Introduction

Every Eye sees differently. As the Eye, such the Object.

WILLIAM BLAKE[1]

Before it can ever be a repose for the senses, landscape is the work of the mind. Its scenery is built up as much from strata of memory as from layers of rock.

SIMON SCHAMA[2]

This book traces the unique role of the desert in Australian culture – from traditional Aboriginal beliefs and observances to the literature, art and film of the last two hundred years. In the process of writing it I have drawn on the insights of numerous other disciplines, including ecology, geography, archaeology and geology; and rather than adhere to a single, consistent viewpoint I have taken a variety of approaches – post-colonial, feminist, post-structural and comparative – where these seemed most helpful in illuminating the topic.

Why the desert?

In his recent book *Landscape and Memory* historian Simon Schama explores the way in which people's view of landscape is conditioned by the cultural myths that have come to surround groups of natural features and the connotations they carry for us, even from the fairytales we heard as children. Schama's childhood was spent beside the River Thames so, not surprisingly, one of his three categories is water. The other two are woods and rocks, also central to the European consciousness. In a similar vein the French philosopher Gaston Bachelard writes of forests as having a 'before-us' essence, 'whereas for fields and meadows, my dreams and recollections accompany all the different phases of tilling and harvesting. . . . But forests reign in the past.'[3]

In Australia it is the desert that epitomises this 'before-us' quality. In our collective imagination the site of ancient myth, of spiritual dimension and cultural rebirth is peculiarly the desert, a landscape that for more centuries than

European civilisation can lay claim to has symbolised the land's endurance, provoking creative reappraisals of our place in Nature and the meaning of our existence. When we read of progressively older geological and archaeological finds setting the age of the continent at more than 800 million years, the River Finke in Central Australia at 350 million years, and Aboriginal habitation nudging 50,000 years we are scarcely surprised.

In geographical terms, seventy per cent of Australia is classified as arid, making it, statistically, the driest continent in the world after Antarctica. However, statistics mean little in the Centre. The average annual rainfall in these arid areas may fulfil the definition of being less than 250 millimetres but months of flooding may alternate with years of total drought. In 1996 the publican at William Creek, a one-pub, one telephone-box (solar-powered) 'town' near Lake Eyre, told me that the Bureau of Meteorology in Adelaide had rung him recently to ask whether he would agree to monitor the rain gauge in the area. He said okay, he would, but wasn't his neighbour up the track doing it? He was, in theory, the Bureau said, but he was useless; he hadn't registered any rainfall with them for eighteen months. 'Well,' drawled the publican, 'that just could be because it hasn't rained here for eighteen months.'

As well as extremes of rainfall, the Australian arid region is notable for the extraordinary diversity of its landforms, vegetation and fauna. While the spectacular red sand dunes of the Simpson Desert and the familiar landmarks of Uluru (Ayers Rock) and Kata Tjuta (the Olgas) may be the most widely known features, the arid terrain includes a great variety of surfaces and textures: chains of mountains such as the MacDonnell Ranges, the Musgraves, the Kimberley and the Hamersleys, rising up like the ribs of an ancient carcass; the striated 'beehive' structures near King's Canyon in the George Gill Range, and in the Pilbara; the most extensive areas of woody scrubland (mulga) in Australia; oases of rare plants – ancient cycads and the unique Red Cabbage Palm, *Livistona mariae* – clustered in a few refuge areas that retain the underground moisture levels of an earlier and wetter climatic period; the brilliant white coastal dunes of the Great Australian Bight and, inland from them on the north-east edge of the Nullarbor Plain, the 35-million year old dunes, probably the oldest in the world, that mark the one-time coast of the continent; inselbergs, like Uluru, Kata Tjuta and Mount Connor, seeming to rise sheer from the desert plain; hot mound springs like Dalhousie Springs where the emerging temperature is forty-three degrees Celsius; claypans with a thin crystalline skin or a surface of baked mud, fissured into chocolate-coloured plaques that curl at the edges; and salt lakes, most notably the mirage-haunted Lake Eyre, the lowest depression in the continent and the driest, with an average annual rainfall of less than 100 millimetres per year.

In Aboriginal culture this bountiful variety of geology and biology is documented so richly and in such minute detail that even the smallest mound or declivity has, for the local people, a complex history and meaning. But variation has featured rarely in non-indigenous Australian art of the desert and even more rarely in its literature. Diversity offends against the image conveyed by the European notion of 'desert' as wilderness – vast, empty, monotonous. In these post-modernist times we recognise that the landscape we observe is a cultural construct based on our desire for either a mirror to reflect particular social values (the orderly constructed landscapes of the Enlightenment, the alpine crags of the German Romantic sublime, the Manifest Destiny school of American wilderness paintings in an age of expansionism) or a dialectical complement to our deficiencies (rural scenes as an escape from industrialism, cubism as an alternative to political and social complexities). Even at the base level of selecting what natural features we consider to be worth observing and editing out those that fail to interest us, we are continually creating the landscape that we 'see'. Add to this the multiple ways in which landscape may be depicted, the emotional content of the work, and the culturally conditioned response of the reader or viewer, and we can see what heterogeneous images the supposed 'mirror' held up to nature may reflect. But few other landscapes have been so variously perceived or have elicited such diverse responses as the Australian desert. In the two centuries since European settlement of the continent it has been promoted from 'best forgotten' oblivion to centre stage prominence. Once execrated for its failure to provide an inland sea, the Centre is now the most exported image of Australia: in tourist offices around the world Uluru vies with the Sydney Opera House as *the* icon of the continent. Why is this? How has such a reversal occurred? This book attempts to answer these questions.

3

Reinventing the void

As we shall see in Chapter 1, traditional Aboriginal understanding of the land was uniquely personal and spiritual, an I–thou relationship that embraced all aspects of life including religious and cultural values. The land was the source of life, creativity and renewal and this was as true for the desert as for the rainforest. Antithetical to such a relational interaction with the land was the Cartesian philosophy on which the observations of the Europeans were predicated. The cultural studies critic Ross Gibson argues that 'modern Australia is precisely a product of the Renaissance mentality that instigated the notion of an environment other than and external to the individual ego. This is the mentality that the English Colonial Office sent to the continent'.[4] This mindset is epitomised in the obsession with mapping that drove Europeans to the ends of the Earth to name and measure every geographical feature. As critic John Vernon remarks, 'It is no coincidence that Descartes, who formulated the subject–object dichotomy, also invented co-ordinate geometry, which made the theory of functions and accurate, scientific map-making possible.'[5] The map spells the end of the I–thou relationship because, once space is mapped (that is, enclosed, objectified and localised in relation to all other spaces), the observer is perforce either a detached subject locked out of this world and observing it from a distance, or else included within the map as another object.

Chapter 2 examines not only this Cartesian preoccupation but also the cultural resonances associated with the notion of 'desert' that European settlers brought as part of their baggage.

The obsession with mapping the continent ran in tandem with the settlers' desire for more pastoral and agricultural land, but for both purposes the desert presented a front of obdurate non-cooperation. Chapter 3 traces the nineteenth-century explorers' dismal attempts to subdue the wayward geography of Australia's central desert to the domination of the map. Seeking landmarks and peculiarities to record, they found for the most part only a vast and monotonous sameness. During his expedition to the Great Victoria Desert in 1875 Ernest Giles wrote in high dudgeon, 'Geographical landmarks have been terribly scarce upon this expedition ... the land is featureless and only the water [one spring] is name-worthy'.[6] To the explorers, then, the desert was a 'hideous blank'[7] where named features should be: nothing, void. Little wonder that they began to write of themselves as embarked on an archetypal journey in the tradition of Melmoth the Wanderer or the Ancient Mariner 'alone on a wide, wide sea', an image peculiarly apposite in a terrain of wave-like sand dunes or the sea-mimicry of glistening salt lakes and Fata Morgana. For Charles Sturt, obsessed with finding an inland sea, the imagery was overpowering. As we see in Chapter 4, the explorers became adept at constructing in their mind a desert that complemented their self-image of heroism, even in defeat. In their published reports exploration gave way to exploit.[8] Defeat in an 'impossible' task becomes more honourable than success, since the latter presupposes an easier assignment. The desert explorers succeeded in convincing not only themselves but also their contemporaries and successive generations of writers that they were heroic in defeat and that their endurance was of more lasting importance than the original goals of their expedition. Vilified as the destroyer of the nation's heroes, the desert was cast as antagonist in the evolving history of a nation that had fought no wars against military oppressors until the mythology of Anzac offered a rival testing ground.

If the desert was a map-maker's nightmare, it was equally inimical to artists' requirements for the standard conventions of framing and perspective. Chapter 5 outlines their frustration with the refusal of the desert terrain to conform to the criteria of contemporary landscape practice, and how this caused them to hammer it into an approximation of the lineaments prescribed by the European schools of the Picturesque or the sublime. For an artist such as Ludwig Becker, fixated on notions of the sublime, the desert, with its ghostly mirages, its potential terrors to survival and the lure of mystical enlightenment, was the counterpart of the Alps for the Romantic artists, especially his personal hero Caspar David Friedrich.

In the latter half of the nineteenth century, when Britain's confidence in its empire was shaken by uprisings in India and Africa, it became fashionable to see the colonies as contributing the flower of their manhood to reinvigorate a worn-out imperial centre. In the ripping yarns of the 1890s the Australian desert offered an alternative to Rider Haggard's Africa as a venue for masculine adventures that simultaneously glorified the empire and allowed men to indulge their desire to escape the restrictions and responsibilities of a society they perceived as petticoat-governed. These fictional desert-darers, however, unlike their real-life predecessors the explorers, are rewarded by both fame and fortune, the latter usually involving the discovery of a mountain of gold. Underlying the construction of this role for the desert as the scene of both danger and wealth was a dual political motive – the provision of soldiers for the empire and a statement of colonial optimism in the nation's future.

So attractive was this manly image of desert conquest that when it ceased to provide novelty in fiction it continued to supply a role model for the documentary writings of travellers such as Ernestine Hill, C.E.W. Bean, George Farwell, 'Bill' Harney and others. The opening of the Trans-Australian Railway in 1915 vastly increased the accessibility of the Centre, and public interest was fuelled by diverse factors, not least a belated interest in the country's indigenous inhabitants, now concentrated in the desert regions. Having signally failed to fulfil Darwinian predictions of an early demise as an inferior race, the Aborigines had been subjected to a blanket of silence until it became advantageous to appropriate them as objects of scientific and cultural investigation. The anthropological publications of Baldwin Spencer and Francis Gillen, highly regarded internationally and later supplemented by the work of Charles Mountford and T.G.H. Strehlow, not only allowed Aborigines to be cast as nonthreatening but, by a sleight-of-hand transfer of their characteristics to their predominantly desert habitat, reinforced British rights to the continent. Since the Aborigines were regarded as a primitive race it was reasoned that their ancient culture (how ancient was not then realised) had remained fossilised, unaltered through centuries – a fallacy that has only recently been challenged.[9] By extension the desert was declared to be an unchanged land, geologically and geographically. In retrospect we can see this as a classic example of what the critic Fredric Jameson has called the 'political unconscious'.[10] The popular notion of the Australian desert as unchanging, the land that time forgot, conveniently accorded with and embellished the British political myth of *terra nullius*: before 1788 Australia had been not only a land of no people but a place where nothing of significance had happened, a Sleeping Beauty land passively awaiting the arrival of its princely (and pre-ordained) colonists.

During the 1930s and 40s the Australian desert was discovered by painters. Aridity became interestingly different and a red landscape was suddenly beautiful; its simple shapes and lines were seen to provide ready-made Modernist studies; and vastness and monotony provoked artists to devise new forms of composition. Chapter 9 traces the origins of this visual revolution in factors as diverse as the artistic record of Australia's role in the Middle East campaigns of World War I, air transport, modernism and the ready availability of colour film. Russell Drysdale's paintings of emaciated figures in a surreal outback landscape and Sidney Nolan's aerial panoramas of Central Australia were, in turn, to have a profound impression on literature, suggesting a powerful local metaphor for existential angst and a modernist perception of spiritual poverty in both the individual and the nation. The desert assumed a Gothic role in psychodramas that enacted a mythic journey into the self.

Inevitably the symbolic journey into the interior recalled the inland explorers of the previous century and again, as will be seen in Chapter 11, artists provided the immediate stimulus. Nolan's Burke and Wills series, as well as Albert Tucker's 'Antipodean Heads' and his subsequent identification of the explorer with the relief map of the continent, inspired writers to revise the psychology of exploration. The patriotic hero, conquering a treacherous land for the good of nation and empire, was replaced with an arrogant monomaniac, careless of his companions' survival and obsessed with acquiring public fame or personal fulfilment. Patrick White's novel *Voss* and Francis Webb's explorer poems are the best known of many literary representations in which the explorer's journey becomes a metaphor for a personal spiritual quest. In such treatments, the desert provides a uniquely symbolic landscape, overlaid with powerful imagery drawn from the Judaeo–Christian tradition of self-renunciation in the wilderness.

More recently the desert, representing as it does the antithesis of materialism, has been recast to epitomise the concerns of environmentalism and a worldwide interest in indigenous cultures. So-called 'eco-tours' to the Centre, especially those featuring an 'Aboriginal experience', attract tourist dollars approaching the fabled wealth of Lasseter's reef. Such tours not only provide the intrinsic interest of novelty but contrive to promote a residual glow of virtue: travelling in the desert, even within the comfort cocoon of an airconditioned bus and with five-star overnight accommodation, suggests a satisfying element of self-renunciation, of anti-materialism, perhaps spiritual rebirth. New Age cults and the lucrative market in Aboriginal artefacts are drawn as if by a magnet to Alice Springs, capital of desert land, and to its internationally famous icon, Uluru.

Ironically, then, the desert, considered for more than a century of white settlement to be a national disgrace, has begun to liberate Australian landscape and consciousness from its subservience to European dominance. The Centre, now recognised as home to the world's oldest surviving culture, provides Australia with a claim to the antiquity and historical respectability that its white settlers, marginalised by the European Centre, have craved for two hundred years. In an age of sensitivity to over-population and urban over-crowding, the immensity of space that so terrified British colonists has become an enviable asset. Silence, immensity, and ancientness, the characteristics of the desert, are now eminently marketable.

The question of ownership

Where does this burgeoning interest in the desert leave the indigenous communities? Has their culture once again been appropriated through the demand that it remain locked in its traditions as stereotyped for tourist consumption, the archetypal primitive frozen in time? Chapter 15 looks briefly at the ways in which Aboriginal artists (performing as well as visual) are evolving new representations of the desert as the source of their spiritual identity, focus of political aspirations and symbol of reconciliation with white Australians. When I first began researching this book (in the wake of the Mabo legislation)[11], and while drafting it (during the time of the Wik decision)[12], I was optimistic about such a synthesis. Now I am not so sure that we are not about to re-run the tragic film of white Australian arrogance, capitalist greed and spiritual blindness, with even less excuse than the first time around. I hope I am wrong and that, as a nation, we may once again discover that 'from deserts the prophets [rather than merely profits] come'.

I owe an obvious debt of ideas to such seminal writings as Tim Bonyhady's *Burke and Wills: From Melbourne to Myth*, Paul Carter's *The Road to Botany Bay*, Wally Caruana's *Aboriginal Art*, Robert Dixon's *Writing the Colonial Adventure*, Simon Ryan's *The Cartographic Eye*, Robert Sellick's unpublished thesis The Epic Confrontation: Australian Exploration and the Centre, and *Dreamings* edited by Peter Sutton, to name only a small selection. However, I believe that this work is original in its scope and in its tracing of interconnections and influences between literature, art and science to provide an overview of the cultural importance of the Australian desert.

Part I

ENCOUNTERING THE DESERT

'One Land, One Law, One People'
Ngangatja apu wiya, ngayuku tjamu–
This is not a rock, it is my grandfather.
This is a place where the dreaming
comes up, right up from inside the ground.

GEORGE TINAMIN[1]

These creatures, these great creatures, are just as much alive
today as they were in the beginning. They are everlasting and
will never die. They are always part of the land and nature as
we are. We cannot change and nor can they. Our connection to
all things natural is spiritual.

SILAS ROBERTS[2]

Today most people have their first encounter with the Australian desert from
an aeroplane window. Flying across a vast stretch of seemingly featureless country with no sign of a straight line, that characteristic signature of civilisation, is
an experience that some find depressingly monotonous. Others take comfort
in reflecting that there still remains a tract of pristine wilderness unmarked by
human beings. Both views are fundamentally wrong. At ground level – even
apart from the spectacular MacDonnell Ranges, the monoliths and boulders
strewn across it and the deep gorges carved by ancient rivers – the Australian
desert is enormously vibrant and diverse for those who are able to relate
to what is actually there, rather than measuring it against preconceived notions
of landscape. In terms of human settlement this land has been home to the
world's oldest known culture, that of the indigenous Australians, for a period
of time that is now agreed to amount to at least 50,000 years. Looking from
his plane window, Aboriginal poet Jack Davis saw something entirely
different:

Some call it desert
But it is full of life
pulsating life
if one knows where to find it
in the land I love.[3]

To begin to understand Aboriginal people's perception of the desert we must appreciate the inseparable trinity that is fundamental to their culture and beliefs: the Ancestors – spiritual beings who created and continue to nurture the land in which they dwell; the biological species, including humans, that the Ancestors created; and the living, sustaining land. In this unique ideology the land is the vital nexus between the physical and the spiritual, between the temporal and the eternal, for, as the continuing dwelling place of supernatural beings, it participates in both realms. Consequently, unlike the myths of origin of most religions, Aboriginal creation stories locate the creative power not remotely in the heavens but deep within the land itself. Originally, it is believed, the land was flat and featureless, but during the Dreaming, a concept that will be discussed below, mythical creative spirits came forth from the earth, appearing in the form of humans, animals, plants, or even inanimate elements such as fire and water. The 'birth places' from which the spirits emerged became the first sacred sites, endowed with the life and power of these super-natural entities.[4] By their presence and actions, and particularly during their legendary travels, these autochthonous Beings (that is, coming from the earth itself), male and female Ancestors of all that is, created the landforms that have existed since this time and remain permeated by their presence. So the level, treeless plains or *Yarntayi* that lie between the long parallel sandhills or *jilji* of the Great Sandy Desert are believed by the local Walmajarri people to have been formed by two giant mythical snakes travelling from east to west and forcing a swathe through the *jilji* and trees in their path,[5] while two ancestral sisters, crawling across the land, imprinted a winding creek bed.[6]

Having completed their epic work of creation, the Ancestral Beings sank back into the earth, in many cases at the site where they had first emerged, or else transformed themselves into topographical features – rocks, trees, water-holes, claypans, declivities – which, along with the sites of their particular exploit, are revered as continuing foci of supernatural power. The radius of influence emanating from them is not visually defined, but its extent is known precisely to the clans of the area and rigorously respected.[7] After a life spent with the Aranda people of Central Australia, Ted Strehlow wrote:

> In the scores of thousands of square miles that constitute the Aranda-speaking area there was not a single striking feature which was not associated with an episode in one of the many sacred myths, or with a verse in one of the many sacred songs, in which aboriginal religious beliefs found their expression.[8]

These landmarks are further venerated as visible reminders of the 'Law' laid down by the Ancestors and passed down through traditional observance. The 'Law' comprises obligations to perform religious ceremonies, to obey rules of behaviour such as kinship laws and food prohibitions, and to observe zones of avoidance associated with places or sights forbidden to particular age or gender groups. So intimate is the connection between the Dreaming and the 'Law'

12

that the same word is often applied to both – *jukurrpa* in the language of the Warlpiri, *tjukurpa* in Pitjantjatjara. In particular the 'Law' specifies the responsibility of the people for their land. As the land nurtures them both phys- ically and spiritually, so they have a duty to care for it physically (by clearing waterholes, by regularly firing patches of grass) and spiritually (by performing the appropriate ceremonies to restore its fertility and honour the Ancestral Beings within it). Thus poet George Tinamin's triad – Land, Law and People – quoted at the head of this chapter is a trenchant statement of the fundamental, intimate and enduring connection between the land, the Ancestors of the Dreaming as givers of the Law, and the communities who commemorate them.

Although Aboriginal culture recognises two spheres of being, one approx- imating to the physical world and the other to an invisible realm inhabited by spiritual beings, these are not separate but coexist in continuous communica- tion.[9] People may enter the spirit world through the process of dreaming and, conversely, spirits may be induced to enter the physical world during the per- formance of the ceremonies they have instituted. The spirit world, often called the Dreaming (a translation of the Aranda word *ulchurringa* derived from *altjerri*, to dream)[10], is eternal and self-sufficient, but the physical world too is not merely temporal and contingent; it is indwelt by that eternal dimension. This numinous quality of the land means that there is no distinction, such as Western culture understands, between external object and inner meaning, between signifier and referent.[11] Since the seventeenth century Europeans have been taught to look at the world around them as a set of material objects. The primary sense of investigation, sight, is used to define, objectify and sepa- rate what is observed from the observer. The mechanical exploitation of such a reified world is regarded as logical and necessary. Aborigines' perception of their environment is entirely different. It is a profoundly respectful and reli- gious relationship, not with objects but with spiritual entities. It also carries a permanent responsibility to observe the Law and to act as co-creators with the Ancestors in the ceremonies prescribed to renew the land. The sacred songs and ceremonies that honour the deeds of the Ancestors are believed to have been given to the people by those same beings. There is thus a strong obliga- tion to ensure that they are performed and transmitted unchanged through generations. On the other hand, a sense of spiritual power is believed to emanate from the sacred places. Aboriginal writer Ruby Langford, who was born at Box Ridge Mission, Coraki, in the mid-1930s, describes her surprise at this unexpected insight on her first visit to Uluru:

13

> It was like a huge animal that was asleep in the middle of nowhere. We came
> closer and I could feel the goosebumps and the skin tightening at the back of
> my neck. Everyone else was quiet. It made me think of our tribal beginnings,
> and this to me was like the beginning of our time and culture. Time was
> suddenly shortened to include all of history in the present, and it was stretched
> to a way of seeing the earth that was thousands of years old.[12]

The spirit of the land

All Aboriginal peoples are individually linked to a particular geographic site which remains their spiritual home and provides their identity.[13] It is significant, in this regard, that they, possibly alone among indigenous peoples, have no myth of alienation from nature equivalent to the Genesis account of the Fall in Judaeo–Christian tradition. To them the desert is not a place of punishment, a wilderness for those banished from Eden; on the contrary, like the most fertile country, it is imprinted with spiritual meaning and riches, invisible to the pragmatic gaze of Europeans. Because natural species are used as symbols to identify and distinguish social groups, Aboriginal culture could be described as totemistic in Levi-Strauss's terms.[14] But this identification is less for the material purpose of ensuring the increase of a food source than to commemorate the totemic Ancestors.[15]

Unlike Western science, then, Aboriginal knowledge is embedded in a complex teleological framework that can never be deduced from observation, but only by initiation into the traditional lore that provides the contextual key. For the Aborigines, the whole land is semiotic, a complex web of signs, pointing beyond themselves to a spiritual meaning. As anthropologists Catherine and Ronald Berndt have remarked: 'The whole land is full of signs: a land humanised so that it could be used and read by Aborigines . . . read as clearly as if it were bristling with notice-boards.'[16] But without the spiritual context no one can read the country, any more than we could decode the road signs for approaching curves without understanding the convention that the bottom of the sign represents the nearer part of the road and the top the part further away. For Aborigines, the signs of the country both point to, and are explained by, the continuing presence of the particular beings that created these landforms and now reside within them.

The divergence between this Aboriginal ideology of the land, as spirit-filled and teeming with life, and the materialist philosophy of the European colonists is nowhere more starkly apparent than in their respective understandings of the desert regions. As we shall see in the next chapter, Europeans, coming from a culture focussed on the visual, saw in the Australian desert only an enormous absence, a dearth of animals and plants, a featureless, useless and monotonous expanse, a 'hideous blank' forever reproaching them at the centre of the continent. By contrast, the indigenous peoples of the desert regions celebrated their land in sung narratives, dancing and many forms of visual art.

Narrating the land in song and dance

Aboriginal myths have played a vital part in reinforcing the intimate connection between the topography of an area and the spiritual presences that produced it. Understandably in the culture of a nomadic people, most myths focus on narratives of a journey, usually a journey of the Ancestors, and

14

the particular epic dramas in which they engaged (fights, meetings, transformations) to create the features of the land. The journey narratives – in the form of songs – indicate the paths to be followed by the tribal groups of that area, either for seasonal wanderings to find food and water or for ceremonies with other tribes. Thus every part of the land is a map for some group, a map studded with the precious jewels of physical survival (waterholes), and the equally significant spiritual sites. Because trade routes have also tended to follow the Ancestors' paths, these have been of pragmatic as well as spiritual significance.[17] The Dreaming tracks also determine kinship. Members of all areas on the track of the same *tjukurpa* heroes are regarded as siblings.[18]

Non-indigenous Australians have difficulty understanding the inestimable importance of these song narratives in connecting Aborigines directly to their mythic history and to the most powerful spirits of the land. The nearest counterpart in Western writing is the more individually focussed search for family roots. Discussing the work of twentieth-century Australian writers concerned with the past, critic Andrew Taylor points to their emphasis on discovering moments of origin at the far end of a time line that is sustained by narrative. He sees this 'narrativization of the past ... as a manoeuvre to keep the past apparently accessible to the present. ... If the past is where we, both as a culture and as individuals, come from, then to lose access to it would be such a drastic truncation of identity as to threaten identity entirely.'[19] This is precisely what has happened to Aboriginal identity in the last century. In many cases the fragmentation of tribal groups has broken the link between the present and the Dreaming so that the system of beliefs expressed in oral and artistic tradition has been lost. When the traditional owners of the stories were forcibly relocated to alien places, the ceremonies and songs could not be performed. *My Place*, Sally Morgan's account of her search for her Aboriginal family in the north of Western Australia, is prefaced by words that extend her individual search into the wider Aboriginal quest for identity, and resonate with suggestions of the complex identity that involves both people and place:

> How deprived we would have been if we had been willing to let things stay as
> they were. We would have survived, but not as a whole people. We would never
> have known our place.[20]

The words of Silas Roberts, Chairman of the Northern Land Council, to the Ranger Inquiry in 1977 – 'Without land we are nothing. Without land we are a lost people' – are not metaphorical but literal.

While the thousands of individual myths and song cycles that have been recorded for publication are widely diverse, it is possible to identify certain basic components. In their *Speaking Land: Myth and Story in Aboriginal Australia*, which recounts 195 myths, Catherine and Ronald Berndt list as recurrent elements: 'conflict as a normal feature of social living, a familiar natural environment never quite harnessed to the service of human beings, and a countryside that could on occasion become terrifying'.[21] One example – the Rainbow

Snake – may indicate the role of such myths in connecting land and sky, spiritual and physical, eternal and temporal, the Ancestors and the Aboriginal people.

Of the many thousands of mythical beings the Rainbow Snake is the best known, not only because stories about such a snake were current all over mainland Australia, but also because of its popularity in Aboriginal art.[22] The Rainbow Snake, or its equivalent under a different name, is nearly always connected with waterholes, where this usually male serpent normally lives, and thus with rain and fertility; but he is also associated with great journeys across the desert, creating watercourses and swales by his tracks. The rainbow reflected in a waterhole is a sign of his presence, while the rainbow in the sky images the immense track of his journey. In many stories a Rainbow Snake pulls unwary children down into a waterhole and swallows them, later vomiting them up in a changed form, suggesting a transformation from one spiritual state to another, as through initiation. In some creation stories a female Rainbow Snake gives birth to the first people by vomiting them up and licking them dry with her tongue. Thus Rainbow Snakes, like Kali in Hindu mythology, symbolise the simultaneously destructive and beneficent powers of nature and characteristically the myths avoid assigning moral judgements to the events they relate.[23]

The songs and associated dances 'belong' in trust to a particular group or family, having been given to them by an Ancestor; therefore they may not be altered. The same reverence for preserving the tradition obtains in the visual arts since the artist is simply reproducing a design devised by the Ancestors. Anthropologist Peter Sutton points out that when a 'new' sacred song or design originates with an individual artist it is always said to have been 'sent' by the Ancestors and 'found' by the artist in a dream or some other occurrence.[24] The late Rover Thomas once explained that his 'original' sectionalised image of the Rainbow Serpent, *Wungurr (Rainbow Serpent)* (1994), was given to him, along with an associated song cycle, in a dream during which he was visited by a recently deceased female relative and the Rainbow Serpent.[25] Hence artistic originality, so much prized in Western culture, would be considered irreverent, even impossible, in traditional Aboriginal art.[26] As we shall see in Chapter 15, this repudiation of originality is changing under the influence of Western parameters.

Art and the land

Whereas European artists, confronted with the desert's apparent dearth of physical features, could find little to record in visual terms, Aboriginal art of the desert expresses the abundance of life and spiritual meaning with which this region is endowed. To the indigenous people the 'empty', barren landscape is filled not only with ever-replenished sources of food, but with spirit beings who continue to provide a framework of purpose and meaning. The

ABOVE
Anmatyerre women's ground design of Ngarlu Dreaming, Yuendumu, 1985.
Courtesy Françoise Dussart.

RIGHT
Detail from a painting of a ground design by an Aborigine of Papunya, 1971.
Courtesy R.G. Kimber.

ABOVE
Pintupi men preparing for ceremony involving body painting, 1984.
Courtesy Françoise Dussart.

BELOW
Edward Frome (Australia 1802–90), *First view of the salt desert – called Lake Torrens*, 1843, watercolour on paper, 18.0 × 27.8 cm, Art Gallery of South Australia, Adelaide. South Australian Government Grant City Council and Public Donations, 1970.

poet Judith Wright has succinctly expressed the conceptual divide between European notions of a landscape derived from the perspective of an empowered observer, whose magisterial gaze calls an appropriately aesthetic prospect into being, and the Aboriginal understanding of a spirit-filled landscape through which individuals access their identity:

> This very word 'landscape' involves, from the beginning, an irreconcilable difference of viewpoint, and there seems no word in European languages to overcome the difficulty. It is a painter's term, implying an outside view, a separation, even a basis of criticism. We cannot set it against the reality of the earth-sky-water-tree-spirit-human complex existing in space–time, which is the Aboriginal world.[27]

Traditional Aboriginal paintings are rarely concerned with material and visual aspects of landscape in isolation or for their own sake; they are reflections of its spiritual significance. Whether the art overtly depicts Ancestral forms such as the *Wandjina* of the Kimberley, the *Mimi* figures of Arnhem Land or the ubiquitous Rainbow Serpent, or offers a map–painting of the land, to the initiated eye both the land and the spirit beings are inextricably present. Because of the religious obligations inherent in the art, traditionally everyone

Rover Thomas, *Wungurr (Rainbow Serpent)*, 1994, ochre on canvas, 100.4 × 200.2 cm, Collection Jeffrey Hall (Grant Samuel & Associates, Sydney), Grant Samuel, Collection of Contemporary Art. Courtesy the Artist.

17

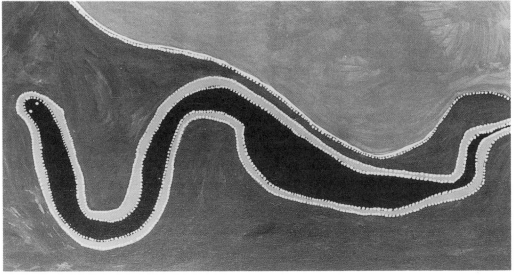

is expected to participate in some form of art, whether body painting, ground paintings (see illustrations following page 16), rock engravings, bark paintings, or the decoration of utilitarian objects. The visual element may be mimetic, a copy of the form or event that leads into the meaning; it may be mnemonic, a reminder by association; but it is never an end in itself. Even a map-like painting is not merely concerned with giving information about the location of wells in a district and the tracks joining them; an equally important purpose is to celebrate the Dreaming tracks of the Ancestors who crossed the territory, creating these wells in the process.

Essentially, then, Aboriginal art of the desert depicts the land from the inside out, as a spiritual presence apparent to the initiated eye within the external forms of stones, trees and waterholes. Thus even art that appears to display no natural features is, in effect, a landscape, linking in a more or less explicit narrative the natural features of place, the Ancestors, the artist's people and, implicitly, their whole cosmology. As Peter Sutton writes, 'The centrality of place – particular lands and sites of significance – in this imagery enables even the religious sculptures to be regarded as "landscapes".'[28]

The traditional art forms whereby Aboriginal clans throughout Australia once sought to re-initiate the relationship with the spirit beings of a particular place varied from the most ephemeral – body or ground paintings, produced only for a particular ceremony and destroyed immediately afterwards – to the most enduring rock engravings. But they were always purposeful, never random, and their purpose was invariably spiritual, never merely secular or aesthetic. An important aspect of this was the reflection in the art of universal order and the patterns of life laid down by the Ancestors to preserve such harmony. To this day, men and women produce different religious designs, focussing on diverse aspects of a Dreaming. Thus women's art or *yawulyu* (a Warlpiri word also used for the women's ceremonies) emphasises sexuality, fertility, growth of natural species and people, and the well-being of the land. It also tends to reflect an intimate knowledge of details in the landscape, consistent with the women's role as gatherers of plants and berries and as hunters of small burrowing animals. The men's designs or *kuruwarri*, on the other hand, often express a broad-scale, epic view of the countryside, reflecting their perspective as hunters of larger, above-ground animals.[29] The ground mosaics, for example, which were created only by men, represent an aerial view of an extensive area of land.

In a unique way, too, traditional Aboriginal art has been not only *about* the land; it is literally *of* the land. It has been produced exclusively with materials derived from the land (earth pigments, ochre, clay, charcoal and stones) or its 'children' (birds' feathers, flowers) and is painted, incised or arranged on natural surfaces. There is thus a total connection, symbolic and actual, between the art and the land.

The traditional colours of Aboriginal painting are those of the desert because they once were literally that – made from the desert itself, just as the painting was, and still is, regarded as having an intimate spiritual relationship

18

with the desert, not merely representing or imitating it. But the colours are also transformed by a level of brilliance (derived from the effects of contrast in the design) to indicate the spiritual ingredient of the land, the powers and beauty of the Ancestors.[30]

The most spectacular traditional art form of the desert regions is the ground mosaic, which may extend over one hundred square metres and include in its design artificially raised and decorated mounds.[31] After the land is levelled and cleared of any vegetation, it is spread with a layer of crumbled termite mound to produce a hard surface. Leaves, stems and flowers of native plants are finely chopped and mixed with animal fat and birds' feathers – ideally the white fluff of eagle down. Half of this pulp is dyed with powdered red or yellow ochre,[32] and the other half with white clay or black charcoal. The variously coloured pulp is then pressed into small round pellets which are laid on the ground to create the geometric elements of the design. This detailed and time-consuming preparation of the mosaics is carried out only by the older men, custodians of the tribal knowledge. In the centre of the design there is usually a hole into which a pole of phallic significance may be placed. These mosaics are never produced in isolation but only in association with the performance of sacred rituals designed to 'open' the surface of the land and induce the creative power of the always-present spirits of the Dreaming to emerge. The mosaics therefore represent both the surface of the earth from an aerial perspective and the spiritual dimension beneath that surface. Together with the associated ceremonies, they serve to re-enact the creation of the land, restoring its fertility. Thus, however elaborate and beautiful, the ground mosaics are invariably destroyed by the ceremony for which alone they have been produced.

Describing the Aranda ceremonial cycle of the *Krantji* kangaroo clan, Strehlow commented that during this part of the ceremony fully initiated members of the clan would saturate the ground with blood from veins in their arms, since

> new kangaroo 'life' could come out of the ground only after some of the life of
> the original kangaroo totemic ancestors had been poured down upon it; and
> the blood which flowed from a man of the *Krantji* kangaroo totem was regarded
> as sacred in this special sense when the appropriate *Krantji* kangaroo charms
> had been sung during the laying down of the ground painting.[33]

In the ceremony that followed, each kangaroo performer, having a ceremonial phallus attached to his head, approached the ground painting and blew into its central hole. When each performer had done so, the whole group brought the phallic pole into contact with the ground painting and the feather down stripped from it was put into the hole. This was then covered by down stripped from the ground painting and branches were heaped on the top. The ceremony involved dancing on the mosaic, which was necessarily destroyed in the process; but this did not affect its sole purpose, which was to ensure a large increase of kangaroos after the next summer rains.

19

Body painting of the dancers was an equally important part of the ceremonies for which the ground mosaics were produced. The body was greased and the designs painted on using fingers or sticks and the same pigments and down as for the ground paintings. Like the production of the latter, the group body painting process was part of the ceremony and accompanied by the singing of traditional songs to enlist the spiritual powers of the Ancestors. For a ceremony the bodies of the participants were elevated from their mundane state to a spiritual one by the application of brilliant colours to suggest the radiance of the spiritual power that would be transmitted through them.[34] The white fluffy down was an important part of both the design and the ceremony since, as the dancers moved, the fluff floated off their bodies and drifted to the ground, symbolising semen and the distribution of fertility. Thus, during the ceremony, the performers *became* the Dreaming Ancestors, bestowing their fertility on the land.[35] The brightly coloured pellets of the ground mosaics were the inspiration for the now more widely known acrylic dot paintings of contemporary desert art (discussed in detail in Chapter 15), and determined their characteristic planar perspective.

Geometric shapes could also be endowed with spiritual significance and, reproduced on the exterior of persons or objects, could transform them from a secular to a sacred state. From his extensive study of Aboriginal art and customs, anthropologist W.E.H. Stanner wrote:

20

> My hypothesis is that the geometric forms enter the general system of symbolism as *conventional signs*. Their significance, which is always one of a completed and final action, is a kind of command for an exemplifying action by living men as the appropriate response.[36]

The Western Desert region was the home of the traditional carving and painting of wooden artefacts such as the curved wooden carrying dishes or coolamons, spear throwers and boomerangs often decorated with particular designs. Like other art of the desert, these patterns were both geometrical and semiotic in their relation to the associated stories. Classical desert art is also found on incised boards and stones or *tjurunga*, which have highly secret and sacred significance.

To non-Aboriginal viewers, the most accessible Aboriginal art forms are those featuring human and animal figures, since these seem to offer a parallel to Western art. However, as with landscape art, the focus is rarely on the physical figure or animal for its own sake; rather, they are most often depicted as spiritual beings intimately associated with the land. Three distinct kinds of figures are found in desert rock art: the Bradshaws, the *Mimi* and the *Wandjina*, of which only the last are traditionally associated with shaping the land.

Bradshaws, named after Joseph Bradshaw, the first European to see them (in 1891), are the oldest known Aboriginal figurative images. The slender forms of the Bradshaws, usually depicted in motion (dancing or hunting), and wearing elaborate head-dresses and tassels hanging from their hair, neck, waist, arms and legs, are reminiscent of figures in Minoan art or Indonesian *wayang*, the latter analogy suggesting, perhaps, the influence of very early immigrants to the continent from Indonesia. However, Bradshaw himself, along with several other anthropologists, claims that none of the costume elements depicted is significantly different from those worn in the area.[37] Some of the figures hold boomerangs and barbed spears that predate the modern stone-tipped spears introduced some 3000 years ago. This suggests they are much older than the *Wandjina* with which they are frequently overpainted. Most recent evidence from optical dating of quartz grains embedded in wasp nests built directly over one of the figures gives a minimum age of 17,000 years (the peak of the last Ice Age).[38] The question of whether or not these figures were produced by the ancestors of the Ngarinyin, the present-day Aborigines in the area, or a different cultural group (possibly from South-East Asia) remains highly controversial, as do the nature and extent of their spiritual significance.

Mimi or 'dynamic style' paintings of West Arnhem Land and Kakadu depict characteristically thin spirit figures that can pass through cracks in the rock. Unlike most of the Dreaming Ancestors, the *Mimi* are credited not with creating topographical features but with teaching the people how to paint the so-called 'X-ray' images of animals with which they are associated.

By contrast with the Bradshaws and the *Mimi*, the *Wandjina* images of the Kimberley are regarded as a source of great spiritual value. To Westerners the appeal of these mouthless figures lies in their large, dark, heavily lashed eyes and a slightly gamin, 'lost' expression, but such aesthetic considerations play no part in their cultural importance. For the Aborigines of the Kimberley region they are embodiments of the Ancestral *Wandjina*, spirits of the clouds, who emerged from the sky and sea at the Dreaming, bringing rains and consequent fertility to the region and shaping the contours of the land during their journeys before imprinting themselves in huge images (up to six metres high) rendered in ochre and white clay on the walls of caves in the area. The *Wandjina* have no mouths – allegedly because, as well as the lightning and thunder, they carry the rain, which would fall unceasingly through their mouths. The halo-like circles surrounding their heads, often with radiating lines as in some Medieval depictions of saintly figures,[39] represent both their hair, and clouds with radiating lightning. These symbolise the cyclonic clouds associated with the wet season and hence, by extension, the fertility that follows this rain in the desert. The predominance of white clay in the depictions of the *Wandjina*, traditionally painted on overhanging rock faces or in caves, magnifies the impression of brilliance and hence of spiritual power. The figures are almost invariably painted in large clusters, reinforcing the lesson that Aboriginal people need the tribal group to survive in the harsh conditions of this country.[40] Although *Wandjina* are regarded as anthropomorphic manifestations of the Rainbow Serpent,[41] the creative force particularly associated with waterholes, they are also often depicted with the plants and animals associated with a given site, suggesting that the fertility of all species derives from the *Wandjina*. Drawings of the *Wandjina* are believed to be the work of the

21

Wandjina themselves and must be ritually restored before each wet season to ensure that the rains will bring fertility.

Even this brief overview of Aboriginal culture of the desert indicates the strongly unified belief system that has traditionally integrated the people with their spirit Ancestors and with the land. This relationship is expressed in behavioural codes, in cultural values and in all forms of art. Unlike European or Western art forms grounded in aesthetics, economics and enjoyment, the ritual song and dancing cycles, with their associated body and ground painting, enact a spiritual dialogue: an offering of religious observance and a receiving of creative power. This dialogue occurs both through the land and in order to revitalise the land that gives essence and meaning to all aspects of life.

The explorers and settlers who came to Australia during the eighteenth and nineteenth centuries saw the land through eyes very different from those of its indigenous inhabitants (though with no less entrenched mythology), and it was to take nearly two hundred years of settlement before a Eurocentric culture could begin to appreciate the Aborigines' rapport with the desert.

Forms, Images, Imaginings

Just as none of us is outside or beyond geography, none of us is completely free from the struggle over geography. That struggle is complex and interesting because it is not only about soldiers and cannons but also about ideas, about forms, about images and imaginings.

EDWARD SAID[1]

A picture held us captive. And we could not get outside of it for it lay in our language and language seemed to repeat it to us inexorably.

LUDWIG WITTGENSTEIN[2]

They [the Plains] are not . . . a vast theatre that adds significance to the events enacted within it. Nor are they an immense field for explorers of every kind. They are simply a convenient source of metaphors for those who know that men invent their own meanings.

GERALD MURNANE[3]

Unlike the North American continent, where the early European settlers were religious pilgrims, led by the desire to found a spiritually based society free from the persecution and restraints of the Old World,[4] Australia's origins as a white settlement were almost wholly secular. Whether we assign the major impetus for the founding of Britain's antipodean colonies to scientific curiosity, the desire to keep the French from establishing a Pacific empire, or the need to relocate the superfluity of felons overflowing from British prisons, there is nowhere a suggestion of religious intent. Whereas the founding fathers of America believed that they had been given a continent in which to build the new Jerusalem, the Europeans who came to Australia acknowledged no such manifest destiny. On the contrary, the most characteristic response, even of those who were not convicts, was a sense of alienation and exile.

For the newcomers the visual sense was fundamental and the gaze (or way of looking at things) was a means not only of locating themselves within the land but of claiming possession. Such dominion might be economic (in the exploitation of the land for primary industry), aesthetic (in the construction of a picturesque prospect designed to conform to criteria established elsewhere), or scientific (in the collection of information and objects that were taken to define the land). Explorers were particularly instructed to cultivate the scientific gaze in order to ransack Nature's vast 'museum' and return with a *cabinet* of natural history exhibits for the education and delectation of their fellow Europeans. With the practice of having scientific artists attached to expeditions, the landscape itself became a collectible item of scientific interest. Scenes of exotic places were composed in conformity with patterns of prior expectation deriving from contemporary theories of natural history, such as catastrophism or gradualism, vulcanism and neptunism.[5] Even the scientific travel account, as art historian Barbara Stafford has shown, conformed to the tradition of voyages to past civilisations, with their accompanying moral lesson of eternal mutability.[6] This manipulation of observation in the service of a theory of cataclysmic nature and cultural decay was diametrically opposed to the Aboriginal view of the land as essentially numinous and continuous with the past.

Imagining the Orient

Edward Said's revisionist classic, *Orientalism: Western Conceptions of the Orient* (1978), has inexorably led a generation of readers to a chastening realisation of the extent to which Europeans have progressively fashioned an imaginary concept, 'the Orient', against which the credibility of all things south of the Mediterranean and east of Greece were measured. Said did not, however, consider the curious case of Australia, a continent further east than the Far East, and burdened with the full weight of centuries of hypothetical expectation, even before any European sighting of it was recorded.[7] Arguably this is because, despite its geographical location, Australia was not initially associated by Europeans with the east but rather, as indicated by the name they bestowed on it, with the south.[8] Indeed the continent was regarded by the British as an imperial possession to be protected from its oriental neighbours[9] as much as from rival European powers. Even the strangeness of Australia was depicted not as oriental, but as peculiar to this antipodean 'other', whose unique plants and animals were regarded as so many jests of a playful Nature. Early colonists, suffering from the 'black swans and songless birds' syndrome, were obsessed with compiling catalogues of opposites to their European counterparts. In due course, however, as the Australian colonies developed a more secure foothold and settlers, surrounded with their cultural icons, prepared to entice other immigrants, parallels with Europe began to outweigh the shock of contrast. Even the 'Bush', formerly vilified, was gradually accepted as the counterpart of wild Romantic nature, providing a moral contrast to urban corruption.

However, the desire to regard Australia as a user-friendly extension of Europe received a major setback with the realisation, during the 1840s, that an extensive area at the centre of the continent was desert. For Europeans of the late eighteenth and early nineteenth centuries 'desert' meant either North Africa or the Middle East, areas endowed with centuries of recorded history and culture. Although the inhabitants of these deserts were perceived as strange, as indicated by their exotic clothes, culture and religion, they were not regarded as necessarily inferior in consequence. The respect that Egypt had enjoyed from classical times, and the religious associations of the Holy Land, ensured that their differences even served to elevate rather than demean them. Egypt excited admiration as a vast treasure house of ancient history, while the Turkish empire, although characterised as cruel and pagan, was also identified with a heady mix of opulence, sex and decadence, as popularised in the Romantic Orientalism of the French artists, Géricault, Gérôme and Delacroix, and the English poet Byron.

Much of the frustration and bewilderment expressed by the inland explorers sprang from the disparity between the Australian desert and these Orient-generated expectations. The Australian desert offered no regular oases, no paradisal walled gardens, but only, it seemed, the overwhelming monotony of interminable parallel dunes, spinifex and mulga scrub. At best there was the infrequent native well or stone basin such as Ernest Giles encountered and named, with determined and extravagant imagination, after Scottish glens and tarns and Arcadian vales.[10] Worse, it offered no human monuments analogous to the pyramids, to indicate occupation by an ancient civilisation, although, as we shall see in Chapter 7, the notion of a forgotten antique culture was a popular theme for adventure novels and science fiction of the 1890s.[11] There was therefore no historical context to which Europeans, hungry for a past but unable to appreciate Aboriginal culture, could relate. Even though he settled in Australia in the 1890s and wrote compassionately of life on outback sheep stations, the French writer Paul Wenz voiced this sense of absence in terms that most of his contemporaries would have understood:

25

> There is no history; the childish primitive legends that peopled the great deserts died with the tribes. . . . In Australia there is a total lack of ruins that are the tangible past, of the old castles and the old temples that form part of the history of a people.[12]

Equally stark was the disparity between the exotic images of dignified Middle Eastern desert sheiks, resonant with echoes of the Crusades, and the nineteenth-century perception of the Aborigines as filthy, irreligious savages, little better than animals. Eastern women, depicted in Western art as either mysteriously veiled for the street or half-clad odalisques in harem settings, were rendered more erotic by their differences from European women, and adaptations of Eastern costume became fashionable in portraiture. By contrast, approaches made by naked Aboriginal women were regarded by the explorers as particularly disgusting on aesthetic as much as moral grounds. 'When they knew we would not let them stop [stay], they abused us as roundly as so many Billingsgate Fish Fates,' wrote Daniel Brock, a member of Sturt's expedition to

Central Australia, of six Aboriginal women who had come to offer sexual favours,[13] while Ernest Giles, who at times jocularly described young Aboriginal women as lively and handsome,[14] was more usually as derogatory about their looks as their intelligence and their general right to live there.

Edward Said has argued that Europeans were able to form their own image of the Orient because they ignored the Orient's account of itself. But whereas 'Orientalism' was essentially a textual construction, supported by a vast literature of contact or speculation dating from classical times, Australia had no such literature, so extraneous ideas could be applied without check. European descriptions of the Australian desert carry implicit cultural and textual references to one of two opposing prototypes. One cluster of images, which we may call the wilderness image, presents the desert as harsh, infertile and punitive; the other, which can be identified as visionary, constructs it as a place of spiritual enlightenment. Ironically, given what has been said about the predominantly secular imperative for the settlement of Australia, both views derive originally from the Judaeo–Christian tradition. With minor modifications these two prototypes have been consistently applied to the Australian desert in literary and artistic judgement for two centuries, sometimes with one or other predominating, sometimes in an ambiguous alliance.

The wilderness condemned

In Hebraic tradition the desert wilderness is not only a perpetual reminder of the Fall (Genesis 3:17–19); it is a warning that disobedience to God will perpetuate the curse: 'the earth that is under thee shall be iron. The Lord shall make the rain of thy land powder and dust' (Deuteronomy 28:23–24). In the Eden story the desert stands in contrast to the garden, the oasis, and by extension to the cultivation that both sustains and emanates from civilisation. Cultural geographer John Rennie Short points out that 'wilderness' is a social notion that emerged at the time of the agricultural revolution some 10,000 years ago, because only with settled agriculture could 'a distinction be made between cultivated and uncultivated land, savage and settled, domesticated and wild animals'.[15] In the tradition that built on this dichotomy, land had meaning only in terms of human use and history. Hence wild places are, in classical terms, devoid of significance. The progress of civilisation depends on the taming of the wilderness, on making the desert blossom like the rose as promised by the prophet Isaiah: 'For the Lord shall comfort Zion: he will comfort all her waste places; and he will make her wilderness like Eden, and her desert like the garden of the Lord' (Isaiah 35:1 and 51:3). This view has been implicated in a theology of subjugation that emphasises a particular translation of the Genesis injunction to subdue the earth and have dominion over all living things (Genesis 1:28).

This biblical directive was implicit in the declaration of Australia as *terra nullius*, an empty space belonging to no one, not only conveniently available for the taking but even morally demanding settlement in order to be put to use.[16] There are starkly obvious generic parallels with the American myth of conquest wherein the virgin wilderness was 'inhabited by nonpeople called savages ... incapable of civilization' whom it was the moral and religious duty of Europeans to subdue.[17] More typically, though, as geographer Yi-Fu Tuan has pointed out, European attitudes to that specific form of wilderness, the desert, are characterised by a strong element of denial, a conspiracy of silence about the very existence of deserts because they appeared as a moral flaw in the creation. By posing a threat to fundamental human needs for food and water, they suggested not just a lack of resources but a slur on the wisdom and beneficence of the Creator. This view was so strong that 'empirical evidence on the extent of deserts, gathered over the centuries by traders, missionaries, and explorers who crossed them, was over-looked in the interest of maintaining a reassuring physico-theological theory of the earth'.[18] The push to settle the centre of the continent was consistent with such a view, being based on the premise that Australia represented an Eden, still pre-industrialised and innocent, a southern Arcady conferred by Providence to absorb Britain's excess population.[19] All these operations could be readily justified in terms of prevailing theological views. In his *Second Treatise on Government*, the British philosopher John Locke wrote:

> And hence the subduing of the Earth, and having Dominion, we see are joined together. The one gave Title to the other. So that God, by commanding to subdue, gave Authority so far to appropriate. And the Condition of Humane Life, which requires Labour and materials to work on, necessarily introduces private possessions.[20]

27

Faced with the dawning realisation that vast areas of the continent remained obdurate desert, successive generations of Australians, heirs of eighteenth-century optimism, have interpreted this as a challenge to restore utility and meaning to the land by subjecting Nature to science. Over time proposals to transform the desert into fertile plains have included the diverting of rivers, irrigation by piped water, flooding the Lake Eyre basin with sea water to produce precipitation, desalination of sea water, cloud seeding with iodide crystals and even towing icebergs from Antarctica. The manifest failure of most of these schemes to deliver the pastoral dream[21] has encouraged the race to derive mineral wealth from beneath this otherwise useless land. From de Rougemont's fiction of an Australian El Dorado, through the gold rush days of the 1850s and Lasseter's unlucky search for a mythical gold reef, to the lucrative exploitation of iron ore, nickel, oil and gas, the Australian desert has been the target for numerous modern variations on the theme of global reconstruction inherited from the Enlightenment and its underlying theology of utility. William Ramson notes that the evolving 'lexical landscape' of Australia in the period 1788 to 1838 was strongly utilitarian. Thus the American usage of 'to improve', in the sense of bringing land into cultivation or pastoral use, began to be widely adopted in Australia during the 1830s.[22]

During the twentieth century the desert acquired a further element of condemnation in psychological terms. To an immigrant population separated from its cultural roots, traditions and family support systems, the loneliness of this eerie continent was understandably traumatic and Harry Heseltine has argued that the perceived alienation of the Australian landscape, combined with convict history, underlay the existential angst that became an enduring preoccupation in Australian literature.[23] When the Bush was the frontier, it was identified as a brooding emptiness spurning settlement, a threatening place of death which Marcus Clarke so famously identified as 'weird melancholy'.[24] Judith Wright has suggested that 'probably this loneliness caused her early inhabitants to exaggerate her strangeness – the lost and ancient quality that Lawrence later felt'.[25] As the settlement marched inland, the central desert, the new and final frontier, inherited this psychological topography. It not only epitomised the cumulative sense of loneliness but also, as we shall see in Chapter 10, slid into metaphorical use for the spiritual barrenness of its few inhabitants, depleted in morality as in energy by their arid land. It was not long before the physical emptiness, the 'hideous blank' at the centre of the map, was taken to signify an even more disturbing wilderness, the metaphysical void at the centre of the national identity.

In search of spiritual enlightenment

Precisely by virtue of its material desolation, the desert also offers, in Judaeo–Christian tradition, a means of spiritual purification and salvation. The Children of Israel spent forty years in the wilderness, including the terrible Negev Desert, as a prerequisite to inheriting the Promised Land; and throughout Israel's history the prophets not only came from the desert but periodically returned there to purify their hearts. In the New Testament, John the Baptist and Jesus both isolated themselves in the desert wilderness to prepare for their ministry, a practice that was adopted by the Desert Fathers during the first four centuries of Christianity as a necessary program for spiritual growth. Saint Jerome, who allegedly declared, 'To me a town is a prison, and the desert loneliness a paradise',[26] provided a popular subject for religious art. The notion of 'desert' suggested in many of these fifteenth- and early sixteenth-century depictions of the saint, such as those of Sano di Pietro, Jacopo di Arcangelo and Joachim Patenier,[27] is perceptual rather than actual, more a matter of voluntary exile from a nearby town than a place of extreme isolation. The significance of the desert in these works was its ability to generate a sense of the numinous, of religious awe. Three of the predominant responses recorded by the explorers of the Australian desert – terror at its starkness, awe at its immensity and fascination at its wildness – align precisely with the sensations of *mysterium, tremendum* and *fascinans* associated by the theologian Rudolph Otto with the experience of the numinous: 'Empty distance, remote vacancy, is, as it were, the sublime in the horizontal. The wide stretching desert, the boundless uniformity of the steppe have real sublimity and even in us Westerners they set vibrating chords of the numinous.'[28]

Seeking spiritual enlightenment, the pilgrim strives to transcend physical surroundings and to triumph over bodily discomfort. In such a quest the otherwise inimical aspects of the desert become virtues. Absence of material comforts promotes concentration on the spiritual; hardships provide not only a physical test of survival, but a trial of motivation; the vast, isolated expanse tests the individual's ability to overcome loneliness and stand alone before God. In this construction the desert operates as the European version of a tribal initiation into self-reliance, a spiritual Outward Bound course. More specifically the desert was, and largely still is, conceptually a man's place. Thus an important part of the self-denial associated with the desert was sexual abstinence, with a concomitant rejection of women, at least implicitly perceived as inherently sinful, the source if not the active perpetrators of sexual temptation. Even when literal residence in the desert was considered impractical or superfluous, it remained a powerful metaphor for spiritual pilgrimage and a test of manhood, its very barrenness suggesting sexual abstemiousness along with rejection of debilitating 'softness', luxury and decadence. So the thirteenth-century German mystic, Meister Eckhart, taught: 'Be like a desert as far as self and the things of this world are concerned' in order to discover the 'desert of the Godhead'.[29] This interlocking complex of belief about the desert wilderness in Judaeo–Christian tradition is usefully summarised by George Williams:

29

Sano di Pietro (1406–1481), called Lo Spagna, *St. Jerome in the Desert*, wood panel, 39×81 cm, Louvre, Paris. Courtesy Service Photographique de la Réunion des Musées Nationaux, Paris.

> We shall find in the positive sense that the wilderness or desert will be interpreted variously as a place of protection, a place of contemplative retreat, again as one's inner nature or ground of being, and at length as the ground itself of the divine being. . . . In its negative sense the wilderness will be interpreted as the world of the unredeemed, as the wasteland, and as the realm or phase of punitive or purgative preparation for salvation.[30]

The happy coincidence of facilitated tourism (Thomas Cook undertook the first commercial tourist enterprise in 1841) and the religious revivals of the nineteenth century produced a growing fascination with the Holy Land, both as a living museum to illustrate the Bible and as a place where, it was hoped, contact with the actual scenes of the Gospel and the early Church might revive a simple faith under siege from science and history. The Reverend Thomas Hartwell Horne's *The Biblical Keepsake: or, Landscape Illustrations of the Most Remarkable Places Mentioned in the Holy Scriptures* (1835) and Alexander Kinglake's bestseller *Eothen: or Traces of Travel Brought Home from the East* (1844) inspired and informed the many British tourists who began to descend on the Holy Land in the 1840s. By the 1870s there were highly organised tours to Palestine, typically with more than a thousand European tourists camped there at any one time, absorbing the 'religious' atmosphere of the desert.

In more secular times an aesthetically or emotionally uplifting experience in response to the immensity of the desert was substituted for that of spiritual illumination. Edmund Burke's *Philosophical Enquiry into the Origin of Our Ideas of the Sublime and Beautiful* (1757) popularised the notion of strong emotions, especially terror, in the face of natural grandeur as being aesthetically uplifting:

> Whatever is fitted in any sort to excite the ideas of pain, and danger . . . or is conversant about terrible objects, or operates in a manner analogous to terror, is a source of the sublime; that is, it is productive of the strongest emotion which the mind is capable of feeling.[31]

At first this sense of the sublime was associated almost exclusively with mountain scenery, but as accounts, and more particularly illustrations, of the eighteenth-century voyages of exploration became known, the sources of sublimity were expanded to include forms of horizontal expanse as well – the ocean, broad tracts of steppe, and deserts. Thus the rejection of desert as unproductive wasteland was subsumed in the Romantic celebration of Nature's immensity, unsullied by human contact. Indeed the concept of 'desert' became so popular that the term was applied to almost any vast, uncultivated area.[32] The desert signified a place of few visual objects but seemingly limitless space where time seemed stationary, giving rise to the view of the desert as unchanging and charged with a sense of the infinite. The French philosopher Gaston Bachelard remarks on the synthesis of opposites whereby the immensity and emptiness of the external space are 'annexed to inner space', concluding that 'immensity is within ourselves'.[33] But he also considers this experience to be part of a two-way process, evident in the poet Baudelaire's *L'art romantique*: 'man's poetic fate is to be the mirror of immensity; or even more exactly, immensity becomes conscious of itself, through man.'[34] In this view the notions of the desert's vastness and the observer's consciousness of its immensity are mutually created. Bachelard also suggests that, in general, we make ourselves feel less strange in the universe by marking out a space for ourselves, a space decked with familiar objects and events to provide emotional meaning. This familiar space is domesticated and defined by its difference from other spaces around it in the process that Edward Said calls 'imaginative geography'.[35] In a secular society, experiences that would once have been designated religious can be described only in such phenomenological terms or, ironically, in terms of other cultures' religions. Thus, in the late twentieth century, another form of the Romantic absorption with the desert has involved, as we shall see in Chapter 14, an attempt by white Australians to appropriate the Aboriginal understanding of the desert as spiritual presence.

Myths of the interior

Coming, historically, at the intersection of these two perspectives derived, in turn, from two antithetical biblical constructions of desert wilderness, it is not surprising that British exploration of the interior of Australia was frequently characterised by conflicting ideological premises. Desiring to disprove reports of arid wasteland at the heart of the continent, the British explorers set out optimistically to re-create the Centre, conceptually as much as factually, according to a preconceived wish list that included fertile plains and an inland sea – which, if actualised, would have annihilated its generic desert character. Necessarily they failed in these endeavours: for the most part the land stubbornly retained its character of unredeemed wilderness. But in the process the explorers evolved a new myth in which the desert was recast to define the expedition leaders by complementarity: the harsher the desert, the more heroic and saint-like the explorers. The impressions of the desert conveyed in their diaries, reports and pictorial records were progressively modified through successive waves of public response to those explorations, and reflected in theliterature and art of subsequent generations.

One of the most notorious European allegations about the interior of the continent was its negligible indigenous population. It is estimated that, when John McDouall Stuart made his first attempt to cross the continent from south to north, the Aboriginal population of the central desert region was of the order of 10,000, a number that already showed the impact of a smallpox epidemic responsible for some 5000 deaths. However, apart from a very few descriptions of skirmishes with 'unfriendly natives', the prevailing impression to be gained from written accounts of the desert, whether by the explorers or by the early pastoralists, was of virtually unoccupied land, a particular and most exemplary case of *terra nullius*. Obviously there were strategic reasons for this.

31

As we shall see in the next chapter, the explorers in particular had a brief to bring back good news of the land they traversed, and that certainly included large tracts of unoccupied and potentially productive land awaiting settlement. If they could not always deliver news of fertility, they could at least imply that it was free of potential conflict from hostile indigenes. Mary Louise Pratt has pointed out, with respect to Africa, that such failure to acknowledge the presence of indigenous people in written accounts projects the notion of a 'primal' virgin landscape awaiting the pastoralist, the cultivator, and eventually the urban planner, and conveniently paves the way for the literal depopulation of indigenes by the encroaching settlement. Pratt calls these absences from the records 'anti-conquest' strategies of innocence, since they absolved the travellers of the odium attached to the older style military imperialism.[36] The power of their evasive accounts as propaganda in the cause of colonialism can be gauged from the expectations they generated: when the pastoralists did subsequently encounter Aborigines determined to protect their traditional lands, there was an immediate sense of outrage that the latter should attack peaceful settlers who had harmed no one, and reprisals followed swiftly.

It was further assumed that the desert was spatially and temporally uniform. We have already noted the great variability in terrain of the desert areas, but these differences were largely erased by the explorers' accounts, which dwelt instead on the monotony of the land and its vegetation, permitting a simple stereotype to be contrasted with a diverse Western culture.

Similarly, in the temporal dimension, the desert is most frequently characterised as timeless and pristine. It is true that some of the rocks in the Centre are among the oldest in the world – nearly 2000 million years old – but it is also an area of immense and visible geological change: the ancient Finke River was flowing before the MacDonnell Ranges were laid down on top of it; the now dry watercourses and heavily eroded mountains and chasms are witness to the dynamics of geological time; indeed, until 350 million years ago, the whole central desert area was covered by a shallow sea, while the MacDonnell Ranges, now eroded to a mere 1000 metres, reached 9 kilometres, the height of the Himalayas, at the time of their emergence 300 million years ago.

Some of this historical variation was perceived and understood by the explorers. Charles Lyell's *Principles of Geology* (1830–33) was well known and Sturt, who repeatedly cited evidence for the inland sea he so eagerly sought, acknowledged at the end of his published accounts that such a sea existed only in a remote geological past. Yet the myth of an unchanging desert persisted because, like the parallel doctrine of *terra nullius*, it could be used to sustain implications that provided a convenient justification for conquest. The changeless land, so the myth went, had been asleep for eons, awaiting only the arrival of the Europeans to awaken it into activity and progress, Hence it was theirs by right, a gift held in trust for them, the reward for their quest. Although not specifically couched in terms of negation, these strategies – which served to remove the desert from spatial and temporal concerns – were effectively methods of nullifying its substance. In such a discourse of negation the land cries out for the European settler to give it identity, meaning and legitimacy.

The notion of changelessness ascribed to the desert was easily transferred to its inhabitants. Aboriginal culture was declared to be a 'stone age' one, an ethnic fossil, clear indication that such people could not adapt to change and were thus inevitably headed for imminent extinction. It is salutary to realise that Aborigines, contemplating the mores of their conquerors, must have been struck by a parallel sense of impoverishment and absence in white Australians' constructions of the land. Rhys Jones has described the culture shock experienced by Frank Gurrmanamana from Gidjingali country in the 'Top End' on his first visit to Canberra:

> The ordered streets and geometric vistas of the planned capital city of Australia left him totally uninterested. . . . The idea of buying and selling land like any other commodity and of attachment to the land only as a matter of transient convenience was totally alien to Gurrmanamana, and he regarded it with a mixture of suspended belief and with some mild revulsion, as if there was something deeply wrong with this state of affairs. Here was a land empty of religious affiliation; there were no wells, no names of the totemic ancestors, no immutable links between land, people and the rest of the natural and supernatural worlds. Here was just a vast *tabula rasa*, cauterised of meaning. . . . In his own words, 'this country bin lose 'im Dreaming.' He was disturbed by this.[37]

The nineteenth-century exploration of Central Australia led to further stereotyping of the land. The expedition leaders were almost obliged to vilify the desert in order to account for their failure to deliver the hoped-for reports of fertile acres awaiting settlement. As we shall see in subsequent chapters, this detraction was increased by the nation's desire to consecrate those who had triumphed over it and, even more, those who died in the attempt. Myths of national heroism demand an enemy and the land was readily sacrificed to that end. The greater its horrors and intractability, the greater the honour accorded the individuals whose initiative, bravery and endurance redounded vicariously and symbolically on the whole white population.[38] Thus Burke and Wills are popularly believed to have died in the desert when in fact they were camped by Cooper's Creek, with no shortage of water, in an area where local Aborigines easily obtained a varied and adequate diet. But by focussing on the horrors of the desert, these myths generated both national martyrs and an expectation that White Australians 'deserved' the land and anything else they could wrest from it, as minimal recompense for the sufferings and death of their heroic representatives.

Anthropology of the desert

In parallel with this defamation of the land, Europeans came increasingly to discredit the surviving indigenes. W.E.H. Stanner noted the deteriorating attitude of Europeans towards the Aborigines:

> In the early years of settlement insensibility towards the Aborigines' human status hardened into contempt, derision and indifference. The romantic idealism, unable to stand the shock of experience, drifted through dismay into pessimism about the natives' capacity for civilisation.[39]

More than any other geographical region, the desert was associated with the Aborigines. This was the last stronghold to which they had been effectively driven by the expansion of settlement from the coastal fringes, and since it remained the area most inimical to Europeans it was readily ceded to them until it began to acquire commercial and strategic value for mining or nuclear testing. This association between Aborigines and the desert was not, however, a simple empirical matter; it resonated with political and ideological implications in a bitter preview of the 'land rights' issue that has continued to bedevil Australian history. The fact that Aborigines had been successfully inhabiting these 'inhospitable' tracts of land for tens of thousands of years was either carefully censored or, if considered, was taken as further evidence of the inferior humanity, even the subhumanity, of the race. It was used to condemn both the land and its indigenous people as being equally primitive and inimical to civilisation. This view was bolstered by various tactics, notably the casting of the Aborigines as infantile, or as savage and primitive scientific curiosities. With few exceptions, they were treated as backward children, to be distracted and entertained by glass beads, pieces of cloth or shiny metal and thereby induced to impart their knowledge about the location of water supplies. Even their survival skills were denigrated as an indication of their primitive needs. For nearly two centuries there was little or no attempt by Europeans to inquire into the indigenous knowledge of the land or its flora and fauna, except as an aspect of anthropological study. Attempts by Aborigines to speak English or to wear European clothing, and the unconventional use to which they put European gifts, were derided as further evidence of their intellectual inferiority. Deconstructing some of the accounts of contact between Europeans and Aborigines, we occasionally glimpse on the part of the Aborigines an element of derision or amazement as to the stupidity of their visitors, but such notions of mimicry and and critical judgement remained unsuspected by the colonists.

34

Aborigines were almost universally regarded as being among the most primitive of all peoples – if indeed they could be classified as human beings – inferior to Africans and manifestly beneath the New Zealand Maoris and Polynesian races. Their customs, if inquired about at all, were recorded as scientific curiosities, appropriate to and further testifying to their primitiveness and separation from any form of civilisation. When the explorer George Grey observed Aboriginal cave paintings he concluded they were too sophisticated and well delineated to have been produced by such a primitive people and declared them a relic from some invading race. In the early decades of white settlement it was assumed that the Aborigines would quickly die out, being unable to withstand the benign diseases carried by Europeans or the competition with a stronger (and hence morally superior) race.[40] Darwinian theory soon legitimised these vague notions as a 'law of nature': the concept of survival of the fittest was assumed to vindicate the European conquest of indigenous peoples as inevitable. In an amazing passage of special pleading Ernest Giles even managed to combine Darwinian theory with the will of God:

> The Great Designer of the universe, in the long past periods of creation, permitted a fiat to be recorded, that the beings whom it was His pleasure in the first instance to place among these lovely scenes, must eventually be swept from the face of the earth by others more intellectual, more dearly beloved and gifted than they. Progressive improvement is undoubtedly the order of creation, and we perhaps in our turn may be as ruthlessly driven from the earth by another race of yet unknown beings, of an order infinitely higher, infinitely more beloved than we.[41]

Thomas Henry Huxley had been the first to compare skulls of Australian Aborigines with a recently discovered Neanderthal cranium and to claim similarities between Aboriginal artefacts and those of primitive Europeans,[42] but Giles was quick to apply Darwinian terms to Aborigines in this typically jocular account: 'the old man was so monkey-like – he would have charmed the heart of Professor Darwin. I thought I had found the missing link and I had thoughts of preserving him in methylated spirits, only I had not a bottle large enough'.[43] Elsewhere he describes the Aborigines he meets as 'the lower organism of God's human family'.[44] Throughout *The Descent of Man* (1872) Darwin contrasts 'savage' and 'civilised' peoples (the former characterised as practising infanticide), and in his final paragraph affirms that he would rather be related to a baboon than to 'a savage who delights to torture his enemies, offers up bloody sacrifices without remorse, treats his wives like slaves, knows no decency, and is haunted by the grossest superstitions.'[45] Darwin presumably was not averse to claiming biological relationship to those responsible for the enslavement or genocide of an indigenous people.

It is alongside these images, introduced from a European tradition, that we must locate the views of the Australian desert expressed in the literature and art of the emerging nation. In some cases the inherited images were too strongly inscribed to be erased even by actual experience of the desert and travellers saw only what they had set out intending to see; in others they were progressively modified, leading to an eventual reversal in the estimation of the desert from economic disaster to tourist Mecca, from loathsome wilderness to the locus of spiritual rebirth.

35

The 'Hideous Blank'

Give me a map; then let me see how much
Is left for me to conquer all the world.

CHRISTOPHER MARLOWE[1]

Let any man lay the map of Australia before him, and regard the
blank upon its surface, and then let me ask him if it would not be an
honourable achievement to be the first to place a foot in its centre.

CHARLES STURT[2]

... as long as there are new regions to explore, the burning charm of
seeking something new, will still possess me; and I am also actuated
to aspire and endeavour if I cannot make my life sublime, at least to
leave behind me some 'everlasting footprints on the sands of time'.

ERNEST GILES[3]

In Joseph Conrad's novel *Heart of Darkness* (1902), set in the Belgian Congo,
the narrator Marlow explains his fascination with African exploration in the
following words:

> Now when I was a little chap I had a passion for maps. I would look for hours
> at South America, or Africa, or Australia, and lose myself in all the glories of
> exploration. At that time there were many blank spaces on the earth, and when
> I saw one that looked particularly inviting on a map (but they all look that) I
> would put my finger on it and say, When I grow up I will go there. The North
> Pole was one of those places. ... Other places were scattered about the Equator,
> and in every sort of latitude all over the two hemispheres. ... But there was one
> yet – the biggest, the most blank, so to speak – that I had a hankering after.[4]

Half a century earlier, one of these blank spaces had been the centre of
the Australian continent. To some this geographic enigma was an alluring
challenge; to others it was, as the *Argus* newspaper of Melbourne called it, a
'hideous blank'.

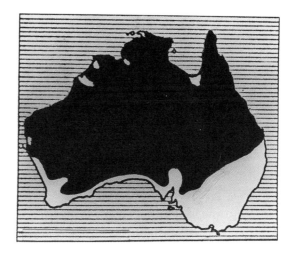

The 'hideous blank'. The
white areas show the limits of
mainland exploration, 1842.

By the 1820s the push for economic development and the cry for more land
arose in all the expanding young settlements nudging the boundaries of
coastal fertility, and successive expeditions were drawn as though by a magnet
towards the centre. As historian Ray Ericksen remarks:

37

> This need [to make use of every part of the continent], widely and urgently felt,
> gave special impetus, as well as sanction, to the reckless speed with which our
> pastoral frontiers expanded in advance of orderly control. It also helps to
> account for the appalling swiftness and thoroughness of our destruction of
> Aboriginal society. . . . the decisive motive was our insistence on a superior right
> to possession and use of the land.[5]

Major exploratory expeditions were exorbitantly expensive and those who
underwrote them, whether from government coffers or the private purse,
expected to see their money multiplied as a result. Fame and the promise of
wealth awaited the first explorers to return with credible accounts of good land
for agriculture or pasture, or of a mineral find. Well-known explorers, carrying
with them the hopes of the colony for expansion and gain, were farewelled
with great festivity. The day that Charles Sturt's expedition left Adelaide for
Central Australia, 10 August 1844, was declared a public holiday in the city and
a lavish breakfast was held in Sturt's honour, attended by the leading citizens
and the governor, Captain George Grey. But this gathering was eclipsed by the
crowd that gathered in Melbourne on 20 August 1860 to catch a glimpse of the
departing Burke and Wills and marvel at their exotic beasts and elaborate
retinue. Despite the optimistic departures, the homecomings often told a

different tale. By the 1840s it was becoming uncomfortably clear that the middle of the continent was desert, or at least surrounded by desert, still shrouded in a cloud of speculation as to its extent, its ferocity and whether it could ever be tamed for settlement.

The quest for an inland sea

For the first half of the nineteenth century the most glittering prize in the exploration of the interior was reserved for the discoverer of a great inland river system or an inland sea. Here, as in so many cases, geographers were seduced by analogy. Europe had three such river systems conveniently crossing the continent, and all the other settled continents had at least one. An orderly universe demanded no less from Australia for, as Sir Joseph Banks had proclaimed in 1778: 'It is impossible to conceive that such a body of land as large as all Europe, does not produce vast rivers capable of being navigated into the heart of the interior.'[6] Soon the existence of the great central river system was 'confirmed' by its appearance on a published map. T.J. Maslen, a retired officer of the East India Company, had never visited Australia but he was not, on that account, deterred from cartographic largesse. His book *Friend of Australia*, compiled in 1827, was illustrated with a map of the continent showing a major river (which he named tellingly the Desired Blessing) flowing conveniently from the south-east of the continent and entering the Indian Ocean on the north-west coast in the vicinity of what is now King Sound.

38

North American parallels in desert exploration are also illuminating in this regard. The northern half of the Great American Desert was referred to by the early Spanish explorers as 'the northern mystery' and for nearly three centuries their descendants hoped and believed that there was a navigable inland waterway flowing from the Atlantic to the Pacific, thereby opening up a direct route to India.[7] Despite notable lack of success in discovering the mouth of such a waterway, the desire for its existence led waves of immigrants to invent names, hypothetical locations, and even fictitious maps of the alleged passage.[8] Belief in this inland waterway still ran high in 1801 when Thomas Jefferson became third President of the United States. He therefore commissioned Meriwether Lewis and William Clark to lead an expedition across 'the immense trackless desert of the West' in order to locate 'direct communication from sea to sea formed by the bed of the Missouri and perhaps the Oregon.' After an epic journey of two years, during 1802–4, Clark produced an imaginative map of the Far West showing the desired inland waterway, thereby perpetuating the myth.[9]

During the first decades of the nineteenth century analogy ran rife and, in addition to a Mississippi-like inland river system, a Great Lake system was confidently predicted for inland Australia.[10] Although there were sceptics, there were equally passionate believers in the inland sea, most notably Edward John Eyre and Charles Sturt. In his expedition of 1828–29 Sturt had come upon the Darling River near Bourke and taken this as evidence of the existence of a great body of water, a belief which he continued to cherish despite his subsequent discovery, in 1829–30, that the river system of south-east Australia flowed south. In his expedition to Central Australia in 1844–46 he optimistically set out on a drought-stricken track with a whaleboat for sailing on this sea, and regularly had it painted along the way, in readiness for launching. As soon as he encountered a declivity in the land, Sturt 'could not but think that we had approached to within a tangible distance of an inland sea.'[11] When he eventually proved, even to himself, that there was no such body of water, he

T.J. Maslen, *Sketch of the Coasts of Australia and of the Supposed Entrance of the Great River,* drawn for *Friend of Australia,* 1827.

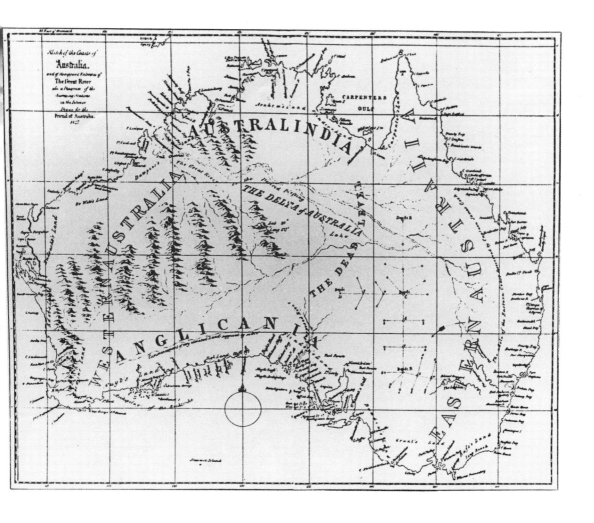

turned to the geological evidence of the remote past, surmising that Australia was formerly an archipelago of islands which some convulsion had raised up along with the intervening sea bed.[12] This theory was, of course, closer to the truth. Some 25,000 years ago permanent freshwater lakes existed in the Lake Eyre basin and 450 million years ago (in the Cretaceous Period) an inland sea stretched nearly 2000 kilometres from King's Canyon to the Western Australian coastline, as evidenced by the many fossils of squid-like nautiloids in what is now stony desert.

Routes of the explorers of Australian desert areas.

The zeal with which the hypothetical inland sea was pursued, in the face of so many deaths and against all reason,[13] indicates that its existence was more than just an economic advantage; it was an ideological necessity, reminiscent of the long-term European belief that a great southern continent must exist because it was 'needed' to balance the northern continents. This widespread Enlightenment belief in balance and order as an innate quality of nature was implicitly reinforced by reference to the ever-ready model of the Orient where green oases studded the sandy wastes; Australia's southern Sahara must do no less.

Psychological and social factors also contributed to the lure of the desert: the quest for fame and the need, in a time of peace, to establish proof of manhood and heroism; the demonstration of conspicuous loyalty to Queen and Empire; a declared concern for the public good; and the desire to inscribe reassuringly familiar names upon the vast blank space in the centre of the map, thereby endowing it with a meaningful history.

Fame

Of the diverse motives that drove professional explorers, fame was the one most widely sanctioned in mid-nineteenth-century British society, which derived many of its role models from Ancient Rome. Certainly it was the one most readily and unselfconsciously put forward in the published accounts, to an extent that embarrasses the modern reader. Sir Thomas Mitchell began the account of his first expedition to discover the alleged River Kindur with words which today unhappily recall Conrad's strictures on the Eldorado Exploring Expedition:

41

> It seemed to me that even war and victory, with all their glory, were far less alluring than the pursuit of researches such as these, the objects of which were to spread the light of civilisation over a portion of creation as yet unknown, though rich, perhaps in the luxuriance of uncultivated nature, and where science might accomplish new and unthought-of discoveries.[14]

Charles Sturt had no hesitation in enrolling himself on the list of famous names in exploration. His naked ambition is apparent in the letters he dashed off to former governor of NSW and a personal friend, Sir Ralph Darling,[15] asserting theatrically that 'it would be better for me to run the risk of letting my bones blanch in the desert than to remain where I am without any prospect of advancement',[16] and to Lady Darling: 'I would not choose to fall more enviably than so as to have my name placed with Cook and Humboldt.'[17] Fame was the reward for evidence of exceptional endurance and self-sacrifice, conceived as a statement of superior masculinity, especially when employed in the service of some higher good. The explorers were thus constrained to construct their narratives so as to draw particular attention to both their physical prowess and the noble cause to which it was allegedly dedicated. For British explorers such a cause – the Empire – was readily at hand.

For Empire and the country's good

The cause of Empire was further elevated by the degree of reverence accorded to the Queen. Victoria, if not a Virgin Queen, was nevertheless cast as the chaste and virtuous Mater Imperatrix. Franz Xavier Winterhalter's painting *The First of May (1851)*, a classic Adoration of the Magi composition,[18] depicts her as an almost emblematic recipient of the devotion expressed in explorers' narratives, such as Ernest Giles's account, in *Australia Twice Traversed*, of finding and naming Queen Victoria Springs and the Great Victoria Desert.[19]

The umbrella of Empire suggested both comparison and rivalry between its colonies. For Australian explorers, the exploits of Livingstone and Stanley

Ulrick J. Burke, *24th of May – 'The Queen'*, from Peter Egerton Warburton, *Journey Across the Western Interior of Australia.*

and of Burton and Speke in Africa had established the pantheon in which it was important to be numbered.[20] Giles goes on to urge a claim, albeit nicely understated, that his expedition has been more difficult, and hence more meritorious, than those of his more famous African counterparts, David Livingstone who had named the Victoria Falls and John Speke who 'discovered' Lake Victoria and provided the information that led to the European 'discovery' of Lake Albert Nyanza:

> In future times these may be celebrated localities in the British Monarch's dominions. I have no Victoria or Albert Nyanzas, no Tanganyikas, Lualabas, or Zambezes, like the great African travellers to honour with Her Majesty's name, but the humble offering of a little spring in a hideous desert, which, had it surrounded the great geographical features I have enumerated, might well have kept them concealed for ever, will not, I trust, be deemed unacceptable in Her Majesty's eyes, when offered by a loyal and most faithful subject.[21]

John Forrest's account of his return to Perth after his journeys included without demur a report of fervent welcome speeches, placing him in the company of '. . . such men as Mungo Park; Bruce, who explored the sources of the Nile; and Campbell, who, labouring in the same cause, traversed the wilds of Africa; and that greatest and noblest of all explorers, the dead but immortal Livingstone!'[22] The Sydney newspaper, the *Empire*, resorted to similar comparisons in its praise of John McDouall Stuart's first undisputed crossing of the continent from south to north. 'Henceforth Mr Stuart's name will rank with those of the discoverers of the North-west Passage and the sources of the Nile; his labours possess the additional recommendation that they can be turned to profitable account.'[23] The Royal Geographical Society obviously agreed. It had already presented Stuart with a gold watch in acknowledgment of his 1858 expedition; it now awarded him the Patron's Medal (the Victoria Medal), making him the only person besides Livingstone to receive both awards.

43

While imperial accolades may have represented the pinnacle of personal fame, in the colonies the profession of acting for the public good carried more immediate appeal and expedition leaders almost invariably alleged this to be one of their main considerations. In the preface to his *Narrative of an Expedition into Central Australia*, Sturt asserted that he had sought and entered upon

> the field of Discovery . . . not without a feeling of ambition, I am ready to admit, for that feeling should ever pervade the breast of a soldier, but also with an earnest desire to promote the public good, and certainly without the hope of any other reward than the credit due to successful enterprise.[24]

This statement ill accords with his financial bargaining before the expedition and his subsequent machinations to obtain a knighthood for his endeavours. In the appendix to the *Narrative*, addressed to the Right Honourable Lord Stanley, he declared himself a loyal public servant desirous only of 'endeavouring, by personal and honourable exertion, to benefit my Country and mankind'.[25] However, despite such high-flown statements about his public-spirited motivation, several remarks in his *Journal*, not intended for publication, make it clear that financial reward was also high on his list of priorities; and in an unguarded moment he even wrote to the governor of South Australia, Sir George Grey, of his wife and children as 'those for whose good alone I have sought this desperate task.'[26] It is arguable, however, that all these considerations were indeed subsidiary to his personal obsession with vindicating his belief in an inland sea and being the first to reach the centre of the continent. In the introduction to her edition of his *Journal* Jill Waterhouse astutely remarks:

> Sturt, though he often claimed otherwise, was fully aware of the probable length
> and dangers of the journey, and what tormented him was he knew in
> his heart of hearts that he would have embarked on it whatever the dangers.
> Had he been single, he certainly would have gone; now that he was married, he
> had to rationalise his desire so that it became a duty. . . . A duty to whom? To
> his family? To himself? To the nation?[27]

Conjunction of opposites: heroism and glad tidings

Despite the many complex factors involved in the success of an expedition, the explorers' popular fame was assessed in direct proportion to the dangers encountered. Those who died in the cause were accorded the highest honours, even if their expeditions achieved little of economic importance. Leichhardt's overland journey from Moreton Bay to Port Essington in 1844–45, during which he was presumed dead, was remembered more than Gregory's more productive explorations around the Victoria River in 1855–56, and his final disappearance in 1848 ensured his lasting pre-eminence, along with Burke and Wills, in exploration mythology, even though these latter expeditions contributed virtually nothing to knowledge of the land, the flora or the fauna.[28] The correlation between death and fame was well understood by the Adelaide citizen who allegedly said to Giles, after his first, unsuccessful attempt to cross the Nullarbor to the west coast, 'Ah, Ernest, my boy, you should never have come back. You should have sent your diary back by Tietkins [his second-in-command] and died out there yourself.'[29]

In reporting on their journeys, explorers were therefore faced with an almost insoluble dilemma. To guarantee their heroism they were required to emphasise the extreme physical trials of their journey, the threats from Aborigines, the mental hardships, the testing of the human spirit. But to validate the expedition funding, certainly to secure more, and to win the gratitude of governments and the public alike, there was a virtual requirement to return, if at all possible, with favourable news of the development potential of the newly charted land. For this it was necessary to depict the terrain quite differently – ideally it should be well watered and fertile, readily accessible, and preferably free from native visitation, especially of a hostile kind. Without such a report, an expedition, however heroic, risked condemnation as a failure. One sees contemporary reviewers of Eyre's *Journals* struggling with this perplexity, condemning the 'unsatisfactory results' while acknowledging 'the sufferings, escapes, and spirit of endurance' of Eyre himself.[30] In many of the explorers' narratives, particularly those intended for publication, there is a delicate balancing act in progress, a careful sculpting of an ambivalent landscape designed to throw the protagonists into heroic high relief without precluding economic potential. George Grey took no chances; he declared his triumph as part of his title – *Journals of Two Expeditions of Discovery in North-West and Western Australia, during the Years 1837, 38, and 39, under the Authority of Her Majesty's Government, describing Many Newly Discovered, Important, and Fertile Districts* – and then proceeded to demonstrate his heroism throughout. Ernest Giles, the last of the major nineteenth-century explorers, the only one to cross Australia from east to west and back again, and the only white person known to have crossed the infamous Gibson Desert on foot, ended his two-volume account of five separate journeys with words that bravely attempted to accommodate these contradictory requirements:

> It is with regret I have had to record the existence of such large areas of desert land encountered in my travels in Australia. The emigrant, however, need have no fear on that account. The scenes of his avocations will be far removed from them. They are no more a check to emigration now than fifty years ago. . . . Anyone who is sufficiently interested to read these pages may well understand the trials and dangers that have beset my path. The number of miles of previously unknown country that I have explored reaches to the sum of many thousands. The time I expended was five of the best years of my life.[31]

45

John McDouall Stuart described the dangers of his journeys clearly enough, particularly his skirmishes with the Aborigines, but he took care also to deliver to the South Australian colonists periodic rosy pictures of the country's potential for settlement. 'After leaving it [the Finke River], on a bearing of 329°, for nine miles, we passed over a plain of as fine a country as any man would wish to see – a beautiful red soil covered with grass a foot high. . . . I have not passed through such splendid country since I have been in the colony.' The area around the Adelaide River elicited similar enthusiasm: '. . . a grassy plain of a beautiful black alluvial soil, covered with lines and groves of the cabbage palm trees, which give it a very picturesque appearance. . . . The country gone over to-day, though not all of the very best description, has plains in it of the very finest kind – even the sandy table-land bears an abundant crop of grass.'[32] These glowing accounts were almost certainly a major factor in generating the continued South Australian support for Stuart's six successive expeditions. Eyre, on the other hand, who had no wish to continue in the field of exploration, unambiguously condemned the terrain encountered on his abortive attempt to reach the centre of the continent and on his subsequent journey around the Great Australian Bight from Streaky Bay to King George's Sound. Instead of promises of desirable real estate, he promotes his own sense of duty and heroic endurance, more relevant considerations for the public career he wished to embark upon. His preface, written in the third person, includes the frank disclaimer:

> the author would observe that he has been led to engage in it [publishing his *Journals*] rather from a sense of duty, and at the instance of his friends, than from any wish of his own. The greater portion of the country he explored was of so sterile and worthless a description, and the circumstances which an attempt to cross such a desert region led to, were of so distressing a character, that he would not willingly have revived associations, so unsatisfactory and so painful.[33]

Public response to the expeditions and their leaders was heavily influenced by such considerations. Hence the poor initial reception Sturt received when he not only failed to discover an inland sea in his Central Australian expedition of 1844–45 (at the time of his setting out probably only Sturt still believed in such a phenomenon)[34] but declared virtually all the land he had traversed unsuitable for settlement. An editorial in the *Sydney Morning Herald* praised Ludwig Leichhardt's journey from Moreton Bay to Port Essington by contrasting it with Sturt's failure:

> The joyous, the exultant sensations which this brilliant deed has inspired in the breast of the colonists is the greater from its having followed the gloomy disappointment caused by the disastrous issue of Captain Sturt's last expedition. Sturt's announcement struck daggers into our Australian hearts; Leichhardt's has applied a balm that has neutralised 'the poison and healed the wound'.[35]

It is a retrospective irony that much of the terrain traversed by Sturt in a year of severe drought, and rejected by him as impossible for settlement, was later to yield not only adequate grazing land but rich mineral deposits. Four decades later Ernest Giles wrote critically of Sturt's adverse assessment of the land:

> A great portion, if not all the country, explored by that expedition is now highly-prized pastoral land, and a gold field was discovered almost in sight of a depot formed by Sturt, at a spot where he was imprisoned at a water hole for six months without moving his camp. He described the whole region as a desert. . . . Sturt's views are only to be accounted for by the fact that what we now call excellent sheep and cattle country appeared to him like a desert, because his comparisons were made with the best alluvial lands he had left near the coast.[36]

Similarly, the Burke and Wills expedition, by most criteria an embarrassing disaster,[37] was judged a success at the time as the result of the explorers' account of apparent fertility in an area previously assumed to be totally desolate.

Fighting the desert

Although Leichhardt remained one of the best known of inland explorers, and a significant number of Germans were attracted to the expeditions, mainly as naturalists, most desert exploration was conducted under British command. The leaders of these expeditions came predominantly from a military background, a factor that was to have a considerable effect on their subsequent reports and on long-term attitudes to the land. The army was regarded by organising bodies and financial backers as the most effective training for leading an expedition, for making and enforcing necessary decisions, for disciplining 'the men', for surveying and mapping, and, perhaps most importantly, for physical and mental endurance. Complementing this perception was the fortuitous availability of military officers to undertake leadership of such expeditions owing to the sheer success of the Pax Britannica. With the exception of the brief Crimean War (1854–56) there was little opportunity for promotion in the British army between the end of the Napoleonic Wars in 1815 and the beginning of the first Boer War in 1880, but for adventurous young men an alternative path to advancement and heroism was to transfer to one of Britain's colonies and there secure the leadership of an exploratory campaign instead of a military one. Given the rigours of the terrain, the notion of a war waged against the land seemed more than metaphorical and death in the desert, whether delivered by an Aboriginal spear or the more lingering agony of thirst and malnutrition, no less honourable than death on the battlefield. For the successful survivor, on the other hand, there were significant material rewards in the form of land grants or money, honours from the Royal Geographical Society, possibly even a knighthood,[38] and the still more lasting fame of naming a geographical feature, an honour not available to even the highest ranks of the military. Consequently many of the most famous names in Australian desert exploration, including Sir Thomas Mitchell, Sir George Grey, Charles Sturt, Peter Egerton Warburton and Robert O'Hara Burke, were drawn from the officer class of the British army.

The influence of this military metaphor on the ideology and language of exploration has been all-pervasive. The surveyor's need for height is translated into the tactical language of war and the verb 'to command' features prominently in journals of exploration as leaders assert their visual conquest over surrounding territory from some local prominence.[39] But, given that exploration was viewed as a military campaign, the question arises: against whom was it waged? who or what was the enemy? There were only two candidates for this role: the allegedly hostile natives, whom the history of exploration rendered all but obligatory; or the land itself, depicted as an antagonist to be subdued.

Conquering the 'savage tribes'

Although there was never any serious belief that they constituted a major threat, the Aborigines represented, by default, the Australian counterparts of African tribes, North American Indians, and New Zealand Maoris. Few in number and helpless against firearms, they were an object of pity rather than fear, though they did, at times, successfully ambush unsuspecting Europeans, infrequently causing death.[40] The attitudes of the desert explorers to the Aborigines they encountered were coloured not only pragmatically, by the contacts of settlers with the indigenous people, but also theoretically, by contemporary European ideas about 'primitive' races.

The Enlightenment concept of the 'noble savage' readily stretched to include the Polynesian peoples, but the Australian Aborigines, along with the Maoris and Fuegians, were less easily accommodated, and recent commentators have distinguished between a 'soft' primitivism applied to the former and a 'hard' primitivism applied to the latter. As art historian Bernard Smith points out,[41] soft primitivism was more closely associated with deistic thought and neoclassical values, and the Polynesians were appropriated pictorially as inheritors of Classical Greek physique and poses. The Aborigines, however, were less easily pressed into this mould, and disappointed early colonists reverted to attitudes resembling the abhorrence expressed by William Dampier in 1697: 'The Inhabitants of this country are the miserablest People in the World ... who have no Houses and skin Garments, Sheep, Poultry and Fruits of the Earth. ... They differ but little from Brutes.'[42]

Moreover, the rise of evangelicalism and European missionary endeavour during the nineteenth century led to a hardening of attitude towards non-Christian people; their culture was seen as necessarily depraved, redeemable only by conversion to European norms and the Christian faith. Ironically, Darwinism tended to confirm the evangelical assessment since it was popularly believed to provide 'scientific' evidence of the conviction that non-white races were, by definition, inferior to Europeans in biological development, understanding, morality and culture.

These views were still flourishing at the end of the nineteenth century and statements such as 'a race very low in the intellectual scale of humanity', 'the mental degradation of the autochthones of Australia', 'the zero, so to speak, of all anthropological analysis' were still being bandied around.[43] However, during the decades of desert exploration both attitudes – the neo-classical model, reinforced by the Romantic estimate of primitive peoples as naturally free from the evils of civilised society, and the view that they were a biologically and culturally inferior race – were current and reports of encounters with desert Aborigines show allegiance to one or other of these prevailing stereotypes (or sometimes both). Discussions of Aboriginal intelligence, estimated according

48

ABOVE
S.T. Gill, *Country North-west of Tableland*, 1846, watercolour, 19.1 × 30.7 cm, National Library of Australia, Canberra.

BELOW
S.T. Gill, (Australia 1818–80), *Invalid's tent, Salt Lake, 75 miles north-west of Mount Arden*, 1846, watercolour on paper, 21.4 × 34.2 cm, Art Gallery of South Australia, Adelaide. Morgan Thomas Bequest Fund, 1944.

ABOVE
Ludwig Becker, *Crossing the Terrick-Terrick Plains, August 29, 1860,* 1860, watercolour and pen-and-ink, 12.5 × 17.7 cm, La Trobe Collection, State Library of Victoria.

BELOW
Ludwig Becker, *Border of the Mud-desert near Desolation Camp*, 1861, watercolour, 14.0 × 22.8 cm, La Trobe Collection, State Library of Victoria.

ABOVE
Nicholas Chevalier
(Australia 1828–1902),
*Memorandum of the Start of
the Exploring Expedition*,
1860, Melbourne, oil on
canvas, 97.4 × 153.2 cm,
Art Gallery of South
Australia, Adelaide. M.J.M.
Carter Collection, 1993.

BELOW
Henry Short, *Our Adopted
Country. To the Memory of
the Lamented Heroes of the
Victorian Exploration*,
1861, oil on canvas,
70.0 × 90.7 cm, La Trobe
Collection, State Library
of Victoria.

William Strutt, *The Burial of Burke*, 1911, oil on canvas, 122.0 × 207.5 cm, La Trobe Collection, State Library of Victoria.

to the arbitrary criteria of the explorers and ignoring survival skills, almost invariably inclined to the 'inferior race' stereotype. Sturt professed to provide scientifically based evidence of this view: 'If there is any truth in phrenology, they must have their share of the brutal passions. The whole appearance of the cranium, indeed, would lead to the conclusion that they possess very few of the intellectual faculties.'[44] Giles subscribed to a similar estimate, dismissing the cave paintings of the 'Troglodytes' as:

> hideous shapes, of things such as can exist only in their imaginations, and they are but the weak endeavours of these benighted beings to give form and semblance to the symbolisms of the dread superstitions, that, haunting the vacant chambers of their darkened minds, pass amongst them in the place of either philosophy or religion[45]

The assumptions of inferiority on the part of the Aborigines frequently surfaced under the guise of concern for their inevitable extinction. In the preface to his *Journals of Expeditions of Discovery into Central Australia*, Eyre professed regret for 'a people who are fast fading away before the progress of civilization which ought only to have added to their improvement and prosperity', and quoted Polish explorer Count Strzelecki's words that the attitude of the Europeans to the imminent demise of the race was 'like an inquest of the one race upon the corpse of the other, ending for the most part with the verdict of "died by the visitation of God".'[46] Four decades later Giles even accepted some blame, in his capacity as explorer, for hastening the inevitable demise of the race: 'On me, perchance, the eternal obloquy of God's doom may rest, for being the first to lead the way, with prying eye and trespassing foot, into regions so fair and so remote'.[47]

Few of the explorers seem to have realised that the negative reception they sometimes elicited from the indigenous desert people was the result of their inevitable competition for scarce supplies of water. The Aborigines, accustomed to surviving in arid conditions through their abstemious habits, were no doubt horrified to see the amount of water consumed by these new arrivals and, even more, by their animals. Hospitable at first, they were soon doing everything in their power to dissuade the intruders from their territory. Stuart, victim of several well-conceived Aboriginal ambushes, had no cause to consider them inferior opponents: 'If they had been Europeans they could not better have arranged and carried out their plan of attack.'[48] Giles, too, recorded that it was only by chance that his party was not murdered by a surprise attack as they sat at supper. He also remarked, seemingly unaware of the irony entailed, that this attack was occasioned by the tribes' resentment when several of them were ordered away from his camp. 'I ordered these *intruders* out [my italics]. Thereupon they became very saucy and disagreeable and gave me to understand that this was their country and their water.'[49]

In the main, however, confrontations with Aborigines were played down. They appeared more often as the subject of a regretful analysis[50] of their inevitable demise as a species, an occasion for the writer to demonstrate

49

humanitarian concern in the certain knowledge that any problems of cohabitation would shortly be resolved in favour of the Europeans. They were thus relegated to the status of passive objects, to be vivified, like features of the landscape, only when noticed by the recording eye. This ability of the Europeans to determine whether or not the Aborigines would be included in their narratives, as well as how and when, conferred a new level of power on the explorers and put the indigenous peoples on the same level as native fauna, waiting on the sidelines for scientific analysis and classification, or even edited out of the narrative entirely.

Conquering a gendered land

Infinitely more implacable as an enemy of inland exploration was the land itself. Early writing about the Australian desert is characterised by three exceptional, if not unique, features. Firstly, because we know exactly when the public exploring expeditions[51] were mounted and have access to almost all the accounts produced,[52] we can pinpoint very precisely when this body of material appeared, and thus contextualise it with reference to European influences. Secondly, the early records were written not by people who actually lived in the desert, but by travellers, so the views expressed, often based on preconceptions, were formed quickly rather than after a long period of reflection.

Thirdly, the visitors were all men. Until the arrival of Daisy Bates on the edge of the Nullarbor in 1912, there were no Australian counterparts of the renowned British female travellers Lady Mary Wortley Montague, Lady Hester Stanhope, Amelia Edwards or the 245 British women who published travelogues on the Middle East between 1821 and 1914.[53] Women travellers, as Pratt has shown, had a different agenda. In general they were less intent on conquering and possessing the landscape than on understanding themselves through the process of considering and assessing colonial societies, and constructing what Pratt calls personal 'feminotopias' that were critical of male travel writing.[54] Recent studies also suggest that women travellers in the Orient, whether or not they were themselves artists, celebrated the women they encountered in aesthetic rather than erotic terms, erecting a respectful distance between the European observer and the observed.[55] These kinds of insight, strikingly different from the records of male exploration, are virtually absent from the nineteenth-century literature of the Australian desert, an absence that was to have major ramifications in national responses to the interior of the continent.

The gendering of the land in Western culture can be seen as part of the more general categorising of nature as female,[56] and hence as an extension of Plato's mind–matter dualism. In this binary system the elements of mind, the male principle and rational or cultural pursuits were regarded as inherently superior to physical matter, the female and nature. A 'female' land was thus a ready metaphor for male explorers to use, identifying an alien terrain with the alien sex, and thus constituting it as doubly 'other'. Also implicit in the image of a female land was the notion of conquest and possession. Consciously or not, the inland explorers conceived of their endeavours in terms of a classical struggle or *agon*, in which they themselves were the protagonists and some conceptual composite embracing nature, the land, the feminine, the 'other', was cast as antagonist.

However, contrary to the expected outcome of the gender war, the desert proved to be no passive, acquiescent 'lady'. Ernest Giles, for example, wrote, 'I was pitted, or had pitted myself, against Nature, and a second time I was conquered. ... In vain the strong will and the endeavour which for ever wrestled with the tides of fate'.[57] Accounts of expeditions to the interior of the continent commonly have recourse to the imagery of sexual conquest, the removal of the veil as a visual metaphor for dis-covery[58] and the penetration (a word that occurs with extraordinary frequency in exploration literature) of the 'inner recesses' of the land. The notion of unveiling the land conforms closely to feminist theories of the gaze, whereby the male observer constructs an image of the female as both the passive object of study and the willing object of desire.[59] Sturt wrote of his earlier expedition in search of the great inland river system: 'The veil has only as it were been withdrawn from the marshes of the Macquarie, to be spread over the channel of the Darling.'[60] At the end of his fourth journey he moralised: 'His [the explorer's] duty is to penetrate it [the country]. ... The successful penetration of such a region must ... have its value'[61] and he writes of 'penetrating the deserts from which he [Eyre] had been forced back'.[62] Perhaps most revealingly Sturt also counterpoints masculine rationality against the quasi-feminine country in a process that he describes as a siege: 'Such a country can only be penetrated by cool calculation and determined perseverance. I have sat down before it as a besieger before a fortress to make my approaches with the same systematic regularity.'[63] Eyre, too, was obsessed with reaching 'the vast recesses of the interior of Australia, to try to lift up the veil which has hitherto shrouded its mysteries from the researches of the traveller'.[64]

The explorers' characterisation of an implicitly gendered land, and of the desert in particular, was an important component of their public self-construction as intrepid heroes. However, the most highly mythologised heroes of Australian exploration, Sturt, Leichhardt, Burke and Wills, are those who, in terms of conquering the land, could only be considered failures. Indeed, Christina Thompson has suggested that in Australian exploration narratives:

> in order to convey the omnipotence of the desert, its indifference, its
> superiority, and conceivably its malignancy ... the explorer is sexually
> characterised as perverse, as infantile, as masochistic, as deviant in some respect.
> The explorer as a sexual figure becomes subservient. The love story which
> results – the romance of exploration – is a 'romance' in most uncertain terms.[65]

51

As we shall see below, the Gothic imagery used by many of the explorers suggests their representation of themselves as victims of a malignant land, counterparts of the imprisoned Gothic heroine.

It has been noted that in most colonial landscape imagery the land is doubly subordinated: 'on the one hand a rich, fecund virgin land is supposedly available for fertilisation; on the other hand, a libidinous and wild land has to be forcefully tamed and domesticated.'[66] But while these two images have been liberally applied to America, the West Indies, Africa, and the Pacific island nations, Central Australia defied such characterisation. Other 'female' stereotypes were then resorted to. Contrasting the Australian attitudes towards the land with the pantheistic affection of Finns for their country, historian Miriam Dixson has concluded that 'Australia is like the body of an unloved woman'.[67] The infertile, drought-ridden land was characterised as an old hag, barren and past her time; the irregularity of seasonal rainfall, the erratic rivers and the mirages that teased the struggling explorers were readily construed as expressions of female fickleness and deception, a wilful shrewishness that required taming through the well-worn tropes of conquest and possession. This magisterial attitude to the land was further reinforced by the assumptions implicit in the science of surveying and the underlying ideology of cartography.

Surveying and mapping the land

After the army, the second great recruiting ground of expedition leaders was the Government Survey Office where it was assumed that, if they had not learned leadership, they had at least been trained in the principles of cartography. Augustus Charles Gregory and his brother Francis, John and Alexander Forrest, William Christie Gosse, George Woodroffe Goyder, John McDouall Stuart and David Lindsay were all trained surveyors, while in 1827 Major Thomas Mitchell stepped sideways from an army career to appointment as surveyor-general of New South Wales, in which role he duly appointed himself leader of four major exploring expeditions.[68] While curiosity and the desire for fame and adventure were certainly not lacking among the Australian explorers, the predominant public service mentality, whether emanating from the army or the Survey Department, was significantly different from the motives which drove the British explorers of the African and Middle Eastern deserts. Few were interested in the intrinsic character of the desert or the culture of its inhabitants: there was no Richard Burton, no Hester Stanhope or Charles Doughty, no T.E. Lawrence 'embodying in his person', as Simmons says, 'all the nostalgia the English people felt for the purity of the desert, the nobility of its people, and an earlier period of chivalric warfare.'[69] There was, in Australia, little notion of cherishing the desert for its own sake, for its uniqueness; rather it was perceived as an object for conquest.

Simon Ryan has outlined some of the ways in which the rhetorical structures of cartography have affected notions of the imperial frontier and in particular Australian exploration and the mythology of heroism that emanated

from it.[70] He points out that the gaze of the explorer/surveyor was characterised as god-like, isolated, objective, licensing him to construct the land for
posterity. A fundamental part of that process was the cult of the map as an icon
of scientific accuracy and objectivity. In it was allegedly enshrined the truth
about the land, without regard to the power relationships encoded in such
innocent-sounding concepts as perspective, the privileging of the visual (a
focus inherent in the technical use of the terms 'surveying' and 'observations')
and the notion of separation from the object of observation. These attributes
of cartography are only a special case of the Newtonian paradigm of the distanced, uninvolved observer, surveying the universe and perceiving behind its
unruly facade the orderly laws that determined its behaviour. By a process of
logical slippage, it was a short step from deriving natural laws to imposing
them, a divine prerogative which his contemporaries all but literally ascribed
to Newton.[71] It is within this framework of the physical sciences that the major
exploratory expeditions into the central desert, carried out under the aegis of
the Royal Geographical Society, must be positioned. The Society defined both
the goals of such scientific expeditions and the terms in which the official
reports should be written. In return, the Society dignified the expedition as a
scientific venture and conferred on its leaders the status of scientists, with the
concomitant presumption of ethical nobility, altruism and a brush with Truth.
Such implicit vindication from the scientific world, especially when confirmed
by the gold medal of the Royal Geographical Society,[72] swept along in its train
the more doubtful ideological premises associated with a gendered 'other' and
colonial domination.

53

Naming the desert

In the classical journey narratives, the traveller-hero typically came to places
already inhabited and hence named. But during the great eighteenth-century
voyages of discovery the most fundamental possession ritual of British exploration was the naming of geographical features, on the assumption that before
the advent of Europeans they had no local name, or none worth perpetuating.
John Oxley, when surveyor-general of New South Wales, wrote, 'The naming of
places was often the only pleasure within our reach; but it was some relief from
the desolation of these plains to throw over them the associations of names
dear to friendship, or sacred to genius.'[73] At the time this custom was regarded
as innocent, natural, even necessary, but recent revisionist readings of colonial
practices have, by reference to the Genesis myth of Adam naming the plants
and animals and thereby assuming domination over them, reinterpreted them
as sinister, manipulative and yet another weapon of imperial subjugation. Post-
colonial critics see an imperial power imprinting its particular cultural codes,
prejudices and criteria of value on what it took to be a *tabula rasa*, since the
indigenous peoples were regarded as devoid of culture or appreciation of
abstract values.[74] To the settlers the desert represented the ultimate example of
such uninscribed space, an unparalleled opportunity to impose echoes of what

Fredric Jameson has called the imperial 'master code'. We have seen evidence of this in Giles's naming of Victoria Springs and the Great Victoria Desert, an exercise which not only conferred a compliment on the Queen, Giles's explicit intention, but represented a perhaps less conscious desire to tame the hostile colonial periphery, the threatening 'other', by linking it to the unassailable focus of the familiar, the monarch herself. Ultimately, by such a process of naming the land *after* the representatives (monarchs, home secretaries, governors) of Empire, the whole continent would be verbally positioned in a state of dependence and posterity, the very words freighted with notions of spatial and temporal subordination.[75] It seems not to have occurred to Giles that there would be a local name for such springs or that he might acknowledge it.

Of all areas of the continent, the desert remained most resistant to this domesticating process, as the names bestowed on so many of its hills and mountains testify. The central importance of elevations for the purpose of surveying and mapping the country made it essential that the explorers should seek out such eminences to 'command' the scene, preferably with 360° vision of the surrounding terrain,[76] but inevitably they also hoped for a prospect, if not of prosperity, at least of difference from the monotony around them. The catalogue of their baffled frustration is eloquently expressed in the names they conferred: Mount Hopeless, Mount Deception, Mount Dreadful, Mount Misery, Mount Barren, Ophthalmia Range, Mount Disappointment, Mount Destruction, Mount Desolation, Mount Terrible (originally named Mount Damnable until a later, more puritanical generation came to regard this as blasphemous), Mount Delusion and Mount Despair. Here the only satisfaction left to the imperial conquerors is the Pyrrhic victory of name-calling on a grand scale, a victory that simultaneously announces their defeat.

54

The conceptual attack on the desert

The British imperative to subdue the continent conceptually as well as geographically and economically (and indeed often in defiance of economic best practice) also led to the nineteenth-century obsession with crossing the continent from south to north and from west to east, tying it up like a neat parcel with latitudinal and longitudinal 'string'. These journeys were concrete enactments of the idealised grids that were regarded as the self-evident basis of location. Deriving ultimately from the Augustan–Georgian fascination with Roman military precision and Greek classicism, the British colonial obsession with straight lines was intended to erase both the natural order and any evidence of indigenous occupation.

Paul Carter has commented that the explorers 'were expected to arrest the country, to concentrate it into reversible roads which would summarise its content; they were expected to translate its extension into objects of commerce. They were, by a curious irony, meant to inaugurate a form of possession that would render the dynamic of their own journeys invisible.'[77] The imposition of a geometrical system of measuring the landscape, assumed by the colonists to be scientific, natural and neutral, was, in fact, a means of intellectual appropriation which ignored the parameters suggested by the contours or other innate qualities of the land itself, 'for, by definition, the grid plan equalizes parts, rendering everywhere the same'. The motive behind this was the desire to reduce a whole continent, frightening in its immensity and strangeness, to the comforting order of a universal scientific system, as valid in the Antipodes as at home, the transformation of a vast, alien land to a measurable, homely space.

Ernest Giles took pains to emphasise that his expeditions advanced in straight lines, as though some singular merit derived from this: 'For several years previous to my taking the field, I had desired to be the first to penetrate into this unknown region where, for a thousand miles in a straight line, no white man's foot had ever wandered, or, if it had, its owner had never brought it back, nor told the tale. ... On that expedition [1872] I explored a line of nearly 700 miles of previously unknown country, in a straight line from my starting point.'[78] Burke had forced his way north from Cooper's Creek to the Gulf of Carpentaria in almost a straight line, as though this were a matter of strict principle, and only the fact that he travelled in a season with an exceptionally good supply of water allowed him to survive along this route.

Superimposed on these spatial considerations was the obsession with the particular spatio-temporal event of being the first European to set foot upon the exact geographical centre of a continent, even though it was not unanimously agreed where that point might be. Integrally related to reaching the centre was the need to establish possession by the phallocratic act of planting a flag in this quasi-magical spot – a flag that no one but Aborigines, happily unaware of its intended significance, would see. Sir Thomas Mitchell had hoped to reach it by sailing down the fabled River Kindur, allegedly a tributary of the Darling, while for Charles Sturt the idea of being the first white person to stand at the centre of the continent became a ruling passion.

When Eyre set out from Adelaide in 1841, it was Sturt who had the honour of delivering to him the 'silken union' worked by Miss Hindmarsh and Miss Lepson, 'to be unfurled by him in the centre of the continent'.[79] Eyre failed to achieve that goal. Having mistakenly assumed that the present Lake Eyre was a continuation of a horseshoe-shaped Lake Torrens barring the way to the centre of the continent, he had, he declared, 'no alternative but to turn back from so inhospitable and impracticable a country' and retreated from the 'dismal scene'.[80] But Sturt certainly saw himself as the inheritor of that commission. Less than three years later he wrote grandiosely to Sir Ralph Darling, 'I have a kind of presentiment that I shall unfold the Interior of the World'.[81] Indeed, with the benefit of hindsight, he added, 'So strong has this feeling been upon my mind that I did not expect Mr Eyre wd [sic] succeed in gaining the Centre when he undertook his last fearful journey.'[82] On his expedition to Central Australia in 1844–45 Sturt, too, carried a huge flag, lovingly embroidered by Miss Cooper, the sister of Judge Cooper, a patron of exploration, and her friend Miss Conway, to plant for his Queen in the geographical centre of the continent.[83] Despite his hopeful premonition, he was no more successful

55

than Eyre. Nevertheless, at the end of his abortive expedition, he wrote, 'I can only say that I would not hesitate again to plunge into those dreary regions that I might be the first to place my foot in the centre of this vast territory, and finally to raise the veil which still shrouds its features, even though, like the veiled prophet, they should wither the beholder.'[84]

Leichhardt's last journey (1848) was motivated by his desire to reach the centre from the east, while Augustus Charles Gregory attempted to come at it from the north-west and later from Moreton Bay. However, the honour was reserved for John McDouall Stuart, who had accompanied Sturt as draughtsman, and who, in 1859, successfully led an expedition from Adelaide to Port Darwin, through what he considered to be the centre of the continent.[85] Stuart's laconic style is rarely disturbed by flights of eloquence, but he too becomes unusually emotional about the planting of the flag on the elevation nearest to what he estimated as the centre, Central Mount Stuart. Like Sturt's earlier outpouring on the Murray,[86] Stuart's account, couched in terms which

Nicholas Chevalier, *The Great Australian Exploration Race*, 1860, *Melbourne Punch*, 8 November 1860, p. 124.

now carry a bitterly ironic twist, displays a naive confidence that the significance of this piece of coloured cloth on a pole would be understood in the same terms by the Aborigines:

> Built a large cone of stones in the centre of which I placed a pole with the British flag nailed to it. Near the top of the cone I placed a small bottle, in which there is a slip of paper, with our signatures on it, stating by whom it was raised. We then gave three hearty cheers for the flag, the emblem of civil and religious liberty, and may it be a sign to the natives that the dawn of liberty, civilisation, and Christianity is about to break upon them.[87]

Such were the parameters of the public sphere from which the desert explorers drew their motivation and within which their success was judged. The next chapter examines their own considered reflections on their journeys, as recorded in the heavily revised popular accounts of the expeditions – the first and most influential literature to emerge from the desert.

George French Angas, *Planting the Flag on the Shores of the Indian Ocean*, from *The Journals of John McDouall Stuart During the Years 1858, 1859, 1860, 1861 & 1862*.

Geography Is Never Innocent

Chapter 4

> When efforts are made to describe terrae incognitae, extrapolations
> from the known become confused with the believed, conjectured or
> desired. The white light of knowledge may be seen dispelling the
> shadows that have hidden unknown lands from the sight of man.
> But geographical knowledge is not white light – it is a spectrum with
> wave-lengths of differing sizes and values. And in analysing the
> spectrum it is difficult to separate what is truly known from what is
> thought to be known.
>
> JOHN L. ALLEN[1]

> It is fiction that determines the way we read history, history that is
> contingent on fiction, and not the other way around.
>
> STEPHEN SLEMON[2]

> There was room for snowy mountains, an inland sea, ancient river and
> palmy plain, for races of new kinds of men inhabiting a new and
> odorous land, for fields of gold and golcondas of gems, for a new flora
> and a new fauna, and above all the rest combined, there was room for
> me!
>
> ERNEST GILES[3]

To a greater extent than anywhere else on the globe except Antarctica, the
nineteenth-century explorers shaped the Australian desert for posterity, invest-
ing it with the character and significance it continued to bear for over a century. Their writings not only provided the records and measurements expected
of such expeditions, but the analogies, metaphors and interpretations in which
they couched their impressions became an inseparable part of the message
they brought back. Because the desert experience was for several generations
virtually unavailable to others, the complex matrix of their scientific, emotional and iconographical reporting determined how the desert would be
viewed by the writers and artists who came after them. Unwittingly they generated the Gothic fairytales with which the nation still periodically frightens itself
so that images of treachery in and by the desert lie dormant in the

collective memory ready to erupt at every conforming incident. Two young jackaroos die of thirst in the desert when their car breaks down; baby Azaria Chamberlain is killed by uncertain means at the symbolic centre of the desert: immediately a wave of intense personal fear and anger is unleashed against the desert or its dingoes. Even people who have never been near the desert respond to this psychological power.

The explorers did not set out to deceive. They undoubtedly believed they were delivering an objective account of what they had seen and experienced. But they, as much as their contemporaries, were insidiously seduced by the power of their stories. They not only reinvented themselves as solitary heroes; they changed the accepted goals of exploration, gradually substituting personal endurance for economic good news, exploit for exploration. The uniquely Australian exploration myth of a glorious defeat began with Eyre's account of his epic journey across the Bight, continued with Sturt's obsessive expedition into Central Australia in search of an inland sea, drew sustenance from the many hypothetical accounts of 'lost Leichhardt' and culminated in the fiasco of the Burke and Wills disaster. By drawing strength from each incident the myth was able to subsume successive individual 'defeats', reinterpreting incompetence and poor planning as the malevolent actions of a sinister, implicitly personified desert.

The myth was created not from any factual material but through the literary power of the published accounts, the most famous Australian explorers being those who created for themselves a fictional heroic persona. Consciously or not they modelled themselves on Coleridge's Ancient Mariner, translating his experience of alone-ness 'on a wide wide sea' into a parallel one of existential loneliness at the centre of a continent. Eyre, ignoring the presence of his Aboriginal companion Wylie, told a tale of lonely endurance pursued by the spectre of thirst throughout a journey of unimaginable terrors. Sturt painted a desert landscape that focussed all the 'desolation and destruction' of the Gothic sublime. Leichhardt presented himself as the patient scientist consecrated to the service of God. Stuart on the other hand was so keen to promote the land he had travelled through that he underplayed the significant suffering he endured, while Giles, who endured hardships arguably greater than those of more famous explorers, debarred himself from the role of tragic hero by the cheerful tone of his published account. By describing his difficulties with wit and humour he made them too accessible to a public that craved superhuman heroes. So effective were the accounts of Eyre, Sturt and Leichhardt in defining the expectation of what great explorers should be that the lack of documentation from the Burke and Wills expedition was the opportunity for these ill-fated explorers to have the service performed for them. King and Gray were virtually edited out of the story, the terrain was recast in the format of Sturt's burning desert, and Wills inherited from Leichhardt the mantle of disinterested scientist patiently studying the works of the Creator.

A necessary condition of these tales of heroism was the construction of a landscape of terror. Few would now disagree with Foucault that 'the quest for truth was not an objective and neutral activity, but was intimately related to the "will to power" of the truth-seeker. The "knowledge" they conveyed was thus a form of power presented in the guise of scientific disinterestedness'.[4]

Writing the adventure narrative

The continuing popularity of Homer's *Odyssey* testifies to the perpetual fascination of travellers' tales independent of their credibility. However, in eighteenth-century Europe, the Homeric formula of interweaving the everyday and the exotic with minimal regard for probability was modified by a new requirement, scientific realism. Influenced by the flowering of Francis Bacon's project of building an immense, worldwide data base of information, readers of the Enlightenment were encouraged to expect that accounts of the wonderful and strange would be viewed through a filter of objectivity and accuracy. The sponsoring of journeys by scientific bodies such as the Royal Society and its various specialist counterparts, notably the Royal Geographical Society, imposed rigorous criteria of observation, measurement and classification within a systematic framework. The accepted formula for presenting results to these learned societies discouraged undue speculation or imaginative language. Captain James Cook's voyages to the Pacific and Alexander von Humboldt's journeys in the Americas provided the prototypes for this new style of adventure narrative. But while the Royal Society applauded Cook's journals as the model for such factual discourse, the British Admiralty, which had provided the ship and the personnel for the first voyage, seems to have been well aware that Cook's log and original journals were somewhat deficient in narrative interest. It commissioned John Hawkesworth, a freelance writer, to produce a version with more popular appeal. Both the text and the newly devised illustrations of Hawkesworth's three-volume *Account of the Voyages Undertaken by the Order of His Present Majesty for Making Discoveries in the Southern Hemisphere* (1773) transformed Cook's restrained, factual account, embellishing it with allusions to classical mythology and transforming the Fuegians and Australian Aborigines into modern Spartans contemptuous of luxuries in their deliberate espousing of Greek virtues.[5] Decried by purists for such changes, Hawkesworth's *Voyages* was nevertheless immensely successful with the public,[6] immediately providing a model for popular exploration literature.

Both these modes of travel discourse, the scientific and the popular, were still much in evidence throughout the nineteenth century and the Australian inland explorers were well aware of the importance of satisfying both kinds of readers. Most produced at least two published accounts of their journeys: the official narrative for the Royal Geographical Society, the State Parliament, or other funding body, and a later popular version. The former asserted its credentials by being closely based on the log books and diaries written during the expedition, and claiming historical veracity. Authors therefore resisted literary devices such as metaphor and closure, except insofar as the return of the expedition provided the latter element. They also privileged the visual over other modes of knowing, classifying objects solely by their visible features, and relying heavily on measurement as a guarantee of first-hand experience and scientific accuracy. The implicit purpose of such documents was to edit the observer out of the account, to imply that the observations, being recorded with total objectivity, carried universal validity and relevance: they were 'the facts' with no value added. We recognise, now, that such affectations of disinterestedness mask a hidden agenda. Selection of what is observed and what is reported, the ordering of elements within the account and the language used are but some of the ways of introducing a value system. For Europeans, the most fundamental signifier of possession of new territory was the map: only when land was satisfactorily mapped was it brought into conformity with the Enlightenment ideal of order.[7] Hence, along with the comprehensive list of the Latin names of all flora and fauna observed en route, the map accompanying the account was assumed to provide unassailable evidence of the first-hand experience and scientific objectivity of the writer. As such it carried a talismanic quality as the precious thread the explorer unwound through the labyrinth of the unknown land to show the way to those who came after.

Ironically, although maps were revered as the guarantee of authenticity, the cartography of the inland expeditions was far from accurate. As well as frequent failures of surveying equipment and discrepancies between the measurements obtained by different members of the group, the major problem was the large element of subjectivity involved in the estimation of distance. Toiling at a snail's pace across unfamiliar and tortuous terrain, the explorers understandably tended to overestimate the distance travelled in a day and, when one day after another brought the same monotonous scenery, to omit whole days from their calculations. When the English cartographer, John Arrowsmith, attempted to produce maps from Sturt's *Journal* of his 1844–46 expedition into Central Australia, he had immense difficulty in matching the distance the explorer claimed to have traversed with that indicated by the relevant latitude and longitude positions.[8] Sturt's *Journal* record for 20 August 1845, for example, states that the party covered a distance of 15 miles (24 kilometres); in the later 'Condensed Account', prepared for the Royal Geographical Society, the entry for that date has stretched the distance to 45 to 50 miles,[9] while Arrowsmith's map shows it as 12 miles. At the point where he finally turned for home Sturt wrote in his *Narrative* that he 'was at that moment scarcely a degree from the Tropic, and within 150 miles of the centre of the continent'.[10] In fact the distance to Central Mount Stuart was 400 miles (650 kilometres), of which 300 miles were across the terrible Simpson Desert, and Sturt was considerably more than one degree south of the Tropic.[11] With the benefit of hindsight we may now realise that 'maps do not reflect reality but produce it in a number of ways, and in so doing represent particular interests and create various realities'.[12] As a result we may be tempted to censure the explorers for their gross exaggerations, suspecting them of arrant

61

self-aggrandisement. But such facile condemnation ignores the different genres, each with its own parameters, in which they were writing.

If the official account intended for the Royal Geographical Society omitted the explorer, the popular narrative reinstated him with full honours. For the general reader the explorer was necessarily and of right the hero of his own picaresque novel which derived its structural organisation from his continuing presence, personality and commentary on the passing panorama of his journey. Knowing that the author had returned in safety to tell the tale may have decreased the suspense, but the circular journey from settlement to wilderness and back to habitation provided the reader not only with vicarious participation in the achievements of this courageous representative, but with a satisfying metaphor of formal closure. In the popular accounts of his journey the explorer's subjective responses were made more explicit: his speculations and feelings were allowed full rein to qualify the strictly visual experience and it was this web of impressions, psychological as much as visual, that provided the basic fabric for the mythology lovingly embroidered upon it by successive generations.

Even though the explorer-as-expedition-leader was at the mercy of the land and its inhabitants, the climate and the state of preparedness of his party, the explorer-as-narrator had the power to re-create the journey in much greater conformity with what he would have wished it to be, to gloss over errors of judgement, to re-emphasise the successes and minimise the failures, above all to explain his mistakes after the event, invoking mitigating circumstances. False starts, detours and abortive forays out from a safe camp could be excluded from the narrative or made to seem inevitable. By means of such cosmetic surgery, he was able to provide for posterity another classic text of exploration, complete with a courageous, commanding hero, cool-headed in decision-making, generous to the Aborigines unless provoked beyond reason, selflessly enduring a hostile environment for Queen, country and science, and inspiring his party to similar feats of heroism. Many years after the event Giles could declare with conviction:

> I represented that we were probably in the worst desert upon the face of the earth, but that fact should give us all the more pleasure in conquering it. . . .
> I had sworn to go to Perth or die in the attempt, and I inspired the whole of my party with my own enthusiasm.[13]

Random events, too, could be endowed with special significance by repositioning in time, by emphasis and by editing out conflicting interests. John Eyre's nightmare journey around the Great Australian Bight from Streaky Bay to King George's Sound is consciously constructed as an almost classic narrative of exploration around a series of dramatic events, pre-eminently the death of his only white companion Baxter at the hands of two rebellious Aborigines. This incident is positioned strategically at the mid-point of the story as a fitting climax at the end of volume I: 'I was horror-struck to find my poor overseer lying on the ground weltering in his blood, and in the last agonies of death.'

Volume II begins with the full emotional impact on Eyre in the midst of a Gothic scene that owes more to *Hamlet* than to the Royal Society's prescriptions for the presentation of observations.

> The frightful, the appalling truth now burst upon me, that I was alone in the desert. . . . At the dead hour of night, in the wildest and most inhospitable wastes of Australia, with the fierce wind raging in unison with the scene of violence before me.[14]

Eyre's highly dramatic reconstruction, with its word play on the 'dead hour of night' paralleling the dead man, wilfully ignores the presence of the remaining Aborigine, Wylie, who faithfully accompanied him to the end of his journey. This is partly because Wylie is not perceived as a human companion, a comrade in the field, but only as a 'native'; but more centrally because Eyre is intent on recording not primarily the event but *his feelings* in response to it. With the realisation that in this immense and barren expanse he is suddenly bereft of the one person with whom he could share his experience, his overwhelming emotions are terror and a sense of almost cosmic loneliness. Similarly the amazing, comic-opera hiatus in the midst of the trek across the Bight, when Eyre was taken aboard the French ship *Mississippi* by its Captain Rossiter and revived with food, clothes and comfort before setting out on the last stage of his journey, is played down as merely a providential incident within the great undertaking. So, too, Sturt's desperate and futile forays out from Depôt Glen, so many crushing defeats on the path to the inland sea and the centre of the continent, are dramatically reworked as part of the mounting suspense regarding the party's survival.

63

Most importantly, although the motivating force behind the expedition itself was primarily economic (the perceived need to 'open up' more pastoral or agricultural land for settlement) and secondarily ideological (to assert domination over the continent by bringing it into the realm of the documented and the known), the reader of the adventure was more interested in the human factor, the experiences of the heroic leader. The published accounts of exploration changed from being records of discovery to become narratives of epic journeys. The explorer-as-narrator was encouraged, even expected, to embellish his journal with emotional elements, to reconstruct it in the manner of letters home, combining a sense of immediacy with a confessional style, while guaranteeing its veracity by implicit reference to the official account already presented to the scientific body. While it may appear that these successive versions of the journey – log books, diaries, letters, scientific reports, and popular accounts – represent a progression from spontaneity to self-consciousness, none of the accounts escaped mental editing. All the explorers structured their narratives, and probably their innermost thoughts, to conform to the expectations cherished by the recipients of their various communiques.[15]

Where we have multiple reports from one person, or accounts from several members of the one exploring party, we can more readily see how the journey, the other expedition members, and the landscape itself were progressively constructed, like a palimpsest, to accommodate these requirements. On his ill-fated expedition to Central Australia in 1844–45, Sturt kept a journal addressed to his wife Charlotte Christina and written in an intimate, apparently spontaneous style. However, one clear subtext of the journal is Sturt's desire to conceal from Charlotte (who was opposed to his expedition and sceptical of the existence of an inland sea), and no doubt from himself, his real motives, while rationalising his personal obsession with reaching the geographical centre of the continent in terms of his duty to his family and the nation.[16] Subsequently he extracted from his journal and official papers 'A Condensed Account of an Exploration in the Interior of Australia', which was presented to the Royal Geographical Society in 1847. Two years later still he published his carefully constructed *Narrative of an Expedition into Central Australia* (1849). Here he presents himself as one obsessed with a vision of serving the public good and prevented from delivering to humanity the news of an inland sea only by the most insuperable difficulties in a land worse than any other on earth. The *Narrative*, intended for a wider public, is clearly dramatised relative to the journal. In it Sturt introduced an emotional scene at Moorundi and claimed that the sight of the Stony Desert took his breath away and forced upon him the unwilling decision to turn back. In fact, as the journal makes clear, this was the second time he had seen the Stony Desert and thus he had little cause for surprise, whatever the degree of abhorrence he might be experiencing. From the same expedition we also have the diary of Daniel Brock, a well-educated man employed by Sturt as an armourer and bird collector. His diary, intended for his mother at home in England, 'the fireside book for a reverend parent',[17] is written in a self-consciously pious, confessional style, especially in the Sunday entries. To prevent fraudulent land speculation, it was a government requirement that all documents produced by the members of an expedition be surrendered to the commander until his own official report had been delivered in writing. Apparently Sturt was rigorous in enforcing this convention since Brock recorded early in the journey: 'orders are issued no letter is to be sent home, till it has been seen by Capt. Sturt – Sturt is a most mean man, or a very suspicious one.'[18] It therefore seems likely that we owe the survival of Brock's subversive journal to the fact that he had hidden it in his coat lining. Brock had his own unique agenda for the expedition: he regarded the desert as a vale of soul-making, rejoicing in its barrenness and hardships as a path to salvation. A third journal surviving from the expedition is the unfinished one of Dr John Harris Browne, surgeon.

These multiple narratives frame and construct the desert landscape in subtly different ways. Mindful of his brief to report favourably on grazing conditions, Sturt began by enthusiastically proclaiming the potential of the land near Lake Bonney because it was well watered, but Brock and Browne recorded a very different estimate. Brock writes:

> what a pity such wretched country should be watered by so noble a stream – nothing but scrub, sometimes sand, and sometimes stone, but never soil that

would raise even a radish – except in the flats which at seasons are overflowed. When Capt. Sturt published his account of his memorable expedition he stated that this country was adapted (highly so) for pastoral and agricultural purposes. 'Travellers see strange things.'[19]

Browne, not being an expedition leader, could afford to be more frank in denigrating the land and even declaring the expedition a failure:

> It is a most inhospitable desert. In fact nothing more can be said for the whole country between this [and] Moorundi. . . . its resources are now proved beyond a doubt to be very limited. . . . I do not at present think any benefit whatever will accrue to the Colonists or to Britain from this Expedition. Suppose a good country to be found, it will be too hot for sheep and useless as an agricultural district on account of the difficulty of access. . . . Captn. Sturt does not agree with me in this opinion, but thinks such a country if found would be immediately occupied and says the difficulties I speak of would render it more valuable on account of the great security they afford to such a place.[20]

Eventually Sturt, continually frustrated by the desert's refusal to produce that grand oasis of his dreams, the inland sea, ceases to hold out any hopes for the country to the north and depicts it as a wilful, deceiving antagonist:

65

> . . . it was now clear that the effects of refractions had entirely misrepresented them [the mountains] to me, that the whole were similar to the hill on which I stood, and that the whole country was impenetrable. My heart sank within me, Dearest, at seeing my hopes blasted one after the other in such a way.[21]

Similar though perhaps less extreme amendments to accommodate their readers' expectations are to be found in the writings of Stuart, Warburton, Leichhardt and Giles.[22] Giles especially showed how well he could cater for the popular market of the time. In *Australia Twice Traversed* he vividly conveys the details that particularise his experiences. Mock heroic accounts of his battles with flies and ants, a liberal scattering of literary quotations (and misquotations), scraps of homespun philosophy, outrageous puns, jokes and purple passages, snatches of doggerel that make a modern reader cringe, witty observations about his fellow expeditioners, and reconstructed conversations with Aborigines constantly enliven the observations of an often monotonous terrain. Whatever their literary extravagances, Giles's accounts of his five journeys are arguably the most readable travel writing to emerge from the exploration of the desert.[23]

In many cases, the published accounts were successively modified for other purposes again, becoming propagandist exercises to encourage immigration from Britain or, since Aboriginal habitation was edited out or otherwise repudiated, to re-legitimise imperial conquest on the grounds of primacy of access.

There are three particular facets of the explorers' perceptions of the desert that were to have an enduring effect on later writers: its capriciousness, its significance as religious experience and its Gothic terrors.

A wayward land

With an erratic rainfall from year to year and consequent fluctuations of drought and fertility, the climate of Central Australia is indeed extremely variable. The British geologist J.W. Gregory, having journeyed around Lake Eyre in the summer of 1901–2, remarked of the area between Lake Eyre and the Simpson Desert, for which he coined the name 'the dead heart':

> According to Eyre and Sturt, it was a desert of the worst type; according to Howitt, Davis, and McKinley – all three of whom went there to search for the lost expedition of Burke and Wills – it was a fertile land of lakes and rivers and meadows, and was well adapted for pastoral settlement. . . . Cattle stations were founded where Sturt had found existence intolerable and barely possible, and where Burke and Wills had perished of starvation.[24]

The nineteenth-century explorers, however, interpreted this changeableness metaphorically, in quasi-moral terms – as wilful resistance by a deceitful and fickle female Nature. Three specific aspects of this inconstancy recur in their reports: the failure to provide the inland sea that order and symmetry required; erratic river systems that flooded one year and were dry creek beds the next; and treacherous mirages that misled the traveller desperate for water.

THE LOST SEA

In 1844, the same year as John Charles Frémont's expedition set out to map the hypothetical American waterway, Charles Sturt set out, determined to discover an inland sea for the Australian continent. Like a Roman augur, he believed that its existence had been shown him by the flight of birds. As early as 1828–30, while exploring the Macquarie–Darling region in expectation of finding a great river system, he had noted the flight paths of birds heading west-north-west away from the arid area during the summer. On moving to Adelaide, he again noticed migrating birds, this time flying directly to and from the north.[25] Combining these observations, he derived what he believed to be a clear indication that a large body of inland water must exist where the two flight paths of the birds intersected.

> As I felt assured of two lines of migration thus tending to the same point, there could be little doubt but that the feathered races migrating upon them rested at that point, for a time, so I was led to conclude that the country to which they went would in a great measure resemble that which they had left – that birds

which delighted in rich valleys would not go into deserts and into flat country ... so the point at which migration might be presumed to terminate would be found a richer country than any which intervened.[26]

In 1840 he wrote to Gipps, 'Everything tends I believe to prove that a large body of waters exists in the Interior' and, later in 1843, he became convinced that Lake Torrens was an estuary connected with an inland sea, beyond which lay the fertile land, 'a better country', to which his birds were certainly bound.[27] In the light of Sturt's confidence in the capabilities of the birds to locate the inland sea, the comment by his servant, Joseph Colley, on 13 February 1845, as he and Sturt surveyed the stretch of desert immediately south of Cooper's Creek, carries special significance. Sturt wrote to Charlotte: 'Just as we turned to go back a parrot flew over our heads with loud cries of alarm, it went thro' the air with a zig-zag flight, and appeared to be just as much at a loss as a bird that has been driven out to sea by a gale. "That bird, Sir," said Joseph, "does not seem to know where to go." "No", said I, "he does not indeed, and if he cannot see a place on which to rest, how shall we find one?"'[28]

Eyre had been less than enthusiastic about Sturt's obsessive belief in an inland sea, especially as, in 1839, he himself had already travelled in the direction where Sturt imagined it to be and found only desert. Even while Sturt was staying with Eyre at Moorundi, en route to the Centre, the latter showed him a letter he had just written to Lord Stanley, Secretary for the Colonies, volunteering to conduct an expedition from Moreton Bay to Port Essington, in the course of which he explicitly dissociated himself from Sturt's optimistic views: 'I am unwillingly forced to the conviction that the great mass of the interior of New Holland consists of salt beds of extensive lakes, barren scrubs or desert sands. With every deference for the opinion of so intelligent and experienced a traveller as Captain Sturt, I must confess that I cannot ... see any data from which to infer either the existence of a fine country ... or of a deep inland sea.'[29] Sturt chose to interpret this as a failure of purpose on Eyre's part, commenting in the *Narrative*: 'Should I, their leader, be one of those destined to remain in the desert, or should I be more fortunate in treading it than the persevering and adventurous officer whose guest I was and who shrank from the task I had undertaken'.[30] The following year, 1845, Eyre published his *Journals of Expeditions of Discovery into Central Australia and Overland from Adelaide to King George's Sound in the Years 1840–1* in which, after discussing the question of an inland sea at length, he concluded: 'I have never met with the slightest circumstance to lead me to imagine that there should be an inland sea, still less a deep navigable one, and having an outer communication with the ocean.'[31]

Undeterred by Eyre's opinion, Sturt set out into the desert and, predictably, saw reminders (to his mind, evidence) of a sea all around him. Certainly there are many features of the desert landscapes which invite such a comparison and Sturt was by no means the only traveller to mention them; it is more a question of focus and degree. His *Journal* and *Narrative* are studded with marine imagery to describe the desert landscape which, for him, is virtually predicated on its similarity to the sea. In the Simpson Desert '... the sand

67

ridges became closer succeeding each other like waves of a tempestuous sea', the similarity being heightened by the presence of 'spinifex, a thick wiry grass generally found on the sea shore'.[32] He repeatedly describes the sand dunes as 'land waves' and the view was, 'as it were, over a sandy sea'.[33] Even when there was no such visual analogy before his eyes, Sturt's mind returned morbidly to such comparisons: 'we were as lonely as a ship at sea, and as a navigator seeking for land'.[34] At the farthest point of his search Sturt gazes upon the stony desert and sees 'a plain as extensive as the sea covered over with the shivered fragments of former mountains. There were hills over which the floods must have swept clad if I may say so with the same imperishable materials. . . . No horse would willingly have faced that iron sea,' and a few days later:

> We had no object on which to steer but were like a ship at sea. We
> traversed a region for eleven miles that it is impossible for me to describe to
> you . . . the whole span looked like a sea beach on which fragments of rocks
> of every size had been thrown.[35]

Proceeding up a dry creek bed, he notices 'vestiges of tremendous floods on every side, but not a drop of water to be seen. . . . It was indeed evident that no flood had occurred in the impetuous and momentary water course for many many months.'[36] A line of hills that 'formed a steep wall to shut out the level country below them' remind him of cliffs: 'One might have imagined that an ocean washed their base, and I would that it really had been so'.[37]

Not only does Sturt, by such analogies, repeatedly characterise the desert as cheat, deceiver and arch-ironist; he also advances geological theories about an inland sea remarkably similar to those proposed by the geologist James Hutton in 1788.[38] Struck, as every traveller to the Simpson Desert must be, by the parallel sand ridges which 'followed each other like the waves of the sea in endless succession', he ponders:

> What . . . was I to conclude from these facts? – that the winds had formed these
> remarkable accumulations of sand, as straight as an arrow lying on the ground
> without a break in them for more than ninety miles at a stretch, and which we
> had already followed up for hundreds of miles, that is to say across six degrees
> of latitude? No! Winds may indeed have assisted in shaping their outlines, but
> I cannot think that these constituted the originating cause of their formation.
> They exhibit a regularity that water alone could have given, and to water,
> I believe, they plainly owe their existence. It struck me then, and calmer
> reflection confirms the impression, that the whole of the low interior I had
> traversed was formerly a sea-bed, since raised from its sub-marine position by
> natural though hidden causes; that when this process of elevation so changed
> the state of things, as to make a continuous continent of that, which had been
> an archipelago of islands, a current would have passed across the central parts
> of it, the direction of which must have been parallel to the sandy ridges.[39]

By the time he was back in London, preparing his *Narrative* for publication, Sturt was willing to acknowledge that wishful thinking may have played a part in structuring his views:

> I commenced my investigations under the impression that I should be led to that point, in tracing down any river I might discover, and that sooner or later I should be stopped by a large body of inland waters . . . perhaps this opinion was fostered by the hope that such would be the case.[40]

But he was not prepared to relinquish the hypothesis of an inland sea existing in prehistoric times when the continent was little more than an archipelago, until some convulsion raised the central part of the continent above the sea.[41]

ERRATIC RIVERS

Inland Australia presented geographers with another alarmingly subversive experience – impermanence. Rivers flow – sometimes; in other years they do not exist. Lakes may be deep and extensive, rich in bird life; or they may be salt-pans, even rock-hard racing tracks. William Hardman, editor of Stuart's *Journals,* wrote in his preface to that volume of 'the caprices of Lake Torrens, at one time a vast inland sea, at another a dry desert of stones and baked mud'.[42] The early explorers in their capacity as surveyors record their deep frustration, even outrage, at this apparent frivolity of the land, which defies their most strenuous attempts to chart and fix it. A map of the Australian desert can be, at best, only a statistical approximation. Sturt writes peevishly about the deceptive character of Australian rivers: 'Such . . . is the uncertain nature of the rivers of those parts of the continent of Australia over which I have wandered. I would not trust the largest farther than the range of vision; they are deceptive all of them, the offsprings of heavy rains, and dependent entirely on local circumstances for their appearance and existence.'[43] While searching in vain for water, he repeatedly finds ironic evidence of devastating floods in an earlier season. 'There were indeed the ravages of floods and the vestiges of inundations to be seen in the neighbourhood of every creek we had traced, and upon every plain we had crossed, but the element that had left such marks of its fury was no where to be found.'[44] While detained for six months by drought at Depôt Glen, Sturt notes 'the ravages made by the floods' and reflects:

69

> how fearfully that silence must sometimes be broken by the roar of waters . . . we observed the trunks of trees swept down from the hills, lodged high in the branches of the trees in the neighbourhood of the creek . . . whilst the line of inundation extended so far into the plains that the country must on such occasions have the appearance of an inland sea.[45]

Thirty years later Giles records finding the debris of Sturt's boat on which that explorer had 'vainly hoped to have ploughed the waters of an inland sea'. Ironically it had been carried by a flood twenty miles down the watercourse in which Sturt had despairingly abandoned it.[46] It was Giles's theory that the lost Leichhardt expedition of 1848 must have been buried in the mud from a flash flood in Cooper's Creek, which is known to fill the whole valley to a width of sixty to eighty kilometres without any rain having fallen in the actual region.[47]

This perplexing transience of the terrain is not only seasonal, but occurs even on the small scale with desert sandstorms which, in a few hours, can obliterate tracks and landmarks and completely disorient people. These occurrences, too, are assimilated into the image of an unpredictable and capricious land, venting its rages on the innocent travellers attempting to cross it.

MIRAGES

The irony of topographical reminders of an inland sea was increased by the appearance of Fata Morgana, a common enough phenomenon in deserts, but one for which few Europeans were prepared, especially when the mirage parodied their own desires. Eyre describes the mimetic power of such an experience:

> From the extraordinary and deceptive appearances, caused by mirage and refraction, however, it was impossible to tell what to make of sensible objects, or what to believe on the evidence of vision, for upon turning back to retrace our steps to the eastward, a vast sheet of water appeared to intervene between us and the shore, whilst the Mount Deception ranges, which I knew to be at least thirty-five miles distant, seemed to rise out of the bed of the lake itself, the mock waters of which were laving their base, and reflecting the inverted outline of their summits. The whole scene partook more of enchantment than reality, and as the eye wandered over the smooth and unbroken crust of pure white salt which glazed the basin of the lake, and which was lit up by the dazzling rays of a noonday sun, the effect was glittering, and brilliant beyond conception.[48]

Because of his intense desire to believe in an inland sea, Sturt was only too ready to accept the account of a large body of water brought him by one of his men, Poole. Without checking the report, he dashed off a letter to his friend John Morphett who immediately published it in the *Adelaide Observer*, complete with its postscript which stated confidently:

> Poole has just returned from the ranges. . . . He says there are high ranges to N. and N.W. and water, – a sea extending along the horizon from S.W. by W., to then E. of N. in which there are a number of islands and lofty ranges as far as the eye can reach. . . . Tomorrow we start for the ranges, and then for the waters, – the strange waters on which boat never swam, and over which flag

never floated. But both shall ere long. We have the heart of the interior laid open to us, and shall be off with a flowing sheet in a few days. Poole says that the sea was a deep blue, and that in the midst of it there was a conical island of great height.[49]

There was to be a bitter ironical truth in the words 'the strange waters on which boat never swam'.

The 'scene' described by Poole included characteristics of the classic mirage, particularly the large expanse of deep blue water at the horizon, but it conformed too closely to Sturt's obsession for him to question its veracity. Two days later, still in a state of euphoria, he wrote to the colonial secretary: 'We seem on the high road to success with mountains and seas before us ... it will be a joyous day for us to launch on an unknown sea, and run away towards the tropics.'[50] Later he suffered agonies at the thought of the mirth his hasty and ill-advised letters must have created in Adelaide, and in subsequent accounts he denied any such belief on his part, simply recording that Poole had brought an unfavourable report of the country.[51] Another member of Sturt's party, Brock, perhaps wise after the event, wrote in his journals the following day: 'During our travelling we observed the delusive mirage, it causes the unwary traveller to believe his parching thirst will soon be relieved. The appearance of water could not be more so, if veritable water it was, but it is a refraction.'[52]

Mirages continued to deceive, especially when they appeared to confirm the heartfelt wishes of travellers. In 1857 George Woodroffe Goyder, assistant surveyor-general of South Australia, reached what is now Lake Frome, then believed to be a continuation of Lake Torrens, and he was most excited to find that it contained fresh water, not the brine which characterised the western Lake Torrens. Goyder reported that the lake was of great extent, a veritable freshwater sea, with vast tracts of fertile land surrounding it.[53] But the jubilation of the inhabitants of Adelaide was short-lived. When Freeling, the surveyor-general, hastened to explore this desirable land he found that Goyder had been misled by a mirage.[54] The persuasive power of this phenomenon was not to be underestimated as even Stuart, who never admitted to being deluded, conceded: '... the mirage is so powerful that little bushes appear like giant gum-trees, which makes it very difficult to judge what is before us; it is almost as bad as travelling in the dark. I never saw it so bright nor so continuous ... one would think that the whole country was under water. Camped without water.'[55]

A vale of soul-making: the desert as religious experience

Like the 'discovery' of Australia by Captain Cook and its subsequent settlement as a British penal colony, exploration was, as already mentioned, a fundamentally secular project. The expedition leaders were men of science or public ambition rather than pilgrim fathers in search of religious freedom. Yet, when the desert refused to capitulate to the apparatus of a military campaign, and simple models of heroism proved inadequate, the explorers had frequent recourse to Old Testament imagery, reviving the theology of suffering in the Book of Job, or invoking a promise of spiritual exaltation as a reward for endurance in the wilderness. The scriptural prototypes of the wilderness thus reinforced the secular, militaristic estimate of the desert as an opponent which it was praiseworthy to subdue. In this parallel spiritual *agon* the desert itself was cast in the role of Satan, the opponent with which the pilgrim must wrestle, and from which only Providence could rescue him. Both biblical metaphors – the desert as earthly hell and the desert as spiritual testing-ground – loom large in the narratives of exploration, even though both were essentially at odds with the official purpose of expeditions funded for specifically material objectives. There is thus, from the outset, an uneasy disparity between the devotional mode of discourse and the secular inclinations of the writers. When Sturt begins his *Journal* for Charlotte with the preamble 'Prosperity, Dearest, was the blessing of the Old Testament, Adversity is the blessing of the New, and the knowledge of this should be a useful lesson to us, and if it please GOD to permit my return to you, it may be that this long and fearful separation will be another proof of what both religion and reason point out to us that, "whatever is, is right" ',[56] he is clearly indulging in special pleading, invoking Scripture to justify the course of action he is determined to pursue, regardless of Charlotte's wishes and his own family responsibilities. Moreover, by associating both prosperity and adversity with the desert, he implicitly provides a metaphor for the presence of the inland sea of his dreams as the reward for endurance.

72

Religious references were also advantageous in suggesting a predestined mission on the part of the explorer, a vocation, like that of Moses, to lead others to the Promised Land. Sturt had frequent recourse to such arguments to justify his *idée fixe* in the face of opposition at all levels, from vice-regal to domestic. The claim to a God-given destiny permits him to do as he wants while playing the part of the humble Christian, obedient to his call. More than any other explorer, Sturt makes frequent appeals to Providence to sustain both his expedition and his family at home[57] and ascribes critical incidents in the party's survival to divine intervention. Desperately short of water on his earlier expedition, Sturt's party had followed a pigeon to a small puddle, just sufficient to sustain them temporarily. Sturt was quick to ascribe to Providence this ironic reversal of the dove leading Noah to dry land:

> . . . we began to wander round our lonely bivouac. It was almost dark, when one of my men came to inform me that he had found a small puddle of water, to which he had been led by a pigeon. It was, indeed, small enough, probably the remains of a passing shower; it was, however, sufficient for our necessities, and I thanked Providence for its bounty to us.[58]

Similarly, even when effectively blockaded by drought in the Depôt Glen, Sturt can still see in his party's survival the hand of the Almighty: 'Providence had, in its allwise purposes, guided us to the only spot in that wide-spread desert, where our wants could have been permanently supplied, but had there stayed our further progress into a region that almost appears to be forbidden ground.'[59]

If Providence was critical in furnishing Sturt with reasons for embarking on his expedition to Central Australia, it was even more essential in providing justification for an honourable return. To die in the desert was a heroic course of action; to return without either finding the inland sea or reaching the centre of the continent meant ignominy and defeat unless it could be shown that his decision to withdraw was not wholly voluntary. This premise is hinted at in the last words of the passage just quoted. If the region to the north is 'forbidden ground' – that is, forbidden by God – then it is futile for Sturt to persist. In the *Journal* for Charlotte (whose chief desire was to have him safely home) he wrote: '. . . an almost irresistible desire to push on took possession of me, but an unknown and secret influence prevailed and at length determined me to turn back.'[60] Thus, for Charlotte, he constructs an Everyman struggle between a good and a bad angel: on the one hand an 'almost irresistible desire' which is presented as implicitly evil, since it would lead to his death and those of his men, and on the other a benign 'secret influence' which returns them to safety. In the second-last entry of his *Journal*, he can accept the necessity (which he construes as punishment) of turning back without having achieved his goal of reaching the inland sea or the centre of the continent, only by interpreting this as God's will. In a piece of typical Victorian domestic piety he writes to Charlotte:

73

> If it should please God to unite us once more, Dearest, it may be that even this heavy punishment, I can see it in no other light, may have been intended for my ultimate benefit – to make me bend more submissively and view more calmly those trials and afflictions which it may be are my portion of human trials and afflictions. It may be this has been as a lesson to me to teach me moderation, to oblige me to limit my wants to the means I may have of attaining them, to stoop to gather the blessings of this life, and to cast from me those oppressive and irritable feelings which so sear the heart and deprive the man who gives way to them of all mental tranquillity. If such has been the merciful object even of this severe punishment I shall be truly grateful.[61]

However, in the later *Narrative* written for the general public, the 'unknown influence' counselling return has become tyrannical – an imperative 'necessity' overriding Sturt's innate and noble desire to persevere regardless of danger to himself: 'Nevertheless, though thus convincing my understanding, I felt that it required greater moral firmness to determine me to retrace my steps than to proceed onwards. . . . I turned from it [the prospect before him] with a feeling of bitter disappointment. . . . I may truly say, that I should not thus have abandoned my position, if it had not been a measure of urgent and imperative necessity.'[62] Daniel Brock, a member of this expedition, believed that when, on 6 October 1845, Sturt determined to make one last attempt to press towards the north with just three men, he was seeking death rather than facing the dishonour, as he considered it, of failure. Brock wrote in his diary, 'Sturt has failed, and that most signally failed, and he would care nothing if he perished. His pride is hurt – he has done nothing.'[63]

Later in the *Journal* Sturt invokes John Harris Browne's alleged illness from scurvy as the principal reason why, as a responsible leader, he must turn back: 'If my own life were the only sacrifice, I would willingly risk it to accomplish my purpose; but it seems that I am destined to be disappointed; man proposes, but the Almighty disposes, and his will must be obeyed.'[64] According to Sturt's field journal Browne's illness did not occur until after the decision to return was taken, but Sturt inverts the sequence to invoke a causal relationship between the two events. Nevertheless, like Captain Walton in Mary Shelley's *Frankenstein*, Sturt vacillates to the end: 'God knows I repine not even now.' Here we see an interesting reversal of the traditional view in which the religious significance of the desert depends on its opposition to worldly ambition and pride. In Sturt's case, instead of being a place to induce renunciation of earthly aspirations, the desert itself is the goal of his worldly ambition, the source of pride. It is not his going into the desert, but his turning back from it, that marks the crisis of spiritual growth, the literal conversion. Even so, the tension in this entry suggests that, had there had been a viable alternative in physical terms, Sturt would not have returned without achieving his goal, and would equally vehemently have interpreted his perseverance against all odds as obedience to God's will. After all, he had argued as strongly at the beginning of his account that it was his God-given destiny to reach the centre of the continent and discover the inland sea.

There are other elements of ambivalence in Sturt's piety. The material advantage to be gained from leading a successful inland expedition is never far from the surface and frequently becomes explicit. On hearing from George Grey that Lord Stanley had given permission for such an expedition, he replied in what now seems a calculated mixture of piety and self-conscious public spiritedness, 'I trust that under the guidance of the same Good and beneficent Power which directed my steps on former occasions, I shall be the humble means in the hands of Providence of benefiting my Country, the Province and Mankind.'[65] As we will see in Chapter 12 this fluctuation between outward humility towards God and the spiritual pride of the man pushing at the boundaries of physical endurance has attracted twentieth-century writers to re-create the inland explorers as prototypes of the inspired but arrogant overreacher.

Daniel Brock's religion, on the other hand, was troubled by no such grand ambitions. He constructed his account of the expedition in pietistic, Methodist terms as a spiritual journey. Redolent with religious fervour, his account repeatedly enunciated his hope that 'with fresh struggles I find fresh grace'.[66] In his case the journey was given supernatural sanction by being foretold in a dream. In June 1844, his former stock inspector's job was finished, his baby son William was seriously ill, and he had no other prospects of employment. In such straits he experienced a dream encounter with a strangely clothed individual from whom he learned for the first time of Sturt's projected expedition. The next day this whole incident was enacted in reality and was instantly interpreted by Brock as a leading from heaven, especially as he was subsequently chosen from 300 applicants to accompany the expedition.[67] Given this auspicious start, it became increasingly difficult for Brock to align the miseries of the journey, exacerbated by what he perceived as the limitations of its leader, with a holy plan, except through the trope of physical suffering as a prelude to spiritual growth. The desert became pivotal, therefore, in the justification of his position. He alternately romanticised the journey as the crossing of a new frontier ('we might now say we have passed away from the dwelling of civilised man, our future home will be in the wilds and wastes of this singularly constituted land') and abhorred the land and the conditions: 'The heat in these sand hills is intolerable, the air being charged as if from a furnace'; 'The country is horrible, none in the world can be much worse'; it is a 'Climax of Desolation – no trees, no shrubs, all bleak, barren undulating sand. Miserable! Horrible!'[68] This phrase, a 'Climax of Desolation', with its resonances of *The Pilgrim's Progress*, is characteristic of Brock's struggle to extrapolate from 'intolerable' conditions to spiritual elevation, a perplexity rendered more acute by the implicit desire for praise and comfort from the pious mother, for whom the journal was intended. He endeavoured to find spiritual consolation in the view that his trials had a purpose. 'Whom the Lord loveth he chasteneth – before I was afflicted I went astray – ... out of my present trials I believe I shall come forth a better man.'[69] Yet in case the worst should befall him, Brock, too, had a spiritual fall-back position, albeit different from his leader's. Perhaps unconsciously he had been constructing it almost from the beginning of the journey. An avid Lord's Day observance man, he was deeply affronted by hearing Sturt remark early in the trip, 'There are no Sundays in the bush'.[70] The weekly refrain in his diary is: 'Sunday – yet no regard to the day.'[71] How can such an endeavour prosper when the men are godless and even the leader flouts God's will by non-observance of Sundays?

75

> Sunday. No cessation from labour – can a blessing be expected to rest on us when the Lord's day is so desecrated? ... it shows a contempt and disregard to God – manifested by our Chief Officer – which must lead to bad results. ...
> Sunday – As usual no rest – we moved away about half past seven ..
> <u>No Prayers</u>. (Brock's emphasis)[72]

Thus the biblical precedents of prophets seeking spiritual purity in the desert played an important part in providing sanction for expeditions conducted, like Sturt's, in the face of domestic and governmental disapproval and for abandoning them; in offering a martyr's crown for the explorer who perished there or suggesting reasons for the unworthiness of a party to deserve such spiritual honours.

Even the cheerful, practical Ernest Giles, not given to demonstrations of piety, reported a spiritual experience in which he was the recipient of a message from heaven. The passage, with its liberal sprinkling of archaic language, rhymes and biblical resonances, deserves quotation at length for, despite its apparent similarity to Brock's dream of being chosen by God, it is sharply differentiated from the earnest Brock's account by the confident, even self-regarding tone that belies its overt spiritual affirmation.

> I fell into one of those extraordinary waking dreams which occasionally descend upon imaginative mortals, when we know we are alive, and yet we think we are dead. . . . At such a time the imagination can revel only in the marvellous, the mysterious, and the mythical. The forms of those we love are idealised and spiritualised into angelic shapes . . . while lying asleep, engrossed by these mysterious influences and impressions, I thought I heard celestial sounds upon mine ear; vibrating music's rapturous strain, as though an heavenly choir were near, dispensing melody and pain. As though some angels swept the strings, of harps ethereal o'er me hung, and fann'd me, as with seraph's wings, while thus the voices sweetly sung: 'Be bold of heart, be strong of will, for unto thee by God is given, to roam the desert paths of earth, and thence explore the fields of heaven. Be bold of heart, be strong of will, and naught on earth shall lay thee low.'[73]

Giles's Providence is invariably encouraging and cheerful like himself, slotting easily into ready-made phrases:

> I could not help believing that the guiding hand of Providence had upon that occasion prevented me from obtaining my heart's desire to reach them [the Alfred and Marie Ranges]; for had I then done so, I know now, having proved what kind of country lay beyond that, neither I nor any of my former party would ever have returned. Assuredly there is a Providence that shapes our ends, rough-hew them how we will.[74]

Indeed Giles appears to regard himself as almost an equal partner with Providence. In the worst extremity of his life, when he realises that Gibson will not be returning with a relief party and that he must walk some sixty kilometres back to the camp with no food and very little water, through the most hostile desert, he remarks stoically: 'I concluded that if I did not help myself Providence wouldn't help me'.[75]

A Gothic desert

> The eye of God looking down on the solitary caravan, as with its slow, and snake-like motion, it presents the only living object around, must have

contemplated its appearance on such a scene with pitying admiration, as it forced its way continually on.[76]

The most alarming prospect faced by the inland explorers, coming from the confines of heavily populated Britain and Europe, was that of void. This was particularly true of the desert with its repeated vistas of empty horizontal planes under a cloudless, overarching sky. It therefore seems paradoxical that this vast expanse of apparently empty space was so frequently described, in their accounts, in Gothic terms of enclosure and entrapment. However, when we examine the sources of Gothic literature, we can see insistent parallels with the physical and psychological conditions experienced by the desert explorers. The fears exploited by Gothic writers were analogous to those that Edmund Burke had identified with the sublime. In European Romanticism the immensity of Nature, the essential ingredient of the sublime, was provided by precipitous mountains – the Alps or the Pyrenees – or by the ocean. In Australia the central desert was cast as the scene of such immensity, rendered more acute by its association with waste and void. Sturt writes:

> It appeared as if we were the last of creation amid the desolation and
> destruction of the world. There was a solemn stillness around, not a living
> thing to be seen, not an ant, not a cricket, or a grasshopper. The horizon was
> unbroken from north all round to north again, nor was there a shadow of hope
> in that dreary and monotonous wilderness.[77]

77

The sensationalist interest of many Gothic novelists in the supernatural can be seen as part of a broad reaction against the prevailing cult of rationalism, scientific materialism and reductionism. Haunted castles, ghosts and other apparitions constituted a counter-catalogue of elements defying logical explanation. Similarly, the characteristic Gothic scenery of wild mountains, deserted moors or overgrown areas rank with weeds rebuked the order of the carefully landscaped Augustan garden. In symbolic terms it is now widely recognised that the Gothic provided a particularly appropriate mode of speaking on behalf of women and of the colonial condition, insofar as it expressed otherwise suppressed knowledge of alienation, disjunction, oppression, terror and conflict. Gothic fears were readily engendered by the immensity of the Bush that confronted the early settlers, and by the perceived hostility of that landscape, exacerbated by the presence of Aborigines (the dark enemy) and escaped convicts threatening the safe structures of society. But the desert presented new and different terrors.

In a country bereft of a built environment in the European sense, ruined abbeys, burial vaults,[78] subterranean passages or convent cells were replaced as motifs of imprisonment by the physical barriers erected by a seemingly hostile Nature, and by the equally effective detention produced by drought, heat, thirst and the legitimate fear of being lost, both physically and spiritually.[79] Like the horrors of the Gothic novel, these naturally produced terrors mocked the failure of European rationality to exert control. The sense of confinement was particularly acute when exploring parties found themselves walled in by ridge after ridge of towering sandhills. Sturt records the sense of futility following each thwarted attempt to find a path through them (ending with a sentence not inappropriate for utterance by a Gothic heroine):

> The plain was surrounded on all sides by sand hills ... I saw therefore that there was no hope in that quarter. We therefore turned back and I ultimately made up my mind to try a westerly course in the morning. .... At a mile we encountered an immense sand hill that had been hid from our view by trees. From its summit we saw that we were already on the margin of the salt formation. The valley below us was dark with samphire bushes, and white with salt that blew into our faces and eyes like snow drifts before the heavy breeze ... and to the westward there was a succession of sand hills gradually increasing in height as far as the eye could reach. My heart sank within me at so hopeless a prospect.[80]

Similar descriptions recur as the party floundered and toiled over the long parallel sand ridges, up to 300 kilometres long and 30 metres high, of the Simpson Desert.[81] Sturt was even moved to ascribe volition to them, 'the sandy ridges once more rose up in terrible array against us ...', before he was forced to turn south again.

Even in the absence of such natural 'walls', the sense of detention is equally acute when the party's advance is blocked by the invisible 'barriers' of monotony and thirst. The unvarying, featureless landscape, relentlessly presenting the same outlook despite days of laborious travel, assumes a character of bizarre enchantment from which the travellers cannot escape, even by the most strenuous exertions. Sturt's unfortunate party was forced by continuing drought to camp for six months[82] at Depôt Glen (a name with ironic connotations of a picturesque, well-watered Scottish valley) on Campbell Creek while attempting to reach the Centre. The several accounts by members of the expedition contain repeated references to a sense of 'detention' or 'prison'. Afraid to move from this spot because they cannot find another source of water, the normally unemotional Browne records: 'It is impossible to move forward until rain comes. It would be equally impossible for us to retrace our steps. ... We are thus completely imprisoned.' And later: 'Another month is near its close and here we are still in the same place. ... Our confinement is every day becoming more irksome. We cannot go more than two days' journey from the camp as the whole country is destitute of water.'[83] Reflecting on their 'ruinous detention' at the Depôt, Sturt's entry for 27 January 1845 records: '... it became evident to me, that we were locked up in the desolate and heated region, into which we had penetrated, as effectively as if we had wintered at the Pole'.[84] At best he speaks of trusting to 'the goodness of Providence to release me from prison when He thought best' and of giving up 'all hope of success in any future effort I might make to escape from our dreary prison'.[85] When, finally, rain falls, Sturt records it in terms of liberation: 'we have at length obtained our freedom.'[86] However, the relief is temporary; the land remains obdurate and Sturt finally bursts out: 'the idea of detention in that horrid desert was worse than death itself.'[87]

Sturt's drought-stricken party was not unique in its response to the desert experience. The normally phlegmatic Peter Warburton, recording an attempt to cross south-west from Alice Springs to join John Forrest's tracks, describes the waterless condition of his party in similar terms of confinement: 'Without water we are helpless. We are hemmed in on every side; every trial we make fails.'[88]

Not only this sense of imprisonment but also solitude, stillness, desolation and an unspecified sense of dread are repeatedly ascribed to the desert – just as, in earlier decades, such states had been associated with the Bush.[89] Sturt, with his melancholy temperament, was particularly sensitive to such impressions and his *Two Expeditions into the Interior of Southern Australia* as well as his *Journal* and *Narrative* abound in references to 'that fearful solitude' of the desert in which there is no sign of animal life. In his account of the first expedition he writes:

> There was scarcely a living creature, even of the feathered race, to be seen to break the stillness of the forest. The native dogs alone wandered about, though they had scarcely strength to avoid us; and their melancholy howl, breaking in upon the ear at the dead of night, only served to impress more fully on the mind the absolute loneliness of the desert.[90]

79

This passage, with its no-doubt conscious echoes of Wordsworth's 'Lines composed a few miles above Tintern Abbey', shows Sturt examining his own responses as he constructs the scene in which he now assumes the place of Wordsworth's hermit. In reporting on his second expedition, he has recourse to similar Gothic imagery to describe the plains of the Morumbidgee (*sic*), indulging in the Gothic eroticism of death:

> It is impossible for me to describe the kind of country we are now traversing, or the dreariness of the view it presented. The plains are still open to the horizon, but here and there a stunted gum-tree, or a gloomy cypress, seemed placed by nature as mourners over the surrounding desolation. Neither beast nor bird inhabited these lonely and inhospitable regions, over which the silence of the grave seemed to reign.'[91]

Again Sturt selects the features which, either by English poetic tradition (the 'gloomy cypress') or by association with it (the 'stunted gum-tree'), support his melancholy mood. These preliminary skirmishes with the Gothic culminate in his experience in Central Australia where he is assailed with the dual sense of detention and desertion by all other forms of life, apart from occasional visits from birds of prey. 'The stillness of death reigned around us, no living creature was to be heard; nothing visible inhabited that dreary desert but the ant, even the fly shunned it . . .'.[92] Predatory kites, swooping down low over the party, are the only other living creatures visible. 'That they came to see what unusual object was wandering across the lowly deserts over which they soar, in the hope of prey, there can be no doubt.'[93] Then the birds, too, disappear.

Sturt's most frequently used adjective in describing the desert is 'gloomy': 'gloomy and burning deserts', he calls them; 'the most gloomy regions that man ever traversed'; 'the whole landscape ... was one of most gloomy character'; gigantic red sandhills are separated by 'gloomy valleys'. The Stony Desert is 'dark, dark, dark ... in no direction could I see a glimmering of hope' and when he traverses a baked mud plain cracked into deep crevices, he is immediately reminded of graves: 'the horses ... kept constantly slipping their hind feet into chasms from eight to ten feet deep, into which the earth fell with a hollow sound, as if into a grave'.[94]

If Sturt's reactions may be construed as the response of a depressed personality, others less pathologically morbid were moved to similar descriptions. Daniel Brock writes: 'The appearance among the ranges is desolation – gloomy – no verdure – but peak rising upon peak'; and 'an immense plain lay before us farther than the eye could reach. Bareness and desolation was the picture'.[95] The normally imperturbable Giles was sometimes acutely sensitive to a feeling of desolation. Between Wynbring and Mount Finke he exclaims, 'I could not help thinking it was the most desolate heap on the face of the earth', and while crossing the Great Victoria Desert he remarks, 'It was totally uninhabited by either man or animal, not a track of a single marsupial, emu, or wild dog was to be seen, and we seemed to have penetrated into a region utterly unknown to man, and as utterly forsaken by God.'[96] Even the businesslike Stuart records, of the view from Mount Finke, 'The prospect is gloomy in the extreme! I could see a long distance but nothing met the eye save *a dense scrub as black and dismal as midnight. ... A fearful country* ... it is even *worse* than Captain Sturt's desert. ... To-day's few miles have been through the same *dreary, dreadful, dismal desert* ...'[97] (Stuart's emphasis)

There were macabre elements, too, in the behaviour which these extreme conditions elicited, indicating the extent to which the explorers had been driven back to an elemental level of mere survival. The punitive treatment that Burke, with the connivance of Wills, meted out to Charles Gray (who, in advanced stages of scurvy,[98] had stolen some flour from the rations) almost certainly killed him. Worse still was the sense of extreme loneliness endured by some of the explorers. The individual in the desert was perpetually dogged by recollections of the original derivation of 'desert': from *desertum* = abandoned, desolate. In a manner not formulated in words until later in the century, the desert, because it was not planted or reaped by the Europeans, spoke an existential truth to the nineteenth-century explorers: they found themselves alone in a neutral universe. Having expected Nature to be essentially amicable and accommodating, they subsequently interpreted its indifference as active hostility. Such a realisation, which exposed as illusion the sense of human superiority and cosiness fostered in the centres of population, was soon to be

John Longstaff,
*The Arrival of Burke, Wills
and King at the Deserted
Camp at Cooper's Creek,
Sunday evening. 21st April,
1861*, 1902–7, oil on
canvas, 282.0 × 429.2 cm,
Gilbee Bequest, 1907.
National Gallery of
Victoria, Melbourne.

ABOVE
George W. Lambert,
Anzac, the Landing, 1915,
1918–22, oil on canvas,
190.5 × 350.5 cm,
Australian War Memorial,
Canberra.

BELOW
George W. Lambert,
The Road to Jericho,
c. 1918, oil on canvas,
35 × 46 cm, Art Gallery of
New South Wales, Sydney.

ABOVE
Hans Heysen, born
Germany 1877, arrived
Australia 1884, died 1968,
*Guardian of the Brachina
Gorge*, 1937, watercolour,
49.5 × 63.5 cm, Felton
Bequest, National Gallery
of Victoria, Melbourne.

BELOW
Hans Heysen (Australia
1877–1968), *The Land of
the Oratunga*, 1932,
Hahndorf, South Australia,
watercolour on paper,
49.2 × 64.2 cm, Art Gallery
of South Australia,
Adelaide. South Australian
Government Grant, 1937.

ABOVE
Russell Drysdale (Australia
b. 1912 d. 1981), *The Walls of
China, (Gol Gol)*, 1945, oil on
hardboard, 76.2 × 101.6 cm,
Art Gallery of New South
Wales, Sydney.

BELOW
Russell Drysdale (Australia
b. 1912 d. 1981), *Man Feeding
his Dogs*, oil on canvas,
51.2 × 61.4 cm, collection
Queensland Art Gallery,
Brisbane. Gift of C.F. Viner-
Hall, 1961. Reproduced by
permission of Lady Drysdale
and Queensland Art Gallery.

Ernest Giles, *Alone in the Desert*, from *Australia Twice Traversed: The Romance of Exploration, being a Narrative of Five Exploring Expeditions into and through Central South Australia and Western Australia from 1872 to 1876.*

81

reinforced by nineteenth-century astronomy and post-Darwinian biology, and later by twentieth-century psychology. In all these sciences alienation became the order of the day, overturning the comfortable Romantic belief in a quasi-spiritual union with Nature. Unlike Sturt and Browne, Daniel Brock was unusually responsive to the beauty of the desert landscape, which he sometimes endows with elements of the picturesque,[99] but he, too, remarks on the qualifying effects of loneliness on his appreciation of the scene:

> The broken yet magnificent ranges – the sinuous course of the creek, traceable a long way by its shining sandy bed and the line of timber on its banks – a beautiful picture lay before me – here away from observation did I enjoy sweet intercourse with heaven. The day was closing in, the sun had set – everything wore the air of consummate quietude, the fly had ceased her humming, the mosquito was not on its wing – all spoke peace, yet I felt I was away from home, from those I loved. The charms of scenery like this I am now looking on lose much of their attractiveness when thus viewed in <u>loneliness</u>.[100]
> (Brock's emphasis)[100]

The ultimate experience of loneliness, however, must be that of Ernest Giles. In 1874 he walked back alone from the terrifying Gibson Desert after his companion, Gibson, who had taken their only horse to get help, vanished. Having also travelled alone for long stretches of the journey from Geraldton to Adelaide,[101] he strongly disputed the virtues ascribed to solitude by the Romantic poets.

> I felt somewhat lonely and cogitated that what has been written or said by cynics, solitaries, or Byrons, of the delights of loneliness, has no real home in the human heart. Nothing could appal the mind so much as the contemplation of eternal solitude. Well may another kind of poet exclaim, Oh, solitude! where are the charms that sages have seen in thy face? for human sympathy is one of the passions of human nature.[102]

The very emptiness of the desert, as seen through European eyes, led the explorers to people it with ghosts. Even without the discovery of sacred caves with piled bones and arcane wall paintings, they tended to ascribe to this land the mystery of Aboriginal ritual, past as well as present. Giles, normally the most cheerful of the explorers, confessed to superstitious feelings in the vicinity of Fort Mueller, south of the Rawlinson Range, and his description of the spot abounds with echoes of the same sound effects as provided the stock-in-trade of the Gothic novel. Although he rightly attributes them to natural causes, their subterranean origin, their unpredictability, and above all the feelings of dread which they elicit, clearly engendered in Giles a powerful Gothic frisson.

82

> Fort Mueller . . . was really the most astonishing place it has ever been my fortune to visit. Occasionally one would hear the metallic sounding clang, of some falling rock, smashing into the glen below, toppled from its eminence by some subterranean tremor or earthquake shock, and the vibrations of the seismic waves would precipitate rocks into different groups and shapes than they formerly possessed. I had many strange, almost superstitious feelings with regard to this singular spot, for there was always a strange depression upon my spirits whilst here, arising partly perhaps from the constant dread of attacks from the hostile natives, and partly from the physical peculiarities of the region itself.

> 'On all there hung a shadow and a fear,
> A sense of mystery, the spirit daunted,
> And said, as plain as whisper in the ear,
> This region's haunted.'[103]

Giles records that he was only too glad to leave the place to the 'native owners of the soil' and turn his back on 'Their home by horror haunted/ Their desert land enchanted.'[104] Although none of the explorers explicitly attributed their defeats at the hand of the Aborigines to magical powers, twentieth-century writers of fiction were not slow to do so. As we shall see in chapters 6 and 7, novelists as diverse as Catherine Martin and Ion Idriess exploited the idea of tribal magic as a potent ingredient in their evocation of the dangers of the desert. As late as 1939 the geologist Cecil Madigan, generally given to understatement, also resorted to frankly Gothic elements in his description of Lake Eyre:

> Notwithstanding the flowers and the grasses, and occasional small birds, the Lake Eyre region has still cast its queer spell over us. All who have travelled there have felt this haunting sense of desolation and death. The song dies on the drover's lips; silence falls on the exploring party. It is like entering a vast tomb; one hesitates to break the silence. The rivers are dead, the trees are dead, but overshadowing all the qualities of death is the very heart of the region, the great lake itself, a horrible travesty, a vast white prostrate ghost of a lake. Here time seems to have stood still for ages, and all is dead. We had seen one sluggish vein quickened in the north, the Warburton. Sea and river birds had gathered there, bringing a show of life that threw into greater relief the deadness of the rest, but the Dead Heart, the focus of a drainage basin of four hundred and fifty thousand square miles of country, will never throb again.[105]

Here, as in the nineteenth-century explorers' accounts, melodrama and insistent intrusions of the supernatural are heavily overlaid on the geographical facts that give them transferred legitimacy. These tropes and images, through constant repetition, have assumed a degree of actuality that justifies the legend of a malevolent, personalised desert waging unequal war on the nation's heroic explorers. Although the explorers claimed a special authenticity for their accounts by virtue of their personal knowledge of their journeys and the terrain they described, and although the accounts were read as privileged scientific narratives, they were, nonetheless, to some extent all fictional. In their appropriation of the desert for their own purposes, the explorers presented reconstructions of a 'reality' heavily selected and coloured by their education, rationale of selection, cultural expectations and personal quest for heroism. Because of the continued isolation of the Australian desert areas, many of these first recorded impressions of the fathers of exploration remained unchallenged for decades, determining what Australian settlers and the many in Britain and Europe who read them believed about the interior of the continent. By extension, they also became extraordinarily influential in the literary and artistic representation of the central desert, and thus over the subsequent direction of Australian history.[106] As Stephen Slemon remarks, '[I]t is fiction that determines the way we read history, history that is contingent on fiction, and not the other way around.'[107]

Once the desert had been invoked to provide the nation with its unique brand of hero – the hero as victim – it necessarily continued to be vilified as harsh, violent, treacherous and unrelenting. Even during the 1890s, when a wave of nationalism, glorifying the pastoral, reclaimed large tracts of the Bush from the odium that had previously attached to it, the desert remained

83

convicted of the deaths or near-deaths of noble men, and was characterised as almost wilfully resisting progress and nationhood. In a country that had experienced no battles on its territories other than the long-term, undeclared war waged by Europeans against the Aborigines, explorers, especially dead ones, provided attractive substitutes for national military heroes, and were honoured accordingly. Condemned by history, and an embarrassment in the present, Burke and Wills nevertheless remained in the wings, still candidates for the role of national heroes in popular culture when that part should again be required. And as chapters 6 and 12 demonstrate, the cult of the inland explorers has continued to provide a major emphasis in Australian literature of the desert.

Chapter 5

Perspectives on the Desert

We call landscape beautiful if it reminds us of pictures we have seen.

GINA CRANDELL[1]

The Trinity of God, Man, and Nature was central to the nineteenth-century universe. Nature itself was illuminated by another Trinity: art, science, and religion.

BARBARA NOVAK[2]

When Joseph Banks argued for the inclusion on the already-crowded *Endeavour* of two scientific draughtsmen, it was the first time that skilled artists had accompanied scientific expeditions to give visual impact to the written reports. This was not a subsidiary process. The exquisitely detailed drawings of Sydney Parkinson, the natural-history artist on Cook's first voyage, were an essential part of the knowledge brought back for the edification of Europeans from their newly opened museum of the Pacific. Although *Endeavour* carried home a treasure trove of more than 1500 new specimens, the artistic records, subsequently engraved for publication, provided symbolic collections, more durable than the specimens on which they were based. In England they excited first wonder, then controversy when some of the fauna would not be pigeon-holed within the existing Linnaean classification system.[3] Part of the great scheme advocated by Francis Bacon for the accumulation of knowledge, they also confirmed a peculiarly European approach to understanding the world, and as such had an important effect on the artistic recording of the Australian desert.

Where the Aborigines understood the meaning of the land in both spiritual and mundane terms, the former element existing deep within the earth and hence invisible to the eye except in ritual, Europeans engaged with the land almost exclusively through visual observation. Identifying it with the separate, measurable objects positioned upon it, they assessed their power over the continent in terms of their knowledge of these entities. In the grand project of naming, listing and categorising the new objects within the European scheme of knowledge, artists were vital participants. Although they were assumed to be objective recorders of what 'was there', they in fact exercised a considerable degree of subjective autonomy, not only in selecting what they would record, but in determining how it would be understood and in what context. Their overarching philosophy of the natural world as a collection of objects that had been slotted neatly into their appropriate places and, importantly, their adherence to the requirements of their funding bodies, whether governments or powerful patrons, were both important factors in the process. Banks wrote to the plant collector Claes Alstroemer of the regimen aboard the *Endeavour*, 'We sat till dark by the great table with our draughtsman [Parkinson] opposite and *showed him what way to make his drawings*.[4] (my emphasis) With such mentors, more interested in science than in art, Parkinson was encouraged to focus on selected details of the specimens and hence to display them analytically, often with exploded diagrams of particular parts, rather than suggesting their ecological context.

Whether they knew it or not, the natural-history artists were assisting a procedure aimed at the long-term economic exploitation of these indigenous treasures. British naturalists were effectively acting as intelligence scouts for the Empire, ransacking new lands for information about plants, animals and geological specimens. Similarly, Australian natural-history painting of the early nineteenth century was undertaken as part of the process of mapping the land and documenting its contents, as a wealthy man might make an inventory of his possessions. For artists making their way inland from the east coast, there was at first great scope for representation. Thomas Watling, a convict artist, described the Sydney area in 1792 as a 'luxuriant museum' and waxed lyrical about its treasures:

86

> Should the curious Ornithologist, or the prying Botanist emigrate here, they could not fail of deriving ample gratification in their favourite pursuits in this luxuriant museum. Birds, flowers, shrubs, and plants; of these, many are tinged with hues that must baffle the happiest efforts of the pencil ... but we have a variety of fishes, the greater part of which, are dropped and spangled with gold and silver and stained with dyes transparent and brilliant as the arch of heaven.[5]

A very different scene awaited the observer of the central desert, where few animals and plants were obvious to the recording eye and those that were visible offered little economic potential. Reports from the early ad hoc forays of pastoralists seeking new grazing land offered minimal encouragement for natural-history artists, while the leaders of later expeditions, even those conducted under the aegis of scientific bodies, were unwilling to be slowed down by a naturalist or an artist stopping to collect specimens or to be lumbered with their equipment. It is therefore not surprising that, with few exceptions, desert exploration produced little of artistic merit. The exceptions were significant but in many cases they were immured in libraries or in the little-visited works-on-paper collections of art galleries. Thus the work of the long-suffering natural-history artists who endured the gruelling conditions of desert exploration had less influence on the nation's evolving iconography of the desert than the written accounts of the expedition leaders.

Painting the desert

Landscape painting, soon to become the dominant art form in Australia, at first adopted as its rationale the agenda of natural-history art. In recording this 'new' land landscape artists were understandably preoccupied with difference, focussing on the features that most distinguished Australia from Europe. With the shifting frontier of settlement the signifiers of difference changed – from the shoreline itself to the fern valleys of the Blue Mountains and Mount Wellington, to the haunting, misty quality of the Bush (an image that had already been consciously constructed in Romantic literature by the time artists were depicting it), to the ultimate 'other' of the central desert. What we think of as the most 'obvious' characteristics of the desert – its dryness, harshness, immensity and silence – are qualities ascribed to it by contrast with Europe. Indigenous people, as we saw in Chapter 1, characterise it quite differently.

Gina Crandell's comment quoted at the head of this chapter, 'We call landscape beautiful if it reminds us of pictures we have seen',[6] is nowhere so obvious as in relation to Central Australia. Now so familiar from calendar photographs, tourist posters, magazine feature articles, tee-shirts and advertisements for everything from four-wheel-drive vehicles to coffee, the desert is the nation's most widely publicised landscape. The vivid colours, the stark outlines of Uluru or Kata Tjuta and the geometric perfection of the parallel red dunes in the Simpson Desert are perceived as strikingly beautiful and we imagine that this is self-evidently so. Yet the desert offered little of interest to nineteenth-century artists, who generally regarded it as antithetical to artistic representation. Indeed, it represented a classic example of the rejection, even the invisibility, of a landscape that fails to conform to prevailing aesthetic expectations.

The desert was considered deficient on at least four counts. Lacking economic interest for patrons or prospective immigrants alike, such a subject offered little market potential; artistically, it was perceived as a visual non-entity, impossible to integrate into the prevailing canons of artistic composition; theologically, it seemed a slur on the benevolence or the ability of the Creator; and logically, it was inaccessible to artists except on specific and restrictive terms. It is worth considering each of these briefly as they conspired virtually to banish the desert from the landscape agenda until the mid-twentieth century.

LACK OF MARKET

To be economically successful within the small colonial market, landscape painters needed to cater for the tastes and expectations of their patrons. Newly rich landowners wanted to see on their walls paintings that expressed both their hope for a new life, materially better than that which they had left behind in England, and, at the same time, nostalgia for 'Home', remembered in its most attractive form as green fields and valleys – a celebration of absence but with subtle implications of growing prosperity. This latter factor was especially closely linked with the economic impetus for Australian settlement. Belief in the promise that wealth would succeed hardship, as freedom had succeeded convict beginnings, was the faith that had brought British colonists across the world, the materialist counterpart of the overtly spiritual motivation of American settlement. The stately home in an arcadian/pastoral setting fulfilled the dual requirements of promise and nostalgia. Tastefully framed in a proscenium of dark vegetation, the house was ideally situated in the middle distance on a slight eminence signifying dominance and conquest of the land. Bathed in full sunlight, suggesting the blessings of fortune, it affirmed its owner's power in the new land, elevating him and his family to equality with the aristocracy. The distant prospect of pastoral acres, with their promise of plenty, confirms the message of power and success announced by the house: that God and Nature have combined to bless this patron with material riches in an idyllic land of social harmony. Through such well-understood iconography these paintings expressed a complex coded statement of domination – political, administrative, economic, agricultural, and social – a statement all the more powerful for being implicit.

88   The desert on the other hand was perceived as a land of absences, an unconquerable expanse, as inimical to the requirements of art as to settlement. While poets, as we will see, could incorporate notions of immensity and void into their work by focussing on the emotions generated by such aspects of the sublime, pictorial art had no such accommodating framework. No cooperative foliage framed a vista suggestive of habitation; no *coulisses*, natural or contrived, invited the eye into the world of the picture; no distant hills suggested the pleasant variety of Nature. Instead, the flat expanse of featureless landscape presented only barrenness, frustrating both expectation and memory. By extension, spatial monotony suggested temporal changelessness, equally inimical to the prevailing cult of progress. The visual depiction of prosperity and power on the grand scale was an important element in the popularity of the moving panorama[7] that offered the spectator the illusion of travelling in space and time from scene to varied scene in a purposeful march of progress, signified by the burgeoning of cities upon the landscape – 'the course of empire', as the American landscape artist Thomas Cole had called it.[8] In such a satisfying scheme the central desert was clearly an embarrassment, a gaunt skeleton in the colonial cupboard that had been hidden for as long as explorers confined their endeavours to the coastal fringe and believed in an inland sea. What patron, interested in progress and the display of icons signifying ownership of the land, would wish to be reminded of an unconquered and unprofitable terrain?

LACK OF AESTHETIC APPEAL

Most limiting, technically, was the absence of compositional models for depicting such terrain. Aborigines looking down at the ground saw at every step a myriad of interesting features – animal tracks, variations in texture, claypans, low clumps of spinifex. But European art, enthralled since the Renaissance with conventions of perspective, invariably viewed landscape as a vertical slice. From such a viewpoint the desert was, indeed, virtually unpaintable. Its flat, monochrome appearance, lack of variation in vegetation and apparent absence of fauna, as well as its emotional monotony, defied the 'realistic perspective' approach based on progression from foreground to background.[9]

Artistically, an important part of familiarisation with the new continent was the need to locate it within European pictorial conventions. At the beginning of the nineteenth century these derived from the Picturesque style popularised by French-born Italian painter Claude Lorrain. To see and paint Australian scenes in this style was the painterly equivalent of mapping the land, signifying the settlers' power over it, since the Claudian formula, especially the panoramic view with its suggestions of wider dominance, moulded and stereotyped the gaze of later artists.

Moreover, the flatness of the desert nowhere drew the eye of the beholder towards heaven; its stunted trees, if present at all, proclaimed only drought and desolation; its manifest lack of history, culture and habitation (as defined by Europeans), its vastness and emptiness, all magnified the settlers' sense of dislocation, exile, alienation and insignificance. Almost by definition, the desert mocked the interlocking iconography of European landscape art, where water was a visual focus loaded with semiotic significance. Apart from its obvious Christian symbolism, water, by its variety, suggested also changing moods and emotions, from tranquillity to tempest. Rivers gracefully leading the eye into the pictured expanse suggested movement and progress; cataracts crashing to the valley floor demonstrated the sublime power of Nature; placid lakes mirrored the sky, suggesting the unity of earthly and heavenly blessing, and an eternal natural cycle. Equally, the sun, conceived of in European cultures as benign, creative and sustaining, becomes in the Australian desert malevolent, destructive and life-threatening. All these precious cultural resonances were forfeited by the desert.[10] It is not surprising, then, that nineteenth-century artists of the desert focussed either on particular details of scientific interest or on the heroic potential of the explorers.

THEOLOGICAL SUBVERSIVENESS

The desert wilderness was not only economically and aesthetically unattractive; it was also religiously subversive. Natural theology found its strongest overt support in the first half of the nineteenth century, from scientists as well as divines, possibly because the cracks in its argument from design were becoming uncomfortably clear. In 1833 the geologist Adam Sedgwick wrote that 'the beautiful and harmonious movements in the vast mechanism of nature' proved the existence of God,[11] but where, in the desert, was the evidence of divine order or of God's Holy Plan? Where, indeed, was God? St Hilary had asked rhetorically, 'Who can look on Nature and not see God?' but in the desert the answer seemed to be 'almost everyone'.

INACCESSIBILITY

Perhaps most importantly, the desert was dangerous and inaccessible. An individual artist dared not venture there on his own terms, in his own time. If he were permitted to accompany an exploring party, his program was subservient to that of the expedition; he was there as a recorder of natural history, to produce a pictorial register for scientific or economic purposes. Expedition artists thus became, if they were not already, surveyors, topographical artists or illustrators of natural history or ethnography. This inevitably limited their way of looking at the desert.

Art as natural history

As the early written accounts of the desert were produced by explorers rather than writers of fiction, so the early depictions of the desert were the work of surveyors rather than professional artists. The training of surveyors and army officers included topographical and perspective drawing and all explorers were expected to make sketches of the terrain and particular features. Usually their rough impressions were redrawn by professional artists to provide the basis for etchings in publications of the expedition. However, confronted with the monotony of the desert, they increasingly included figures in their sketches, partly for scale and partly to impart some variation to the sameness of the scene. Figure drawings were also included to convey some impression of the explorers' life in the field. Ernest Giles's *Australia Twice Traversed* includes, for example, Giles's impression of Mount Olga and a sketch of himself trudging alone through the Gibson Desert carrying his water keg. While these sketches are full of interest in showing us the rigours that exploration entailed at the time, the core of this chapter focusses rather on the more finished landscapes and associated natural-history illustrations of Edward Frome, George French Angas, S.T. Gill, Ludwig Becker and Hermann Beckler, before considering the role of nineteenth-century artists in promoting the cult of the heroic desert explorer.

EDWARD CHARLES FROME: THE HOPELESS PROSPECT

The first pictorial records of the desert landscape resulted from the field work of Edward Charles Frome, surveyor-general of South Australia. After training at the Royal Military Academy, Woolwich, Frome had obtained a commission in the Royal Engineers in 1825. He spent six years in Canada surveying and supervising the construction of the Rideau Canal before becoming Instructor of Surveying and Engineering at Chatham and then being offered, in 1839, the position in South Australia.[12] From 1840 to 1843 he led expeditions beyond the settled areas of the state, supervising and collating the small independent surveying teams of the colony.

On his last expedition he travelled north of the Flinders Ranges with fellow surveyor James Black Henderson,[13] making pencil sketches which he later worked into watercolours that suggest both his professional interest in geographical features and an artist's need to find a focus for his picture. Whereas Henderson's diary entries bemoan the desolation of the area, Frome endeavoured to convey its unique and delicate characteristics. In *The Razor Back from the Top of Mount Bryan* (c.1845), for example, he has chosen an unusual rock formation, the Razor Back Hill, and, by selecting an elevation from which to look down upon it, has emphasised its geographical peculiarities. These are further highlighted by the flat and featureless plain which is obliquely divided by the hill, leading the gaze into the distance. This technically difficult subject suggests an attempt by Frome to adapt his training as a surveyor to the situation, to select the best compromise he can in the terrain at hand. Another version of the Mount Bryan sketch was used for an engraving in Charles Sturt's 'Account of the Sea Coast and Interior of South Australia', appended to his *Narrative of an Expedition into Central Australia*. Frome's series of watercolours of the Depot, Black Rock Hills, all show a similar landform, with long rows of parallel rounded hills separated by tracts of flat land like the swales between dunes. Other watercolours from this expedition show his interest, as a surveyor, in geological formations and shapes. *Prewitt's Springs* shows particular innovation in its use of the irregular planar faces of rock walls as the focus of the composition.

More poignant on several counts is Frome's *First View of the Salt Desert – Called Lake Torrens* (1843) (see illustration following page 16) with its implicit word play. A lone figure on horseback, either Henderson or Frome himself, surveys (in both senses) a perfectly level landscape in which he and his horse provide the sole visual interest. His telescope, through which he searches in vain for some distant geographical feature, is held parallel to the horizon, emphasising the unredeemed flatness and mocking the imperative for a surveyor to make his measurements from some eminence in the region. The visual emptiness is intensified by the fact that more than three-quarters of the picture is devoted to an equally featureless expanse of sky, unrelieved by even a puff of cloud. The colour of the sky – shades of cream to pale mauve but without a vestige of blue – and the lack of shadow cast by the figure, suggest the effect of midday heat haze. The artist's gaze, like that of the observing figure in the painting, implies a perspective elevated above the plain, thereby further flattening its surface, ironing out irregularities such as the tufts of low scrub, which doubtless sheltered a wealth of animal life but which are here undifferentiated and reduced to insignificance.

91

The desolation expressed in the painting is both imputed to and impressed on the land, but its real source is the external expectation of fertility, which created the context of both the journey and the painting that expressed its result. The title, with its juxtaposition of 'desert' and 'lake', underlines the irony that was already becoming apparent to European settlers of the country north of Adelaide. Lakes that were rich in fish and bird life one year might, for a decade, revert to a hard salt bed, glittering in the sun like a sea. We saw in Chapter 4 that George Woodroffe Goyder, assistant surveyor-general of South Australia, was deceived by the reflection off the salt surface of Lake Torrens, reporting fertile land to a prematurely exuberant Adelaide. A further irony, one unknown to Frome, is enshrined in his title, for the lake in the painting was 'called Lake Torrens' because of an enduring mistake first made by Eyre and perpetuated by Frome and Sturt. By chance, on each of his attempts to reach the centre of the continent, Eyre had found his way blocked by one of the semi-circle of lakes (Torrens, Frome, Callabonna and Blanche) around the northern Flinders Ranges. He was thus deluded into believing them parts of a single horseshoe-shaped lake 'stretching away as far as the eye could reach' and 'bending around to the North East'.[14] Frome's delicate water-colour expresses not only the unrelieved monotony of the area for which the citizens of Adelaide had cherished such expectations but also the hopelessness experienced by their representative observer.

92

GEORGE FRENCH ANGAS: OBJECTS IN THE LANDSCAPE

Where Frome had been trained in surveying, another traveller–artist, George French Angas, had studied natural-history art. In his youth he had avidly collected shells along the Devonshire coast, cultivating an interest in conchology that was to dominate his later years. While still at boarding school, Angas had read *Travels to the Equinoctial Regions of America* by the famous German geographer–traveller Alexander von Humboldt and been fired with a desire to travel and record his impressions in similar style. As the eldest son of a wealthy family he had ample opportunity to realise his ambitions to travel, and duly prepared himself by taking lessons in drawing from the natural-history artist Benjamin Waterhouse Hawkins. When his first expedition to Malta and Sicily led to a publication, *A Ramble in Malta and Sicily in the Autumn of 1841*, Angas decided to embark on a more ambitious journey to the Antipodes, 'actuated', as he later claimed in a fine Humboldtian phrase, 'by an ardent admiration of the grandeur and loveliness of Nature in her wildest aspect' and doubtless also by the fact that his father, George Fife Angas, owned the South Australian Company. Angas was particularly interested in recording 'savage life and scenes' before British civilisation inevitably, as he believed, destroyed them, and in preparation for recording his ethnographical observations he also studied anatomical drawing and lithography.

Arriving in South Australia in January 1844, Angas almost immediately attached himself to an expedition through the Mount Lofty Ranges to the Murray River and down to the Coorong. In April, he was off again on a more prestigious expedition organised by the governor, Sir George Grey, from the Coorong inland to Mount Gambier. This was one of the first opportunities for a trained artist to record impressions of desert-like landscape, but despite the variety of Angas's illustrations he virtually ignored this aspect, focussing instead on natural history and Aboriginal artefacts. Angas was perhaps aware that his artistic skills lay more in the area of detailed observations than in landscape, a point made by critics of the first exhibition of his watercolours, in June 1845. After travelling in eastern Australia and New Zealand, he returned to England where, in the following year, 1847, he published *South Australia Illustrated, The New Zealanders Illustrated* and *Savage Life and Scenes in Australia and New Zealand*. The latter, which includes a record of his journey with the Grey expedition, has illustrations of an 'Elevated native tomb' and 'Kangaroo at bay'[15] but there is no attempt to convey pictorially the wild landscape, of which he writes so evocatively in the manner of the sublime:

> The scene that we thus entered upon was wild and desolate in the extreme: a region of the most dreary and melancholy aspect lay before us, where the white man's foot had never before trod, and pervaded by a profound stillness, scarcely disturbed by the low moaning of the ocean. Some of these sand-hills or dunes are of immense height presenting the appearance of barren mountains; and in one place a vast chasm, resembling an extinct crater, rent these sandy heights, surrounded by masses of sandstone and projecting rocks.[16]

93

With an eye to the British sales of his proposed work, Angas selected and annotated those scenes that would encourage immigration by illustrating fertile plains beckoning the settler to a life of prosperity. The illustration of *Waungerri Lake and the Marble Range, Beyond Point Lincoln*, as it appears in *South Australia Illustrated*, is made more alluring to the prospective settler by the comment: 'In a few years, no doubt, all this district will be thickly settled and cultivated; the margin of Waungerri Lake presents an enticing spot for a settler's homestead; and should I ever again visit this locality, the sights and sounds of civilisation and busy industry, will no doubt have taken the place of the kangaroo feeding silently.'[17]

From 1853 to 1860 Angas was secretary of the Australian Museum where, along with administrative duties, he supervised and classified the first collection of Australian specimens, producing copious illustrations in the field of conchology.[18] Bernard Smith has remarked that 'little real distinction can be drawn between the intentions of a scientific illustrator, like Gould, who dedicated himself to the production of fine bird books, and a picturesque artist like Angas, who sought to advance science by means of the information contained in his paintings'.[19] Certainly Angas's early fascination with natural history and ethnography always dominated his art, overshadowing the landscape interest.

CHARLES STURT: THE EXPLORER AS ARTIST

Though most of the inland explorers had studied elements of drawing during their training as surveyors, only Charles Sturt prided himself on his artistic abilities. A keen amateur naturalist (while in Sydney he was a member of the committee set up in 1836 to manage the Australian Museum and the Botanical Gardens), Sturt made careful drawings during all his expeditions with the intention of using them as illustrations in his published journals. While at Depôt Glen he made watercolours of two birds, probably a wedge-tailed eagle (*Aquila audax*) and a chirruping wedgebill (*Psophodes cristasus*),[20] and later a pencil sketch of a jerboa. Sturt had an ulterior motive for drawing this creature. His rival, Major Mitchell, had made a plate of a jerboa and Sturt was keen to show up its inaccuracies. He wrote in his *Journal*:

> We have captured one of those little animals called the Jerboa about which Major Mitchell makes such a fuss in his book and I have it alive and well. It is a beautiful little animal, something between the mouse and the kangaroo in shape, with a very long tail having a brush at the end of it. It is very elegant in its movements, and Major Mitchell's plate is as much like it as it is like the Hottentot Venus, a most absurd resemblance of the little creature altogether. [21]

Particularly interesting in relation to his written account is Sturt's wash drawing *The Depôt Glen* (undated) of the waterhole where drought forced his party to remain for nearly six months during his 1844–45 expedition.[22] His description of the scene in his *Journal* reads:

> The creek was marked by a line of gum-trees, from the mouth of the glen to its junction with the main branch. . . . The Red Hill (afterwards called Mount Poole) bore N.N.W. from us, distant three and a-half miles; between us and it there were undulating plains, covered with stones or salsolaceous herbage, excepting in the hollows wherein there was a little grass. Behind us were level stony plains, with small sandy undulations bounded by brush, over which the Black Hill was visible, distant ten miles, bearing S.S.E. from the Red Hill . . .[23]

But despite Sturt's interest in geology, and although his drawing attempts to indicate the rock formation of the cliff, the work is far from being the strictly objective depiction of a surveyor. Compared with his written account, the painting appears heavily romanticised, an effect heightened by the sepia wash. Although the cliffs are rocky, their outline is softened by the trees and there is no hint of the blinding heat that afflicted the party, nor the sense of imprisonment repeatedly referred to in Sturt's accounts of the place (see Chapter 4). The painting is also shot through with unconscious irony. The only two living creatures are the man with the gun and the bird he is attempting to shoot. This reflects Sturt's fascination with birds and recalls his erroneous conclusion that the intersection of the prevailing birds' flight patterns indicated the presence

94

of the inland sea that was the goal of this expedition. In this picture, the bird hovers in a patch of light, like a heavenly visitor, yet the man is firing at it. On the other hand a line of sight from the gun barrel would suggest that the bird has little to fear!

SAMUEL THOMAS GILL: THE ARTIST IN THE PICTURE

The first professional artist to concentrate on painting the desert was Samuel Thomas Gill. Before emigrating to South Australia in 1839, Gill had trained in London as a draughtsman and watercolourist at the Hubard Profile Gallery, an establishment specialising in the then-popular silhouette art. Conversant with the current Romantic trends in British art and the tradition of book illustration, he quickly obtained a commission to provide sixteen paintings depicting human activities associated with the months of the year, in the tradition of gardening and agriculture guides. The resultant watercolours were effectively only a transposing of conventional English rustic activities to the month appropriate for the Australian seasons. All were composed in the framed style recommended by the eminent English landscape theorists William Gilpin and Uvedale Price.[24]

In contrast to this 'safe' commission, Gill was soon to show his innovation in both technology and technique. Not only was he the first artist in Australia to make use of the camera, having imported the first daguerreotype apparatus to Adelaide in 1845, but he moved from the known and familiar to the unknown landscape of the desert. At first he was employed to make detailed drawings from the rough field sketches of the explorers. In this role he contributed illustrations to Eyre's *Journals of Expeditions of Discovery into Central Australia*.[25] Later he produced watercolours of several of Sturt's expedition drawings, to be used as the basis for the engravings in the *Narrative of an Expedition into Central Australia* (1849). One of the most striking of these illustrations is *Chaining over the Sand Dunes to Lake Torrens* (1846), a vivid picture of the laborious process of chaining then used in surveying. Carrying the heavy twenty-metre chain under the conditions of this journey must have been exhausting at any time, but Sturt made the original sketch for this particular scene close to the point where, 210 kilometres from Depôt Glen and 80 from the nearest water, he finally turned back. When he painted *Chaining*, Gill had not been to this area but he had travelled widely in other parts of South Australia and he captures brilliantly the surface glare, the deceptively flat horizon of terrain that is actually row upon row of parallel sand dunes, and the desolation of a country where the only vegetation is a spattering of spinifex bushes. Like Frome, Gill dispensed with any attempt to employ the principles of picturesque landscape construction; if anything, he emphasises their absence and instead creates interest by focussing on the people and their manifest problems. His expeditioners are tiny but gallant individuals pitted against a vast, hostile landscape.

In the same year, 1846, Gill seized the opportunity to see the desert at first hand. He joined the expedition of John Ainsworth Horrocks as an unpaid assistant, although he clearly hoped to receive remuneration subsequently,[26] as well as to sell paintings based on his experiences. The small party of six men, with their horses and a pack camel called Harry (the first to be used in Australian exploration), was sponsored by a group of Adelaide citizens who hoped for the discovery of good pasture to the west of Lake Torrens, although Eyre had already described this country as a 'dreary prospect' offering neither food nor water.

On 1 September 1846 an advance party comprising Horrocks, Gill and a third man, Kilroy, reached a small salt lake (which Horrocks called Lake Gill but which was later renamed Lake Dutton) near the southern end of Lake Torrens. This was to prove the farthest point of the expedition, for here Horrocks, preparing to shoot a 'new' species of bird, accidentally shot himself instead, when Harry lurched and caught his pack in the cock of the gun, discharging the barrel. The shot blew off the middle finger of Horrocks's right hand and entered his cheek. While Kilroy walked nearly 110 kilometres back to the base camp for help, Gill remained with Horrocks and, to fill in the four weary days of waiting, made sketches which he was later to rework as watercolours, along with a series showing the slow return of the party carrying Horrocks to the base camp. There a doctor finally operated on Horrocks's gangrenous hand, but it was too late. The patient died four days later, just seventy-five days after the party had set out from Adelaide. Before he died, Horrocks wrote, 'Mr Gill showed himself to be a brave and steady companion by remaining with me. He has taken several sketches of this country which will show to those interested how very impossible it is that any stations can be made to the west of Lake Torrens.'[27]

Gill's diary from the expedition, published in the *South Australian Gazette and Colonial Register* (1846), emphasises the deep sense of alienation that he and his companions experienced, assailed by the heat, flies, lack of water and hostile Aborigines. These latter encounters, such as that depicted in *First Interview with Hostile Blacks North-west of Spencer's Gulf* (1868) with Uro Bluff in the background, changed Gill's earlier attitude towards Aborigines. Formerly he had supported the official line that they were harmless, well intentioned towards white settlers and even, under certain circumstances, employable; afterwards, his depictions of Aborigines are decreasingly sympathetic.[28]

From his sketches of the Horrocks expedition Gill produced thirty-three watercolours, exhibiting them with great success in Adelaide in January 1847. These paintings intrigued the citizens of Adelaide, not just because they were the first pictorial records of the Flinders Ranges by a trained artist, but perhaps more because of what they conveyed about the sense of being there. Gill depicts himself experiencing the events and the landscape and indicates his emotional responses. With this element of personal drama Gill, more or less by accident, and in violation of his own training as a landscape artist, evolved a new and viable method of recording the desert in a manner with which a viewer could identify. He was quick to realise the success of this formula: for more than twenty years he continued to produce variations on the ill-fated Horrocks expedition and the scenery of the Flinders Ranges.

Watercolours based on the earlier sketches, made when the party was still hopeful of sighting the grazing land they had been funded to find, show them striking a pose, metaphorically and visually claiming conquest over the territory. Both *Looking South-west to Spencer's Gulf, August 10, 1846* and *Country North-west of Tableland* (see illustration following page 48) glorify the process of exploration in this way and it is not accidental that these were the two pictures bought by Charles Sturt and presented by him to Queen Victoria.[29] However, despite the complacency of the figures, there is an element of qualification as well. In *Country North-west* . . . Gill depicts two of the party, probably himself and Horrocks, on the table-top hills near Eyre's old camp in the hills of Depot Creek.[30] Like Frome's even more poignant painting, which has only one human figure surveying a similar scene, Gill contrasts the human figures with the vast expanse of featureless desert before them. Although he has shown them on an eminence looking down on the plain, the implied conquest over the territory they survey is ironical. As far as they – and we – can see, there is no land worth the taking. The painting seems designed to deliver to the citizens of Adelaide an unambiguous message about the hopelessness of their venture.

Gill's work shows meticulous attention to detail, not only of objects, but of subtle effects of the light. Like Frome he conveys the delicate shades and textures of saltbush and spinifex under the harsh light and the sheen of salt lakes but without romanticising the landscape. Ironically, while it intrigued his contemporaries, Gill's inclusion of figures, such as the expedition members and Aborigines, often exhibiting frank and undignified responses, probably contributed to the relatively low esteem in which his work has since been held, compared with the more austere landscapes of von Guérard or Chevalier. It smacks of the cartoon images that Gill was later to employ in his more famous paintings of the Victorian goldfields. The macabre *Grim Evidence* (n.d.) depicts a skin-clad Aborigine showing a well-dressed European the skeleton of a man who has died of thirst in the desert. He has fallen with one arm outstretched, dropping his tin mug. The skeleton of his dog, the bones picked totally bare, lies curled next to him, while the remains of his horse lie to one side and crows hover overhead, temporarily disturbed from their picking. The observer holds his hand in front of his face in a gesture which might be horror, or might be an attempt to block the smell of the corpse. The murderer accused by the 'grim evidence' is clearly the desert itself, since its blistering heat and dryness have caused the traveller and his animals to die of thirst.

Invalid's Tent, Salt Lake, 75 Miles North-west of Mount Arden (1846) (see illustration following page 48) also stresses the vulnerability of the individual in this alien land where only the miscreant camel seems at ease. Again the interest of the picture is centred on the solitary human figure, Gill himself, lying outside the tent where the wounded Horrocks awaits help. Despite the title, Gill characteristically paints himself as the focal point of his picture; but unlike that of

Frome's lonely surveyor, his gaze is not aligned with ours. He looks off to the side, suggesting that as the direction from which help might be expected to come, but his apathetic posture indicates that the scene he contemplates to the left is as desolate and hopeless as that presented to us. The picture provides today, as it did in Gill's time, an interesting inventory of such an expedition's equipment, but it is a carefully selected statement. Against the immensity of the desolate scene the pathetic tent, the two mugs, the small water barrel, the binoculars hanging unused on the tent pole because there is nothing to look at, and the guns, one of which had been the instrument of disaster, all serve to emphasise the fragility of existence in such a place and the passive resistance of the land in which the human figures are intruders. In another depiction of this waiting period, *Invalid's Tent on Salt Lagoon, Horrocks' N.W. Expedition, S.A. 1846*, Gill again stands near the opening of the tent, revolver in his belt, looking off to the left like a sentry, but powerless against a faceless enemy – the land itself.

In 1847, as a result of his series on the Horrocks expedition, Gill was commissioned by the South Australian Mining Association to paint a series of watercolours at Burra Burra, a successful copper mine.[31] *Kooringa, the Burra Burra Township, April 7 1848*, a composition of which there are several versions, indicates Gill's retention of many aspects of the Horrocks paintings – the bare landscape that dwarfs not only the figures of the Aborigines in the foreground but the town itself, occupying no more than a slight depression in the desiccated and alien landscape.

Despite these successes, Gill was declared insolvent in the Supreme Court in Adelaide on 10 September 1851. He migrated to the goldfields in Ballarat, leaving Adelaide without a landscape artist of significance until the next century when Hans Heysen began to paint in the Flinders Ranges.

LUDWIG BECKER: NATURAL HISTORY AND GERMAN ROMANTICISM

If Robert O'Hara Burke had had his way, Ludwig Becker would have been omitted from the Victorian Exploring Expedition. Burke was particularly unwilling to be encumbered with a naturalist, a role which he regarded as useless and time-consuming, when his only goal was to beat his South Australian rival John McDouall Stuart across the continent. Nevertheless, despite his leader's protests, Becker was appointed by the Exploration Committee, and the forty exquisite drawings and watercolours that he completed during the expedition,[32] many under the most testing conditions, are arguably the most significant results to emerge from this ill-advised and ill-fated venture. Becker was officially appointed as artist, naturalist and geologist, a cumbersome title devised to demarcate his functions and thereby avoid offending William Wills and Hermann Beckler, the other members of the expedition with scientific abilities. Yet the title aptly described not only Becker's multi-disciplinary training and interests but also the outcome of his labours, for he produced work of both styles – meticulous, analytical drawings of desert plants and animals, and superbly evocative renderings of the landscape in the manner of the Romantic sublime.

Born in Darmstadt, Germany, Becker had received little formal training in either art or science, but he compensated for this by his persistence in self-education and his dedication to the cause of exploration science. At school he had already begun a lifelong friendship with Jakob Kaup, later one of Europe's foremost zoologists, who encouraged his interest in the natural sciences and in 1826 engaged him to illustrate his *Galerie der Amphibien*. It seems likely that he studied lithography at the Städelsches Institut in Frankfurt, one of the foremost European centres of art studies at the time. In 1846 Becker had accompanied the renowned zoologist Louis Agassiz on a fossil-hunting trip through the Rhine valley. His fascination with pursuing all branches of natural history and searching for interconnections in the style of his hero, von Humboldt, was already evident when he arrived in Australia in 1851. After eighteen months in Tasmania and two years on the Victorian goldfields, Becker moved to Melbourne where he worked as a natural-history draughtsman and lithographer for the *Transactions* of the Philosophical Institute, and illustrated scientific papers for Ferdinand von Mueller and Frederick McCoy, two doyens of the Victorian scientific scene. He also sent botanical drawings to Sir William Hooker for his *Journal of Botany and Kew Gardens Miscellany* (1849–87), produced twenty-six scientific papers on topics in zoology, geology, ornithology, astronomy and mineralogy, and became an active member of the Royal Society of Victoria.[33] Becker's application to join the expedition was strongly supported by both von Mueller, government botanist of Victoria, and Georg von Neumayer, director of the Flagstaff Observatory; but, even so, it was probably only through the recommendation of Sir Henry Barkly, the governor, that Becker was appointed against the wishes of Burke.[34]

Annoyed at Becker's appointment, and concerned that if a 52-year-old man survived the journey the Victorian public would scarcely be disposed to believe in its rigours, Burke ordered Becker to begin loading the camels with 180-kilogram bags at 5 a.m., to desist from his scientific investigations, and to work and walk with the rest of the men. Soon Burke was able to report cheerfully 'To load four camels and then march twenty miles is no easy task. After the first two days poor Becker was all in and I don't think he's able to carry on much longer.' Later, in his report to the Exploration Committee, the second-in-command, George Landells, wrote: 'I was particularly requested [by Burke] not to allow Dr. Becker to ride, the leader observing that "if Becker accompanied the expedition, and got through, people would say that it would not be difficult to cross to Carpentaria, and that he was to be walked until he gave in"'.[35] Becker complied with this gruelling regimen, but continued to make his scientific records and sketches when the rest of the camp slept. He was one of the party ordered to remain with Wright's group at Menindee for three months from October 1860, and it was here that he completed most of his water-colours, despite being plagued by heat and flies.[36] At the end of January 1861

99

Wright's party advanced to Torowoto where Beckler, Becker and Purcell, the last two suffering badly from scurvy, remained while Wright and a small party proceeded towards Cooper's Creek. In April they moved on to Bulloo where Becker died from the effects of severe dysentery and scurvy.

Becker's natural-history drawings and watercolours were second to none in their time. They included a series of freshwater molluscs from the Darling River, a Gullomalla pigeon, a Long-haired or Plague Rat, the fish Silurus, numerous geckos and even a drawing and description of a parasite found in the armpit of one of them. All are executed to display biological peculiarities, and are amplified by the verbal descriptions appended to them. His study of *Children's Python* (not a pet but named after J.C. Children, a naturalist at the British Museum) is drawn one-third its size, each scale carefully represented. Ink drawings show the disposition of different-sized scales on those parts of its undersurface not visible in the watercolour. Similarly, his various studies of geckos, fish, moths and birds include separate magnified diagrams of unusual details and marginal notes about their habitat. Atypically, Becker also added, where possible, the indigenous name for the organism. His models were the European botanical illustrators, beginning with the Medieval herbals, where illustrations were used for identifying plants rather than for artistic merit.

Unlike the other members of this and most nineteenth-century expeditions, who were intent only on surviving in a hostile environment and conquering the desert, Becker shows in these meticulous sketches that he was interested in the desert for itself and in all the varied organisms it sustained. The delight of the naturalist in finding and recording another species allowed him to transcend, intellectually if not physically, hardships that destroyed the other members. When Becker wrote from Darling Depôt to Dr Macadam, honorary secretary of the Royal Society of Victoria, 'Hard work in the camp want of vegetables & of fresh meat, great heat with flies & moskitos [*sic*] – are not apt to support one whose greatest desire is to try to unveil some of the mysteries of this country',[37] he had in mind something very different from Sturt's unveiling of the mysteries; Becker's mysteries were those of von Humboldt, to be understood by patient study of Nature's differences as part of an infinitely varied cosmos.

In addition to his scientific drawings, Becker's landscape paintings show a broad range of desert scenery and a degree of experimentation in recording the desert not apparent in the work of any other nineteenth-century artists. In these works the naturalist's desire to record minutely what he sees is combined with German Romantic sensitivity to elements that transcend physical and material explanation, effects more felt or imagined than visual or measurable. An admirer of the work of Caspar David Friedrich, Becker was conscious of looking for an antipodean equivalent. This is why he, unlike his English contemporaries, was able to exult in the immensity of the Australian desert as sublime rather than threatening, and to interpret it visually in the German Romantic tradition of grandeur. It is this rare combination of insights from his two role models – the Romanticism of Friedrich and the scientific regimen of von Humboldt – that makes Becker's desert landscapes unique.

100

One of his boldest compositions was the early Sketch No. 2, *Crossing the Terrick-Terrick Plains, August 29, 1860* (see illustration following page 48), showing two diverging lines of men emerging from an invisible central point beyond the horizon. On the left are those mounted on camels, led, no doubt, by George Landells, the second-in-charge and the man responsible for bringing the camels to Australia. On the right is a line of horseriders and horse-drawn covered wagons. In the middle of the painting rides Burke on his prancing horse, Billy. The almost diagrammatic composition reflects the lengthy disputes that had dogged the Expedition Committee as to the relative merits of camels and horses. The line of camels proceeds, unheeding, towards the skeleton of a cow

Ludwig Becker, *Gecko*, 1860, pen-and-ink and pencil, 17.2×12.3 cm, La Trobe Collection, State Library of Victoria.

101

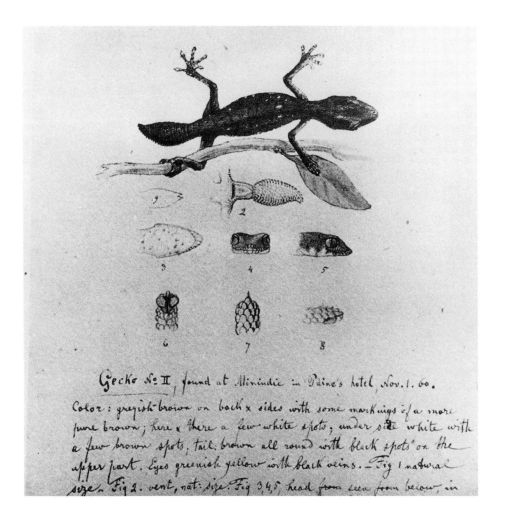

in the left foreground, as though prefiguring the disastrous end of the expedition. Ironically, too, in terms of the outcome, both riders and mounts have a translucent look, by which Becker wished to convey the shimmering heat rising from the plains to the almost white sky, but which also imparts a ghostly quality to the figures.

In the reports accompanying the sketches and watercolours Becker frequently amplified the complex visual effects. Describing his Sketch No. 13, *Banks of the Darling near Bulwaka Camp*, for example, he writes on 2 October 1860:

> A peculiarity noticed already at the river Wakool, is here again visible, viz. the regularity of the banks of the Darling as if the stream were running through an artificial canal. The waters of that river sometimes rise to such a hight as to overflow by four feet the banks. The marks of such floods are about 25 feet above the level of the Darling at the time this little sketch was made. The old big tree on the left had its roots washed out by those high floods and presents now a picturesque view: the tree seams standing on its owen roots, which look like crooked columns. forming grotesk arches, on the top of which the hollow stem of that old Eucalyptus towers. [This quotation retains Becker's spelling.][38]

Another landscape, '*Mallee Sand-Cliffs*' at the Darling Oct. 12, 1860, although measuring only 12.2 cm x 17 cm, expresses both Becker's geological interest in the sedimentary layers of sand and the effect they had upon an imagination formed by European experiences and a Romantic world view. His lengthy report of 12 October 1860 describes in detail his complex response to the scene, of which the following is a part:

102

> It will be seen that the foot of the 'cliffs' is composed of brownish-red sand, which colour changes, higher up, gradually to yellow, when it becomes nearly white at the top of the cliff. These different layers of sand all horizontal are very distinct: the separating sheets of calcareous matter are less affected by the rain water, they being harder, it renders the eye to count and messure correctly those deposits of sand of which we at present do not know to what geological period they belong, as, so far as I know, no fossils were found in that formation. The first impression of the scene upon me was a very striking one – I did not know what to make of it. It looked to me as if it were a sort of model for an alpine formation, the pines on the bottom of the cliffs still more reminding one on some scenery in Switzerland; – then again it was to me as if I were in the Gallery of an enormously large play-house and looking down upon the stage and at the painted back-ground illustrating some scene out of 'William Tell' or of 'Linda di Chamouni'. As it is, however, these sandcliffs are entirely the result of natural forces, and human hands had no play in it: no sand pits, no excavations are to be seen. [Again, the quotation retains Becker's spelling.][39]

In this account, as in the painting, we have a glimpse of Becker, the Renaissance man, with his inimitable combination of skills: the artist's minute observation of colour and texture, the scientific explanation, the emotional and imaginative reaction generated by the parameters of memory, art and Romantic philosophy, concluding with a scientific statement as to origins. Had Becker lived to become familiar with Darwin's *Origin of Species*, he might well have produced a unique response to this proposed ordering of Nature and transformed nineteenth-century art in this country.[40]

Becker's most intriguing desert landscapes are those in which he experiments with the effects of light in a manner reminiscent of Turner to re-create the sense of blinding heat and glare that conjure up a mirage. His knowledge of meteorology, derived from his expeditions with von Neumayer, made him particularly analytical of atmospheric effects, and he attempted to re-create these in his paintings. In his Sketch No. 3, *Terrick-Terrick Hills, Bearing N.b.W.* of 29 August 1860, he shows the flat, featureless Terrick-Terrick plain in the foreground, with the hills on the distant horizon to the left. The horizon to the right shows a mirage of a lake, with trees around its edge, and the actual Mount Hope, forty kilometres distant, appearing to hover above the fantastic lake. Becker adds in his notes on the sketch, 'Trees & other objects near the horizon affected by the <u>Fata morgana</u>'. In *Border of the Mud-desert near Desolation Camp, March 9th, 1861* (see illustration following page 48) the shapes of the dingoes and emus, which remain unaffected by the conditions, assert that this is no fantasy; yet the line of riders on their camels, emerging out of the glare, undermines our confidence in interpreting the material world. Are they real or illusory? Their ghostly appearance suggests at once their alienation from this stark land where the dry mud cracks before our eyes in the foreground, and, in hindsight, a premonition of their ephemeral nature. The visual effects in this watercolour suggest that, when in London, Becker may have seen and admired the controversial landscapes of Joseph Turner. There is the same fascination with the problem of representing light and its effects on our seeing, a feat even more difficult to achieve with watercolours on paper than with oils on canvas.

Under the extreme conditions of the expedition and denied the art materials he repeatedly requested, Becker resorted to a method he had devised earlier, adding eucalyptus gum, his makeshift equivalent of gum arabic, to his dry pigment in order to provide a hard surface. This could be hatched with Indian inks to accent shadows. He then selectively added a clear wash and varnish to produce opaque effects in the foreground while leaving a suggestion of transparency in the distance. With this armoury of makeshift techniques Becker contrived to produce some of the most delicate and evocative landscapes ever to emerge from the Australian desert.

HERMANN BECKLER: THE FASCINATION OF FATA MORGANA

Hermann Beckler, medical officer and botanical collector to the Victorian Exploring Expedition, also brought a specifically German perspective to what he saw. Like Becker, Beckler had been greatly influenced by Alexander von Humboldt, whose *Kosmos* he had studied in detail. Attuned to von Humboldt's attempt to reach a holistic understanding of Nature, he studied climate, geography, geology, astronomy and ethnology as means of understanding the universe and was fired with a particular desire to travel to the interior of the continent. He wrote to his brother Carl, 'Only God knows – there is nothing I want more than to travel on an expedition into the interior'; and a few months later, 'Just how the magical prospect of a miserable, hard life in the wilderness can affect one's whole being – this you can hardly comprehend.'[41] Even under the most uncomfortable conditions he could write enthusiastically:

> There was no question – we had entered a new land. What we saw before us today, unfolding every hour before our eyes and beneath our feet, we had never seen before. Descriptions of the Sahara came to mind; it was clear that genuine desert lay in front of us. The animals sniffed with wide open nostrils, turned their heads alertly to left and right, and waded into this hell-like air. One could almost believe they felt themselves transported into some desert of their homeland. But, poor animals, do not trust this deceptive picture! This was a desert without wells.[42]

Mirages, in particular, fascinated Beckler and he was careful to analyse them in detail as in the following two examples.

> Today, the horizon in front of us appeared to be filled with a row of small, isolated acacia trees of rounded shape and light-green foliage – a strange illusion, one from which we could not free ourselves for a long time. Yet we could never reach this row of trees for they stood, or more correctly, moved away before us at a distance of a quarter of a mile. They proved to be the above-mentioned small species of *Atriplex* [to 20 centimetres high] as magnified by the mirage.

> Looking out in various directions, the eternal fata morgana conjured up smooth, broad sheets of water to the dulled eye, and in the uniform, peaceful blue of the chimeric water shimmered the ragged image of a marvellous island.[43]

To supplement his written account, Beckler also produced more than forty sketches to illustrate his publication, *Burke's Expedition: A Journey to Central Australia*. While far inferior artistically to Becker's, they are competent enough. *Duroadoo* (Beckler's version of Torowatto) shows two camels grazing among spindly scrub. In this sketch, as in *Dry Lake Bodurga*, the horizon is almost unbroken and the foreground consists only of insignificant bushes. In the watercolour *View of a Distant Range of Mountains, Seen from Gogira Hills*, he attempts to give some sense of compositional interest to his difficult subject by seeming to plait the intersecting slopes of the low hills in the foreground. Surprisingly, given his vivid written descriptions, Beckler seems to have made no attempt to paint a mirage. He was clearly happier depicting more lush and mountainous areas, which he presented in the wild Picturesque style of

Salvator Rosa. His watercolour *View of the Gully with Rocky Waterholes, Gogira Mountains*, shows horses grazing on a steep slope, with fir trees and a mysterious cave against which one of the horses is outlined.

After the Victorian Exploring Expedition natural-history painting was superseded by photography in the recording of specimens.

The iconography of exploration

Until Lambert's Gallipoli paintings became part of the nation's homage to its military heroes, Australian history offered artists little in the way of epic subject matter for the construction of a national iconography. Colonial origins were far from glorious and although early exploration offered a potential theme it lacked a national focus. However, the departure of the major expeditions into the desert, bearing with them the hopes of the colonists and celebrated with a carnival atmosphere, provided attractive visual and emotional material for the artist with an eye to the local market, and preserved social details for posterity. Strangely, the ironical disparity between the ceremonial departure and the ignominious return seems to have presented no problem for artist or partici-pant. J. Neil's engraving of Edward John Eyre's 1840 expedition setting off from Adelaide, *Departure of the Expedition*, was chosen by Eyre to adorn his two-volume *Journals of Expeditions of Discovery into Central Australia*. It shows the immaculately dressed party, accompanied by well-wishers, galloping down a street with the air of gentry starting off on a hunt. The carts bearing the equip-ment are relegated to the rear so as not to detract from the glamour of the expedition and its upper-class leaders.

105

S.T. Gill was so optimistic about the market potential of exploration that he painted no less than three watercolours and a wash drawing of the ceremo-nial departure of Sturt's ill-fated expedition to Central Australia from Adelaide on 10 August 1844. One, reproduced in the explorer's *Journal*, shows Sturt, dressed in formal suit and top hat, and mounted on a white horse, leading his party down an Adelaide street watched by clusters of admiring citizens. In another version, Sturt and his elegant party have receded to the middle dis-tance, the foreground being occupied by a group of working-class spectators and Aborigines whose empty bottles have been thrown carelessly over a picket fence. A third ironically includes the boat, drawn on a bullock dray, on which Sturt intended to sail upon the inland sea. The 'departure', like many a more recent 'official opening', was frequently no more than a spectacle to entertain the public. Those on horseback could easily give the loaded drays a start of sev-eral days, so they commonly doubled back to the comforts of home for as long as possible. Sturt's 'departure' was no exception. Having set out in style and journeyed as far as Dry Creek, he and favoured members of his party returned to Adelaide for some days.

All previous depictions of departing explorers were eclipsed by those cel-ebrating the departure of Burke and Wills, as that spectacle itself towered over earlier events. The Victorian Exploring Expedition was part of a belated bid by 'Marvellous Melbourne' to achieve prominence in the history of exploration by funding the party that would be first across the continent. Despite the best intentions of the Royal Society of Victoria, the organiser of the expedition, the emphasis as far as the public was concerned was on being 'first' rather than on any potential gains to science or even on economic potential. Knowledge of the imminent departure of the South Australian candidate Stuart, already a celebrated explorer, added competitive spice to the proceedings. Indeed the colourful canvases depicting the formal departure of the expedition have all the air of a crowd at a fashionable horse race.

The day of departure, Monday 20 August 1860, had not been declared a public holiday but Royal Park was packed with between 10,000 and 15,000 excited spectators (half to three-quarters of the entire population of Melbourne)[44] taking a last look at the camels, Esau Khan, their exotic oriental attendant, and the striking figure of John O'Hara Burke, darling of the crowd. Nicholas Chevalier, one of the best known colonial artists of the day, captured the colour, the movement, the excitement and above all the theatrical performance aspect of the event in his *Memorandum of the Start of the Exploring Expedition*, 1860 (see illustration following page 48). All the major players in the drama are clearly recognisable in this self-consciously historical painting. Burke, a disproportionately small figure mounted on his dappled grey horse, commands a cleared space in the centre foreground. The horse's withers shine brilliantly white from the surrounding tones of brown and black, suggesting a heavenly blessing, and Burke with characteristic flamboyance waves to the dignitaries, including Richard Eades, the mayor of Melbourne, who raises his hat to the departing hero. Behind Burke, the camels tower haughtily over the crowd, one ridden by Becker and one by George Landells, at that stage Burke's second-in-command (though he subsequently resigned to be replaced by Wills) who had been responsible for importing them. The covered wagons are banished to the rear of the proceedings. Chevalier's scene is suggestive of a circus arriving in town, with Burke, uncharacteristically wearing a formal top hat, as ringmaster. Although it is unlikely that he intended such an irony in this painting, Chevalier was certainly not unaware of the circus-like nature of the expedition since he had contributed a cartoon entitled 'The Great Australian Exploration Race' (1860) for the *Melbourne Punch*.[45]

Compared with the brilliant but orderly pageant of Chevalier's oil painting, the muted tones of William Strutt's watercolour and pencil version of the event, *The Start of the Burke and Wills Exploring Expedition from Royal Park Melbourne* (1861), suggest an expedition out of control. Burke still dominates the foreground on his cavorting horse, but with less assuredness than Chevalier's figure. He touches his high-crowned bushman's hat, but it is not a gesture of authority and his figure is hardly differentiated, visually, from the confused group behind him, as horses attempt to bolt sideways, and a mounted policeman threatens the disorderly crowd. The Melbourne dignitaries who offer their blessing in Chevalier's painting are conspicuously absent.[46]

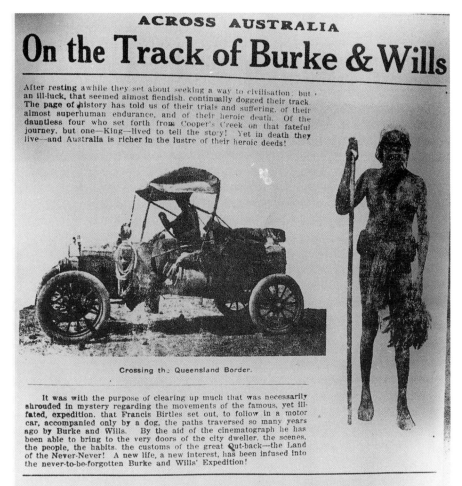

Publicity material for Francis Birtles's *Across Australia on the Track of Burke and Wills*, 1915. Courtesy Mitchell Library, State Library of New South Wales.

After such a euphoric start, the expedition's dismal conclusion struck the more forcefully. When it was known that Burke, Wills and Gray had died of starvation and exhaustion and that three other men, including Ludwig Becker, had died as a result of privations endured on the expedition, it was perceived not as Victoria's tragedy but as the nation's. This disastrous end of an ill-conceived and badly executed operation, under the command of an incompetent leader, was reconstructed by a nation in need of heroes as an epic undertaking of ennobling failure. Although it was widely known that Burke was a wilful and incapable leader and Wills obedient but ineffectual, this did nothing to detract from the mythologising of the two men. The Burke and Wills Expedition, as it came to be known, with John King, the survivor, as an attendant deity, was converted into the centrepiece of exploration mythology, flanked by the equivalent disaster of Lost Leichhardt's last expedition. The defeat of the nation's heroes was not seen as inglorious for they were the victims of an implacable and malignant enemy, the desert.

With the deaths of Burke and Wills, the iconography of Romantic suffering was given full rein. They were immortalised by artists as providing the first incident of nationhood, a subject demanding history painting on the grand scale. The only deterrent was the shortage of commissions for such works. Public bodies undoubtedly felt that enough money had already been spent on the expedition. Indeed Strutt's watercolour of the expedition's departure had still failed to find a buyer when he decided to return to England, so he was forced to raffle it. Henry Short, a specialist in flower and fruit painting, a genre which might seem to have little connection with dead explorers in the desert, ingeniously designed an elaborate allegorical study, *Our Adopted Country. To the Memory of the Lamented Heroes of the Victorian Exploration* (1861) (see illustration following page 48), involving an improbable melange of flowers, fruit, medallions of three dead explorers, a gold locket of King's, marble and gold urns, all set on a table in a misty garden. Not surprisingly, Short, too, was obliged to dispose of his painting in an art union lottery offering 120 shares at a guinea each.

Montagu Scott, chief cartoonist for the *Melbourne Punch*, focussed on the death of Wills, a less morally ambiguous hero, perceived as obedient unto death. *The Last Hours of Mr Wills* was engraved as the frontispiece of William Wills senior's *Narrative of a Successful Exploration through the Interior of Australia* (1863), encouraging the artist to embark on another work, *Natives Discovering the Body of William John Wills* (1865). An emaciated Wills lies on the ground in a position that echoes Henry Wallis's cult painting of *The Death of Chatterton* (1856). His extended arm reaches towards an empty cup and billy, suggesting (wrongly) death from thirst, as five Aborigines express their grief.

William Strutt was commissioned by the Melbourne Club to produce a portrait of Burke, but not the grand historical study he had wished to execute and had, indeed, prepared for by making preliminary drawings of the major participants, the camels and their attendants before the expedition departed. The full length portrait shows Burke, arms folded, in a barren landscape, his prominent blue eyes staring morbidly into the distance as though foreseeing the disastrous end of the expedition. A saddle camel lies behind him and two pack camels stand in the background. It was to be fifty years before Strutt, by then returned to England, finally completed *The Burial of Burke* (1911) (see illustration following page 48), his record of an incident previously neglected by artists in favour of the return to Cooper's Creek or Burke's death. Vivid in its colour and dominated by the huge Union Jack in which Burke's body, completely invisible, is being lowered into its grave, the painting could, as far as its background is concerned, be an autumn scene from Constable, rather than Cooper's Creek. Yet, believing in the sanctity of the events, Strutt paid scrupulous attention to detail, acquiring from the members of Howitt's rescue party an exact description of the place where they had found the bodies and how they had buried them. Anything less would, to Strutt and his contemporaries, have been tantamount to misrepresenting the events of the Crucifixion. Strutt also included in the painting indicators of his own moral judgement on the personalities. William Brahe, regarded by Strutt as the villain of the piece for his failure to remain longer at the appointed meeting place, stands apart from the group, dressed wholly in black as recognition of his guilt, while Alfred Howitt, leader of the rescue party that found King and the bodies of Burke and Wills, dominates the group.

Meanwhile, the best known of all the Burke and Wills paintings, the huge canvas by John Longstaff, commissioned by the National Gallery of Victoria and permanently on display there, continued to dominate public perceptions. Entitled *The Arrival of Burke, Wills and King at the Deserted Camp at Cooper's Creek* 109 (1907) (see illustration following page 80), it shows the three explorers in front of the D.I.G. tree (beneath which Brahe had buried a message and supplies), their exhaustion reflected in the two camels lying down behind them. Burke stands despairing as he reads the message left by Brahe, Wills sits on the verge of collapse, while King lies stretched out on the ground. These attitudes are clearly intended to symbolise the relative moral stature accorded the three men, with Burke remaining the leader to the last and King being the least important. The scene, dimly lit by a rising moon, stressed the humanity rather than the heroism of the explorers, and recalls the striking coincidence, whereby the exhausted explorers arrived at the meeting place on the evening of the very day that Brahe and his group, who had already waited a month longer than the agreed time, departed. The cruel irony of the timing, which was popularly seen as implying an extra element of fatalism in the affair and reinforcing its pathos, is fully exploited in the painting, insuring that it became a dominant element in the ensuing legend.

Works on canvas were insufficient to record the colony's grief. The English sculptor Charles Summers, then resident in Victoria, was commissioned to produce a 3.5-metre-high statue (the first bronze statue cast in Australia) of the two complementary figures of Burke and Wills, the former stepping eagerly forward, the latter sitting, looking up from his diary, representing respectively *vita activa* and *vita contemplativa*.[47] The granite pedestal incorporated four bronze *bas reliefs* depicting the start of the expedition, the return to Cooper's Creek, Aborigines weeping over the body of Burke, and the finding of King. Erected in Collins Street in 1865, the monument was a focal point of the city's identity until it was later moved to Royal Park. It has since been returned to the city centre, where it stands today on the corner of Swanston and Collins streets. An engraving of it featured as the frontispiece to E.C. Booth's *Australia Illustrated* (London, 1873). The state's heroes had become the nation's heroes and the Burke and Wills memorial is arguably the first 'war memorial' in Australia, commemorating as it does the death in action of the nation's brave 'soldiers' while fighting a more powerful enemy, the land.

After the collapse of the Burke and Wills dream, the desert ceased to interest Australian artists for sixty years. Only when Hans Heysen began to paint the Flinders Ranges was a barren landscape reclaimed for art. While this was, at the very least, an unfortunate reduction of subject matter, it had an even more diminishing effect on the depth and philosophical complexity of Australian art. Carrying the contrary implications of spiritual enlightenment and pitiless conditions where the struggle for survival is most evident, the desert potentially offered an ideal arena for artists to agonise over the Darwinian debate. As the watercolours of Becker indicated, the complexities of geology, biological variation and survival of the fittest were all present to be explored artistically. In Australia this opportunity was virtually lost for more than half a century as landscape art focussed, instead, on the pleasant and philosophically unchallenging Bush landscapes of the Heidelberg School.

110

Writers, on the other hand, were not so prone to discard the desert as subject. As we shall see in the next chapter, lack of personal acquaintance with the desert did not prevent poets from reworking the stereotypical scenario of innocent explorers or settlers lost in the desert and threatened by the awful spectre of death by thirst. If anything, the Burke and Wills debacle sanctified all such endeavours. When, later in the century, the element of *Boy's Own Paper*-style adventure and the possibility of finding gold were added to the mix, the desert as subject would even spill over from literature into popular fiction.

'On the Tracts of Thirst and Furnace'

Chapter 6

DEAD EXPLORERS AND NATIONAL IDENTITY

Deserts thorny, hot and thirsty, where the feet of men are strange,
And eternal Nature sleeps in solitudes which know no change.
HENRY KENDALL[1]

Europe has her knightly legends,
   And her names that cannot die;
We have Burke, and Wills and Stuart
   Is their glory not as high?
Though they did not fight in battle,
   'Mid the great ones of the earth,
Yet they made a country's history,
   And they gave a country birth.

F. SESCA LEWIN[2]

Our myths are proud lies that help us to walk tall.
DAVID MYERS[3]

The impact of the inland explorers' journals on the literature of the emerging nation was even more powerful than on its art. This influence derived from two specific but closely related qualities of the narratives: firstly their ability to provide heroes for a country that had hitherto not considered itself worthy to do more than admire from afar the great figures of European history and literature, and secondly their construction of a unique, epic landscape of almost limitless literary potential. Paul Carter argues that '[i]t was the explorer–writer's talent for forging a metaphor of himself as traveller that makes the narrative heroic, not the country and even less the personal qualities of the explorer';[4] but in terms of their literary influence these three aspects were inseparable. The journals provided later writers, who in most cases had never been near the desert, with a new and terrible terrain, rendered credible by the assumed factual nature of the reports. Equally importantly, they supplied a vocabulary for translating the desert into a nightmare landscape within which the deepest fears of the European colonists – isolation in an alien land, drought and thirst hitherto unimaginable, and the fear of a lonely death far from home – could be encoded, identified and confronted. By encountering these widely felt but vague terrors in a precise and literal sense, the desert explorers acquired an emotional status exceeding that accorded more 'successful' expeditions returning with news of practical and economic benefits. Eyre, Sturt, Leichhardt, Burke and Wills were the champions whose exploits gave the nation cathartic comfort and a stake in heroism. What was more, their heroism was virtually contemporary, a rare quality in a century when English writers, from Byron and Carlyle to Matthew Arnold, bemoaned the short supply of great men. In colonies whose recent past was tarnished with the stain of convicts and prisons, and where heroes were in even shorter supply, writers were not slow to recognise the potential of such figures as protagonists.

Poets were the first in the field. Seizing on the immense literary potential of these narratives, they proceeded to extend, modify, embellish and mythologise them, not only keeping the stories alive and accessible, but universalising them. By interweaving individual accounts they evolved one prevailing notion of *the* explorer, subsuming separate journeys across vastly different terrain in one archetypal journey through one specific landscape – a burning desert from which all other life has departed. Later explorers were readily slotted into the evolving legend. The disappearance of Leichhardt's third expedition without trace was in the public mind both 'explained' by, and seen as further confirmation of, the terrible experiences of Eyre and Sturt. Later still, the cumulative emotional investment in this composite heroism elevated even the Burke and Wills disaster into a myth of national greatness. By frequent repetition this landscape became as familiar to Australian readers as the woods and glades of European poetry so that, through the nineteenth century, we can trace the evolution of the desert in literature from nightmare to necessity. Beginning as the malevolent antagonist of the explorers, it became, in the hands of the poets, the necessary component of a uniquely Australian form of heroism. Youthful bards could contribute to the 'Little Laureates' Corner' of *The Town and Country Journal* their mite of praise for Australia's brave men, couched in all the accepted language of desert nationalism. Gradually the desert experience became accessible to those at the outskirts of settlement – drovers and swagmen – offering to them, too, the opportunity to become small heroes, and providing material for socialist contributors to the *Bulletin* to castigate the urban rich.

Wanted: Heroes (preferably dead)

The traditional heroes of the past had been military conquerors or, more remotely, knights embarked on a journey of enormous difficulty through a landscape that was both dangerous and evil. The goal of their quest was often vague or symbolic and, in the long run, unimportant; the main point was to endure the test or, in Tennyson's words, 'to strive, to seek, to find, and not to yield'. This formula was readily adapted to the explorers of the desert. The

ABOVE
Russell Drysdale (Australia b. 1912 d. 1981), *Emus in a Landscape*, 1950, oil on canvas, 101.6×127 cm, collection National Gallery of Australia, Canberra.

BELOW
Russell Drysdale (Australia b. 1912 d. 1981), *Desert Landscape*, 1952, oil on canvas, 102.9×128.3 cm, Art Gallery of New South Wales, Sydney.

Jon Molvig, *Untitled
portrait: Sleeping Aboriginal
Woman and Child*, 1958,
oil and enamel on
hardboard, 106.5×137.5 cm,
private collection.

ABOVE
Sidney Nolan, born
Australia 1917, arrived
Great Britain 1953, died
1992, *Central Australia*
(1949), ripolin enamel
and oil on composition
board, 92.1 × 121.9 cm,
purchased 1950, National
Gallery of Victoria,
Melbourne.

BELOW
Sidney Nolan, *Desert Storm
Nos 6 and 7*, 1966, oil
on hardboard, each
152.3 × 122 cm, Art Gallery
of Western Australia, Perth.

Fred Williams, *Trees in Landscape, Hammersley,* 1979, gouache on Arches paper, 76.3×56 cm, private collection. Courtesy Lynn Williams.

published accounts of Eyre and Sturt had taught their contemporaries to look beyond economics and to value the moral stature of endurance for its own sake. Celebration of these heroes was not confined to Australia. Henry Kingsley published a two-part eulogy of Eyre in *Macmillan's Magazine*, recounting the explorer's tortuous journey around the Bight as an instance of 'almost unexampled valour'.[5] The series of contests with the powers of evil undertaken by the aspiring knight was translated into the recurrent hardships imposed by the climate and the terrain. The land was therefore cast as both dangerous and evil, bent on destroying the explorer – physically through the torment of heat and thirst, and spiritually by tempting him to despair and luring him into the void. To aggrandise Eyre, Kingsley declared Nature senile when she fashioned the Australian Bight: 'A land which seems to have been formed not by the "prentice" hand of nature, but nature in her dotage. A work badly conceived at first, and left crude and unfinished by the death of the artist'.[6]

As the public expectation of exploration passed from the hope of material wealth to the celebration of heroic deed, the job description of the heroic explorer changed too. The first requirement was what historian Robert Sellick has called the 'heroic contract', according to which 'the conditions are usually quite explicit: the price is hardship or privation or suffering of a sufficiently demanding sort and the reward is fame or glory'.[7] For the reward of ongoing national fame, the price was high: death in the desert. It is not fortuitous that, in Sellick's study of thirty-four poems about individual explorers in the period 1813 to 1900, sixteen are devoted to the celebration of Burke and/or Wills and twelve to Leichhardt, while little attention is paid to Stuart (three poems), Giles (one) or Warburton (one), whose record in exploration far exceeded that of the first three but who returned alive from their expeditions.[8]

By other criteria the desert travellers were by no means the only outstanding figures of Australian exploration, nor was their path always through desert. Leichhardt's first overland journey to Port Essington was through well-watered terrain virtually all the way, while Burke and Wills, travelling in a particularly favourable season after good rain, were short of water only once when their waterbags did not hold as well as they had expected.[9] Wills recorded that the country was 'of the finest description for pastoral purposes. The grass and saltbush are everywhere abundant, and water is plentiful, with every appearance of permanence.'[10] As they approached the tropics, 'the country improved at every step ... everything green and luxuriant'.[11] But this was not at all the kind of scenery required for a testing, epic journey and writers almost invariably rejected it for a landscape closer to that so vividly described by Sturt as a desolate, burning desert, abandoned by plants and animals, deserted even by birds. The desert was thus constructed to fill a need on the part of the writers as much as on the part of the explorers. From the supposed death of Leichhardt in 1845 during his first expedition to the profusion of outpourings called forth by the deaths of Burke and Wills in 1861, poems celebrating the inland explorers adhered to a formula for evoking the desert, with heavy reliance on a set vocabulary involving the words 'wild', 'weary', 'gloomy', 'weird', 'waste' and 'lone', to create a composite landscape that was both monotonous and terrifying in its immensity and loneliness.

Essentially, literature about the desert recapitulated the pattern of writing about the continent that had preceded it. As what had formerly been regarded as uninhabitable, barren bush (or 'the Bush') was converted to grazing land, the areas designated desert comprised the only remaining wilderness, the only unknown. The shrinking 'interior' therefore inherited in concentrated form the earlier hostile pronouncements on the continent – the vastness and monotony of the terrain, the fear of being lost and dying alone, and the realisation of the fragility of European civilisation confronted by the incontestable power of Nature and separated from the moral resources of 'the centre', whether that centre was perceived as Britain or the fringe of coastal settlements.

The ultimate horror associated with the desert was the fear of dying there, not only far from civilisation and the last rites of the Church, but without the comfort of a companion in the hour of death. This struck a frisson of terror into the hearts of readers who could enjoy with equanimity the most harrowing Victorian deathbed scene. 'Death in the Bush', a nineteenth-century poem by Margaret Thomas, 'suggested by the death of Burke and Wills', enumerates the many absences experienced by the solitary dying heroes – 'To feel some message . . . yet with none to hear;/To long . . . for the last solace human hands bestow'. Thomas spares her readers nothing of the violence enacted by a pitiless Nature:

> To know not if thy wasted form shall lie
> And shrivel 'neath the sun's all-scorching eye;
> Or if the warrigal with rapture grim
> Shall tear thee piece from piece, and limb from limb;
> To know thine eyes may gaze unclosed to Heaven,
> Till from their orbs by crows and swamp-hawks riven.[12]

The explorer dying alone in the desert inherited the accumulated emotion invested in the familiar motif of the child lost in the bush. Both have, as it were, been swallowed up by the land, overpowered by natural forces against which men and children are equally helpless. The frequent recurrence and particular appeal of such images in nineteenth-century literature suggests that they carried deeper resonances. Lost explorers and lost children were only specific instances of lost colonists separated from their cultural source and struggling against a hostile land at the margins of the known world. The great figures of exploration can be seen as enacting that continuing element in Australian literature that Harry Heseltine has called the 'sense of the horror of sheer existence' and 'the terror at the basis of being'.[13] Indeed they achieve their rank in the nation's pantheon of great men not merely through the fearful reputation of their antagonist, the desert itself, but through its power to evoke a universal response: the image of the traveller dying alone in the interior epitomised in its starkest form the colonists' dread of dying in an alien country, separated from their loved ones 'at home' in England.

Lost Leichhardt

When there was no report of Ludwig Leichhardt's first expedition from Brisbane to Port Essington for six months after it was expected, a search party was sent to locate the explorers (or, as it was feared, their remains), and Leichhardt's friend, Robert Lynd, favoured the searchers with 'Lines Addressed to the Party proceeding on the Track of Dr. Leichhardt'. Never doubting that Leichhardt was dead, Lynd exhorted the search party, when it found the explorer's remains 'whit'ning on the waste', to give them a Christian burial, albeit without benefit of clergy, in a spot more reminiscent of a European scene 'where some mountain streamlet flows . . . by its mossy bank'. The desert where the explorer was presumed to have died was not considered worthy to retain the hero's body for this would suggest that the land, his enemy, had conquered it. In fact the search party found no such remains – for the best of reasons. In March 1846 Leichhardt reappeared aboard the *Heroine*, having successfully reached Port Essington and sailed back to Sydney. He received a hero's welcome for his achievements, £1,000 from the Legislative Council for a subsequent expedition, and numerous tributes to his bravery and leadership. Notable among these was 'Stanzas' by A.K. Sylvester. Despite the explorer's own account of well-watered terrain, Sylvester included a gratuitous vilification of a hostile desert because this was what a heroic explorer was expected to confront:

115

> Thou hast battled with the dangers of the forest and the flood,
> And amid the silent desert – a conqueror hast stood:
> Thou hast triumphed o'er the perils of the mountains and the plain –
> And a nation's smiling welcome, is thy greeting home again![14]

Within a few months of his return, Leichhardt had embarked on a second journey (1846–47), intending to cross the continent from east to west. It was aborted in short time but his third journey, another attempt to cross the continent, was farewelled in 1848 with no less optimism. The complete disappearance of this expedition gave rise to the Leichhardt legend. The enigma of 'lost Leichhardt' not only provoked endless speculation as to the ultimate fate of the party but elicited paeans of praise for a national hero, assumed by this time to have endured a lonely death, perhaps having already buried his companions. Most writers hazarded a guess as to the reasons underlying Leichhardt's disappearance. Adelaide Ironside offered a scenario based on a treacherous attack by Aborigines who battered the 'struggling pilgrims'. 'Far in the wilderness they fell, with none to mark the day.'[15] Henry Halloran's 'Leichhardt' assumed that the party died of thirst and, like the Aboriginal attack theory, this was seen as a deliberate act of malevolence by the landscape or its representatives. In Halloran's poem the desert is God-forsaken, even satanic:

> A cloven waste of gaunt and hungry sand
> Hides from the pitying Heaven the Dauntless One . . .[16]

The intriguing mystery of the expedition's complete disappearance, despite the repeated despatch of search parties, kept the Leichhardt legend alive. In the next chapter we shall see the extraordinary adventure stories that emerged during the 1880s and 90s, claiming a connection with the expedition, alive or dead. Several poets compared Leichhardt to Sir John Franklin whose expedition in search of the North-west Passage had been declared lost in 1845: the central desert was as remote and God-forsaken as the Arctic waste:

> But if like him whose fearless soul
> Dared the dread dangers of the Pole,
>   He hath a martyr fallen too;
> And found untimely life's dark goal
>   A deathless name is then his due![17]

The alleged similarity of the two incidents was taken to underline the comparable achievements of the leaders, suggesting that the Australian champion was at least as heroic as his English counterpart. An anonymous poem of 1865 tried to shame readers of the *Australasian* into emulating Franklin's supporters by sending another search party into the desert:

> If famine, thirst
>   Have done their worst,
> And low in dust the honoured head should lie;
>   Shame on them then,
>   As Christian men,
> The rites of Christian burial to deny.[18]

Sellick notes a common thread through the poems concerning Leichhardt and Burke and Wills, namely the refusal to allow the nation's heroes to find their last resting place in the desert. Robert Lynd had instructed the search party to remove Leichhardt's bones from the barren waste to a grave by a purling mossy stream, and similar injunctions were a feature of many later poems about lost Leichhardt, but one deserves particular notice. Henry Kendall's poem 'Leichhardt' (1880) celebrates not merely a daring explorer, but one further sanctified by his devotion to science. The poem tells the 'tale of hero',

> Shining with a theme of beauty, holy with our Leichhardt's name!
> Name of him who faced for science thirsty tracts of bitter glow,
> Lurid lands that no one knows of – two and thirty years ago.[19]

In this geographically confusing poem Leichhardt, as a child of German Romanticism,[20] was, like Wordsworth's Lucy, educated by Lady Nature to absorb the spirit of her mountains and old-world forests:

> Thus he came to be a brother of the river and the wood –
> Thus the leaf, the bird, the blossom, grew a gracious sisterhood.

In due course the 'starry angel Science' persuades Nature to 'lend him for a space, .../So that he may earn the laurels I have woven for his head!' It is Science that leads him to the Australian desert and to death. But Kendall cannot tolerate the thought that his hero should have perished in such an abhorrent place. He ventures to hope, instead, that Leichhardt has passed through the desert to die in some green and pleasant land reminiscent of his German childhood:

> On the tracts of thirst and furnace – on the dumb blind burning plain
> Where the red earth gapes for moisture and the wan leaves hiss for rain,
> In a land of dry fierce thunder, did he ever pause to dream
> Of the cool green German valley and the singing German stream.
> When the sun was as a menace glaring from a sky of brass,
> Did he ever rest, in visions, on a lap of German grass?
> Past the waste of thorny terrors, did he reach a sphere of rills,
> In a region yet untravelled, ringed by fair untrodden hills?
> [...]
> Let us dream so – let us hope so! Haply in a cool green glade,
> Far beyond the zone of furnace, Leichhardt's sacred shell was laid!
> Haply in some leafy valley, underneath blue gracious skies,
> In the sound of mountain water, the heroic traveller lies!

A century later the unreality of such a theory seems all too obvious, even in the verse itself, with its sequence of rhetorical questions and pious exclamations. But, given the poet's reputation, the effect on Kendall's contemporaries was arguably more insidious. The two landscapes between which the poem oscillates – the European forest glade and the Australian desert – are recurrent images in Kendall's poetry, each carrying its psychological and moral correlative. His poem 'Mooni', for example, involves a similar opposition between the River Mooni, representing a world of natural beauty and innocence, hidden from 'sin abhorrent', and 'the burning outer world' of sin and 'sneers and spurning'.[21] Judith Wright remarks that 'Kendall's "Australia" is a place sharply divided between Eden and Hell – between the lush forested clefts where waters fall forever, and the pitiless desert'.[22] 'On a Cattle Track', 'On the Paroo', 'The Fate of the Explorers' and 'Christmas Creek' all evoke a similar landscape of 'bitter hopeless desert' forsaken by Nature and by God:

> ... spheres that no bird knows of, where with fiery emphasis
> Hell hath stamped its awful mint-mark deep on every thing that is.[23]

In 'Leichhardt', this contrast between Edenic forest and hellish desert, with implicit condemnation of the latter, is particularly inappropriate because it denigrates, in effect, the explorer's own decision to journey into the desert, the alleged rationale of the poem. Kendall desires to celebrate Leichhardt for his exploits in the name of science, but cannot countenance the notion of his hero dying in the terrain he chose to explore. A parallel ambivalence runs

117

deeply through many explorer poems of the nineteenth century: pride in the exploit and hatred of the scene, but in Kendall's case, as Judith Wright suggests, the two landscapes reflect the poet's own spiritual turmoil:

> Kendall knew little of inland Australia, but he did know a great deal about the hells of the outcast and the scapegoat and of the divided mind, and the beckonings of the mirage of peace and the return to mindless innocence. These are his real subjects.[24]

However subjective, Kendall's descriptions of these personal longings and sensations of guilt were deeply influential in consolidating the picture of the inland deserts disseminated in literature, and in this sense his poetry looks forward to the more overtly symbolic treatment of the desert in twentieth-century literature. Like the explorers' own published accounts, his poetry filled in the emotional details of a hideous place, 'a bitter hopeless desert' where those who ventured would die of thirst and heat, lost in body and soul.

In poetry the explorers were increasingly depicted in moral and spiritual terms, shielded from any slur of self-seeking or avarice. Their motives were left vague, usually represented as the altruistic desire for knowledge. At first this was scientific knowledge, and in this regard Leichhardt was popularly supposed to epitomise the selfless scientist, although in fact he had been forced to jettison his specimens at a critical juncture to lighten the load on his horses. But most of the Australian explorers were not noted for their dedication to science. Indeed Burke, having actively but unsuccessfully tried to exclude Becker, the naturalist, from the expedition, had forbidden him to make notes or drawings. Most writers, therefore, preferred to leave vague the kind of knowledge that was sought. It came to include self-knowledge that would, in some unspecified way, elevate the nation. The leaders were, however, endowed with every Christian virtue. Leichhardt, for example, as presented in Sylvester's 'Stanzas', is not only a 'pilgrim of the mighty wastes' but an encouraging comforter of his men:

> Oft in the silent wilderness, when meaner spirits quail'd,
> Have thy unfailing energies, to cheer and soothe, prevail'd;
> For well thy hope-inspiring voice, could speak of perils past,
> And bid each coming one appear, less painful than the last.[25]

Even the death of the naturalist John Gilbert from an Aboriginal spear when the party was near the Gulf of Carpentaria is recast by Sylvester as an added sorrow to be borne by Leichhardt when 'they left him in the desert, to his long and lone repose'.[26]

Burke and Wills mythologised

The legend of lost Leichhardt was rendered possible by the sheer lack of documentary information, for in such a void innumerable myths could, and did,

118

proliferate. In the case of Australia's most celebrated exploring expedition, however, the Burke and Wills myth flourished in spite of the evidence. As Robert Sellick remarks, even when the Royal Commission of inquiry made public the dubious nature of the undertaking and the continued mismanagement of the expedition, 'the public's demand for heroes was greater than their desire for truth'.[27] Financially and emotionally, they had invested in a legend and they were determined to have it.

In defiance of Burke's explicit wish, his remains and those of King were retrieved from Cooper's Creek by Howitt and borne back to Melbourne for a public lying-in-state modelled on that of the Duke of Wellington and for the most lavish funeral arrangements ever witnessed in Australia. A storm of criticism broke forth in the press from those who thought the bodies should have been left *in situ*, those who thought Becker and Gray should have been similarly honoured, those who thought the whole ceremony was a mockery of

The Burke and Wills Funeral Procession, 1863, wood engraving, *Illustrated Melbourne Post*, 24 January 1863, pp. 8–9. Courtesy, State Library of Victoria.

British ceremonial reserved for royalty and military heroes, those who felt they were not sufficiently prominent in the proceedings and those who saw the whole affair as shockingly bad taste. Nevertheless, by relinquishing the heroes' bodies to Melbourne for state burial, the 'desert' (as Cooper's Creek was assumed to be) lost its victims, while the city's demand for their return can be seen as a desire to have the relics of its martyrs available for veneration. Notwithstanding all this, the funeral procession on 21 January 1863, for which a public holiday was declared, attracted between 40,000 and 100,000 spectators. Led by 115 of the Castlemaine Light Dragoons, the band of the Castlemaine Volunteer Rifle Regiment and a firing party of police, the specially built funeral car, also modelled on that of the Duke of Wellington, was escorted by hundreds of dignitaries, coaches and pedestrian mourners forming a procession that took hours to pass from the Hall of the Royal Society to the cemetery.[28] The whole exercise, but particularly the explicit references to the Duke of Wellington, clearly demonstrated the desire to proclaim Burke at least, and Wills by extension, as the nation's answer to Britain's military heroes, though no one was prepared to expound the military connection in detail.

Although the poets eschewed such ostentation and military metaphor, they were no less insistent in proclaiming the heroism of the two unfortunate explorers in other terms. The canonisation of Burke and Wills in poetry began almost as soon as the news of their death was received. Kendall's poems 'Oh, Tell me ye Breezes' and 'The Fate of the Explorers, Burke and Wills' (1861) were among the first in the field, the latter appearing in the *Empire* on 9 December 1861, just one month after the *Argus* had printed the first news from Cooper's Creek: 'The Continent Crossed. Death of Burke and Wills.'[29] In this first version of his poem Kendall pays scant attention to the expedition itself or the desert that exhausted the explorers. He focusses on the figure of the dying leader, who emerges as a transplanted Roman general wrestling with death and exhorting his subordinate, King, to preserve the notebooks which will explain 'something of our baffled movements'. This was an unfortunate inclusion as it later became evident that Burke had kept no formal records at all. Kendall's closing stanzas, with their echoes of *Hiawatha*,[30] import Aborigines as Burke's first mourners:

> Came the natives of the Forest – came the wild man of the Wood;
> Down they looked and saw the stranger – he who there in quiet slept –
> Down they knelt, and o'er the chieftain bitterly they moaned and wept.

Kendall later added a prologue which clearly implicated the alien, unresponsive landscape in the deaths of the heroic explorers, invoking all the stock literary attributes of the desert:

> ... deserts weird and wide ...
> ... deserts lonely; lying pathless, deep, and vast,

> Where in utter silence ever Time seems slowly breathing past – . . .
> Deserts thorny, hot and thirsty, where the feet of men are strange,
> And eternal Nature sleeps in solitudes which know no change.

Writers were not slow to realise the narrative potential of the Burke and Wills saga, with its unique combination of dashing leader, devoted scientist, death in the desert and the suspicion of villainy. Most important was the macabre element of repeated cosmic irony whereby the supply group, headed by William Brahe, left the Cooper's Creek rendez-vous on the very morning of the three desperate heroes' return, and a relief party, arriving later, failed to see any evidence of Burke's presence there. Thus despite the Royal Commission's findings and widespread disquiet about the entire undertaking, Burke and Wills (almost invariably bracketed together as one character) continued to inspire verse eulogies, the majority of doubtful merit historically or poetically. Many poets focussed less on the desert per se than on the universalising fact of death, especially death faced in isolation which, in some obscure way, is seen as uniting the nation. R.H. Horne's poem 'Australian Explorers', however, composed just after the elaborate public funeral in Melbourne, was unusual in its emphasis on the actuality of the desert, including its many unheroic trials, recorded by explorers, but largely ignored by poets:

> pestilent clouds of gnats, horn'd beetles, ants,
> Marsupial mice and rats, and, worse than all,
> The ceaseless torment of the common fly
> Attacking mouth, eyes, skin, by day and night.[31] (ll. 68–71)

121

Like most of the eulogists Horne included Burke's injunction to King to leave him unburied with his pistol in his hand, but he was the only poet to deal with the deaths of other members of the expedition and, in particular, to abhor the lack of respect for Ludwig Becker[32] whose artistic record of the expedition shames the fragmentary written accounts. Beneath his complex and obscuring syntax, Horne also saw the literary potential of the desert mirage that had featured in numerous explorers' accounts as a bitter irony, as demoralising as the physical torments:

> Where the *mirage* presents clear pools and lakes . . .
> And men and camels of the Exploring Train
> Travelling along the necromantic *sky*, –
> Another Train, inverted, foot to foot,
> Travelling beneath: both shadows! (ll. 46–9)

Despite the modest disclaimer of his subtitle, 'A plain, unvarnished (but heroic) tale', and the appended note that 'Nothing of what is understood as imaginative poetry is offered in the above story, which is simply an attempt to condense the whole narrative, divested of all its prose details and technicalities, and to give a few touches of local scenery',[33] Horne's poem emphasises in block capitals the universal and timeless significance of the explorers' deaths: 'THE WORLD PROGRESSES BY ITS MARTYR'D MEN'.

Adam Lindsay Gordon's 'Gone', from the *Sea Spray and Smoke Drift* volume (1867), also universalises Burke as our representative, in death as in life – 'that dead man gone where we all must go'. Again, his heroism consists not in victory but in endurance in the face of suffering:

> ... the dust reclaimed from the sand waste lone:
> Weary and wasted, and worn, and wan,
> Feeble and faint, and languid and low,
> He lay on the desert a dying man.[34]

The necessary counterpart of this heroism and sanctification by suffering is the implacable resistance of the desert, depicted in the stark colours of black, white and red:

> ... the sand ... the whitening chalk,
> The blighted herbage, the black'ning log,
> The crooked beak of the eagle-hawk,
> Or the hot red tongue of the native dog. (st. 5)

NATIONAL TREASURES

Increasingly the desert explorers came to be seen not just as exemplars of heroism in general, but as uniquely Australian, and it is the desert experience that distinguishes them from their counterparts in other nations.

Catherine Mackay (later Martin) was only thirteen when Burke and Wills set out from Melbourne, but fourteen years later she was to produce the lengthiest of the many literary responses to this event. Her poem *The Explorers* (1874),[35] drawing heavily on biblical and early Christian imagery of the desert, is unusual in taking as its protagonist not Burke but William Wills, scientist and second-in-command, and even more unusual in including derogatory innuendoes about Burke's ineptitude as leader. Her chorus-figure Bushman remarks:

> Incompetence and self-will have ofttimes been
> The ruin of great purposes, and I ween
> Such fatal qualities are not wanting here.

Part II of *The Explorers* opens with a description of the landscape at Cooper's Creek, drawn in terms (silence, wastes, seas and solitude) that carry clear Romantic resonances, both German and English: 'great woods which in strange silence lie ... vast wastes, (shaded by seas of leaves) ... unbounded solitudes'. In particular, the land is characterised according to the profoundly Eurocentric view common then as timeless, waiting, silent and uneventful, for the arrival of the 'Pioneers'. Part IV returns to the dying Wills, who becomes the recipient of a desert-generated vision, religious and strongly nationalist in its message. In his despairing state Wills dreams of a scene of social degradation in England, under the very gaze of the Queen: 'dark haunts of vice and gaunt despair' where the weak are jostled and trampled and the strong stand by unmoved by their plight because so much is spent by Church and State in charities.[36] Wills vigorously condemns the cruelty and hypocrisy of England and, in a strong statement of anti-monarchist criticism, predicts that wealth, power and outward piety will not save it from a future 'When Monarchies will reel, and the hoarse cry/Of unbelief and Anarchy, on high/Will rise'.[37] Against the evils of Britain, Wills sets the promise of Australia as the natural home of political and social reform based on egalitarian Christian principles, remarkably close to those that Martin herself was intent on ushering in:

> Thank God, there's room and breathing space
> For millions there, o'er whom want never more
> Need tyrannise, who, on that new-found shore
> May live, a race, free, happy, and content,
> The offspring of the men, who long were bent
> Beneath a yoke, more curst than that which weigh'd
> Afric's sons.

123

Wills sees his moral reward in having 'open'd up a realm, where the faint sigh/ And plaints of hunger never need ascend/To vex the sapphire skies' and where 'Great golden harvests, and quiet happy homes/Will yet be seen'. His last words affirm that the vision will become reality: '"No dream/Was this," he murmured ... "I thank Thee, God, that now/I feel and know, I do not die in vain;/And, knowing this, my loss I count but gain."' Thus the dying Wills receives a religious vision of socio–political reform espoused by Martin herself, wherein Australia will be not a desert but a land of plenty for all. Wills is depicted as dying happy in the knowledge that Australia will be blessed with a purer future – though the connection of this future with the expedition and the 'sun-parched sand' is never elucidated.

This realisation of the nationalist potential of Burke and Wills was still flourishing in the next generation. In 1909 Laura Wilson of Ringwood, Victoria, contributed her poem 'Burke and Wills' to 'The Little Laureate's Corner', conducted by Ethel Turner for *Town and Country Journal*. Laura also judges her heroes as superior to any in English history:

> We listen while the poets
>   Tell tales of bygone days;
> Of Arthur and his knighthood,
>   Of Alfred's minstrel lays,

Of soldiers and brave sailors,
  Who many battles fought,
And not their own vainglory,
  But England's honour sought.

But some there are far braver
  We speak with hushed breath,
Who fought not actual battles,
  Yet warred with life and death . . .

The poem trudges on for seven stanzas before reiterating its patriotic point and, interestingly, including Gray in the pantheon of heroes:

Then, hark, all ye Australians,
  And listen while I say,
That men were never braver
  Than Burke, Wills, King, and Gray![38]

Beyond exploration

The sanctity attached to the figure of the explorer was gradually extended to include other travellers in the desert, who were positioned in a pre-fabricated poetic landscape like figures on a felt board. These later writers felt obliged to invoke the stock list of attributes generated over three decades as a guarantee of fidelity to fact. These included not only heat, barrenness, thirst and monotony but also immensity, vast tracts of emptiness, solitude, silence, a sense of eeriness and changelessness. The desert was thus construed as the ultimate other, repository of all the cumulative fears, futility, desolation, frustration and death that haunted both the individual and the emerging nation. The vast, undifferentiated spatial expanse associated with the central desert became, by ready analogy, a featureless tract of eternity in which nothing had changed or would change.

Despite his first-hand knowledge of the desert, the poet George Loyau was unable to resist the power of this accumulated symbolism. His poem 'The Desert' (1877) purports to be the account, by the sole survivor, of three settlers who left Maranoa for Cooper's Creek, seeking cattle runs, and became lost on the sandy plain. Although Loyau makes no explicit mention of Burke and Wills, their shadow, inevitably invoked by the name of Cooper's Creek, hangs over the poem, in the 'forms whose names are in memory'.

The vivid descriptions of 'white volcanic sand', 'bright as glass – dazzling, burning glass' (an elegant reference to the origin of glass) make for some of his most evocative writing, but he is unable to resist the inclusion of a mirage featuring an extraordinary fruit salad of date-palms, banana, lime and orange trees. These features all but dwarf Loyau's pious purpose of exalting the narrator who, alone of the party, survives because of his faith and prayer 'That

Providence would spare my life' (l. 39) while his two companions 'blasphemed and died'(l. 36). Again the emphasis is on the vastness and the 'waste like a great eternity' (st. 1), but the narrator is saved by 'a Heaven-directed shower', bringing hope embodied in a bird. Loyau's desert is terrible, but always subservient to the power of Providence. It acts as the counterpart of the expanse of ocean in the 'Rime of the Ancient Mariner' of which it has recurrent echoes.

> A wild, wide waste; a perfect sea
> Of sand as far as eye could see, –
> There the west wind speaks, and moans and shrieks
>   Of forms whose names are in memory;
>   A waste like a great eternity!
> [. . .]
> And I escaped! I – only one,
> For 'neath a fiercely burning sun
>   I left my comrades dying;
> The sand became their winding-sheet,
> And oft my heart will still its beat
> When mem'ry turns her busy feet
>   To where their bones are lying.[39]

Ernest Favenc, the only other poet of the period to write from first-hand knowledge of the desert, had a more complex response than Loyau. His desert is both more starkly terrible and Darwinian, unmitigated by the hand of Providence, and also more strikingly beautiful. Of all the desert poets, he was the least dependent on stock descriptions because he wrote from extensive experience as an explorer in Queensland and the Northern Territory. Favenc introduced his collection of poems, *Voices of the Desert*, with a personal affirmation of nostalgia and love for the desert, and a discussion of its unique silence:

> If there is such a thing as darkness which can be felt, then the Australian desert possesses a silence which can be heard, so much does it oppress the intruder into these solitudes . . .
>
> Repellent as this country is, there is a wondrous fascination in it, in its strange loneliness and the hidden mysteries it might contain, that calls to the man who has once known it, as surely as the sea calls to the sailor . . .
>
> A land such as this, with its great loneliness, its dearth of life, and its enshrouding atmosphere of awe and mystery, has a voice of its own, distinctly different from that of the ordinary Australian bush.[40]

'In the Desert' (1879), one of the poems included in *Voices*, also invokes a silent, timeless land but is noteworthy in its inversion of the usual power balance. Here the desert is depicted as a sorrowing woman, threatened by the incursion of Western civilisation. This awareness of white settlers as intruders is a theme running throughout Favenc's writing, a reflection of his own restless

125

attraction to the desert silence after the noise of Sydney. He stated in the *Queenslander*, where the poem was first published, that it was written when his own expedition into the desert was battling with loneliness, exhaustion and starvation near Cresswell Creek.[41]

> A cloudless sky o'erhead, and all around
> The level country stretching like a sea –
> A dull grey sea, that had no seeming bound,
> The very semblance of eternity.
>
> All common things that this poor life contained
> Had passed from them, leaving no sign nor token;
> My footfall first broke stillness that had reigned
> For centuries unbroken.
>
> Almost it was as if my steps had strayed
> Into some strange old land or unknown isle,
> Where Time himself, with drowsy hand had stayed
> The shadow on the dial.
>
> A deep, dread silence, save when fitful sighs
> Of wailing wind were wafted from the south.
> Nature seemed dying: the light had left her eyes,
> The smile her mouth.
>
> Only in dreams unquietly she talked,
> In broken murmurs restlessly did 'plain;
> Then came strange sounds, as if a spirit walked,
> Wringing its hand in pain,
>
> Crying, 'No rest! no rest! Who dares intrude,
> And waken silence that for countless years
> Has been unbroken? Must our solitude
> At last know human tears?
>
> 'Leave but a little space, O restless race!
> Free from your carking vanity and care.
> Keep back! keep back!' And then, a phantom face
> Shone lurid in the air,
>
> Gazing in mine, with a strange, earnest look
> Of solemn sadness, more than mortal pain,
> Then vanished, with a bitter cry that shook
> The dim, dead plain.

The desert and moral conscience

By the 1870s the long-serving image of the desert as a malevolent, implacable enemy was being eroded by two factors. On the one hand, the bleak Darwinian vision of a ruthless, inhumane Nature depersonalised the antagonism, though it did nothing to mitigate its intensity; and on the other hand, the broad-scale application of Social Darwinism transferred the condemnation from the desert to class structures. In the decades from the 1870s to 1920 the *Bulletin* and *Town and Country Journal* printed numerous stanzas focussing on the intense drought and privation of settlers, and their imminent or actual death in the desert. In the *Bulletin* these tropes were frequently employed for political purposes consistent with the *Bulletin*'s strongly socialist leanings. In years of severe drought, responsibility for the deaths of the rural poor was laid squarely at the door of those perceived as privileged – wealthy city folk, the banks, the clergy and parliament.

A typical contribution of this time is the short sketch 'On a Dry Plain' by 'Mulga', describing an encounter between an old swagman desperate to reach water and a wealthy man in a buggy. To the swagman's question, 'How far to the water sir?', the man in the buggy replies, '"Eight miles, my man. Good day" and before he had time to ask for a lift salvation had whizzed away through the rents of the quivering mirage-like dream.' The following day, Sunday, sees the buggy-occupant attending church in the nearby town, while 'Away out on the plain the kites and crows hold *their* "Sunday service" on something that was once a man, strong and kindly, something that might still have been a man, strong and kindly, but for the want of a lift across that eight miles of hell to the water.'[42]

In 'The Ghosts of the Desert', published in the *Bulletin* of 1894 – a year of major drought – Favenc targeted the mortgagors who had forced struggling settlers from their lands to die of starvation.

> ... the western downs, where the red sun sank,
> Are held in the name of a tottering bank;
> And the boundless pastures, the verdant sod,
> Belong to an oily man of God.
>
> The cities where vice and crime cry loud,
> Are rearing a stunted and pallid crowd ...

The ghosts of the rural dead indict them:

> 'For greed and plunder our blood was spent –
> For the curse of a rotten parliament.'[43]

127

C. Holdsworth Allen's poem 'How Long?' of 1903 sets up a similar dichotomy between the urban wealthy and the rural poor:

> How plump and sleek you drive each week
>   To offer your Pharisee prayer,
> And thank your God that you have not trod
>   In the sinners' thoroughfare.
> Here is your walk, where the drought-fiends stalk
>   O'er the souls of your brother men,
> Where red suns rise in the waterless skies
>   And sink and rise again. . . .
> Come out, come out, to the angry drought,
>   Ye eaters of easy bread!
> Where the blackened wheat gives nought to eat,
>   And dry is the river-bed.
> And they cry, 'O Earth! bring forth thy life!'
>   And the Earth brings forth her dead.[44]

In line with the *Bulletin*'s political program and ostentatious Bush ethos, these poems and the many like them contrast the affluent people of the city with desperate farmers trying to eke an existence from the edge of a spreading desert. The strong condemnation of Social Darwinism in these poems led to an interesting modification of the moral characterisation of the desert compared with its depiction in poems focussing on the explorers. Although the desert is still harsh and terrible, and as 'King Drought' extends his empire more innocent people die there, the moral indictment for their death has shifted from the land itself to class warfare and social inequality.

Ripping Yarns at the Outpost of Empire

> The Australian ... will still live with the consciousness that, if only he
> goes far enough back over the hills and across the plains, he comes in
> the end to the mysterious half-desert country where men have to live
> the lives of men. And the life of this mysterious country will affect the
> Australian imagination much as the life of the sea has affected that of
> the English.
>
> C.E.W. BEAN[1]

> The adventure tales that formed the light reading of Englishmen for
> two hundred years and more after Robinson Crusoe were, in fact, the
> energising myth of English imperialism. They were, collectively, the
> story England told itself as it went to sleep at night; and, in the form of
> its dreams, they charged England's will with the energy to go out into
> the world and explore, conquer, and rule.
>
> MARTIN GREEN[2]

By the 1880s and 90s the desert was the almost obligatory setting for Australian
adventure stories, ripping yarns in which youthful protagonists, emblems of
the new nation's manhood, braved and subdued the land, wresting from it
long-held treasures of gold, encountering ancient civilisations or stumbling
upon the secret of lost Leichhardt.

If we accept the close imaginative relation between adventure narratives
and British imperialism suggested by Martin Green in the above quotation,
then the central desert offered Australians a unique means of participating in
the glory of Empire while celebrating their own identity. It is not accidental
that the great decades of heroic exploration of the desert, the 1850s and 60s,
were the same decades that extolled the exploits of Livingstone and Stanley,
Burton and Speke in Africa. Hence the importance, as we have seen, of planting the British flag in the centre of the continent, and the symbolic significance of William Strutt's painting *The Burial of Burke* (1911) in which Burke's
remains are completely shrouded in the Union Jack, a feature later revived for
more cynical scrutiny in Sidney Nolan's 1985 painting of the same name.

However, by the 1880s, British confidence in the political and moral superiority of the Empire had begun to wane. Hard on the heels of Darwinian theory came the shocking notion, fictionalised in Edward Bulwer-Lytton's novel *The Coming Race* (1871), that the British might be superseded by a more vigorous race that would displace them from the top of the evolutionary tree. There was increasing nervousness that English manhood had been rendered effete and ineffectual at home and must renew its strength at the margins by engaging in physically testing exploits. Yet as public faith in the Empire dwindled in actuality, it was proclaimed all the more vigorously in fiction. The rise of the adventure story promoting the bravery and racial superiority of British males at the boundaries of the Empire, far from the restrictions of the domestic sphere and petticoat government, was a deliberate attempt to ensure that the next generation would reverse the sorry downward trend of effeminacy and physical devolution.[3] Such stories, set far from England, could legitimate and overtly glorify the violence that nineteenth-century society had officially banished to the wings but which Darwin had wrenched back to centre stage, seemingly discarding altruists and peacemakers for physical aggressors. In his study of the new imperial romance in Australia, Robert Dixon has argued that 'Australia, along with India, Africa and the Islands was actively constructed as a preferred site of adventure, with all the ethical and political ambiguity that the term adventurer came, almost immediately, to imply'.[4]

130

One important location for such adventure stories was the tropical North, with the danger of invasion by Asian races and the need for honest courage to outwit oriental cunning; the other was the desert, which provided a valuable stage for the playing out of the imperial narrative with its male-dominated action, incipient violence and the identity–anxiety of an emerging nation. Patrick Brantlinger has shown that most British adventure stories of the time articulated the anxieties that Britons felt about their imperial status in the last decades of the nineteenth century. Australian adventure stories of the same period explored the corresponding angst of a generation of Australians contemplating independence from the 'mother country' but unsure how autonomy might be maintained in the face of what they saw as the swarming coloured races supposedly threatening the continent from the north and of the less discussed but nonetheless lurking fear of the Aborigines who had failed to succumb to the early genocide so confidently predicted for them.

Emerging in such a climate of brave hopes and scarcely acknowledged fears, the ripping yarns set in the Australian desert have certain characteristic differences from their counterparts in Africa, India or the Far East. During the 1890s, when the genre was most prolific, three foci, specific to the Australian context, were paramount – almost, it seemed, obligatory: the search for the remains of Leichhardt's expedition, the discovery of gold, and the encounter with a lost civilisation. Some of the most sensational novels managed to include all three.

The Search for Leichhardt

The mystery surrounding the complete disappearance of Ludwig Leichhardt provided endless scope for novelists to produce either his grave or, even more improbably, the explorer himself, almost anywhere in inland Australia. In some adventure tales the encounter with Leichhardt (or his remains) is merely another event in a picaresque tale crammed with incidents; in others it is the main purpose of the hero's quest. But in either case the encounter with Leichhardt is the holy grail, reserved for a noble youth who is subsequently rewarded further by finding some earthly treasure. In W. Carlton Dawe's *The Golden Lake* (1894) the manly youth Richard Hardwicke and his cousin Archie seek for a reputed Golden Lake in Central Australia. On the way they find a tree carved with the initial 'L' and the date 1849, an irrefutable sign of Leichhardt's route. Soon the gallant party is attacked by natives and in the process of burying one of their number Hardwicke's shovel strikes a skull which is immediately agreed to be Leichhardt's.[5] The mystery is solved and they can proceed to further adventures and riches.

Another brief encounter with the Leichhardt mystery occurs in *The Adventures of Louis de Rougemont as Told by Himself* serialised in *Wide World Magazine* during 1898. This picaresque saga, professedly autobiographical, was soon exposed as the fictional composition of a Swiss impostor, Henry Louis Grin, erstwhile cook on a pearling lugger around the north coast of Australia. As well as numerous shipwrecks and makeshift survival techniques closely resembling Crusoe's, de Rougemont's adventures take him, in company with an Aboriginal woman, Yamba, back and forth into the desert where they solve not one mystery of Australian exploration but two. Having encountered a half-caste girl 'who I now believe to have been the daughter of Ludwig Leichhardt', they then come across a deranged white man who, miraculously regaining his sanity at the moment of death, convinces them he is Alf Gibson, lost during Ernest Giles's exploration of the Gibson Desert![6]

In James F. Hogan's novel *The Lost Explorer* (1890), however, the search for Ludwig Leichhardt, transparently fictionalised as Leonard Louvain, provides the main element of a bizarre plot that is worth summarising here as fairly typical of the ripping yarns of this period. Louvain's son, Arthur, who has taken up land north of Cooper's Creek, begins his narrative with the modest assertion: 'I, Arthur Louvain, ... was the most advanced pioneer "squatter" in Central Australia. I had an inherited love of adventure, which accounts for my presence at the farthest outpost of colonial civilisation.'[7] Having successfully travelled from Sydney to Port Essington, Louvain senior had set out across the continent, blazing trees with the obligatory 'L' before disappearing somewhere in the Great Stony Desert, 'an impregnable barrier of solid rock which seemed to encircle the desert like the protecting wall of a fortified city of olden time'! Accompanied by a member of Louvain's earlier expedition and Uralla, a devoted Aborigine of Herculean strength, Arthur sets out in search of a reputed waterfall in the desert. They soon meet an Aborigine, Wonga, who tells

131

them Louvain is still alive and offers to take them to him. En route they discover the body of a man who had found Louvain's papers[8] and from these they learn that, although his men had mutinied, the explorer had persevered alone. Louvain is discovered living as an honoured but heavily guarded prisoner in the marble palace of Queen Mocata, leader of a lost civilisation inhabiting a 'mysterious oasis in the heart of the Great Stony Desert'. Father and son are reunited after twenty years but escaping from the Queen and her High Priest Mooroop presents some difficulty, especially as they are about to sacrifice local maidens to the god of the nearby active volcano, Aronga. Luckily a secret passage is discovered, allowing the explorers to escape just before a volcanic explosion destroys the lost tribe. They make a triumphal progress back to Sydney, Louvain honoured and feted everywhere along the way. By way of realism, Hogan has attempted to include reference to the rock art described by George Grey, but his descriptions of a desert awash with lava from active volcanoes, geysers, boiled fish falling from the sky, crests and hollows of billowy lava must have stretched the credulity even of European readers.

Alleged news of Leichhardt's expedition and the rock paintings described by Grey also feature in Ernest Favenc's sensational novel, *The Secret of the Australian Desert*. By way of citing his credentials and claiming historical veracity Favenc begins his preface with a survey of the explorers of the first half of the century: 'Although the interior of the continent of Australia is singularly deficient in the more picturesque elements of romance, it was, for nearly two-thirds of a century, a most attractive lure to men of adventurous character.'[9] After instancing Oxley, Sturt, Mitchell, Kennedy and Stuart, he moves on to the star of exploration, Ludwig Leichhardt. This allegation of continuity links the novel's heroes with the explorers, tacitly appropriating their reputation. Favenc's latter-day adventurers are Morton and Brown, two squatters from neighbouring runs in the far north of South Australia, and Charlie, Morton's young nephew from England, the stereotypical 'new chum' whose role is to be patronised and exhibit the inadequacy of English traditions compared with Australian bush craft. The other member of the party, Billy Buttons, a black station hand, provides an additional source of humour and devotion but general lack of intelligence and initiative.

Favenc avoids formula descriptions of the central desert, presenting it in unusually varied terms – the prickly grass plains with deep red sand, and a great sheet of bluish–grey limestone rock 'over which a heated haze was undulating'. He also takes pains to argue for the credibility of his assertions about the area to which Leichhardt's party penetrated, providing a map of their likely route. And his adventurers do indeed solve the mystery by recourse to contemporary Darwinian paranoia about survival of the physically fittest and racial degeneration. Leichhardt himself is dead but Morton and Brown find that two survivors of the expedition, Stuart and Murphy, have been living with two warring tribes, one group of indigenous Australians, the other the war-like Warlattas, descendants of a 'superior' invading race, probably from Asia. Another member of the expedition, Hentig, has interbred with the local

Aborigines, producing degenerate offspring such as Lee-Lee, a half-caste cripple. Indeed they find out more about the strange tribe than they had bargained for, not merely in terms of its hostility but in terms of possible regression to cannibalism by Murphy and perhaps also Stuart. Morton and Brown are quick to demolish such a suggestion as inconceivable for a 'white man' but, having been raised, the prospect remains.

> 'There is one question that always worries me,' said Brown, . . . 'Do you think that Murphy was compelled to join in their cannibal feasts?'
> 'I have thought of it too,' replied Morton, 'and have come to the conclusion that he was not. At least, while he retained his reason. . . .'
> 'I am glad you think that, as I am of the same belief. I think any white man, no matter how slow his intellect, would prefer death.'
> '. . . I think, and am glad to think, that he had no part in their evil doings or rites until he was irresponsible for his actions.'

Thus the desert is indeed involved in the nation's greatest enigma – not Leichhardt, but the mystery of origins – cannibals, blacks, hybrid races and racial degeneracy. We shall return to this aspect later in the chapter.

Gold

Another popular focus of the desert adventure story was the finding of a gold reef or a gold mountain, alleged to exist in the desert. Although gold had been discovered in the eastern states from 1850, there was a new rush when convincing strikes were made in Western Australia in the 1890s. Romances of the period certainly reflect this contemporary fascination with gold, not only for its intrinsic mystique but because it epitomised the recurrent dream in which a pauper could become immensely rich overnight. But the details and plots of these stories also betray the influence of Rider Haggard's bestselling novel, *King Solomon's Mines* (1885). Interestingly, Haggard had expressed his regret that:

> soon the ancient mystery of Africa will have vanished. . . . When this has come about where will the romance writers of future generations find a safe and secret place? The North and South Poles have been worked out, and though there is still uncropped land in the recesses of Central Asia, doubtless the harvest will soon be gathered there also. Then the poor story teller, should his imagination prove strong enough, must betake himself to the planets.[10]

Although Haggard himself seems not to have conceived of the Australian interior as a likely venue for high adventure, four Australian adventure stories from this decade – John Boyle O'Reilly's *Moondyne: A Story of Western Australia* (1879), Alexander Macdonald's *The Lost Explorers* (1906), Favenc's *The Secret of the Australian Desert* (1896) and George Scott's *The Last Lemurian* (1898) – exploited the Haggard formula, including the discovery of gold as due reward for the intrepid adventurers.

De Rougemont's *Adventures* had included the discovery of a 'Mountain of Gold' in the centre of Australia and O'Reilly's *Moondyne*[11] also employed the well-worn motifs of gold in the desert and Aborigines, but with the added Australian colour of a convict hero. O'Reilly himself was transported to Australia for political crimes in Ireland but managed to escape to Boston where he became a newspaper editor. The novel interweaves the author's own experiences as an escaping convict with those of 'Moondyne Joe', the alias of Western Australian bushranger Joseph Bolitho Jones, also a notorious escapee. The fictional Moondyne Joe escapes from the cruel Isaac Bowman, to whom he has been assigned, and is befriended by Aborigines who show him a fabled goldmine. Recaptured by Bowman, Moondyne barters his freedom for knowledge of the mine but Bowman takes the gold without freeing him. Immorality, however, is duly punished. On his way back to civilisation, Bowman dies in the desert, among the first of many fictional victims of gold fever and the desert, leaving Moondyne safe in an idyllic community. Here, as in many Australian stories of the Bush, the land is involved as judge, sentencer and executioner of evildoers beyond the reach of the law. The unusual feature of this romance is the attitude to the Aborigines, who are presented as kind and generous, in opposition to the evil Bowman. Significantly, they have no interest in the gold except to give it to Moondyne. It is interesting that this novel preceded by some years the realisation of the state's potential in goldmining. One of the earliest Australian films, *Moondyne* (1913), was based on this story, emphasising even more than the novel the theme of punishment for avarice. This Wordsworthian alignment of the desert with some overriding moral purpose was a comforting doctrine; it suggested not only that the innocent had nothing to fear from even the harshest landscape but that Nature could be relied upon to restore the moral order.

134

Intrinsically precious, gold was even more valuable in providing a socially legitimate reason for the adventurers to abandon civilisation and vanish into the desert. In most cases, as in *The Secret of the Australian Desert*, the pursuit of gold was subsidiary to the more morally exalted search for lost explorers, or a lost race; but it also served to reward the heroes' valour and, more importantly, to demonstrate their conquest of otherwise useless land. Ripping a gold reef from the desert, a rape of the land's resources, was revenge for the ignominious defeat of the desert explorers.

In their time, these adventure stories appeared to be not vastly improbable; gold was being discovered in many areas and fortunes were made overnight. Yet the search for the gold per se was not regarded as providing readers with sufficient interest and it was closely linked with at least one of the other motifs, usually the engagement with a lost civilisation. As we shall see in the next chapter, when the story of Lasseter's search for a gold reef was told, it too, was inextricably associated with the fascination of intercultural encounter.

Lost civilisations

European colonists arriving in Australia in the nineteenth century faced a theoretical dilemma. For the sake of a peaceful and morally legitimate settlement of the continent they needed it to be *terra nullius*. But having declared Australia to be technically unsettled, and in the process having denied validity to Aboriginal culture, they soon realised that they needed a history, one significantly different from, but able to be respected by, the mother country. The unexplored interior of the continent offered writers scope to play with the notion that another, older civilisation might have existed, might still exist, in the centre of Australia.

The first of numerous fantasies to pander to the fascination with myths of origin was Lady Mary Fox's *Account of an Expedition to the Interior of New Holland* (1837). Crossing the Blue Mountains, Lady Mary's explorers discover on the Bathurst Plains the utopian cities of a lost civilisation founded by English and German refugees fleeing from religious persecution in their homelands. Written by an English woman who had never been near Australia,[12] the fantasy could be interpreted as a transparent British–European claim to primacy, or as a need to locate a utopian society, based on tolerance, in some hidden place to avoid contamination. The lost civilisation's need for seclusion is invoked explicitly in another fantasy, the anonymous 'Oo-a-deen' (1847). In this story the narrator encounters a handsome but seemingly deranged figure, Grantley, who leaves him a manuscript containing the central narrative. It appears that this Byronic hero, Grantley, has come to Australia from the Old World, having exhausted its pleasures and vices. During his travels in Central Australia he has stumbled upon Ooadeen, the country of the Mahanacumans. 'Through a cleft that had been riven by the force of volcanic convulsions, I looked and beheld a country fair as the "land of promise" seen by the Hebrew Lawgiver from the top of Mount Pisgah'.[13] Ooadeen is an Edenic land with forests of cedars and groves of fruit trees, girt by snowy mountains, great rivers and an inland sea. Its inhabitants are unbelievably beautiful and Grantley predictably falls in love with Yarranee, the daughter of the high priest. Fearing that their culture will be destroyed by a stranger, the Mahanacumans banish Grantley on a raft through a subterranean river. His derangement is the result of his ceaseless efforts to find his way back. At one level the romance reads like a parody of the wish list of the exploring expeditions at the time when it was written – an inland sea, great rivers, fertile land with abundant food – and it ends with a disavowal of seriousness by claiming that Grantley's 'whole account of Ooadeen is probably to be traced to some adventures in that quarter [Mexico], although in his craziness he had confounded its locality with that of Australia.' However, it can also be read as a desire to protect a pristine, natural Eden from the invasion and destruction of Old World influence.

During the 1850s the ancient legend of Atlantis, a land lost beneath the sea, was dusted off and given scientific credibility by the precursors of continental drift theorists. Alexander von Humboldt, among others, had noted the congruence of the coastlines of Africa and South America and the possible fit of the other continents and islands. These vague notions soon led to a flurry of theories proposing specific intercontinental connections that were seized upon by biologists as a means of explaining the distribution of animal species. Of these bizarre proposals, the one that was to have most literary impact in Australia was that of C.L. Sclater, a biologist, who invoked a lost continent stretching between Madagascar and Malaysia to explain the geographical distribution of lemurs. The location of this hypothetical land mass, which he called Lemuria, was hotly debated between 1870 and 1930, and in many versions had little connection with Australia, but the eminent German biologist Ernst Haeckel believed that the Australian Aborigines were direct descendants of the Lemurians.[14] Suddenly the colonial desire for instant history was legitimised and writers claimed the licence to emulate Rider Haggard's creation of Kukuanaland in *King Solomon's Mines* by inventing an ancient civilisation surviving in the centre of the continent. The nature of this hypothetical race was conveniently vague, allowing for a range of possibilities – from the most primitive cannibals to a technologically sophisticated culture, with influences as diverse as Ancient Egypt, Rome and Polynesia.

Although the impetus to create such fantasies was doubtless spurred by the huge market success of Rider Haggard's novels, and although that, in turn, was a function of the age's disenchantment with the boring grey world of realism and naturalism, the ripping yarns of a lost civilisation in Australia were also

part of the struggle for national identity. The lost race was always constructed as the other, but that other was flexible and was in turn used to help define possible aspects of colonial selfhood and to explore Australian fears of cultural annihilation by either the parent culture or the alleged Yellow Peril to the north. 'Oo-a-deen' was followed by a spate of Lemurian adventure tales in the 1880s and 90s, including O'Reilly's *Moondyne: A Story of Western Australia*, Hogan's *The Lost Explorer*, Dawe's *The Golden Lake*, Favenc's *The Secret of the Australian Desert*, Macdonald's *The Lost Explorers* and Scott's *The Last Lemurian*. Four of these have been discussed already as involving lost explorers or gold. This overlap of motif was not fortuitous but an emulation of Rider Haggard's bestselling African adventure novels. However, many of the Australian romances also forge a link with local prehistory. Several use George Grey's descriptions of the rock art he had seen in north-western Australia in 1839 and in particular Grey's observation that the sophistication of the figures depicted seemed to increase with the distance travelled inland.[15] Hogan uses this as 'evidence' for his artistically talented Maluans:

> Sir George Grey was wiser than he knew . . . Had he penetrated farther and
> farther still into the interior; had he succeeded in crossing the Great Stony
> Desert, as we had done; had he struck the oasis of Malua, been allowed to enter
> the Queen's Palace, and feast his eyes on the splendid specimens of native art
> that we were now beholding, any doubt he might have previously entertained
> would have become a conviction like mine.[16]

The intriguing suggestions of Asian influence that Grey had mentioned in relation to the paintings are translated into the mixed race origins of Hogan's Maluans, the offspring of intermarriage between a white race and an inferior black race. Like Darwin's Galapagos finches they have been cut off from the rest of the world for centuries, in their case by a volcanic eruption that has thrown up an impassable barrier around their oasis. Their culture, while advanced in many ways, including its art, is morally decadent – the combined result, presumably, of miscegenation and subsequent inbreeding. There was a none-too-subtle warning here for Australia, an outpost of white civilisation in the vast Pacific region, surrounded by Asian and Polynesian races as well as Aborigines.

Favenc's *The Secret of the Australian Desert* drew even more explicitly on Grey's descriptions to affirm the plausibility of his lost civilisation. The cave paintings of the Warlattas are relocated in Central Australia and described in terms almost identical with Grey's account, which is quoted in the preface, though with an added explicit reference to their possible Egyptian origin. 'The whole figure was of grave aspect, and much reminded me of the drawings I have seen of Egyptian gods.'[17] Within the narrative the paintings are described by Stuart, allegedly one of the survivors of Leichhardt's party, in his journal, with the additional information that they predate and are unrelated to the Aborigines' culture. A century later, Favenc's cave paintings seem surprisingly similar to the Bradshaws of the Kimberley region described in Chapter 1, rock art which also predates Aboriginal culture and suggests an Asian origin. Like the Morlocks in H.G. Wells's more famous study of degenerate races, the atavistic Warlattas prey upon their Eloi-like neighbours, the indigenous Aborigines, but they are finally demolished by the superior power of the white adventurers. The young Australians thus dissociate themselves from their primitive origins by their technological skills, justifying their use of force as a moral necessity to save the peaceful natives, and delicately averting their gaze from the implications of the half-caste offspring of liaisons between Leichhardt's party and the harmless Aborigines. Such miscegenation might well, in the 1890s, have been seen as a slur on the names of the sanctified explorers, but Favenc has taken care to change the names of all but the leader, who is beyond such an imputation. Stuart fears that he 'will become a savage like those around me, and forget what I was.' He therefore clings to his identity by keeping a journal. 'I must write or I shall forget my language, and that I must keep while life lasts.' There are other clear references to fears of racial degeneration through isolation. Leichhardt's party, separated from its European roots, becomes dependent on the indigenous people for food and comfort, producing the crippled, half-caste Lee-Lee, offspring of Hentig; and ultimately, when Stuart and Murphy are captured by the Warlattas, Murphy at least accepts the human flesh provided by his captors. In these novels we see an externalisation of what Robert Dixon has called the 'colonial identity crisis', symbolised in the 'hybrid lost race, whose ambivalent racial and cultural identity was alarmingly close to the new concept of an Australian nation, caught between a lost origin and an undefined future.'[18]

137

The most elaborate and far-fetched of the lost civilisation romances was George Firth Scott's *The Last Lemurian: A Westralian Romance* (1898). Scott's novel combines the elements of *King Solomon's Mines* present in the earlier romances but adds a brew of spiritualist notions about reincarnation. The latter may have been derived from Haggard's later novel, *She* (1887), but spiritualism was already a worldwide fashion at this time, another aspect of the reaction against realism and naturalism. As in Favenc's *The Secret of the Australian Desert*, Scott presents us with a volcanic mountain fortress, this time ruled over by a giant yellow woman, Tor Ymmothe, Queen of the ancient continent of Lemuria. Protected by a terrifying giant Bunyip, she reigns over a pygmy tribe in the gold-rich area of Western Australia. Unlike Favenc's novel with its total absence of women, the Queen is here the most powerful personality, threatening the novel's upright English heroes, Dick Halwood and the 'Bushman', known as Hatter but actually an English aristocrat, with her physical and psychic powers. Descended from the once proud and ancient race of Lemurians, which deteriorated with the advent of an invading race, the Queen now rules over a grotesque, physically degenerate race, with implications of mental and moral depravity as well:

> creatures who seemed to have been made up of an odd collection of limbs, trunks, and heads, and were in every degree of crippled malformity; . . . another, with disproportionate limbs, has only a monkey skull upon its shoulders. . . . They were a nightmare, a vile nauseating spectacle, such as might come in the dark, lonely hours to mock and torment the stricken fancy of a diseased brain.[19]

138

Tor Ymmothe's palace is a marvel of ingenious engineering, with massive pivoting rock doors operated by water power from subterranean watercourses in the middle of the desert. The Queen herself represents the combined threat of Asia (she is yellow), woman (the Hatter is captivated by her psychic powers) and racial degeneration (through her subhuman pygmies).

Alexander Macdonald's novel, *The Lost Explorers: A Story of the Trackless Desert* (1906), has many of the same components. A party of two young Englishmen, Jack Armstrong and Robert Wentworth (who is also looking for a lost uncle), join up with James Mackay, survivor of an earlier venture, the Bentley Exploring Expedition, and set out for Golden Flat 'away out on the desert's fringe beyond Kalgoorlie, and beyond the reach of any civilising railway'[20] in search of 'a vast treasure of gold and gems'. Once again, activities revolve around a huge mountain, 'like a wall' in the desert. Again there are two very different tribes of Aborigines, one degraded, 'more ape than man', and another, the lost race within the mountain, 'gorgeously arrayed, splendidly proportioned', with 'wonderful intelligence'. Whereas the first Aborigines had confirmed the Englishmen's clear sense of superiority, the second group threaten their stereotyping complacency. In the desert, away from the reinforcement of racial superiority, the English sense of identity is threatened.

'There was gradually dawning in him [Mackay] a vastly increased respect for the natives who lived beyond the mountain ... [his] estimate of their powers was far higher than he cared to admit'. Ironically superiority is reasserted when the heroes kill some of the warriors, disguise themselves in their clothes and blacken their faces, thereby becoming morally and visually indistinguishable from the savages they are so keen to exterminate. The adventure comes to the standard *King Solomon's Mines* conclusion when they discover that one of the 'Aborigines' is Richard Bentley, the lost explorer and uncle of Robert Wentworth. Predictably they escape with gold and gems, blocking forever the passage to the interior of the mountain. The intelligent natives, their alter egos, are thus re-imprisoned in the mountain at the centre of the continent, their threat to Anglo-Saxon identity defused and contained.

In each of these novels the superior white race is troubled by black parodies of itself, savages who either embody the Darwinian nightmare by obscuring the clear boundary lines between man and ape, or threaten white racial supremacy by displaying physical strength and beauty, intelligence and civilisation to rival their British counterparts. Both these deep fears for the integrity of species and race were engendered by Darwinism but intensified in areas of the globe where, in Conrad's phrase, Europeans were separated from 'the policeman and the two good addresses'. Africa was one such place; the Australian desert was another.

While the Aborigines were fewer and less war-like than African tribes and, so it appeared to the early settlers, scarcely human, by the 1880s the issue of miscegenation had become significant and with it the perceived threat of degradation of the white race. Non-susceptible to settlement, the desert remained beyond the last outpost of civilisation, and those who entered it therefore left behind the props and security of society. Forced to rely solely on their own self-estimate, taunted with the irrelevance of social forms but having nothing with which to replace them, and fearful therefore of becoming savages themselves, Europeans either found or lost themselves in the desert. Many of the romances focus on a mountain in the desert, within which lurks some shameful secret. Whether cannibal Warlattas, Lemurians or Macdonald's Aborigines within the mountain, these confronting personae erupt and erode the sense of integrity and self-definition of both individual and society. In many of these stories gender is not irrelevant. Hogan's Queen Mocata of the Maluans and Scott's Lemurian Queen, Tor Ymmothe (Tory Mother?), are both dominant and sinister figures, further empowered by the religious authority of a high priest or, in Tor Ymmothe's case, the mythical Bunyip. Arguably this suggests a subconscious reference to the British Queen, enthroned at the centre of Empire as these fictional queens preside at the centre of the continent, limiting the self-determination of the Australian colonies. More generally, it acknowledges the heroes' difficulty in escaping from the domestic sphere. Even when they journey to the most remote regions, there, in the middle of the Great Stony Desert, they are confronted by the power of an evil woman. But, like Haggard's hero, they succeed in outwitting her, escaping from her

139

power and even destroying her empire. The desert is reclaimed as the safe haven, perhaps the only one, for male autonomy.

Like *The Secret of the Australian Desert*, *The Lost Explorers* and *The Lost Explorer*, *The Last Lemurian* enacts, as Dixon argues, Australian fears about national identity when Englishmen encounter other races, and, more point-edly, the dilemma confronting Australians on the verge of nationhood: how to disengage themselves from Britain without losing the civilisation that they saw as the only bastion between them and the savage races surrounding them. The setting of all these narratives in the desert, centre of the continent and hence symbolically the nation's innermost self, locates these fears of invasion at the deepest levels of identity. Yet, running in parallel with this pervasive fear of invasion by other races when the country is severed from England is a sense of moral failing. The desert is also the last stronghold of the Aborigines, and the variations that the writers adduce on the theme of blackness suggest also an enduring sense of guilt about the original inhabitants and the decimation of their culture since the arrival of Europeans. The preoccupation with waves of immigrant races displacing others who then degenerate and die out is a clear expression of Darwinian fears such as those expressed by Bulwer-Lytton in *The Coming Race* (1871), which he described as a fictionalised account of 'the Darwinian proposition that the coming race is destined to supplant our races.'[21] Although these ripping yarns are crude and probably unconscious expressions of atavistic and racial fears, they are precursors of the psychologi-cal novels of Patrick White and Randolph Stow in the twentieth century, where the journey to the desert is a journey into the interior in every sense.

In the early years of the twentieth century, however, there was little room for either individual or national self-doubt. The period of nation-building that accompanied Federation envisaged future conquests of the land through technological progress. The hopes of Sir Sidney Kidman and others of irrigat-ing the interior with artesian water resurrected the belief in an inland sea, but as a reality to be created by human effort rather than merely found. In such a climate there was little time for the cult of failure. In the '"Desert" Myth' chapter of *Australia Unlimited* (1918) Edwin Brady effectively denigrated Sturt, and by extension all the inland explorers, as ineffectual, even redundant in the march of progress. The desert adventurers were equally inimical to the new literary fashion of modernism, essentially urban in its preoccupations and motifs, and cynical of heroism in any form. From the beginning of the twenti-eth century to the end of World War II the desert seemed an embarrassment to a would-be sophisticated nation.

Part II

APPREHENDING THE DESERT

From Dead Heart to Red Centre

Chapter 8

TALES OF TRAVEL AND REEFS OF GOLD

I have used the word desert often enough in these pages, but mainly in
the dictionary sense of desertion. There is water everywhere, could it
but be conserved. The desert soils are rich. Already miracles of
irrigation are redeeming the waste.

ERNESTINE HILL[1]

It might well be known as the Red Centre. Sand, soil, and most of the
rocks are a fiery cinnabar ...

H.H. FINLAYSON[2]

As he looked at the shining particles, it seemed to him then in a sudden
flash, that he understood the land which was his home more completely
than ever before. How was it possible that from so small a centre should
spring so dazzling an illumination?

E.L. GRANT WATSON[3]

Historian James Walter has pointed out that the idea of nationalism became
common in Europe at the same time as the number of native-born white
Australians equalled the number of immigrants. Thus, for the first time native-
born Australians were in a position to redefine the society so as to privilege
their own values and concerns. By 1901, the year of Federation, discussions of
national identity revolved around differentiation from Britain, while avoiding
criteria that might seem to align the new nation with its Asian neighbours.[4]

In order to demonstrate that the rites of passage from colony to nation
had been successfully negotiated there was much concern in the early decades
of the twentieth century with delineating what Benedict Anderson has called
the 'imagined community', namely that which constitutes a nation in the cultural sense.[5] World War I offered one avenue of self-definition. Another was the
establishment of cultural and economic maturity. This latter goal was pursued
through a self-conscious promotion of Australia's pastoral wealth, the flaunting
of golden acres and golden fleeces as displayed iconographically in the

canvases of Tom Roberts. Given that Australia was already one of the most urbanised countries, and that both golden acres and golden fleeces necessitated a wholesale clearing of the native bush, the notion of a national identity grounded in 'the Bush' can now be seen as an extraordinarily artificial construction, but its unrepresentativeness was more than compensated for by its distinctiveness. The editorial policy of the influential weekly magazine the *Bulletin* encouraged a pioneering Bush focus that was claimed to be both realist and nationalist in character.[6] Implicit in this Bush ethos was an idealised self-image of egalitarianism, mateship, resourcefulness and optimism as the qualities that allegedly distinguished Australians from their European counterparts, stereotyped as effete, ineffectual and imprisoned in an imperial hierarchy.[7] This 'othering' of Britain, hitherto the Centre and cultural standard, was less a feature of the 1890s, to which it was retrospectively attributed, than of the 1920s, following the disenchantment with Britain after World War I, but it later seemed wholly appropriate that it should have arisen in the decade leading up to Federation.

Already by the 1890s the desert had succeeded the Bush as the actual frontier, but as a nationalist rallying point it suffered from a definite image problem. Compared with the popular, romanticised depictions of the Bush in the misty canvases of Tom Roberts and Frederick McCubbin, it was a distinct embarrassment. Neither profitable nor picturesque, it offered little potential for either economic or cultural pretensions. The 'hideous blank' remained, psychologically if not geographically, subverting the propaganda aimed to encourage European immigration and capital, and posing an ongoing challenge to the nation's new heroes, the cattle barons and mining magnates.

An obvious way to resolve this difficulty was to deny its existence or at least its permanence. Edwin J. Brady's *Australia Unlimited* (1918), a survey of Australia's resources specifically designed to elicit post-war investment, epitomised this approach. Determined to overthrow the gloomy tradition associated with the centre of the continent, Brady devoted a special section, 'The "Desert" Myth', to showing that, 'Instead of a "Dead Heart of Australia" there exists in reality a Red Heart, destined one day to pulsate with life.'[8] Reviewing the progressive settlement of areas declared 'desert' by the mid-nineteenth-century explorers, he concluded that the so-called desert was shrinking into non-existence, and quoted the surveyor and explorer Lawrence Allen Wells who, when asked about the desert area he had traversed in 1896, replied, 'I believe the country that is apparently desert will be no desert for future generations.'[9]

Sidney Kidman (1857–1935), owner of a pastoral empire of more than a hundred properties and popularly known as the 'Cattle King', was one of Brady's heroes. He was the new-style explorer, inscribing his name on the landscape with a flourish, not merely as geographic appellation – the north-west of New South Wales is known as Kidman's Corner – but in a more literal sense as one who physically changed the land by sinking bores into the Great Artesian Basin and thus watering land formerly unsuitable for stock. 'The Man [Kidman] is a BIG Man: he would be a big man anywhere in modern industrial

Tim Storrier, *An Altitude,*
1977, acrylic on canvas,
200.5 × 200.5 cm.
Courtesy the artist and
Sherman Galleries,
Sydney.

ABOVE
John Coburn, *Nullarbor*,
1980, oil on canvas,
168 × 213 cm, private
collection. Courtesy the
artist and Eva Breuer Art
Dealer, Sydney.

BELOW
Robert Juniper, *The River
Dies in January*, Diptych
1977, synthetic polymer
paint on canvas,
151.5 × 303.0 cm,
collection Art Gallery of
New South Wales, Sydney.
Courtesy the artist;
photograph by Robert
Walker.

Arthur Boyd (Australia,
born 1920), *Paintings in the
Studio: Figure supporting Back
Legs' and 'Interior with Black
Rabbit'*, 1973–4, oil on canvas,
313.5 × 433.2 cm, The
Arthur Boyd Gift 1975,
collection National Gallery
of Australia, Canberra.
Reproduced with the
permission of
Bundanon Trust.

Arthur Boyd, *Orange Tree, Book and Bound Figure,* 1978, oil on canvas, 151 × 122 cm, private collection. Reproduced with the permission of Bundanon Trust.

civilisation. He is one of the biggest men in Australia today. . . . By fire and strength of will, by steel of patience and eternal effort, they [Kidman, and fellow landowners Tyson and MacCaughey] rise like Titans above the crowd. . . . From the Roper River to the Torrens, his name is written in letters of Wealth and Power.'[10] Kidman's irrigation programs were seen as the flowering of an Australian Enlightenment, since this reconstruction of a continent would occur, Brady believed, through the power of science and technology. Artesian water, soil enrichment programs and efficient transport would cause the desert to blossom like a rose, as the Victorian mallee had already been induced to do. This attitude is perpetuated in W.E. ('Bill') Harney's racy poem 'West of Alice', which celebrates the diesel-grader cutting a highway west through the desert, levelling dunes, tearing down the habitats of native animals and destroying ancient fossils:

> . . . The honey-ants are rooted out to roll upon the sand,
> But ever the ramping, stamping fiend goes roaring through the land;
> The tyres grind and the steel blade cuts the pads where camels trod
> And claws at the ground of a stony mound where tribesmen praised their
> God.
> . . .
>
> We hear the grader's engine roar with Sam behind the wheel,
> And I sing my song as we plunge along to the chatter of wheel and steel.[11]

145

Intent on creating a vast area of fertility and pastoral wealth, Kidman not only denied the existence of the desert, he promoted a new national type based on his own public image: a combination of the visionary and the practical man, one whose exploits not only subdued the land but changed its nature, reclaiming for prosperity the unproductive wilderness that the settlers had inherited. His assumption that this ideology of developmentalism was necessarily in the interests of the nation remained unquestioned for most of this century, reflected in government policy, propaganda and films.[12] Such ecological Darwinism both meshed with and reinforced other contemporary forms of domination: the Social Darwinism which, in contrast to the myth of egalitarianism, actually underpinned Australian society, the sexism that excluded women from significance in the public sphere, and the ethnic Darwinism which, with overt but hypocritical regret, predicted the imminent and inevitable extinction of the Aborigines. When the nation's foremost geographer Griffith Taylor called for restraint in the pastoral industry, warned that drought was the norm rather than the exception, and vigorously disputed contemporary predictions of an Australian population between 100 and 500 million, he was lampooned in the press and branded as an unpatriotic pessimist, out to subvert Australia's image overseas and discourage immigration.[13]

However, despite its socio–economic power, the plutocratic ideal has never been a popular one in literature. A more acceptable means of exorcising the accumulated horrors of exploration and the lurking existential fear of this vast unknown space was science. The mid-nineteenth-century expeditions had been geographical or frankly competitive in intention, but those of the 1890s were directed towards a systematic understanding of the desert milieu in terms of geology, biology and, most memorably, anthropology. The most influential of these was the Horn Expedition of 1894, financed by South Australian mining magnate W.H. Horn, whose stated objectives included the recording of the 'manners, customs and appearance of the aboriginals in their native state ... as in a few years they will be all either dead or semi-civilized'.[14] Among the three professors taking part was Baldwin Spencer, professor of biology at the University of Melbourne, who later edited the four-volume report of the expedition. In the process Spencer received the greatest fillip to his career in the detailed knowledge of local Arunta customs collected by Frank Gillen of the Alice Springs telegraph office. During their subsequent collaboration Spencer passed Gillen's data through the filter of his ingrained belief in evolution and Social Darwinism, assuming before he began that the Australian Aborigines were among the most primitive peoples on earth, and finding evidence for this view wherever he looked. His contemporaries were equally delighted to find their racial prejudices vindicated by science. A review in the Melbourne *Argus* of Spencer and Gillen's second book, *The Northern Tribes of Central Australia* (1904), concluded with the remarks:

> The popular impression that the Australian native is the lowest in the scale of civilization, or is the nearest to nature of any living race, will be deepened by this volume. One of the endeavours of the day is to trace man upwards from his savage ancestors, and, so far as any existing people are concerned, the Australian aborigines appear to represent bedrock.[15]

A century after European settlement, anthropology had finally penetrated the national consciousness and it set a new agenda for desert travellers. As historian Tom Griffiths writes: 'The images of the inland generated by the Horn Expedition and especially by the consequent work of Spencer and Gillen were more complex and social than that of the lone explorer or brave pioneer pitched against nature ... [even if] it revealed the richness of central Australian Aboriginal culture only to deny it in the service of Social Darwinism'.[16] Spencer and Gillen's widely read publications, bolstered by Spencer's scientific credentials, ensured that for nearly a century this view of Australian Aborigines as 'creatures, often crude and quaint, that have elsewhere passed away and given place to higher forms'[17] was set in academic concrete. While these later expeditions yielded scientific information they did not significantly bridge the conceptual gap between the desert and the actual experience of the vast majority of Australians. A more important factor in domesticating the desert by vicarious encounter was the published response of individual travellers with whom readers could identify.

Travellers' tales

Writers of desert travel literature in the first half of the twentieth century self-consciously positioned themselves in the tradition of the exploration journal, implicitly claiming both the authenticity of first-hand experience and a share in the heroism of the past. In their narratives the land they traverse remains tough, but their superiority over their predecessors is apparent as much in their ability to perceive its aesthetic qualities as in the ingenuity and bush craft that permit their survival. The format of such popular travel literature is remarkably consistent for some three decades, being modelled on the *Bulletin* style of documentary realism favoured by its editor A.G. Stephens, 'the easy, detached, realistic sketch'.[18] Writers adopted a racy, often self-deprecating humour, akin to Henry Lawson's in the preceding century, affecting to make light of the dangers and difficulties, but with the intention of magnifying their own *sang-froid*. The desert milieu is carefully delineated by reference to the exotic, especially the oriental. Camels, Afghans, the Marree mosque, date palms, oases and mirages feature prominently in this orientalising procedure, which claims kin with travellers' tales of the Sahara and the Middle East. If the Australian desert failed to provide the frisson generated by the dangers likely to beset the infidel entering Mecca in disguise, writers could nevertheless assume their readers' familiarity with the longstanding Australian myth of the alien land, of Nature itself as the enemy, relentless and implacable. The possibility of being lost in the desert and dying of thirst, deeply ingrained in the national consciousness, could be invoked in relation to even the best-equipped expedition. To generate a sense of fear, writers have insisted on the uniqueness of the desert journey. Travellers wear distinctive clothes and there is particular emphasis on unusual, non-urban modes of transport, whether camels or dilapidated vehicles. (Modern tourists to the desert continue this tradition with the obligatory Akubra hat, the four-wheel-drive vehicle, two-way radio and a vigorously asserted enthusiasm for 'bush tucker'.) Tourists are often accompanied by bushmen whose impressive practicality and skills are usually shared by other colourful characters encountered en route.

The first popular accounts were more in the nature of a scientific treatise than travel literature. British geologist John Walter Gregory's *The Dead Heart of Australia: A Journey Around Lake Eyre in the Summer of 1901–1902* (1906), the account of his expedition to Lake Eyre in 1902, was enormously influential, partly because it offered a scientific opinion on the various possibilities of irrigating the centre for pastoralism and agriculture, but undoubtedly also because it was the first optimistic account of the inland by a British writer. An unusual feature was Gregory's juxtaposition of scientific objectivity and subjective experience, prefiguring the post-modern view that landscape is the sum of previous accounts and responses. Gregory conveyed the unique lure of the desert in terms of a mysticism that was universal or oriental rather than recognisably Christian, and included the notion of a Race Memory, a concept that H.G. Wells was beginning to popularise.

The desert . . . not only projects our imagination into the future – not only is it true, as an Oriental proverb says, that 'the desert is the garden of Allah' – but at the same time it recalls instincts and recollections from the past. The simplicity of the desert, the uniformity of its conditions, the merciless severity of its forces, awaken in us the primitive man, lying beneath the carefully built-up fabric of social obligations. . . . It is this combination of the feelings of the past and of the future, that gives the desert its peculiar fascination – as, for a moment, a man sums up in himself the long experience of his race.[19]

Less welcome to his contemporaries was Gregory's verdict on the Australian Aborigines who he had been led to believe were the most primitive and amoral of races: 'instead of finding them degraded, lazy, selfish, savage, they were courteous and intelligent, generous even to the point of impru-dence, and phenomenally honest; while in the field they proved to be born naturalists and superb bushmen.' Gregory concluded that the Aboriginal race was Caucasian rather than Negroid, belonging 'to the highest primary division of mankind'. This revisionist account not only flew in the face of popular Euro–Australian beliefs but contradicted Spencer and Gillen's conclusion that the indigenous peoples were doomed. Although, in the short term, contem-porary readers were more interested in his assessment of the proposal to flood Lake Eyre with a canal from Port Augusta, Gregory's book was eventually pivotal in the cultural reassessment of both the desert and its indigenes. Ironically, its most enduring legacy was its title, intended to refer only to the Lake Eyre area by analogy with the Dead Sea in Palestine, but providing a ready cliché for a pessimistic view of the whole centre of the continent that Gregory was far from sharing.

148

The 1930s, however, saw a spectacular change in attitude to the desert in literature and art. As we shall see in Chapter 9, Hans Heysen's paintings of the Flinders Ranges and Arthur Murch's landscapes painted around Alice Springs suddenly allowed people who had never travelled beyond the coastal fringe to see the Centre glowing with vivid colour, a feature that, incredibly, had received virtually no mention in the accounts of the British explorers with their fixation on green. Gregory's *The Dead Heart* was succeeded in 1935 by another memorable title, *The Red Centre*, by zoologist H.H. Finlayson. Although this book was illustrated only with black and white photographs that did scant justice to his material, it was Finlayson who first put into words the intense colours of the Centre and 'the flood of radiant energy that beats upon the land':

it might well be known as the Red Centre. Sand, soil, and most of the rocks are a fiery cinnabar . . . perhaps the most beautiful picture of the Central vegetation one may see, is of the dainty ghost gums, with chalk-white stems gleaming in the slanting light of a late afternoon, their brilliant green tops thrown into strong relief against the red cliffs.[20]

Like Gregory, Finlayson also noted similarities to the Orient, particularly in his striking description of Mount Olga: 'In the finished symmetry of its domes it is beautiful at all times; but now the sunset works upon it a miracle of colour, and it glows a luminous blue against an orange field, like some great mosque lit up from within.'

Broader in scope than *The Red Centre* was Ernestine Hill's *The Great Australian Loneliness* (1937), dedicated to 'the men and women of the Australian outback, and to all who take up the white man's burden in the lonely places'. Hill was a journalist and her account of five years' travelling in outback Australia across the Nullarbor, then from Adelaide to Darwin via the formidable Birdsville Track and Arnhem Land, confronted urban Australians with a new image of the Centre. Instead of the empty, monotonous and dangerous expanse they had been led to fear and regret, it burst into life and colour as she peopled the desert with 'characters'. The desert section of the book is provocatively titled 'The Living Heart' (a phrase that Queen Elizabeth II was to recycle during her visit to Alice Springs in 1963)[21] and her chapter 'Mysterious Nullarbor' opens with a radical overturning of expectation:

> Across the interior of the Continent, in the maps of our childhood, damnation was written in four words – 'The Great Australian Desert'. By train and truck and car and camel and packhorse, east and west as far as civilisation goes, and further, I was to travel 10,000 miles of it within the year, to prove those words untrue. The allegedly 'dead heart of Australia' is vitally alive.[22]

149

Hill travelled and wrote from within the tradition of intrepid English women such as Gertrude Bell and Freya Stark who shocked their contemporaries as much by their clothes as by their daring and their obsession with journeying to remote and dangerous areas of the Middle East. This image of the resourceful female traveller meshed well with the image of the Australian tom-boy heroine, epitomised by the character of Norah Linton in Mary Grant Bruce's Billabong books, an honorary male doing 'real' work in a masculine world.[23]

Hill reclaimed two stereotypical attributes of the central desert – its immensity and its vast age – as positive qualities: 'Two thousand miles across, wide as the moon and nearly as empty, an age-old country of hills fretted away in the slow alchemy of time, of burnt-out craters, brown stony deserts and rivers that run into the sand . . .' Potential desolation is immediately countered by the promise of wealth: '. . . a country of great mineral and pastoral wealth when all its secrets of water and rare minerals are known – such is the immensity of the centre of Australia.'[24]

To the extent that Hill reiterated the traditional iconography of the desert she did so only to discard it. In her account the fabled inland sea is revived in fossilised form, 'where the dazzled earth shines like a moonlit sea with gypsum and mica', and water is allegedly there in plenty where 'boiling bores of the artesian basin, from hell's kitchens 4000 feet below, send a white drift of vapour into the air'. Dust storms, so terrifying to nineteenth-century travellers, are reduced to storybook 'genii of the Arabian Nights . . . striding across the land'. Temperamentally a child of the Enlightenment, Hill places her faith in that technological marvel, the Transcontinental Railway, to banish any fears lurking in the desert. A 'blackfellow's devil come true', the train not only overcomes the isolation of west from east but, by delivering supplies, permits settlements to exist along its length.[25] Even the notion of 'desert' is severely qualified:

> It has just been discovered . . . that the Nullarbor is not a sand desert, but the roof of a mighty honeycomb of mysterious caves of crystalline limestone and subterranean rivers, icy cold, flowing 50 miles southward to the sea. . . . Bores are being put down with success, and as soon as they can provide sufficient drinking water for increased stock, the frightening Nullarbor will become a fine sheep country.

This was essentially the politically correct doctrine of the day, a paean of faith in the cattle barons' capability to produce Australia Felix.

> I have used the word desert often enough in these pages, but mainly in the dictionary sense of desertion. There is water everywhere, could it but be conserved. The desert soils are rich. Already miracles of irrigation are redeeming the waste.
> Even as I write, the contours of the map are coming clearer. The aeroplane, the radio, and the motor-car are changing the face of nature, and the king-tide of colonization is setting to the full.

A highlight of Hill's desert journey was travelling the Birdsville Track from Marree to Birdsville and back and meeting Ken Crombie, the taciturn mailman. She records her aesthetic response to the colours of Central Australia:

> Land of fierce lights and desolate distances, this hard-baked desert glows like a rose, hills change like rainbows the whole day long, evening shadows burn and fade across the bluebush, slate blue and winey-red and the wind-blown gold of sand. When Australian artists have finished with Sydney harbour and Princes Bridge, some Cortez with a palette in his swag will find a new world.[26]

Hill was apparently unaware that, nearly a decade before this, Jessie Traill had already packed *her* palette and painted the Central Australian landscape, exhibiting her watercolours in Alice Springs and Melbourne in 1928.

Among Hill's cast of real-life 'characters' none was more famous than Daisy Bates who, camped at Ooldea, a siding of the railway line, typified the indomitable, pioneering female figure of the Australian desert. If Bates had not invented herself, Hill would surely have done so. Although Bates's reputation is now a source of controversy, Hill presented her unambiguously as a

150

living saint, a 'quaint little figure' in Edwardian clothing shouldering the white woman's burden as she brought solace to dying Aborigines.

> Living unafraid in the great loneliness, chanting in those corroborees that it is death for a woman to see, she had become a legend, to her own kind, long lost, 'the woman who lives with the blacks.' To the natives, she is an age-old, sexless being who knows his secrets and guesses his thoughts – Dhoogoor of the dream-time . . . guardian spirit of this occult, shy people.[27]

The recorder of 115 native languages, Bates is presented by Hill as a figure of moral strength, unafraid of physical or spiritual dangers, understanding the nomad tribes but transcending their comprehension, giving but never in need of receiving. As such, she embodies both the intellectual and moral superiority of the imperial race. That the desert had been her home for thirty-five years by the time Hill visited her demonstrated that it was indeed habitable by white women; that she gives succour to the blacks, 'poor, hopeless derelicts, wandering with no comprehension', guarantees that the whites are not only evolutionarily more fit to survive but morally superior. Daisy Bates was as sure as Spencer and Gillen of the imminent extinction of the Aborigines, as the title of her most famous book, *The Passing of the Aborigines* (1938), proclaimed, and she saw her task as being, at best, to 'arrest the contamination of civilisation'.[28] Hill quotes Bates as saying, '"I shall not see the last of them, but this century will . . . all I can do is to make the passing easier. There is no hope for tomorrow, but I can help each one of them for today"'.[29] So successful was the Daisy Bates myth Hill helped to create that, even in 1966, Arthur Mee, introducing the second edition of *The Passing of the Aborigines*, writes of her in terms reminiscent of Mary Kingsley in Africa as 'the last friend of the last remnant of this dying race'.[30] This image of Bates as a frail but courageous little woman was a convenient all-purpose one, ready to apply to other heroic women in the desert, from Bates's contemporary Jeannie Gunn on Elsey Station to Molly Clarke at Old Andado in the 1990s. It conferred token admiration while carefully emphasising the extreme rarity of this departure from the female norm of dependence in an overwhelmingly patriarchal society. Hill certainly concurred with Bates's view of the imminent extinction of the Aborigines and advocated actively assisting it. She reported 'experts' as saying that they could be 'eliminated' and 'submerged' by 'breeding them white' and providing them with 'every opportunity to outgrow their heredity'.[31]

In the tradition of the nineteenth-century explorers and conscious of her self-conferred responsibility to rally a nation, Hill ends her book by affirming the prosperous future of this country. Triumphant over the hardships of camel riding, of being bogged on the Birdsville Track and an encounter with a three-metre snake, she extols the magnificence of the country and the heroism and ingenuity of the people who live in it. 'Two thousand miles due west and north of civilisation, where . . . the silence is implacable as death, white men are living in the Great Australian Loneliness, and greeting it each morning as a friend.'[32]

151

The Territory (1951), Hill's best known work, amplifies this confidence, extolling the prosperous future of the Northern Territory where, according to Hill, water and crops are no real problem and only an increased population is needed to make the whole land blossom. Hill's accounts of her travels through some of the least accessible areas of Australia might have been expected to reclaim the outback for women, restoring to them the prestige of being able to survive in this 'male' territory. But ironically they did no such thing. In her zeal to proclaim her own heroism, Hill presents herself as exceptional and the intrepid Daisy Bates as saintly, eccentric, genderless and anachronistic. Neither woman threatens the assumption that Central Australia is a man's world.

A similar style of racy, jocular realism was adopted by two of Hill's contemporaries, Arthur Groom, author of *I Saw a Strange Land* (1950), and the prolific George Farwell, outback traveller and sometime goldminer as well as journalist and broadcaster. Groom not only foresaw the potential of tourism to the Centre and argued for a link between protection of scenery and Aboriginal welfare but also asserted, 'I had come to a definite conclusion that the wilderness areas of Central Australia belong firstly to the natives, and to the white man only on sufferance.'[33] Farwell's *Land of Mirage* (1950), describing his experiences on the Birdsville Track, draws on the standard ingredients of humour, 'characters', yarns and emphasis on the 'otherness' of the Track. This is signalled immediately in the opening description of the mosque at Marree and the inevitable mirage:

152

> Beyond the mosque with its twin date palms, the plain ebbed away over the edge of the world. A mirage shimmered on the skyline, magically raising the distant sandhill to a line of towering red cliffs above a pale lake. A few ragged trees, apparently without trunks, floated on this illusory expanse of water, distant and forlorn. Somewhere out there lay our track.[34]

Equally obligatory is the use of camels for transport, icons of the strangeness of the land with which they are identified: 'Shaggy, gaunt, archaic beasts, they seemed not of this age at all, yet entirely in keeping with the ancient and eroded landscape around the town.' Farwell gives probably the most extended description of the eerie visual effects associated with Lake Eyre, mirage capital of Australia, concluding: 'The thin air, the absence of sound or wind, the brittle surface under my feet, the utter lack of landmarks to give directions, all this created a numbing, sleepwalker's atmosphere. It was a reminder of man's insecurity upon the earth.'

The market for such colourful reminiscences about outback hardships continued well into the 1960s, driven partly by a nostalgic desire to perpetuate belief in the itinerant characters of A.B. ('Banjo') Paterson's poems, free from domestic responsibilities. Clancy and the Man from Snowy River provided an Australian version of the American frontiersman image so widely disseminated through films of the Wild West. Similar in style to Farwell's books, Len Beadell's *Too Long in the Bush* (1965) deftly calls attention to the author's

implicit heroism by reference to Ernest Giles and the ill-fated Gibson.
Reaching the sandhills at the eastern end of the Gibson Desert, he reflects:

> My thoughts were very much with Gibson who had done the same thing, only
> he had mistaken those hills for the Rawlinson Range. I was within a radius of
> perhaps ten miles of where he had ultimately lost his life. . . . I was incredibly
> thirsty and had not been able to eat for two days but I did have some water and
> I knew where I was going or, to be more precise, I knew where I was.

The tone is unfailingly cheerful as the resourceful Beadell takes discomfort in
his stride.

> When the gales hit during the night, we almost have to dig ourselves out next
> morning . . . We find the bread-tin lids and frying pans by determining the
> direction of the wind and driving on a reverse compass bearing through the
> bush for anything up to half a mile.[35]

The 1930s also witnessed a new wave of interest in Aboriginal culture as
the object of study carefully divorced from its living context. The enthusiastic
reception of Albert Namatjira's landscapes and the formation of the
Jindyworobak group of poets (both to be discussed in later chapters) were
complemented by the anthropological accounts of Ted Strehlow and later by
the Australian–American scientific expedition to Arnhem Land in 1948, sponsored by the National Geographic Society and the Australian Government. The
popular *Brown Men and Red Sand* (1948) by ethnologist Charles Mountford,
who led the expedition, and *Adam in Ochre* (1951) by journalist Colin Simpson,
established the desert as a source of scientific curiosity. Mountford characteristically included a wealth of legends, while Simpson focussed on visual descriptions of the people. Both stressed the sense of timeless antiquity of the desert,
Simpson in his title and Mountford in comments such as that accompanying
his description of an Aborigine completing a cave painting:

153

> there a naked brown-skinned man painted a primitive symbol, which was
> comparable in both design and technique with those produced by our
> forefathers of the Old Stone Age in Europe twenty thousand years ago. It
> seemed as if the hands of time had been turned back through all those many
> centuries.[36]

While Simpson was concerned to demonstrate the skills and potential (always
in Western terms) of the Aborigines, and hence to overthrow the charge
of primitivism, he, like Mountford, nevertheless presents the Aborigines as
natural-history specimens expected to perform on demand.[37]

The magazine *Walkabout*, founded in 1934, had also boosted popular
interest in the outback, so that by the 1960s it could be confidently asserted
that this 'magazine, as much as anything else, discovered outback Australia to

the popular imagination'.[38] The theme of the real outback, as opposed to the Bush, had already begun to intrigue documentary film-makers, beginning with Francis Birtles's 1915 film *Into Australia's Unknown*. Even apparently straightforward travelogues conveyed a clear message of the vastness and beauty of this country and most extolled the heroism of (non-indigenous) individuals wresting a livelihood from the desert. The 1946 film *The Overlanders* reiterates this message of the heroism of outback Australians in the context of an actual event. In 1942 85,000 head of cattle were driven from the north of Western Australia to the Queensland coast as part of a scorched-earth policy designed to leave no food for any invading Japanese soldiers. The cattle drovers, including a young woman, face the diverse hazards of the journey with the combination of resourcefulness, skill and humour that had traditionally typified characters of the bush yarn, but far less orthodox is the impassioned socialist outburst by the star, Chips Rafferty, condemning the disinheritance of the Aborigines and the exploitation of the land by wealthy cattle barons.

One of the most interesting documentaries to emerge from the desert was John Heyer's black-and-white film *Back of Beyond* (1954), made by the Shell Film Unit. It follows the mail man, Tom Kruse, on his fortnightly journey from Marree to Birdsville and back, delivering supplies and mail from his battered truck to the little community strung out along the Birdsville Track. Beginning in the style of a Movietone newsreel, with cliché statements about the Aborigines as a 'disappearing race', and the clear intention of presenting heroic, pioneering individuals conquering the outback through the marvels of modern technology, the film develops in depth as it transcends and even subverts this role. The small, isolated community is indeed sustained by fleeting contact with its mail man and by two-way radio link between the stations, but that link is shown to be tenuous in the extreme. When for various reasons it breaks, lives are lost. The courage and resourcefulness of these people living in isolation on the edge of a vast desert, prey to sandstorms, drought and floods, are indeed celebrated; but the question more poignantly raised by the film is: Why are they there? The minimal station homesteads along the route, the crumbling ruins of the former Lutheran mission at Killalpaninna, now inhabited only by a passing 'dogger' with his dingo scalps,[39] the aged Afghan couple performing ritual prayers for the dead, the reference to two children lost in a sandstorm – all suggest not triumph over the desert but defeat or, at best, bare survival. This aspect of the film, subversive of the Film Unit's intentions, most probably sprang from the involvement of the New Zealand-born poet Douglas Stewart who was commissioned to help write the script. As a further result of this 480-kilometre journey Stewart published a poem sequence, *The Birdsville Track* (1955), recording his own impressions of this 'fierce country' where heat, dust, mirages and baking stone gibbers are the only enduring entities:

> Man makes his mark across a fierce country
> That has no flower but the whitening bone and skull
> Of long-dead cattle, no word but 'I will kill'

154

Here the world ends in a shield of purple stone
Naked in its long war against the sun;
The white stones flash, the red stones leap with fire:
It wants no interlopers to come here.
. . .
And man too like the earth in the good season
When the Diamantina floods the whole horizon
And the cattle grow fat on the wildflowers says his proud word:
Gathers the stones and builds four-square and hard;

Where the mirage still watches with glittering eyes
The ruins of his homestead crumble on the iron rise.
Dust on the waterless plains blows over his track,
The sun glares down on the stones and the stones glare back.[40]

Although he sees the intense beauty of the desert in bloom with daisies, cassia and wild hops, and the corresponding optimism of the settlers that 'the cattle [will] grow fat on wildflowers', Stewart's emphasis is on the evidence of mortality. Induced by thirst, heat and the deceptive mirages that haunt the imagination, death stalks nearly every poem in the sequence – death of people, cattle, camels, even a foal betrayed by 'well-meaning' mules unable to suckle it. All life is ephemeral, like the lilies and the helichrysums. Only the evocative place names – Ethadinna, Mira Mitta, Mulka, Mangerannie, Dulkaninna and Koperamanna – remain as evidence of a former settlement, now abandoned. In the desert there is no pity. Marree, the town at the southern end of the Birdsville Track, is, for Stewart:

155

. . . the corrugated-iron town
In the corrugated-iron air
Where the shimmering heat-waves glare
To the red-hot iron plain
And the steel mirage beyond.

Where life if it hopes to breathe
Must crawl in the shade of a stone
Like snake and scorpion:
All tastes like dust in the mouth,
All strikes like iron in the mind.

On the other hand, *Walkabout* (1958), a film commissioned by British television, had all such adverse observations edited out. A screen correlative of Ernestine Hill's journey, its thirteen episodes provided a travelogue–documentary constructed around landscape, interviews with outback 'characters', and a scattering of anthropological curiosity about Aborigines. Its emphasis on ordinary incidents rather than melodrama acted as a guarantee of validity, though there was a careful exclusion of any scenes likely to offend the sensibilities of a British audience or subvert the official policy of national optimism – no killing of animals, no cattle dead from drought. Eventually, however, as the novelty of the documentary wore off, it became increasingly necessary for films of the Centre to provide an exciting narrative or psychological focus, or to present a particularly heroic protagonist, such as Denis Bartell, whose walk from north to south across the Simpson Desert, filmed as *Desert Walker* (1985), is discussed in Chapter 14.

In parallel with the documentary of travellers' experiences, and providing considerably more excitement, were the accounts, both actual and fictional, of the search for gold.

Lasseter and his legacy: the lure of gold

Prompted by the exhaustion or corporate ownership of more accessible diggings in Victoria and New South Wales the notion of reefs of gold awaiting discovery in the desert stepped out of the covers of nineteenth-century ripping yarns and into commercial consciousness when rich deposits of gold and copper were discovered at the Granites and Tennant Creek as well as the better known fields in Western Australia. The exposure of Louis de Rougemont's fraudulent story of a 'Mountain of Gold' in the Centre of Australia, referred to in Chapter 7, did nothing to deter prospectors; indeed thirty years later the continuing allure of the fabled 'mountain of gold' in an otherwise useless desert allowed another impostor, 'Harold Bell' Lasseter, to convince Sydney investors that he had discovered a lost gold reef. It has since been shown that a man called Lewis Hubert Lasseter appropriated the names Harold Bell from an American writer Harold Bell Wright, whose novel *The Mine with the Iron Door* (1923) explored a similar idea. But the Central Australian Gold Exploration Company Ltd, with the ironic acronym CAGE, established to fund Lasseter's attempted relocation of the 'lost reef', entertained no such suspicions. After a series of unlucky occurrences between July 1930 and January 1931 and the disappearance of Lasseter, a search party led by Bob Buck claimed to have found Lasseter's body and buried it in the Petermann Range. Legend quickly inserted the required moral element, claiming that Lasseter had died of hunger and thirst within five days' journey of his gold reef, so that the multiple ironies of the story exploit the universal greed for gold even while overtly censuring it.

Yet Lasseter, his name immediately a national byword, was also lionised, joining the pantheon of noble explorers defeated by the desert. His story instantly overshadowed earlier fictional treatments of the gold-in-the-desert theme and prompted numerous accounts, with varying degrees of fictionalisation, the most famous being Ion Idriess's *Lasseter's Last Ride* (1931).[41] Widely accepted as 'fact' because of its satisfying mixture of popular cliché, Idriess's account includes an El Dorado in a barren land, the explorer–hero dying of thirst in the desert, an aura of unexplained primitive magic and the satisfying moral of avarice duly punished.

Idriess also exploits the dramatic irony implicit in the disparity between Euro–Australian technology and the power of Nature, as understood by the indigenous people. Presented at first as primitive savages, the Aborigines are duly ridiculed for their superstitions and ignorance of such marvels as mirrors, tea and metal tins. The balance of power is assumed to lie with the technological marvels of the CAGE expedition, 'the best equipped prospecting expedition that ever started out in Australia'. Yet even a six-wheeled Thornycroft truck, an auxiliary truck, a Black Hawk plane, seemingly limitless amounts of money for supplies, and a two-way wireless set fail to protect the expedition against the power of the desert and its inhabitants. Planes and trucks are forced to give way to camels and travel on foot; the wireless neither receives nor transmits when needed, though the Aborigines successfully relay complex messages across vast distances by 'smoke-talk'. A moment of carelessness, such as failure to hobble a camel, or to correct a faulty watch, can result in sudden death.

Idriess's desert defeats the white men through its variability. A series of neo-Gothic occurrences, including an apparent incursion of the supernatural that is never explained, subverts their rational plans. Willy-willies snatch their plane into the air and hurl it back to earth in a frenzy of destruction, or fan a smouldering fire into a blaze that destroys a whole campsite and its food. A brief, localised rain storm may save the lives of men dying of thirst, or it may bog the pack animals. Escaping camels abscond with precious food and vital water. Aborigines mislead the travellers about the position of wells and are ever likely to kill a white man for the glory of having their names enshrined in legend. Mountains, salt lakes and dense foliage impede the expeditioners' progress and conceal their whereabouts from would-be rescuers, while spinifex spears, blazing heat and lack of water and food provide subsidiary levels of torture. In such terrain twentieth-century technology is of less use than the 'stone age' equipment but even the Aborigines are at the mercy of blighted yam harvests, dried-up soaks and scarcity of animals. Idriess emphasises that the desert reduces all races alike to clutching at subsistence. Lasseter's death is ultimately attributed to the *kaditcha* spell[42] placed upon him and Idriess implies that this, like the inexplicable experiences affecting the rest of his party, results from mystic powers beyond the explanation of Western science. These are linked not merely to Aboriginal culture but to a more general malevolence of the desert.

Thus Idriess's account of the desert is intentionally ambivalent. On the one hand he affirms its surprising beauty – its flowers, its brilliant bird life, its colours, trees, and varied terrain. In addition, its potential for development is several times asserted by Lasseter and others, not only in terms of its mineral deposits but as pastoral land able to sustain immense herds. In contrast to the Aboriginal habit of returning to the same few wells, there is the confident belief that artesian water and the hard work of white Australians will inevitably convert desert to pasture. But all these predictions turn out to be dramatic irony, voiced by those whose technology fails dismally in the event. Thus

157

Idriess's novel subverts, even while professing to support, the prevailing inter-war confidence in the development of the interior. Instead it revisits the nineteenth-century horror tradition of bleached bones in the desert, victims of thirst, misadventure and Aboriginal treachery.

Lasseter's fate, real or fictional, did not deter other speculators. In 1936 the Sydney businessman H.V. Foy set out to find the alleged reef, taking with him two young film-makers. The expedition failed to recover costs, either by locating gold deposits or in the subsequent film, *Phantom Gold* (1937), which supposedly reconstructed key scenes in Lasseter's search. The film was with-drawn from circulation when Angus and Robertson threatened legal action on the grounds that it infringed the copyright of Idriess's novel.[43] Nevertheless the continuing desire to believe in Lasseter's tale, whatever the consequences, is indicated by the economic success of the Alice Springs casino, named 'Lasseter's' – an irony that presumably escapes its hopeful patrons.

Idriess had refrained from casting his protagonist as a Midas figure whose greed brings only death in its wake but later writers were not so reticent. John Kinsella's *Lasseter* poem sequence links him with Nebuchadnezzar[44] and in Randolph Stow's *Tourmaline*, to be discussed in more detail in Chapter 10, the self-proclaimed diviner Michael Random fails to find water but locates, instead, a gold reef. Although temporarily bemused by this, the town's inhabitants do not need the gold, which brings only misfortune, engendering greed and schemes for domination by evil men. In Mark O'Connor's poem 'Interview in a Desert' (1984) the Western obsession with gold is satirically counterpointed with the Aboriginal evaluation of the metal:

158

> 'We got nother-fella rock,
> little-fella. Not much to see. Sometimes 'im
> hide under other rock. Too soft for spear point.
> But 'im last, oh yes 'im last! Might be
> two hundred piccaninny times. Dat yellow rock
> go on, all same forever.'
>
> 'So you trade this yellow eternity rock?'
> asked the anthropologist,
> propping his notebook on freckled knee,
> 'You got big myth-cycle, big Dreaming, for him?
> You make totem with him?'
>
> 'Nah, dat proper useless Whitefeller rock.
> Only good for kids go play.
> We got no story who put 'im dere.
> But Whitefeller go hunt for dat yellow rock
> to make 'im trade bead. Poor bugga forget place
> where he born. All day out in sun. Only look
> for dat crazy rock. Dat Whitefeller totem;
> we call dat *Rock belong Jesus Dreaming*.'[45]

While most writers fall back on the easy metaphor of gold prospecting as the cult of Mammon, an interesting exception is provided by the novels of Elliot Lovegood Grant Watson which assert a mystical bond between gold and the desert where it is located. Trained as a biologist at Cambridge, Watson came to Australia from England to join the Radcliffe-Brown anthropological expedition to the north-west of Western Australia in 1910–11. To fill in time before the expedition departed he spent some weeks collecting beetles around the Bulfinch goldmine near Kalgoorlie, an experience that gave rise to several novels and stories set in the Western Australian desert. Watson presents his miners and prospectors sympathetically: prospecting is a noble, even religious obsession and gold is described in almost alchemical terms as the pure essence of the desert, the life source. In *Mainland* (1917), for example, a young miner, John Sherwin, teams up with an eccentric Irish prospector, Gilbert, based on a character of the same name whom Watson had met at the Bulfinch mine. The real-life Gilbert was not interested in the commercial prospects of gold – he sent all the money he earned back to his wife in Ireland – but what most intrigued Watson, and accounted for the elevated status his miners and prospectors enjoyed, was the association between Gilbert's 'profound feeling for the bush' and his search: 'it was not riches, or the hope of riches, that lured him on. It was the unknown background that held him in thrall, and the gold was the symbol of the impossible-to-realize centre of all life'.[46] It is, in particular, the essence of the land itself: 'a great country: unexplored and full of metals – miles of it untrodden. That's where I want to be.'[47] Thus Watson presents Gilbert as a fellow-traveller on a common spiritual quest.

159

In *Daimon* (1925) the search for gold is ascribed a status approaching that of a holy pilgrimage. Watson's protagonist Martin O'Brian, a former cattle farmer, returns to the desert to search for gold, not for wealth but as a symbol of the pure and indestructible essence of life. In the tradition of Henry Lawson and 'Banjo' Paterson, Watson idealises prospecting as offering freedom from society, from domestic responsibilities and from the tiring complexities of gender relations. At the Kumana diggings Martin is attracted by the air of excitement and elation, the camaraderie of men with similar attitudes 'intent on their business, and for the most part, self-contained and reticent . . . It was nice to be amongst so many men, and far from his home and the influence of women.' When, after many years, Martin does discover a rich vein of gold, his response is a religious one, appropriate to a mystical epiphany of the land itself:

> Martin looked at the tiny particles. . . . That was gold: the precious substance, fresh and glistening from the earth. It had been there waiting, as it had been waiting for numberless years, till men whose hearts and minds were open to its magic should come, and, at the risk of their lives, and sacrificing all else that their hearts clung to, should seek and find. . . . As he looked at the shining particles, it seemed to him then in a sudden flash, that he understood the land which was his home more completely than ever before. How was it possible that from so small a centre should spring so dazzling an illumination?[48]

Watson's most sustained treatment of gold prospecting was *The Partners* (1933), published under the pseudonym of John Lovegood and focussing on the contrapuntal relationship between a wealthy speculator, Sam Lawson, and his prospector-employee, Tim Kennedy. Lawson is crass, greedy and sensuous, while the latter is ascetic, laconic and fundamentally uninterested in wealth. Each possesses the one thing the other most desires – Tim the knowledge of the gold seam and Sam a beautiful wife. Both men die in the desert, victims of their respective lusts, but not before, in an unlikely sequence, the worldly and sceptical Sam is spiritually transformed by the mystic beauty of the gold and the desert.

Watson's treatment of gold reflects his own unique response to the desert as a place of origins and epiphanies, a stage for the acting out of psychological dramas. Chapter 10 returns to the discussion of this Gothic mindscape in fiction and in film.

To see the desert is like peeling the skin off a landscape.

FRED WILLIAMS[1]

[Nolan] is enchanted with the desolation not because it is a mirror of his soul, but because it comes to his eyes with the freshness of a surprise, full of strange beauties and challenging forms.

JAMES GLEESON[2]

Because Australia is the only island continent, the notion of its centre has acquired a unique significance (we do not conceptualise the centre of any other continent). Indeed, from our perspective at the end of the century, it seems almost self-evident that the Australian Centre, the symbolic blood-red heart of the continent, additionally characterised by its spectacular land-forms, brilliant colours, and unique Aboriginal culture, should occupy a focal position in the national psyche and provide its visual image to the world. Yet five decades ago such a notion would have been met with incredulity. Certainly there was a desire for imagery to cultivate a sense of national identity and pro-claim visually its political independence from Britain. Landscapes painted in the first decade of Federation show a distinct self-consciousness, a gravity about the importance of the Australian scene as distinct from European correlatives and, in particular, a claim for national rather than regional interest. But although the notion of what represented a national landscape was not unani-mously agreed upon, one thing was certain: it was not the desert.[3] In 1902 Arthur Streeton, the nation's foremost landscape artist, had painted Nelson's Column in Trafalgar Square, entitling his canvas *The Centre of Empire*, and its iconographic and emotional power inspired in the viewing public a desire for an Australian counterpart, to be called *The Heart of Australia*.[4] Although no such picture was produced, there could be little doubt as to the subject expected to fit the title. It would be a rural scene, emphasising fertility and prosperity and implying health, wealth and happiness for the nation's fortunate citizens.

The construction of a national image in terms of landscape fell into abeyance during World War I when Australia was stretched to the limit proving its identity on the Western Front and in the Middle East. Along with official historians, artists were commissioned to document and commemorate the involvement of Australian soldiers in this world conflict;[5] for even early in the war, and certainly after Gallipoli, there was a perception that Australians were winning their spurs on the world stage through their bravery and self-sacrifice on behalf of the oppressed. Indeed, the sense of national identity emanating from the war far surpassed that generated by the purely political event of Federation.

With the return of troops from the front, and the Australian Government's program for soldier settlement on farms, it became even more politically expedient to represent the land as fertile, welcoming and benign, the appropriate gift from a grateful nation to its heroes. Not surprisingly there was renewed interest in the works of the Heidelberg School, which achieved considerable post-war popularity as images of a country eminently worth defending even unto death. Art historian Ian Burn wrote that: 'The dominant image of the landscape in the 1920s and 1930s cannot be separated from the experience of the war. . . . The masculine ideals of war were used to promote and validate a particular landscape of peace, an ideal of pastoral wealth and national potential.'[6] Paintings such as Elioth Gruner's *Spring Frost* (1919), Penleigh Boyd's *Morning Light* (1922) and Arthur Streeton's *Land of the Golden Fleece* (1926) not only typified the image of a pastoral utopia that Australians wished to present to the world but provided a mythology against which other versions of landscape could be measured. These paintings served to exorcise the 'weird melancholy' image of the Bush and to present Australian nature as continuous with the Arcadian past, thereby giving the landscape a credible history and relevance. Their images, widely disseminated by the popular press and further cultivated as part of the economic impetus to attract foreign investment, were fiercely protected, even to the extent of imposing censorship on derogatory comments about the land. Films of the severe drought of 1920 were not permitted to be exported and there was federal pressure to suppress even a local showing of Franklyn Barrett's film, *The Breaking of the Drought* (1920), which included footage of drought-ravaged countryside.[7] In such a political and ideological climate the appeal of the desert as pictorial subject had never been lower.

In addition to these ideological disincentives, the whole tradition of European landscape painting was inimical to the depiction of the 'absences' implicit in the notion of desert. Its featurelessness, its apparently monotonous appearance and, in particular, its subversion of accepted rules of perspective and landscape composition constituted an enormous mental and logistical barrier for Western artists. We saw in Chapter 5 that the vast tracts of desert landscape mocked the colonising impulse by seeming to offer themselves for domination while simultaneously subverting that hope with a vision of extreme loneliness and desolation. For Anglo-Australians they offered no historical, aesthetic or emotional context, no recognisable sites for identification with heroic figures, since all places appeared the same. The process of overcoming this perceived difficulty forced twentieth-century artists to supply new centres of interest in their representations of the desert, producing some of the most innovative Australian art.

Sanctification through sacrifice

While the main focus of the war artists had been the Western Front, a significant degree of interest was aroused by their representations of the campaign in the Middle East. Partly this was the result of the special status accorded the Gallipoli campaign where, in popular opinion at least, the Anzacs had commanded the world's attention. It was also intensified by public fascination with paintings of Palestine. Although Australians were more secular than religious in outlook, a current of emotional fervour greeted George Lambert's images of Australian soldiers in Gallipoli (*Anzac, the Landing*, 1915) and the Holy Land (*The Road to Jericho*, c.1919)[8] (see illustrations following page 80). The acceptance of these parched Middle East landscapes, already sanctified by their religious and historical context and now claimed for specifically Australian reverence, obliquely paved the way for representations of Australian aridity. Pastoral landscapes from the 1920s to the 1930s show an increasing use of brown tones, rather than the olive greens and golds favoured by the Heidelberg painters. As art historian Mary Eagle remarks:

> Not only artists but the community at large took note of Lambert's war paintings . . . [Those that] had a public following were huge images of khaki-clad battalions fighting and dying in the embrace of a rocky landscape like that of inland Australia.[9]

163

There was another potent influence, unrelated to the war, that favoured a new vision of the desert – Modernism. Struck by the stark outlines of the Middle East landscapes – the clear-cut shapes of hills bare of vegetation and thus of detail to distract the eye from the contemplation of form – George Lambert wrote:

> The sandhills take on the shapes and curves, cuts concave and convex, interwoven in an entrancing pattern, here rhythmical, there jagged and eccentrically opposed. With all the knowledge the artist may, nay must, bring to bear, he need only copy and he achieves art; but it takes doing.[10]

In addition to their emotional appeal, both *Anzac, the Landing* and *The Road to Jericho* also exemplify these patterned structures. Despite the expectation set up by the title of the former, Lambert relegates the beach at Anzac Cove to the margin of the work, focussing instead on the repetition of diamond shapes in the broken terrain of the foreground and the jagged peaks above. The figures of the soldiers clambering up the transverse gullies are reduced to shadows, accentuating the geometric forms. Similarly, in *The Road to Jericho* the play of light and shadow on rounded hills and hillocks emphasises the repeating pattern of geological structure. These vague and diverse influences awaited only some opportune catalyst to transfer the resonances of Palestine to inland Australia and produce a new and striking image of the desert. That agent was Hans Heysen.

Edging towards the desert: Hans Heysen

Heysen was already well known for his paintings of gum trees in the Adelaide Hills[11] when he made his first visit to the Flinders Ranges in 1926 in response to an enthusiastic letter from his Melbourne dealer W.H. Gill.[12] This arid northern region of South Australia, then virtually unknown to most Australians, so fascinated Heysen that he made ten trips to various parts of the area between 1926 and 1933, and two subsequent journeys in 1947 and 1949. The immediate and startlingly novel impressions he registered were the clarity of vision resulting from the dry air, the sharp topographical outlines and blocks of colour in a country virtually bereft of foliage, and the almost palpable sense of the land's antiquity. A truthful rendering of these features involved radical changes in his painting style and philosophy of composition. Perhaps for the first time the land was determining the art. Heysen wrote to fellow artist, Lionel Lindsay:

> My first impression upon arrival was that of expanse, of simplicity and beauty
> of contours – the light flat and all objects sharply defined; distances very
> deceptive, and no appreciable atmospheric difference between the foreground
> and the middle distances; indeed, hills at least four miles away [apart] appear to
> unite, and scale becomes an important relative factor.[13]

164 Later he amplified this atmospheric effect: 'I have seen it on calm days of crystalline purity when the eye could travel, as it were, to the end of the world, bringing with it that wonderful sense of infinity that a land of moist atmosphere could never give.'[14] Expressing in pictorial terms this confusing sense of distance required radical revision of the rigid distinctions in Western art between foreground, middle distance and background. The indeterminacy of perspective was further compounded by the lack of distinctive features and details traditionally used to define structural divisions within a painting. Heysen was prepared to dispense with these expectations and evolve alternative signifiers.

Equally intriguing was the presence of seemingly ready-made Modernist forms in the exposed rock surfaces of this denuded and geologically ancient landscape, 'rugged and full of primitive character ... the bare bones of the landscape'.[15] Gone are the detailed, close-up eucalypts of his earlier work. If they appear at all they are blackened, distant stumps reduced to gaunt, leafless shapes of contrasting colour in an overall pattern. Heysen later wrote:

> It was in the Flinders Ranges that I was made curiously aware of a very old land
> where the primitive forces of Nature were constantly evident. The barren
> hillsides, incised and torn by nature's forces, hold a peculiar attraction. Their
> geological structure is seldom obscured by foliage, and in many parts where
> great masses of stone are piled layer on layer in regular formation, as if built up
> by some very ancient people, their appearance is given an architectural order.[16]

The immense size of the rock formations and features that he wished to capture forced Heysen to locate them in the distance in his paintings, thereby necessarily simplifying the forms and further accentuating their shapes. Fascinated by the seemingly contemporary artistry displayed by such pristine landforms, he wrote, '... everything looks so old that it belongs to quite a different world. There are scenes ready made, which seem to say "here is the very thing you moderns are trying to paint". Fine big simple forms against clear transparent skies – & a sense of spaciousness everywhere.'[17] Heysen was particularly captivated by the massive sandstone monolith towering 244 metres above Brachina Creek near the entrance to Brachina Gorge in the Ranges, and now known as Heysen's Hill. C. Warren Bonython, an Adelaide naturalist and keen bushwalker who trekked across the Simpson Desert with Charles Mc Cubbin, wrote of this hill: 'The eastern face is the steepest and most impressive, having vertical angular ribs or buttresses which, together with the rock variations – bright red at the bottom and pale cream towards the top – give it the property of changing its aspect with each change of light.'[18] Heysen sketched and painted it many times, the best known examples being *Brachina Gorge*, which won the Wynne Prize for landscape in 1932, and *Guardian of the Brachina Gorge* (1937) (see illustration following page 80) – arid landscapes virtually unrelieved by foliage. Indeed, Heysen rigorously censored green grass from his Flinders Ranges paintings. When he revisited the area in 1928 to find lush new grass springing up after rain, he refused to paint the scene as it was 'most disconcerting and out of harmony'.[19] His most dramatic paintings of the Flinders Ranges – *The Three Sisters of the Aroona* (1927), *Patawarta, Land of the Oratunga, Drought (Arkaba)*, *The Hill of the Creeping Shadow* and *Foothills of the Flinders* (all 1929), *Land of the Oratunga* (1932), *The Bluff, Arkabas, Flinders Ranges* (1933), and the unfinished oil *Yappala Range* (1928–68) – show only the characteristic burnt tree stumps and a land ravaged by five years of drought.

165

Whether or not Heysen knew of Lambert's remarks about the patterned landscape of the Middle East when he began painting in the Flinders Ranges, he was certainly aware of the war artist's work. Art historian William Moore later commented that '[w]hen last in Sydney, Heysen visited the war museum three times to see Lambert's Palestine landscapes'.[20] Lionel Lindsay also noted this artistic quotation, describing Heysen's work as 'a landscape of fundamentals, austerely Biblical',[21] while the historian Sir Keith Hancock later commented on Heysen's 'Arabian landscapes and Arabian names ... dry, flat light, hard skies, clamorous reds and ochres, Dolomite masses and sharp forms – "a landscape of fundamentals".'[22]

Although Heysen's paintings, with their focus on striking monoliths, ranges and red gums, hardly conform to the widely held notion of desert as flat and featureless, his visual representation of desert-like landscape in terms consistent with both biblical reference and the tenets of Modernism triggered a new wave of interest in the symbolism which could be wrested from the Australian wasteland. Heysen's landscapes, nine of which were awarded the

Wynne Prize, dominated the Australian art scene for almost thirty years and, reproduced widely in prints and on calendars and Christmas cards, were important in educating a wider public to see barrenness as beautiful. Other artists soon followed Heysen's lead. Horace Trenerry's *Aroona Valley* (1930) and Harold Cazneaux's paintings of the mid-1930s clearly reflect Heysen's influence, a style that was to determine depiction of the Flinders Ranges for nearly half a century. The intrepid Jessie Traill travelled to areas that were even more remote, holding the first exhibition of Central Australian landscapes in Melbourne in 1928.[23] The extension of the railway line from Oodnadatta to Alice Springs in 1929 made the desert much more accessible, not only physically but conceptually. The Centre became a focus for travellers, writers, photographers and artists, including Arthur Murch who visited the area in 1933 to paint Mount Sonder and the MacDonnell Ranges.

Primitive or prophetic? The work of Albert Namatjira

Following the increasing interest in the Centre, painter Rex Battarbee travelled several times to the MacDonnell Ranges between 1932 and 1936. During one of these journeys he visited the Hermannsburg Mission, where he was asked by Pastor Albrecht to give some lessons in watercolours to a promising young Aranda artist at the mission who was already known locally for his carving and painting with ochre and vegetable dyes. His name was Albert Namatjira. Battarbee encouraged him with some tips on technique and left him with a selection of paints, promising to return and see how he was progressing. On his next visit he was confronted by a display that staggered him. Unlike Murch's landscapes, with their muted Romantic tones, Namatjira's work was a glowing record of the brilliant reds, ochres and purples we have now come to associate with the area around the MacDonnell Ranges. His paintings were first shown with Battarbee's in Adelaide in 1937 and the following year the works in his first one-man exhibition, held in Melbourne, were all sold. But despite the popularity of Namatjira's work outside the art world, he has never been wholly accepted by art critics. His art was judged to be a doubtful amalgam of two incompatible traditions, tribal and Western, satisfying the criteria of neither. In Western terms he was considered too conventional, too literal for the Moderns and too primitive for the traditional watercolourists. More recently, with the popularity of Papunya acrylic painting, Namatjira's works were yet again denigrated as mere copies of Western art rather than emanating from an indigenous tradition. Only recently has it been recognised that the watercolour tradition Namatjira pioneered was an important precursor of acrylic paintings, and that the style he evolved was a complex statement of cross-cultural contact and *rapprochement*. Whereas it was formerly believed that Namatjira had merely pandered to Western taste, selecting scenes that approximated to the rules governing desirable landscapes, it is now realised that this was not part of his intention. Rather, the land he represented was his ancestral landscape,[24] inscribed

166

with the meaning it held for his people and glowing with brilliant colours to indicate its spirit-filled state. 'Empty' with respect to the markers of European settlement, these paintings tacitly assert his perception of the land as created in the Dreaming, long before the arrival of Europeans. Ian Burn has suggested that Namatjira's paintings are 'even about a kind of resistance and repossession consistent with a sense of Aboriginal custodianship of the land.'[25] Burn and Ann Stephen have also argued that Namatjira's art, and that of the Hermannsburg School which he founded, can be read as a form of colonial mimicry, where the land superficially appears to conform to Western landscape expectations but, when examined more closely, 'looks back at us: it meets and deliberately crosses the viewer's gaze (of possession).'[26]

It is characteristic of all the paintings discussed so far that the desert is presented as not only barren but empty of human habitation. Although Heysen wrote about the settlers living in the drought-stricken area of the Flinders Ranges and, to his amazement, maintaining a sense of optimism in a land of 'blasted hopes', such people are absent from his paintings. So, too, are Aborigines. Despite their intimate association with the desert, they were excluded from paintings (though not from photography[27]). This can be seen in part as resulting from the influence of Modernism, with its focus on shapes rather than detail, but it can also be read in a more sinister light – as part of a conscious conspiracy, begun in the 1890s, to erase the Aboriginal presence from the record, whether written or painted. This 'great Australian silence', as the anthropologist W.E.H. Stanner called it, is a particularly glaring example of what Fredric Jameson has termed the 'political unconscious', employed to censor the awkward fact that the Aborigines had not, as was confidently pre-dicted, become extinct. The attempt to erase them from the landscape, to ren-der them visually non-existent, was an aspect of a broader effort to vindicate the doctrine of *terra nullius*.

167

Figures in the landscape: the art of Drysdale and Molvig

The first artists to depict human figures integrated with the desert landscape were Russell Drysdale and Jon Molvig. Despite their very different styles they both evolved ways of including characters without either dwarfing them by the immensity of the scene or subverting the power of nature.

DRYSDALE

Russell Drysdale's interest in stark and barren landscapes began in the 1940s with his paintings of drought in the Riverina and western New South Wales, and his work moved increasingly towards the depiction of scenes from an arid outback that was, in effect, a surreal desert. Drysdale was not the first to see the surrealist potential in the Australian landscape. The twisted shapes of trees and the sharply outlined forms of the Central Australian landscape had already been noted by Heysen, but Drysdale transformed them into something completely new, with little if any reference to the naturalism that Heysen, Trenerry and Murch had never really abandoned. Bernard Smith wrote, 'Drysdale is among the most original of all Australian landscape painters. Few contemporary Australian painters of landscape have been able to escape entirely from the broad terms of reference that his Albury paintings of 1941 began to lay down. ... It was a radical break with anything that had been painted since the days of the Heidelberg School.'[28]

Another innovative feature of Drysdale's desert paintings is his monochromatic palette. Eschewing the brilliant blue skies reproduced by many painters of the inland he opted instead for brown, red–brown, yellow or even green skies, toned to the colours of rocks and earth, as in *Road with Rocks* (1949), *North Australian Landscape* (1959), *Desert Landscape* (1952) and *Emus in a Landscape* (1950) or the striking ox-blood sky of *The Walls of China, Gol-Gol* (1945) (see illustration following page 80). This gives a heightened sense of the unity of land and sky, and the imprisoning experience this can produce. Unlike Heysen who had concentrated on rock masses to provide a focus, Drysdale confronted head-on the technical problems of representing flatness, emptiness and an elevated sky. His method was to import trees and people, most of them exaggeratedly tall and thin, apparently devised to connect land and sky together like the uprights of some flimsy shelter.

Repugnant at first to a public (and critics)[29] unprepared for them, Drysdale's misshapen, anorexic forms of pioneer settlers or solid women with legs like gateposts, survivors of the worst the land has to offer, were later embraced with a kind of affection as depictions of the Aussie Battler. Certainly life is war in Drysdale's desert outback. His figures inhabit a battle-scarred landscape disfigured by heaps of debris, both natural (dead trees) and unnatural (the rubbish of settlement and derelict buildings). They stand as exemplars of evolutionary struggle, surviving, but barely, in a world of natural selection. Art critic James Gleeson affirmed that 'Drysdale ... saw the desert in a more sombre light [than Nolan]. For him it represents a testing ground for man's eternal duel with nature. But Drysdale never doubted that man would win. His faith endows the protagonist with enormous dignity. He may seem to be defeated by drought or loneliness or neglect, yet his spirit is not broken.'[30]

In Drysdale's early paintings the limbs of the figures seem, in an implicit parody of materialism, to double as furniture, pointing to the essential absences of the desert. In *Man Reading a Newspaper* (1941) a gaunt stick figure in singlet and trousers perches on a tree stump, his thighs and lower legs at sharp right angles like the seat and legs of an absent chair, implying the lack of that most basic facility. Another (dead) tree doubles as a clothes rack, as the man's coat, suspended from a branch, suggests a hanged body. Balancing the figure on the other side of the painting is a heap of bent sheets of corrugated iron, possibly the remains of a tin shed that has been blown to rest against the dead trees. The barren ground is littered with farm rubbish, receding past a clump of dead and felled tree stumps to the iron lattice of a windmill tower, the tallest 'tree' in sight. Yet the man is not dejected. Unperturbed by his minimal surroundings, he reads his paper with great concentration. To city viewers, especially Europeans, his predicament, like that of most Drysdale figures, represented ultimate existential loneliness, but Drysdale consistently denied this: 'those people who *do* know, that have been into the back country, there is no loneliness for them at all.'[31]

In *Man Feeding his Dogs* (1941) (see illustration following page 80) the two men and their three dogs are all equally emaciated, scarcely more than stick figures with their limbs projecting at sharp angles. The land they inhabit is bare, flat desert on which the dead tree trunks stand stiffly balanced as though rootless. A broken wheel from a farm cart leans against one tree, while a spindly Austrian chair hangs suspended from the side branch of another tree in the middle distance, suggesting that it was deposited there by a past flood. But the mood of the painting is far from hopeless. There is a strong sense of life, even of sophisticated wit and humour. The elegant greyhound dogs leap joyfully forward to greet the man bringing their food; the distant figure leaning against a tree watches with interest in this major event of the day, as though material deprivation has emphasised the importance of these relationships. Similarly, in *Going to the Pictures* (1941) the potential pathos of the outback family dressed in its best clothes waiting to depart in a derelict car to some unimaginable cinema in the middle of nowhere is subverted by the jaunty attitude of the woman with her flowered hat, handbag and high-heeled shoes, the youth in short trousers leaning in exaggerated patience on the mudguard, and the man in unaccustomed suit and tie carrying an incongruous watering can across the totally barren earth. Drysdale dares us to pity these people, at home in their desert.

169

While these landscapes are not intrinsically alien they are often appallingly disfigured by the discarded rubbish of unsuccessful settlers now departed. Junk iron, a recurrent feature of the paintings of this period, broken windmills, discarded pipes and tins, and derelict houses proclaim the abuse of the land. Yet Drysdale's condemnation is leavened with humour. In *Emus in a Landscape* (1950) (see illustration following page 112) the outlines of the birds in the middle distance are reflected in the curved shapes of the assortment of junk iron piled up in the foreground. Equally, Drysdale suggests the fragility of the land, even in combination with strong shapes and colours. *Desert Landscape* (1952) (see illustration following page 112) with its clear-cut blocks of colour in the piles of rocks in a bare landscape could be merely a stylised Modernist painting but the precarious poising of the rock at the top of the pyramid on the right symbolises the fragile balance of nature here in this harsh, almost surreal environment. The trees, too, if not actually uprooted and thrown to the ground, appear to balance on the surface, ready to be overturned by a passing wind.

It was Drysdale who first incorporated Aboriginal figures into desert land-scapes. The paintings that resulted from his journey to Cape York in 1951 are rich in such figures, sometimes active (*Boy With Lizard*, 1955; *Basketball at Broome*, 1958) but more frequently grouped stiffly in the centre foreground as though posing for the camera – as, indeed, they were.[32] The combination of suggested passivity, expressed in the drooping shoulders and unrelieved immo-bility of the figures, and the anxiety derived from the oblique gaze which emphasises the whites of the eyes has been interpreted as a statement of the hopelessness of their state. The stiff poses of the hatted figures, accentuated by the constricting, Western-style clothes from which black legs and square, flat, bare feet emerge, suggest a pun: a civilisation imposed from the head down, but never quite successfully. In the politicised climate of today, it is hard not to see in *Station Blacks, Mullaloonah Tank* , *Young Man, Mother and Child*, and *Young Station Boys* (all 1953) figures of dispossession, accusing their white observers, but the similarity of their quiescent attitude to that of Drysdale's white outback settlers suggests that we should rather read them as respected survivors, inte-grated into, even extensions of, this harsh landscape.

In 1956 Drysdale, accompanied by his wife and children, drove a battered car across Northern Australia from Pioneer in Queensland to Perth before heading east again across the Nullarbor Plain to the Flinders Ranges and thence to Adelaide. This immensely long journey through the most arid areas of the continent had a profound effect on Drysdale. The sense of space and the mutu-ally respectful encounters with Aborigines, as well as the freedom of attitudes in the outback compared with the stiff proprieties of the cities, changed his evalu-ation of the desert and of those who lived there. The paintings of Aborigines produced from this journey are strikingly different from the earlier ones. They are more assertive, more integrated with the landscape, reclaiming their land and its traditions. As visual evidence of this union, they are frequently painted in the striking, deep-red tones of the desert itself, as in *The Red Shirt, The Rainmaker, The Puckamanni, Red Landscape*, and *Native Dogger at Mt Olga* (all 1958), and *Man in a Landscape* and *Ceremony at the Rockface* (both 1963).

Although the sense of immensity that strikes all serious desert travellers is clearly present in these paintings, it is tempered by a parodic reversal of expec-tation that was to become more pronounced in the desert paintings of Sidney Nolan and Arthur Boyd. Juxtaposition of incongruous objects, personification of the inanimate and reversal of scale all suggest the liberation of the artist from urban conventions to display quirky details against the backdrop of infini-tude. So in *Native Dogger at Mount Olga* (1958) the Aborigine and one of the camels are fused into a single, two-headed entity, mimicked by the two-headed grass stalks in the foreground. But the disparity between the camel's arrogant stance and the man's enigmatic expression, somewhere between bewilderment and humour, subvert the enforced comparison of indigenes with exotics. In the far distance the Olgas (Kata Tjuta) have shrunk to a row of insignificant pebbles. In *The Red Shirt* (1958) the Aboriginal figure, clad only in a red shirt and white headband, stands apparently abandoned against a vast stretch of desert and distant mountains. Yet this view is subverted by other details of the painting. The long emaciated legs beneath the shirt and the elongated fingers of the hands, one hanging down, one slightly crooked, even the hunched shoulders, all suggest an exotic wading bird, temporarily alighted there for its own purpose. In *Man in a Landscape* (1963) Drysdale positions his Aborigine on the other side of a waist-high rock from which he seems to be growing. His red-stained white shirt is associated with the white-stained, red rocks, while his hat, with the right side of its crown hollowed in, mimics the shape of the monolith behind him, with its declivity on the right side. He stares back at us, with intense eyes, as though looking into the far distant space and time, past and future, before the white men came, after they leave.

These paintings of Aboriginal figures never achieved the popularity of Drysdale's earlier works. After initial abhorrence and embarrassment that Australians should be depicted as ugly figures in a hostile land, the public came to accept Drysdale's stocky *Drover's Wife* (1945) and similar paintings. But prevailing attitudes that still confidently expected the imminent extinction of the indigenous peoples could not accommodate these portraits of self-assured, even mocking Aborigines. Possibly these works may yet receive delayed recognition in a changed political climate.

MOLVIG   171

Jon Molvig's desert landscapes were the first to suggest a benign and nurturing desert rather than a harsh and hostile terrain. In this sense they represent a Western counterpart of the Aboriginal belief in a sustaining land. This is not an accidental parallel. In 1958 Molvig travelled for four months in Central Australia in an attempt to give concrete expression to the attraction that Aboriginal symbols of the land and its antiquity had already exerted on him theoretically.[33] As well as this transcription of a spiritual relationship Molvig was also intensely interested in the physical forces that shape the land. In *Centralian Landscape No. I* (1958) Uluru 'looms up like a fossilized tidal wave over their tent',[34] sculpted by rain, wind and abrasion into peaks and troughs similar to the dips and rises of the tent. Yet this power of nature suggests protection rather than alienation. The rising moon emerges from a hole in the Rock itself, leaving behind in the declivity, as on the tent, the white glitter of moonlight. A crow and a goanna are part of this magic realist scene. A full appreciation of this symbolic sculpting is best seen in *Untitled Portrait: Sleeping Aboriginal Woman and Child* (1958) (see illustration following page 112) where the orange–pink dresses of a sleeping Aboriginal girl and her mother are raised into peaks and declivities that, enhanced by their colour, suggest strong parallels with the shape of Uluru and indicate both its protective function in guarding them as they sleep and the integration of the Aboriginal people into the landscape.

The aerial perspective

To the nineteenth-century explorers the desert constituted a barrier: if not a threat to survival, it presented a scene of endless drudgery, such as that expressed so vividly in S.T. Gill's picture *Chaining over the Sand Dunes to Lake Torrens*, discussed in Chapter 5. When four-wheel-drive vehicles made the Centre of Australia more accessible to individuals, artists were able to experience the diversity of the desert; but their perspective was not significantly altered. The radical change came with air travel, which liberated artists from the need to toil over vast distances and from concerns about subsistence, while allowing them to see at a glance the immensity and the physiognomy of the landscape. Yet this experience of being distanced, both literally and emotionally from the desert, while it empowers the viewer, diminishes the artist's sense of involvement. The aerial panoramas of barrenness express, for the first time, control and conquest of the desert. Paradoxically, even as the area encompassed by the gaze expands immeasurably, the desert as environment is diminished, reduced to contours and ultimately to abstract patterns.

NOLAN

172

The first artist known to paint the Australian desert from the air was Sidney Nolan. His initial interest in the desert was sparked in 1931 when, as a student at the Prahran Technical College in Melbourne, he met two painters who had been there. Then, in the 1940s, he saw Drysdale's landscapes of the Riverina drought which, together with photographs of the outback in the magazine *Walkabout*, alerted him to the artistic potential of barren landscapes. In 1948 he set out with his wife, Cynthia, to travel from New South Wales to Adelaide, then north through the Centre to Borrooloola and Darwin and thence to Halls Creek, Derby, Broome, Geraldton and Perth and back across the Nullarbor Plain to Sydney. During this epic journey he clocked up many hours of air travel over the 'dead heart', photographing and sketching his impressions. Cynthia Nolan recorded that when they were flying low over the Musgrave Ranges out to Uluru, 'Sidney gazed with his mouth open and his tongue pushed between his teeth, as he does when painting with the greatest intensity. . . . he was both tremendously excited and repelled by the wind, desolation and phenomenal light.'[35]

For the artist the visual impact of this experience presented a logistical challenge:

> Looking straight down from the plane gave me that questioning I felt on first seeing the flat Wimmera from the back of a motor truck. . . . How to solve it I do not know as yet . . . [it is] a vision without philosophy, distortion, primitiveness, [I] should have gone in an aeroplane a long time ago.[36]

Difficult as it was to interpret on a flat surface, this different perspective enabled Nolan to capture the immensity and ancient geological structure of the land in a completely new way. In *Central Australia* (1949) (see illustration following page 112) the antique, red, craggy hills, like volcanic craters, march endlessly into the far distance, where they meet the pink flush of the sky. By reducing the sky to a narrow strip (scarcely more than one-sixth of the canvas) he increases the sense of distance and creates the illusion of gazing obliquely at the whole continent laid out as a relief map and vast enough to show the curve of the Earth's surface. Through a juxtaposition of colour and deep shadow he contrives to give a deceptive impression of detailed topography. One critic wrote perceptively in 1950 that 'These violently-crumpled mountain faces loom up and disappear on every side. The whole landscape as one travels through it has a calligraphic quality as if it were *written* in multi-coloured shapes.'[37] Nolan's medium for most of these works, fast-drying Ripolin enamel, captured the brilliance of the light in a uniquely startling and (for Nolan) satisfying way. He had once remarked, 'This is a very bright country, glittering in fact, and we might have lived in a studio in Paris or Berlin, for the amount of good it has done us.'[38]

In 1950 Nolan exhibited 47 Central Australian works which he called 'composite impressions', including the spectacular aerial perspectives of the Musgrave and MacDonnell Ranges. These paintings assert the vastness and antiquity of the land, its eroded mountains like bare bones confronting the expanse of monochromatic, brilliant sky. The public response was overwhelmingly positive. One critic tried to convey the immediacy that so struck visitors to the exhibition:

173

> When you enter the gallery the blaze of reddish-brown hits you like a ton or two of real red earth. You have to take a deep breath and sort out the subtle harmonies of colour and the superbly moulded shapes. . . . And how Sidney Nolan feels about Central Australia! He riots and revels among its fantastic landscapes in pictures which have the glow of heat in them, yet retains the bright clear light of his initial enthusiasm.[39]

And James Gleeson wrote:

> Sidney Nolan's exhibition of Central Australian landscapes . . . must be regarded as one of the most important events in the history of Australian painting . . . it may not be too fanciful to imagine that future art historians will date the birth of a predominantly Australian idiom from this exhibition. . . . He makes us feel the oppressive fascination of these stark unpeopled immensities of wind-worn rock and bitter soil. And through them all runs the central theme of grinding heat. The earth is furnace-coloured under dried-up skies.[40]

In 1966 Nolan returned to the Central Australian landscape to produce the massive seven-panel epic *Desert Storm Nos 6 and 7* (1966) (see illustration following page 112), expressing the power and unpredictability of Nature. The first four panels are filled with the light of a blue distance that seems to promise us vision, but in the last three panels a dust storm blows up, characteristically without warning, obliterating the once expansive prospect in a swirling cloud of dark red dust and flying grit. Suddenly we are no longer powerful, disinterested observers of the scene, but victims of its power. This sequence asserts the uncertainty of our attempts to conquer the desert by imposing our view upon it. More specifically, since vision is the pre-eminent sense of the artist, *Desert Storm* represents Nolan's own limitations in attempting to see and paint the scene.

Certainly the overwhelming impression of Nolan's desert landscapes is of an uninhabitable land where the powerful fury of Nature decimates anything in its path. Nolan himself called the country 'cruel ... harsh and barren beyond any other part of the habitable globe. For thousands of miles one sees nothing but red desert, the bones of a few dead animals, and occasionally the sordid remains of a street where somebody looking for gold had tried to build a township.'[41] Yet, like all Nolan's paintings, they have a characteristic detachment: they engage with an intellectual problem. He later remarked, 'I wanted to deal ironically with the cliché of the "dead heart"; I wanted to know the true nature of the "otherness" I had been born into ... I wanted to paint the great purity and implacability of the landscape.'[42] Far from being devastated by what he saw, Nolan viewed even drought with an objective, witty gaze. For him it was an intellectual and aesthetic game and he recorded it dispassionately, delighting in the forms, shapes, colours and ideas it suggests. But whatever Nolan's own intentions, he more than any other artist created a new myth of the Australian landscape, linking it, like all mythographic visions, to a truth that was both individual and universal, topical and timeless, psychological and cosmic.

Later painters using the aerial perspective have distanced themselves even further from the landscape. For Fred Williams, Robert Juniper, Tim Storrier and John Coburn the desert becomes increasingly abstract, providing only pattern, colour or spiritual beliefs.

WILLIAMS

Fred Williams claimed to see all landscapes 'in terms of paint': '... all else is irrelevant. Whatever the content of it is I'm not that interested ... the landscape is just something I can hang my coat on. ... After Cubism the subject was pretty unimportant anyway.'[43] His paintings of the Australian desert are no exception. Williams first went to the Centre in 1967, on a painting trip to Tibooburra with fellow artist Clifton Pugh. He was immediately impressed, as Drysdale had been, with the sense of seeing through to the underlying structures, the bare bones, of the land: 'To see the desert is like peeling the skin off a landscape',[44] he wrote; but he also saw the desert in colours no one had seen before: 'the pure sulphur & Lilac colour of it – reminded me of Persian paintings'.[45] *Aboriginal Grave* (1969) places lines of pure bright colour – sulphur, blue, lilac – against a plain sand-coloured background to make us see their vividness. Williams had been impressed by the simplicity and non-invasiveness of Aboriginal graves near Tibooburra, where twigs were respectfully spread over the burial mounds and the lines in this painting represent those twigs in the brilliant colours that Williams saw. By the end of the visit he had come to the conclusion that 'there is something very similar running through the Australian Landscape (any landscape) so much so that I may drop the regional titles from all paintings'. All landscapes, he believed, could be regarded as a monochrome open space on which lines or dots of colour characteristic of the area were displayed in patterns, representing the surface objects, a notion that he had broached earlier in another form: 'I suppose the most "universal" picture is a map?' This idea formed the inspiration for his *Australian Landscape* series of 1969 which both suggested a debt to Aboriginal art and foreshadowed the aerial views he was to produce in the 1970s. In 1977 he was given the opportunity to visit the Comalco mining operations at Weipa in North Queensland and spent some time cruising over the area. This experience provided him with a map-maker's perspective on the grand scale. He was particularly intrigued by the similarities between the aerial perspective of, say, a river, appearing as a line, and the planar perspective of Aboriginal art. Thereafter, when painting in his studio he would characteristically place his canvas on the floor, standing over it to position the particular marks he wanted, as seen from above.

In 1979, Williams was invited by the chairman of the mining company Conzinc Riotinto of Australia Ltd (CRA), to fly low over the Pilbara in Western Australia, taking photographs and making sketches, with a view to producing paintings that CRA would purchase. Showing the skeletal framework of the land, unveiled by vegetation, his Pilbara series is dominated by the sense of colour and pattern that only an aerial view makes possible, but despite the scale involved Williams is also intent on showing the particularity of detail in shade and shape against the monochrome background. In *Trees in Landscape, Hammersley* (1979) (see illustration following page 112) the chocolate-brown land is varied not only by the bleached eucalyptus trunks and dots of colour, but by the shadings of brown from pink through mauve to black. In *Brumbies Running, the Kimberleys* (1979) the desert is immensely varied, with patches of rose, yellow, blue, green and mauve representing saltpans, scrub, and rock. The wild horses, reduced by the height of the perspective to a mere spattering of black dots, indicate the vastness of scale.

175

STORRIER

Still further removed from engagement with the desert as real-life experience is the work of Tim Storrier, an artist intrigued by the concept of space. He says:

> Of the impact of a given landscape, all that remains by the time I am ready
> to use it in my painting is the impulse that has set in motion other, as yet
> unexpressed, forms ... individual impressions of the outback lose their identity
> and fuse into a conglomerate of sensations that remain as a typically Australian
> canvas. What is permanent is the cool blueness, the detached, impersonal
> excitement of unlimited space.[46]

'Cool blueness' is certainly not often associated with the Australian desert, but Storrier's desertscapes are concerned with 'the feeling of horizon, the atmosphere, the heat haze, the utter stillness ... the sense of space and flatness and the merging of sky and horizon that one experiences in every vast terrain.' Superimposed on this timeless background arise vast enigmatic building shapes – a brick tank of water as in *Tank*, or a pyramid as in *Towards an Innuendo of Impermanence* (1977).

Storrier's fascination with space has led him to produce his aerial studies of Central Australia, not from a low-flying plane like Nolan or Williams, but from the much greater height of a jet aircraft. *An Altitude* (1977) (see illustration following page 144) depicts a remote desert land far below the clouds whose shadows fall upon it. Parallel dunes are faint lines, vegetation minute dots. In *Australian Studio* (1978) the 'stage' is the whole continent – a gridded, physical map of Australia, with feathers, bowls, cloth bags, a flower and pieces of string arranged on it. These distant perspectives represent a curious inversion of the experience of space normally associated with the desert. Whereas previous artists have sought to lose themselves in this vastness, to yield to the power of Nature that immensity symbolised, Storrier dominates it, determined to appropriate on his canvas nothing less than the whole continent to fashion and decorate as he wishes.

Yet monumentality is only one impression to which Storrier responds in the desert. His first trip to the Australian desert was in 1973, in company with John Olsen who was making his second visit to Lake Eyre. Characteristically, while Olsen focussed on bird and plant life and the shape of the lake, Storrier was transfixed by the sense of space.[47] In his work, Storrier juxtaposes space and detail. Indeed, he sees space as a stage on which to arrange a selection of isolated 'objects' such as the leaves, feathers, nuts and berries of *Still Life* (1978).

COBURN

John Coburn reduces the desert to symbols – shapes, as he prefers to call them – that are even more abstract. 'I consider myself to be a shape painter. All my work is deliberately abstract so that people can read into it whatever they like. ... I find that if I paint naturalistically then it loses its symbolic power.'[48] Although Coburn had travelled across the Nullarbor by train during World War II, it was only when he crossed it in a low-flying aircraft in 1960 and saw the abstract patterns made by saltpans that he became interested in its artistic potential. Viewed from above, the massive and imposing monoliths become merely outlines which Coburn further stylises as basic geometrical figures – circles, triangles, dumbbells, trapezia. In his *Nullarbor* (1980) (see illustration following page 144) he arranges a display of such simplified forms in black, brown and sand colour on an intense scarlet backdrop. The effect is like a flag or an altar cloth where iconic shapes carry symbolic meaning. Although more abstract than the leaf and flame motifs of his earlier work[49] these shapes

ABOVE
Lloyd Rees (Australia 1895–1988), *The MacDonnell Ranges, Last Light*, 1976, watercolour, pencil and wax crayon, 38.2 × 56.4 cm, collection National Gallery of Australia, Canberra.

BELOW
Lloyd Rees (Australia 1895–1988), *The Olgas – The Northern Aspect*, 1976, wax crayon, watercolour, pencil and charcoal, 38.2 × 56.6 cm, collection National Gallery of Australia, Canberra.

ABOVE
Scene from *Priscilla, Queen of the Desert.* Courtesy Latent Image Productions, Sydney.

BELOW
Sidney Nolan, *Burke and Wills Expedition, 1948,* ripolin on board, 91.3 × 122.2 cm, Nolan Gallery, Lanyon.

Sidney Nolan, *Burke*,
c. 1962, synthetic polymer
on hardboard, 122 × 122 cm,
Gift of Godfrey Phillips 1968,
Art Gallery of New South
Wales, Sydney.

ABOVE
David Boyd, *Burke and Wills Bed Down for the Night*, 1957–8, private collection. Courtesy the artist.

BELOW
Albert Tucker, *The Last Days of Leichhardt*, 1964, PVA on board, 120.5 × 151.0 cm, Harold Mertz Collection, University of Texas, Houston.

celebrate the beauty, purity, order and wholeness of the desert, rather than desolation and destruction.

In 1988 Coburn travelled extensively in the Northern Territory and from that experience produced a series of paintings based on the desert areas of Central Australia and the Northern Territory. The patterned shapes of *Desert Country*, like irregular stones set in a paving, betray its inspiration in desert claypans, while *Totemic Forms and Stormbird* is inspired by the termite mounds of the Territory, which Coburn compares to the installation of 200 Aboriginal coffins in the National Gallery.

Coburn is an intensely religious artist. He has explained: 'One of the things that I am trying to do in my work ... is to express the spiritual – or human spirituality – through the Australian landscape. ... I sometimes try to paint God and sometimes I just paint the earth.'[50] He finds in Aboriginal art a similar sense of spirituality:

> I think all aboriginal art is very spiritual art, but over the last ten years or more [from 1982] I have been allowing more and more things to come in from aboriginal art. ... I don't feel that I am copying it; I am simply relating to the landscape in the way that the aboriginals do and trying to keep some of the spiritual qualities that they have – that spiritual relationship to the land.

JUNIPER   177

In many of Robert Juniper's best-known paintings, such as *The River Dies in January* (see illustration following page 144) and *Lake Amadeus* (1984) and *Sons of Gwalia Painting* (1987), the aerial perspective of the desert is used to evoke a sense of great distance, detachment and scale, and to emphasise the large-scale patterns of red oxide sand, white salt lakes, grey–black shadows and meandering rivers that are apparent only from the air. But for Juniper the significance of this is radically different from the effect in a Nolan or a Storrier painting. So far from dominating the landscape, his intention is to return autonomy to the land, to create a sense not so much of *looking at* the landscape as of *being in it*, surrounded by it. The signs of human habitation are reduced to insignificance against the vast areas of background in his work: 'Vast empty space and areas of colour with only a few markers of man's passing – mere dots of interest: these are the dominant impressions I get and communicate from the Australian wilderness.'[51] Juniper identifies this with 'the Oriental technique of making the space as significant as the objects placed in it', but it is also related to his conscious recognition of Aboriginal art, especially linear styles of bark painting and the Mimi figures of the Western Central Desert, in his work.[52]

Juniper's *The River Dies in January* (1977) records the intermittent course of the Helena River which, in summer, dries up to a series of discrete iron-stained pools. However, the river bed remains like a calligraphic swirl, signifying not only the topography but 'a metaphor of human suffering and extremity. By extension it is a reminder of survival and renewal.'[53] If the river dies in January it is cyclically reborn in order to die again and thus, like Olsen's images of Lake Eyre that are discussed in Chapter 13, its dry course recalls its counterpart at other points in time – the flowing river of the past and the future. The line of the river bed therefore suggests a journey in time as well as space. Many other Juniper paintings, such as *Lake Amadeus* (1984), *The Grave of Henry Birdsong* (1985), *Sons of Gwalia Painting* (1987) and *The Guardians* (1989), represent a similar map through time, with accretions of events and memories from the Dreaming to the present. To this end he also collects objects left behind by previous generations and incorporates them in his paintings as a way of inscribing human history and indicating the transience of that history relative to the landscape. Juniper believes that, in these compositions, he has 'mapped the growth of white consciousness. These paintings are potent icons of identity and belonging rather than of possession . . . internalised maps of the mind, song-lines for all Australians.'

The Old Ones of Kunturu (1990) and *The Silent Rocks of Kunturu* (1990) present, in effect, palimpsest maps. At one level they record the geological facts about Lake Moore (Kunturu), a dry salt lake 380 kilometres north-east of Perth, with a serpentine arrangement of rock slabs fifty metres out from the shore, some standing, some fallen. At another level they recall the Aboriginal beliefs about Kunturu, a sacred site. 'Landscape, history and myth coalesce into a single form and achieve a unity that makes art of real substance . . . landscape is memory.' In this sense Juniper's art is intended to express the increasing awareness apparent in modern literature that 'the landscape image is inseparable from Aboriginal life and culture and its artistic and mythological representations of the landscape.'

178

The desert as allegory: Arthur Boyd

Whereas Drysdale peopled his desert with emaciated depictions of actual people, and Nolan turned to Australian history for legendary heroes, the inhabitants of Arthur Boyd's deserts are powerful Blakean figures suggestive of an obscure mythology, denizens of a Freudian or Jungian subconscious. In such company the desert setting ceases to be a geographical location and assumes a wholly symbolic function.

Some of the most striking Australian paintings of the 1970s are Boyd's complex allegorical paintings set in a desert landscape: *Paintings in the Studio: 'Figure supporting Back Legs' and 'Interior with Black Rabbit'* (1973) (see illustration following page 144), *Chained Figure and Bent Tree* (1973), *Kneeling Figure with Canvas and Black Can* (1972), *Reflected Figure and Cave* (1976) and *Orange Tree, Book and Bound Figure* (1979) (see illustration following page 144). In each of these the artist himself is depicted in some form of bondage. Whereas in traditional religious imagery the aspiring saint or hermit underwent temptation in the wilderness–desert to purify his soul and develop holiness, for Boyd the saint has been replaced by the aspiring artist, naked in the desert–wilderness, tempted by fame, wealth and ideology which threaten to paralyse him and stifle his artistic creativity.

In *Paintings . . .*, a large canvas measuring 314.2 by 433.7 centimetres, two 'pictures' hang on a charcoal grey background. The smaller of the two, a landscape of gaunt trees growing in sheer sand and almost blinding sunshine, is covered, frame and all, with wire netting. In the larger one, the artist, suspended by the legs (the paralysed wheelbarrow figure recurrent in Boyd's work)[54] is held prisoner by some female demon, whose head and supporting hand are the only features visible. On the ground before the figure lies the canvas on which he tries to paint with three inverted (and hence inactive) paint brushes clutched uselessly in his left hand, while his right hand (suggesting his priority) protects a heap of gold coins: enslaved by the lure of money, he is unable to paint and has turned his back on the natural landscape, the only source of light in the painting. One leg protrudes from the canvas as though he is vainly attempting to escape from his picture. The 'Interior' in the title is ambiguous: it includes reference to the assumed dark 'room' in which the two paintings are hung; it also plays on the connotations of interior/exterior, referring to the framed 'outside' scene of the desert, the Interior of the continent; and it is a cue to read the whole as a *paysage intérieur*, a landscape of the mind.[55]

Chained Figure and Bent Tree depicts the artist bending over to paint but his head is enclosed in a tight metal cage (ideology) which is chained to the tree behind him. Again, the scene is the blinding white desert with the deep blue sky of Central Australia. Similarly, *Kneeling Figure with Canvas and Black Can* locates the artist, in a glittering white desert where stumps of dead or dying trees emphasise the extreme desolation. On his knees before his canvas, the naked artist is held prisoner by a muzzled black dog that mounts him, and again his brushes are inverted.

In *Reflected Figure and Cave* the artist figure, again suspended wheelbarrow-like, this time by a female figure within a cave, gazes narcissistically at his reflection in a pool of water.[56] The gold coins lie on the ground beneath him and a crow flies overhead. Similar dead trees grow out of the blinding white sand around the cave for, despite the pool of clear water, the landscape is still a barren desert. *Orange Tree, Book and Bound Figure* presents yet another white desert landscape in which a chained figure stands with its hands behind it bound to the upright pole of a gallows. In the foreground a stylised, improbably fruiting orange tree grows in the white sand and under it lies an open book on which the bearded head of a man is drawn.

The role of the desert in these allegorical pictures is problematic. Possibly signifying the barren materialist society, inimical to the individual naked artist who is variously imprisoned, incapacitated and impeded from his art, it may equally well symbolise the true milieu of the ascetic artist, where the illumination of nature floods the scene with light.

Immensity and detail

Two other innovative approaches to depicting the desert are apparent in the very different styles and techniques of Lloyd Rees and Jörg Schmeisser.

REES

Unlike most of the other artists so far considered, who journeyed into Central Australia relatively early in their careers or who, like Albert Tucker, painted it before actually going there, Lloyd Rees was already a veteran landscape artist aged 81 when he first visited the Centre in 1976. It is therefore less surprising that, although he, too, was deeply moved by Kata Tjuta and Uluru, and particularly the sense of space and immensity, these impressions were subsumed *within* his aesthetic signature rather than determining it. He looked for, and found, not the brilliant reds and oranges and the sharp outlines that had so impressed themselves on Drysdale and Nolan but the opalescent shimmering effects of light at the interface of rock and sky.[57] He therefore stressed the similarities of Central Australia with the Romantic atmosphere of other places he had painted – Tasmania, Italy, and especially Chartres Cathedral which he had visited shortly before. He has said:

180

> In a strange way my feelings during that initial encounter with the Centre were similar and closely linked to the spiritual impressions I received in the great church. An abiding sense of infinity governs both places, despite the difference in scale. Both are enfolded by aspiring vaults, the one constructed of masonry, the other a canopy of sky.'[58]

Pastel colours of pink, blue and pale green are not the palette generally associated with the desert, but in Rees's paintings it is the shadows and the sky that predominate and determine the texture, rounding the rocks to the softness of human forms very different from the sharply defined geometrical shapes that had struck the other artists. His vision of Uluru and Kata Tjuta is thus more mysterious, closer to the religious presence that these places exert for Aboriginal people. *The MacDonnell Ranges, Last Light* (1976) (see illustration following page 176), with its ink-blue sky, orange clouds and the gold and purple light and shadow on the sheer walls of the mountains, recalls the colours and mood of Van Gogh's *Starry Night*. On the other hand, *The Olgas – The Northern Aspect* (1976) (see illlustration following page 176) emphasises the shapes and the familial community of the rocks. Details are irrelevant; ambience is everything.

SCHMEISSER

Intaglio printing, with its emphasis on minute detail, would seem to be the artistic approach least compatible with the seemingly featureless immensity of the desert, but artist and printmaker Jörg Schmeisser, who studied in Germany and Japan before establishing the Printmaking Workshop at the Canberra School of Art, challenges this view. As one whose travels have included working as draughtsman on an archaeological dig in Haifa, Schmeisser brings to his perception of the desert a particular feeling for the 'small things gathered by the wayside', as a way to record the vast. Such a method recalls the philosophy of the German Romantics, whose emphasis on fragments as the only possible way to experience the world was nevertheless based on a premise of underlying unity and a faith that concentration on any part of the universe would reveal a cross-section of its meaning.

Schmeisser seeks to record a total experience of places, objects and emotions, rather than just an outward view of things arranged according to rules of composition and his prints therefore encompass a variety of perspectives,

Jörg Schmeisser, *Diary and Ayer's Rock/Uluru*, 1979, colour etching, 48.0×61.0 cm. Courtesy the artist.

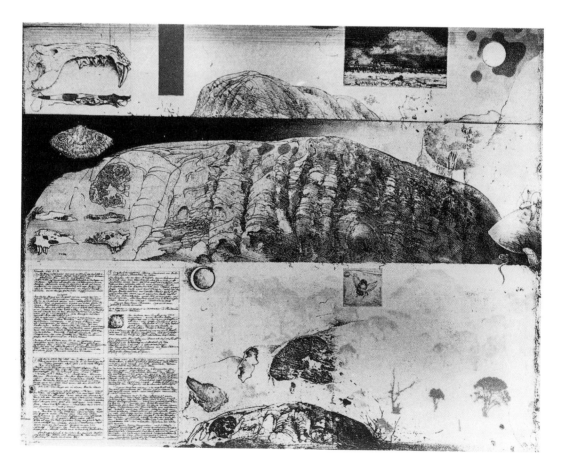

scales, textures and images. *Diary and Ayers Rock/Uluru* (1979) includes four images of Uluru from different elevations and with different degrees of surface detail, silhouettes of trees, careful line drawings of animal skulls found in the region, sketches of boulders, pages from Schmeisser's own diary and detailed studies of insects from the area. He is also fascinated with the possibilities of depicting time as the fourth dimension of an object (as many traditional Aboriginal paintings do)[59] by recording the changes in that object, either through a series of etchings or by superimposed printings and paintings.

Schmeisser says of the desert, 'It is a land of such powerful extremes and great degradation – [from] drought, fires, and heat, to floods and wind erosion. Mostly I wanted to capture its texture, but found it difficult.'[60] Only when he developed new techniques of printmaking was he able to achieve this effect. In 1994 he travelled to Purnululu National Park, the Bungle Bungles, in the Kimberley region of Western Australia, and the series of prints he produced as a result of this experience were made using perspex plates, engraved with a precision power tool originally designed for a dentist's drill to achieve the delicate lines and fine dots he needed. 'You can get a far wider range of colours and different textures using this plastic printing technique,' he has said. 'I think of them more like paintings in print.' *From Kununurra to the Kimberleys*, *Purnululu* and *Purnululu Range* (all 1995) are three very large works composed of individually printed but pictorially continuous squares, a technique also favoured by John Wolseley whose work will be considered in Chapter 13. The works incorporate aerial mapping, close-ups of rock faces, details of texture, and meticulous natural-history drawings, yet they cohere in an organic unity which tells us more about the land and the way we truly experience it than a formally composed 'view'. Critic Merryn Gates writes:

182

> Confronted with the vastness of the Western Australian desert, Jörg Schmeisser has asked new questions from the technique and has given the tools new roles to play. The lines on the plate act as a metaphor for the surface of the rocks they shape, the etched marks forming a parallel to the weathered rough surface of the landscape, pocked and worked on by rain and wind. Where the depressions in the plate hold ink, the rock collects dust and water. They are a profound morphological response to the landscape.[61]

The problem the desert had posed for nineteenth-century landscape artists – how to convey its immensity and monotony as well as its fascination – remained a challenge for all of the artists discussed in this chapter, each of whom evolved a different solution. To achieve the simultaneous perspective of vast space and close detail they increasingly dispensed with the traditional formulae of European landscape art and the obsession with presenting a vertical slice of sky and land arranged according to accepted principles of perspective. Their liberation from this mindset dates from a 1950s technological breakthrough: affordable aeroplane travel. With this innovation came the opportunity to encompass the experience of immensity while being allowed to select the details from a vast range of country, rather than relying on finding those features in conjunction. Although the details for inclusion are selected very differently, the aerial perspective has produced astonishing similarities to the conventions of Aboriginal art discussed in Chapter 1: looking down into the land to discover what is there, rather than requiring the land to display itself according to pre-determined conventions.

183

A Gothic Desert

Chapter 10

> Our fear of the wilderness in ourselves matches its counterpart, the
> wilderness without.
>
> WILLIAM FAULKNER[1]

> Just as the heart of the continent is a burning, insane emptiness, so too
> at the heart of a man is the horror of his prehistory.
>
> HARRY HESELTINE[2]

> Perhaps true knowledge only comes of death by torture in the country
> of the mind.
>
> PATRICK WHITE[3]

Traditionally associated with gratuitous cruelty, with superstition and with claustrophobic imprisonment in some ancestral house, the term *Gothic* seems, on the face of it, to bear no relation to the desert. Yet there are subtle but insistent parallels, suggested even in the journals of Eyre and Sturt. And these have been powerfully exploited by some twentieth-century writers to provide an appropriately intense setting for modern psychodramas in which the desert functions as a mindscape of the horror within. In his introduction to *The Oxford Book of Gothic Tales*, Chris Baldick cites, as necessary components of Gothic, 'a fearful sense of inheritance in time with a claustrophobic sense of enclosure in space, these two dimensions reinforcing each other to produce an impression of sickening descent into disintegration'.[4]

The desert provides just such a synaesthetic experience when the visual perception of spatial immensity is superimposed on the sense of a changeless land. Isolation through distance is no less absolute or terrifying than imprisonment by walls; the unassailable natural powers of heat, thirst and desolation are no less despotic than those of the aristocratic villain; the arbitrary terrors of the Gothic are given physical form in the violent and unpredictable sandstorms that can obliterate all geographical markers in a few minutes; the apparition of ghostly forms is parodied in the phenomenon of the mirage, while a more subtle sense of the supernatural is supplied by the eeriness, silence and loneliness experienced in the desert. A post-Freudian reading of the Gothic as a trope for the suppressed fears imprisoned in the dark atavistic house of the subconscious is equally readily transferred to accounts of the desert. Its indeterminate space of darkness and nothingness points to the culturally repressed dread of alienation and the more extreme metaphysical terror of erasure of the individual through death. David Spurr points out that, in Joseph Conrad's *Heart of Darkness*,

> the name of Africa [is] everywhere displaced by the ambiguous and
> portentous phrase which serves as the title of the text. By means of this
> displacement of the referent, Africa is no longer bound in time and space, but
> becomes the figure of darkness and nothingness. This figure serves at least two
> functions: it transfers historical and geographical space onto metaphysical
> ground while, working from the other side, it transforms nothingness into
> the substantial unity of time and space embodied in narrative form.[5]

The Australian desert, rarely identified with any particular area but instead referred to generically as 'the desert', serves a similar function. Through loss of its specific geographical identity it takes on a wider significance as the epitome of absence, of the metaphysical void.

From the early decades of this century Australian novelists have evolved an extended role for the desert as fictional setting, psychological symbol and metaphysical signifier. In its capacity as setting, the desert may either function as adversary or provide opportunities for violence against the innocent; in its symbolic role, it draws to the surface the subconscious dread of a void within. In traditional Gothic the imprisoning ancestral house was a readily decoded feminist symbol for patriarchal tyranny; in the case of the desert, however, an interesting gender inversion is involved since the individuals trapped in the desert have been almost exclusively male while the land is most commonly troped as female. Yet there are numerous variations on the traditional stereotype of the imprisoned heroine. Against the power of the desert, males, too, may be disempowered; or the villains may be not the land but evil men who are, in turn, punished by the desert; or, very rarely, the female protagonists may emerge victorious.

Victors and victims: white guilt

Feminist critic Kay Schaffer has argued persuasively that 'Australian women have written about the land in fiction in ways which ... challenge man's assumption of mastery over the land ... [They] perceive a different relationship of the male to the earth as opposed to the female to the earth. That relationship, however, remains encased within a masculine order of sameness.'[6] Nevertheless, for two important women novelists writing about the desert in the 1920s, Katharine Susannah Prichard and Catherine Martin, the gender

185

issue is also intimately associated with race and while Schaffer's argument holds well for Prichard's *Coonardoo* (1929), where the elements of race and gender reinforce each other, it is less valid for Martin's remarkable novel, *The Incredible Journey* (1923).

Writing in conscious rebuttal of the derogatory notions about Aborigines that were current in the 1920s,[7] Martin uses the ordeal of a journey across three hundred kilometres of red sand desert to affirm the heroism and resourcefulness of two Aboriginal women and, implicitly, their superiority to the European explorers. In contrast to the main body of nineteenth-century writing about the desert, and even to most of the literature discussed in the present chapter, the enemy in *The Incredible Journey* is not the land but evil men, both white and black. Iliapo and her friend Polde cross the desert to recover Iliapo's son, Alibaka, who has been kidnapped by a white man to work on a distant station. As constructed by Martin the desert functions both as a complex entity in its own right, harsh and beautiful, and as an index of the characters' moral strength. The two women are able to endure because of their determination as well as their intimate knowledge of the land. From their own experience they successfully reason where to find water and where to dig a soak hole to collect water overnight. Accepting the land's conditions they rest during the heat of the day and travel in the early morning and at night. Adept at catching a variety of foods and finding materials for their fire, they also, even in the midst of danger and difficulty, delight in the beauty of the land. Despite a disorienting sandstorm that completely changes the contours of the land, and bewildering mirages, they retain their optimism and determination to recover the boy.

Unlike her predecessors, Martin describes the desert here, as in her earlier desert novel *The Silent Sea* (1892), with intimate knowledge of its variability and appreciation of its beauty, and she insists that this beauty coexists with the rigours of the land. As Iliapo's son reflects on the women's journey he marvels that his mother and Polde have survived such a journey 'over such burning sand, such waste tracts of country, such waterless stretches, in which there were no beasts or birds for food.' *The Incredible Journey* was unique in presenting Aboriginal women as assertive and triumphant, and even more remarkable in its emphasis on the land as active partner with the women. It is the white man who is defeated. Martin's novel was also noteworthy for its sympathetic portrayal of Aboriginal women without any suggestion of authorial guilt for the treatment of them meted out by white settlers.

Written in the same decade as Martin's novel, Prichard's *Coonardoo* offers a picture of the desert that is closer to the essentialist, gendered model identified by Shaffer since, however regretfully, Prichard shows the inevitable domination and destruction of a land that is imaged as female. Although this novel has been read most often in terms of its frank discussion of interracial sexual relations, it also offers an early attempt to explore race relations in terms of responses to the land, to argue for their complementarity, and to give an emic[8] view of Aboriginal beliefs, rather than denigrate them as the foolish ignorance of the black 'other'.[9]

In *Coonardoo*, Hugh Watt, heir of Wytaliba, a cattle station in north-west Western Australia, represents a paternalistic attitude to the land: it is property for which he is responsible, as his widowed mother, Mrs Bessie, was before him. Significantly the Aborigines call her 'Mumae', a word that mimics the child's term 'mummy' but in their language means 'father'. For her, being account-able for the land means negating the natural desert, honeycombing the station with wells and planting a garden with neat rows of vegetables. For Hugh, car-ing for the land means preserving the material prosperity of the family prop-erty (the very word *property* proclaims the fundamental notion of ownership) and caring for the well-being of the Aboriginal workers as an act of benevo-lence that is not without self-interest. 'Generous, kindly their relationship had been, in an overlordship imposed gradually, imperceptibly, until the blacks rec-ognized and accepted it, by conditions of work for food and clothing.'[10] The relationship is one of suzerainty acknowledged by both parties, endorsing the colonialist position of superiority in wealth, education, power and morality.[11]

Coonardoo, an Aboriginal girl of Hugh's own age, represents both the cultural 'other' and the gender 'other', the doubly marginalised. Prichard, however, elevates and dignifies her protagonist through her traditional associ-ation with the land. Her name means 'well in the shadows', and symbolically she represents the spirit of the place, a concept associated with mystical and ceremonial components. Coonardoo enters and leaves the novel singing a song about kangaroos in her Aboriginal language, as inaccessible to the white characters as their complexities of language are to her. Mrs Bessie 'had once come on a half-circle of men squatted before a little girl, and singing to her breast. They looked as if they were worshipping her, squatted there on the wide plains under the bare blue sky. And they were, in their own way, she imagined, venerating the principle of creation, fertility, growth in her.' Coonardoo is cul-turally bound to an association between human fertility and that of the land, and her sexual needs are described in terms of the land. Although repulsed by a white womaniser, Sam Geary, 'she could not resist him. Her need of him was as great as the dry earth's for rain.' Reflecting on the morality of sexual repres-sion taught at school and its inappropriateness in such a barren landscape, Hugh concludes: 'here in a country of endless horizons, limitless sky shells, to live within yourself was to decompose internally. You had to keep in the life flow of the country to survive. . . . How could a man stand still, sterilize himself in a land where drought and sterility were hell?' He sees Coonardoo as 'a force . . . silent and absolute. Something primitive, fundamental, nearer than he to the source of things: the well in the shadows'.

However instinctive these responses may be, they are not proof against the views of white society. Hugh succumbs to the paternalistic view that categorises children, indigenes, animals and the land together as objects for which the white man's burden makes him responsible, not as an equal but as master. Culturally indoctrinated with this role, Hugh is unable either to accept Coonardoo as an equal or to enter into a spiritual relationship with the land. When drought hits Wytaliba the station is returned to desert.

> On the horizon mirages blotted out trunks of the trees. Smooth polished stones, black and red, lying over the plains, shone with the light of dull metal.
>
> The air, at a little distance, palpitated, thrown off from the stones in minute atoms, visible one moment, flown to invisibility the next . . . The sun, an incandescence somewhere above and beyond the earth, moved electric, annihilating. And stillness, a breathless heaviness, drowsed the senses, brain and body, as if that mythological great snake the blacks believed in, a rock python . . . sliding down from the hills of the sky, were putting the opiate of his breath into the air, folding you round and round, squeezing the life out of you.

When Coonardoo is driven from Wytaliba, the property degrades further. Chitarli, an Aboriginal 'mystic', explains:

> A curse was on the place since Coonardoo had gone. . . . Coonardoo's spirit had withered and died when she went away from Wytaliba . . . And that withering and dying of Coonardoo's spirit had caused a blight on the place. She had loved Wytaliba and been bound up with the source of its life. Was she not the well in the shadow? Had she not some mysterious affinity with that ancestral female spirit which was responsible for fertility, generation, the growth of everything?

Coonardoo is here associated with Hugh's *anima* principle, as Jungian soul-image.[12]

In its sympathetic representation of an Aboriginal concept of the land *Coonardoo* was revolutionary, but it probably did little to change ingrained attitudes. The identification of Coonardoo with the land would not have surprised Prichard's readers. Western society has invariably modelled its notion of 'civilisation' on its own practices, while regarding those farthest removed from itself culturally as most primitive, and hence closer to Nature. Even Chitarli's identification of Coonardoo as a timeless spiritual principle serves to 'other' her yet further, without in any sense diminishing the assumption of white superiority. The settlers can never really accept the Aboriginal idea of the land as indwelt by a spiritual presence and drought years are interpreted in fatalistic terms rather than as emanating from human relational deficiencies. Indeed, despite Prichard's condemnation of Hugh, *Coonardoo* remains firmly set in the tradition where Aborigines were depicted as a dying race, a regrettable outcome, perhaps, but a Darwinian necessity attested to by biologists and anthropologists. By implication the desert, the land pre-eminently associated with the Aborigines, must inevitably give way before the technological improvements of the settler culture.

The 1955 film *Jedda* revisited this theme of the Aboriginal girl, this time brought up wholly in a white society and thereby alienated from her own culture. Adopted at birth by a white woman whose own baby has died, and forbidden to have contact with her own people, Jedda is nevertheless instantly attracted to a young Aborigine, Marbuk, who comes to the remote cattle station looking for work. He abducts her, half-willing, half-terrified, and takes her across the desert to his tribal lands where he is punished for violating the tribe's marriage taboos. Finally, hunted by avenging parties from both Jedda's station and Marbuk's tribe, the lovers fall from a cliff to their death. The film was remarkable in its time for its frank discussion of a highly topical issue – the best future for Aborigines brought up by whites, the 'stolen generation' as they are now referred to – but perhaps more for its presentation of the Central Australian landscape. Charles Chauvel, the producer, claimed to have chosen the film's location even before he had a story to 'match the magnificent backgrounds'.[13] For the first time Standley Chasm and Ormiston Gorge burst upon the screen in full colour, astounding audiences with their brilliance. The immensity and grandeur of these scenes dignified the passion and tragedy of Jedda and Marbuk beyond what a script could achieve, presenting the social problem of assimilation (which by 1951 had become the official government policy in regard to Aborigines) as intimately associated with the land itself.

Another view of Aboriginal status and well-being was presented by the 1967 film *Journey out of Darkness*, set in the Central Australia of 1901. Like the very early film *Moondyne*, it developed the idea of an alliance between an Arunta man who is to be arrested for performing a ritual killing, and the white trooper who crosses the desert to apprehend him. On the return journey it is the trooper who learns from his prisoner how to survive in the desert. These films presented a new view of Aboriginal people as handsome and heroic in Western terms, and simultaneously dignified the Western Desert, their home.　189

The trend was continued in the 1971 film *Walkabout* (not connected with the 1958 film of the same name), with its Romantic approach to the desert and to Aborigines as the noble representatives of its ethos. Throughout there is a stark contrast between the pressures and hypocrisy of the city, which drives people to insanity and despair, and the desert, which affirms life, love and naturalness. The film opens with a deranged father taking his two children into the desert with intent to murder them and then kill himself. Wandering off, the children are saved from death a second time by a young Aboriginal boy on a solitary walkabout as part of his initiation. He falls in love with the fourteen-year-old girl and as they approach white civilisation, he dances a courtship dance for her. Because of her white upbringing she is culturally unable to respond to such overtures, and the Aboriginal youth hangs himself in despair. The girl and her brother find their way back to a mining settlement where they are less than welcome, and eventually she returns to the city and marries, but she remains haunted by memories of a different kind of relationship. The journey through the desert is presented in almost mythic images, emphasised by the brilliant colours and endemic fauna. Film historian Neil Rattigan argues that '*Walkabout* displays a far greater obsession with the Australian landscape than any [other] Australian film. ... The landscape is more than a character, more than a visual expression of the film's themes; the landscape *is* the film. Its brooding presence – beautiful, awesome, changing, and ancient – dominates the film to the extent that the narrative (such as it is) and themes are swamped by it.'[14] Here, as in *Coonardoo*, the desert functions symbolically, representing the land before European settlement which, it is implied, has tarnished all that was natural and prevented its people from accessing their spontaneous emotions.

Olaf Ruhen's first novel *Naked Under Capricorn* (1958), set in Central Australia during the first half of the twentieth century, offers an early post-colonial interpretation of the history of race relations between Aborigines and Europeans in the latter's encroachment into the central desert. Tracing the working life of Davis Marriner, from his destitute youth, having been robbed and left naked in the desert, to his emergence as a wealthy cattle king with subsidiary income from mining, Ruhen narrates the history of colonialism in Australia. Initially unable to survive in the land, Marriner is taught self-preservation skills by members of the Eiliuwarra tribe and for this he is grateful and well disposed towards them, entering into a seemingly permanent relationship with one of the girls; but the liaison is always on his terms. Symbolically re-naming the Aborigines with English names, he monopolises their time and energies, diverting them from their traditional lifestyle to undertake cattle droving. His well-intentioned acceptance of Aboriginal culture does not extend to protecting 'his people' against the ravages of other drovers and settlers who rape and kill as of right. Nor does it prevent his re-enacting the appropriation of the continent as *terra nullius*. Already wealthy as a result of his droving ventures along the desert route from western Queensland to South Australia, Marriner is encouraged by his trading associates in Adelaide to file a claim to hundreds of hectares of Eiliuwarra land rich in gold and wolfram (tungsten) deposits. He thereby condemns these once self-sufficient hunter–gatherers to a future of dependence on Western food, clothes and alcohol, and hence to poverty, debt, and social and physical degradation. Marriner is lured into marriage with an Adelaide girl and when she subsequently evicts the indigenous people on his estate from their traditional land, he fails to protect even his own children. Instead, by adopting a habit of assumed powerlessness and denial, he embodies white Australian attitudes to a government policy that led to the removing of Aboriginal children, the 'stolen generation', from their family and traditional culture.

Eventually Marriner comes to a realisation of the enormity he has perpetrated against these people:

190

> Marriner saw vividly and for the first time the whole tragedy of the tribe. And in it he was integral. For the Eiliuwarra people had accepted him, and that was all. That was their only transgression against their laws. They had paid for his meat with their services; to his profit they had lost their land and their inheritance. He had in no way improved their lives: they paid him back their wages to buy the clothes they would not have needed had he not been there. And when he usurped their time . . . he usurped their inheritance. They had let slip the wisdom that had sustained them through the vanished ages; they had put little that was useful in its place. . . . Suddenly it was all very clear to Marriner. His was

the culpability of the bystander; but he was no less to be condemned. The man who watches the rape of the virgin is himself a monster; his culpability is no less than that of the participant.[15]

Like many white Australians, Marriner attempts to make amends, but Ruhen can envisage no return to innocence. At the end of the novel a goldfield is discovered near the traditional lands of the still-tribal Pintubi people, suggesting that they, too, will lose their heritage to the miners. Marriner's Aboriginal friend, Activity, tells him there are plenty more places, further on, where the traditional ways can be preserved, but Ruhen's conclusion clearly implies that such a hope belongs only to the Dreaming.

Like *Coonardoo*, *Naked Under Capricorn* presents a particularly bleak, even deterministic, view of colonisation. The nineteenth-century dreams of a cattle empire and mining riches are attained but fail to bring fulfilment. Aborigines and white settlers alike are the victims of some inevitable process called progress. The antagonist is not, as Marriner at first thinks, the harsh land but rather the attitudes imprinted on even benevolent white settlers: the imperative to dominate the wilderness licenses almost any acts of greed and violence.

A place of evil

In a century in which physical dangers became increasingly uncommon, the desert offered writers a new range of terrors, physical and mental, to supply the horror story and the horror film. Invoking the longstanding nightmare images of the Australian landscape as threatening to swallow up anyone who trespasses there, they focus in particular on the added threat posed by extreme isolation. This kind of Gothic horror was parodied by a brief story, 'Revenge of Charterhouse', published in the University of Sydney undergraduate magazine *Hermes* in 1933. An English aristocrat, Arnold Pytcherley, accompanied by his dingo, Charterhouse, has set out to walk three hundred kilometres into the desert on the recommendation of a drunken Austrologist that he should see 'the native companions dance their minuet'. Pytcherley believes that his faithful hound will stay with him to the end, and indeed he does, for he devours his dying master: 'Arnold did not stir, he was anybody's breakfast'.[16] This macabre preview of the black humour that emerged half a century later in response to the Azaria Chamberlain case suggests the peculiar fascination with the dingo that has infiltrated the national consciousness. The dingo, a wild and allegedly untameable dog (yet ironically, derived from the domestic dogs believed to have been brought by the Aborigines from Asia), subverts the desire of Western Man to believe in a unique affinity between himself and 'Man's best friend', with the latter willingly subservient and faithful unto death. Parodying the guardian role of the sheepdog by its killing of sheep, the dingo represents the dark underside of the comforting illusion that we control Nature as of right.

In twentieth-century horror stories and films it is rarely the land alone that is the agent of terror; it is the evil men who lurk there like the *banditti* concealed in the traditional Gothic landscape.

Kenneth Cook's savage novel *Wake in Fright* (1961), made into a successful film in 1971, focusses on a young Sydney school teacher, John Grant, posted to Tiboonda, a tiny town in far western New South Wales, close to 'the silent centre of Australia, the Dead Heart', and in Grant's eyes 'a variation of hell'.[17] Although the novel (and the film) might be regarded as a moral fable in which Grant's deterioration results from his weaknesses for drink and gambling, and his arrogance towards his neighbours, the emphasis on the desert landscape as a major player in the action precludes this. It is the sheer vastness of the distances and the isolation of characters trapped in one place, in one social group, that inexorably drives the action. Despite modern transport and some sizeable towns, the desert, it seems, remains in control of people's lives. The novel begins with the contrast, ever-present in Grant's mind, between the heat and aridity of Tiboonda, where people, 'their skins contracting and their eyes sinking as their stock became white bones', attempted to coax a living from the semi-desert, and the eastern coastal strip 'where Nature deposited the graces she so firmly withheld from the west'. The film, more immediately visual, opens with a circular pan of an immense, featureless plain. Grant, desperate to escape to Sydney for his six weeks' annual leave, fears that this will imprison him as surely as Depôt Creek did Sturt. Tiboonda itself consists of two buildings, the schoolhouse and the pub: the two poles of Grant's life. Hitherto he has eschewed the pub, despising its inhabitants, but moral degradation lies in store as he succumbs to the aggressive mateship of the pub and its associated activities. These, in turn, emanate from the terrain: heat brings thirst and alcoholism; isolation engenders desire for conviviality; a minimal existence breeds brutality. Forced to stay a night in the neighbouring mining town of Bundunyabba (Broken Hill) to wait for his plane to Sydney, Grant is suffocated by the kindness of the locals. He becomes drunk on free beers, gambles at two-up, loses his plane fare, gets drunk again, walks across the desert, hitches a lift which lands him back in 'Yabba, and is 'befriended' by the alcoholic Doc Tydon who takes him 'home' to his filthy shed. Tydon engineers Grant's participation in a savage and bloody kangaroo shoot which takes on the force of an initiation ritual and Grant is induced to prove his manhood by ineptly butchering a helpless female kangaroo as part of an extended massacre. Escaping into further drunkenness, he is sexually abused by Tydon, though not, it seems, without his consent. At the lowest ebb of self-respect Grant attempts suicide and finally arrives back in Tiboonda, destitute but with greater understanding of his own nature, in time for the next year's teaching.

Scarcely an adventure story, since there is no hero, *Wake in Fright* evokes a distinctly Gothic sense of place, in which the combined forces of harsh terrain and isolation supplant the supernatural as the source of determinism and terror: education, intelligence and innocence are no match for outback brutality, traditionally romanticised as 'mateship', but here deconstructed with the sharp satire that novelist Thea Astley was later to adopt in *An Item from the Late News*. A Kafkaesque web of mateship woven around the pub and the two-up den, Grant's predicament is the inevitable result of his outsider's arrogance and the landscape in which fate, in the likeness of the Education Department, has placed him. Ultimately it is the desert that wins. Like the inhabitants of 'Yabba, Grant eventually learns to position himself humbly in the context of its implacable vastness and even to be 'exhilarated by the brilliant, wild placidity, the riotous order of the stars'. Instead of the conventional moral tale of human weakness in the pub and the gambling den, Cook presents a peculiarly Australian version in which sin is defined not against a socially generated morality but against the code of the land.

Evan Green's novel *Alice to Nowhere* (1984) differs markedly from Cook's in having a recognisable hero, Fred Crawford the solitary mail man, on the legendary Birdsville Track through the Strzelecki Desert. Crawford (a fictional counterpart of Tom Kruse in John Heyer's film *Back of Beyond*), who doubles as general carter of everything, epitomises the bushman tradition – taciturn, resourceful, bashful with women, but brave and intelligent when it counts, given to self-improvement through avid reading and the companionship of a dictionary. Again the desert functions as both setting and major player in the murder mystery that provides the plot. The distances involved, the isolation of the stations totally dependent on their two-way radios, and the difficulty of the terrain, with its towering sandhills and shifting tracks, flooded rivers and the overpowering heat, are all key factors in the theatrical episodes of this journey. It is a variation on the archetypal quest motif, as Crawford sets out to transport the newly arrived nursing sister Barbara Dean from Marree to Birdsville. Green's characters are categorised by their attitudes to the desert. His heroes, the mail man, the policeman and the station residents, well experienced in the nature of the Strzelecki, accept it on its own terms, respecting its dangers; in general they survive. The villains, on the other hand, two escaping murderers, are further condemned by their fear and hatred of the land that, in the end, destroys them. Like *Wake in Fright, Alice to Nowhere* stresses that the power of the desert is not to be trifled with today any more than it was in the nineteenth century. Notions of heroism are revised here; accommodation to the land and its constraints is both a prerequisite for survival and an index of morality.

Holocaust in the desert

Whether in its geographical character as 'hideous blank' or its perceived nature as a place where life can scarcely survive, the desert provides a natural arena for modern notions of the post-nuclear holocaust, but the use to which this arena has been put in recent decades in both fiction and film has varied from cause to effect. In George Miller's Mad Max films (*Mad Max*, 1979, *Mad Max II*, 1982 and *Mad Max: Beyond Thunderdome*, 1985) the desert functions not realistically but strategically and parodically. In providing such a setting, as well as a locus for the enactment of fantastic narratives with a universal hero/anti-hero who transcends culture and time, the desert has both Australian and international significance. By exaggerating the stereotypical attributes ascribed to the Australian desert through clichés, intertextual quotations and a 'comic book aesthetic',[18] the Mad Max films self-consciously parody such a cultural construction. The immensity of the desert is invoked to justify the national obsession with the car[19] and hence with a fuel economy in which gangs murder for petrol; the alleged antiquity of the desert justifies its mythic dimensions; the wildness of the desert, in which all civilised species revert to primitive, ancestral types, accounts for the Feral Child of *Mad Max II* and the whole tribe of lost children in *Mad Max: Beyond Thunderdome*. In its post-nuclear mode, the desert in the Mad Max films sets the scene for a Darwinian struggle in which only the strongest and most ruthless survive. The mystical experience of the desert that is popularly supposed to erode individuality is echoed in the name of the despotic ruler Aunty Entity ('Aunty' as pronounced in the US), while the elevation of Max himself as a folk hero whose story has become a legend parodies the Man from Snowy River, 'a household word today'. By invoking a landscape that so blatantly accounts for everything, the *Mad Max* trilogy spoofs the obsessive, mythopoeic focus on the land throughout Australian literature and film, and the concurrent implication that the land determines narrative, character, ethos, national identity – everything.

Thea Astley's feminist analysis of outback male attitudes in *An Item from the Late News* (1982), a novel written at the height of the Cold War, locates the causes of global conflict at the local level. Situated in the western Queensland desert, her fictional one-pub former mining town, the ironically named Allbut, epitomises an overwhelmingly male culture, not because women are literally absent, but because they are ignored, raped, or forced to disguise themselves as men. The national cult of 'mateship', rampant in this male-dominated town, is swiftly dissected to expose its components: aggression, racism, sexism and exploitation. It becomes clear that this desert is as much a moral as a geographical one. With the exception of Wafer, Astley's androgynous hero, the males of Allbut have drifted there from successive failures somewhere else and despise the boredom and pettiness that is Allbut, this 'desert saucer where the towns have been chucked about like a losing toss of dice on a vast baize of dead felt'. They also fiercely resent any new arrivals. Wafer, however, a twentieth-century Desert Father,[20] has come to the desert with a purpose: he is intent on escaping the nuclear holocaust and the materialism of Western society. Ignoring the warning signs, he challenges the greed, violence and hatred of Allbut, precipitating upon himself its private, inimitable holocaust. His kindness to the Aborigines draws upon him the venom of the town's racial hatred; his protection of young Emmeline Colley from intended rape provokes the assumption that Wafer himself has violated the teenage girl; his pacifism tacitly condemns the war games that entertain Allbut both on television and in the pub; and most of all his rejection of material possessions incites a paroxysm of greed in a town 'always dreaming of the big strike'.

The desert setting of Allbut, with its suggestions of isolation, barrenness, timelessness and the prefiguring of a post-nuclear landscape, recalls the traditional role of the desert as the scene of renunciation and spiritual enlightenment. The Christ-like Wafer's martyrdom, however, when he is shot dead by the town's official agent of law and order, fails to inspire a spiritual rebirth. In terms of action, the only gain Astley's cynical social analysis permits is the belated repentance of Gabby, Astley's narrator, for her Judas role in betraying Wafer to the powers of Allbut. In her role as narrator, however, Gabby assumes a power far in excess of her status as character, voicing Astley's rejection of the linear explanations of space and time imposed by a predominantly male culture. In *An Item from the Late News* the desert functions simultaneously as a moral wilderness, the agent of death, and the path to spiritual enlightenment, but even at its most hostile, the desert landscape is benign compared with the sadism perpetrated by the males of Allbut. In this sense Astley aligns herself with Catherine Martin and Katharine Susannah Prichard, for whom man, not the land, is the enemy.

Dorothy Johnston's bicentenary novel, *Maralinga, My Love* (1988), focusses on the continuing neo-colonial activities of Britain in the Australian desert. The use of Emu Field and Maralinga in South Australia as test sites for the detonation of British nuclear weapons was implemented with the full support of the Australian Government since the Prime Minister of the time, Robert Menzies, was an unquestioning supporter of British policy. Apart from the major test explosions, involving bombs from 1 to 25 kilotons, there were several hundred 'minor' trials, the purpose and nature of which were never disclosed to the Australian Government. While Johnston's primary target is the irresponsible arrogance of the imperial power in carrying out a secret and highly dangerous exercise on colonial soil, her treatment of the desert landscape also functions (like Astley's and Ruhen's) as a moral index of the characters. For the military the desert is already, by definition, an empty wasteland, so using it for a purpose that intensifies this aspect seems self-evidently sensible. The few indigenous inhabitants should simply be herded out of the area. Flora and fauna, if noticed at all, are entirely dispensable. The British soldier stationed temporarily at Maralinga can only condemn this place:

195

> 'It's bloody awful, isn't it? Is it like this all over Australia?'
> 'God, no. Are you ignorant or something?'
> 'I'd want to be ignorant of this place.'[21]

For Graham, the Australian protagonist, however, the desert, even in summer, is fascinating in its many moods. Discovering waste plutonium fragments scattered, without acknowledgment over the site, with a half-life of 24,000 years, Graham voices his anger and condemnation: "'The British've been so bloody careless! They *are* so careless. Australia really is a colony to them, a rubbish dump, a bit of desert to do what they like with.'" Yet even his anger at discovering the extent of the radioactive pollution is not, at first, sufficient to drive him to action. The catalyst comes from the desert itself: 'Graham had another insight, which seemed to come from the stillness of the air and quietness of the desert afternoon.'

In *Maralinga, My Love* the desert is associated not only with the nuclear tests and the personnel associated with them, but also with the Pitjantjatjara Aborigines who, unaware of the dangers of fallout, of blindness from the blast itself and long-term dangers as yet unknown, were still in the area, despite the perfunctory and mismanaged efforts of the army to drive them south to Yalata. Already confused and dispossessed from their land by the white settlement that has disrupted their ancestral ways, they cannot comprehend the obscure warnings issued in administrative jargon by Canberra. Like the Aborigines of Ruhen's *Naked Under Capricorn*, they have no place in a desert appropriated by Western self-interest.

The psycho-symbolic desert

The land, and pre-eminently the desert, becomes the tangible correlative of the tragic element that European literature has traditionally had to supply through some abstract, philosophical or psychological premise such as existential angst. In Australia the physical threat remains actual; the desert can legitimately be cast as the implacable agent of existential terror demonstrating the fragility and absurdity of the human condition. The medical conditions ophthalmia and trachoma or 'sandy blight', so frequently experienced by desert travellers, enact and parody the inability to see meaning or value in a wasteland that is both actual and metaphorical. In addition to its very real physical terrors, the desert generates psychological terrors. In her discussion of fantasy literature Rosemary Jackson describes strange places as 'bleak, empty, indeterminate landscapes which are less definable as places than as spaces, as white, grey or shady blanknesses'.[22] The desert epitomises such a landscape. Perceived as a place of absences, without distractions from the terror of emptiness, a place that mirrors the worse dread of an interior void, of existential loneliness, the desert makes visible the sense of the uncanny. The specific external fears of the nineteenth-century writers – thirst, heat, dingoes, Aborigines – have been translated into more vague and hence more potent fears of dislocation, nihilism. The French feminist Hélène Cixous remarks that the strange, the uncanny, forces a fissure in the façade of realism whereby the supernatural can intrude; it 'infiltrates itself in between things, in the interstices, it asserts a gap where one would like to be assured of unity'.[23] Ironically, as we have seen in Chapter 1, this notion of the interstices through which the spiritual may emerge is, in Aboriginal culture, the source of security and permanence.

The use by Australian writers of the desert at the centre of the continent as a symbol for the cultural and psychological emptiness of its people is generally thought to begin with A.D. Hope's provocative poem, 'Australia' (1939), but nearly two decades before this Elliot Lovegood Grant Watson, a Cambridge-trained biologist, published six novels, some of them discussed in

Chapter 8, in which the Australian desert has a strongly psycho-spiritual role. These relatively neglected novels, written between 1914 and 1935, represent an unusually complex engagement with the Australian desert, affirming views about Aboriginal culture and European settlement that would now be considered post-colonial, even while upholding an estimate of women that remains distinctly pre-feminist. Equipped with a broad literary background, a close knowledge of current psychoanalytical practice and Jungian ideas, a fascination with religious experience and the prior experience of travel in the Middle East, as well as his training in biology and anthropology, Watson was uniquely qualified to translate into fiction his own experiences in Western Australia in 1910–11.

Although, in his autobiographical writing, Watson interpreted his impressions in terms of the psychological and anthropological theories current around the turn of the century and, like Joseph Conrad, identified Aboriginal culture as the subversive force acting on the European mind, his six Australian novels[24] published two decades earlier insisted on the role of the desert itself as the principle that tests, destroys or transforms his characters. With their simple plots and few characters, these novels document as relentlessly as a Greek tragedy the elemental struggle between the rival powers of Western civilisation and Nature (epitomised in the desert) for possession of the European mind.

We saw in Chapter 8 that Watson came to Australia in 1910–11 as a member of a scientific expedition led by Alfred Radcliffe-Brown to study the anthropology of the Aborigines; but he ended up writing about the anthropology of Europeans exposed to the desert. During his time in Western Australia he apparently underwent a profound psychological crisis which led him to question European values and to evolve instead a 'philosophy of the fringe', a notion that 'in the centres of civilisation life was withering away'. 'Human life,' he came to believe, 'was centripetal, having its sources at the circumference, and . . . drove inward towards congestion and death'.[25] In his autobiography *But to What Purpose* (1946) he reviewed the profound impact of the desert and its indigenous culture on him:

> I witnessed daily the power of magic. . . . I only just snatched myself back in time
> to be able to half-believe ever again in the conventions of Europe. . . . I had
> entered the animism of the savage mind, and had found within those mystical,
> sympathetic identifications the open doorways to the unconscious.

Two of Watson's novels in particular, *Desert Horizon* (1923) and its sequel *Daimon* (1925), parallel his own struggle to come to terms with the desert as a metaphysical experience. The two central characters, Martin O'Brian and his English wife Maggie, enact Watson's alternating fascination and revulsion with the land: where Martin wants to immerse himself in the spirit of the desert as a window on eternity, Maggie will not relinquish her European heritage, flawed and exhausted as Watson believes it to be. Although he rejected Darwin's reliance on chance, Watson accepted the centrality of a Darwinian struggle for existence, not only between Man and Nature, but in sexual rivalry for a mate.[26]

197

In *Desert Horizon* and *Daimon* Maggie competes with the desert for possession of Martin's soul and ultimately it is the land that wins.

In these novels the desert functions not only as the place for meditation, as in the hermit tradition of Christianity, but as a gauge of the characters' spiritual development. From his mystical position Watson inverts the more usual judgement of the desert's character. The sense of immensity and void that has so appalled the European explorers and settlers is, to Watson, an essentially positive quality urging the renunciation of material possessions as the necessary prelude to enlightenment. *Daimon* ends with Martin preparing for death by divesting himself of all possessions, even his clothes, as Watson plays on the two meanings of possession: 'He was possessed with one last desire: to be free of all encumbrances; then with long strides, swinging his arms about him, he strode eastwards toward the heart of the desert, singing to himself.'[27]

For Watson the desert is essentially amoral, transcending judgements and defying categorisation. At points along her spiritual journey Maggie too realises this mystery. 'The desert was beyond good and evil, something aloof and opposed altogether to human love and sympathy.' But perhaps the most interesting quality Watson ascribes to the desert is the sense of the numinous. This power affects all his characters who live there for any time, ranging from the sighting of a mirage with its testament to a reality beyond the material, to what Martin dimly understands in Platonic terms as 'the land of his dreams, that symbol of a noumenon life, more real than material things, which are but shadows of the beyond.'

198

Martin and his sister have their first strong intimation of this phantom world as children during an exhausting trek across the desert to find their father after their mother's death. In the midday heat, a white salt marsh shimmers into a haze which takes up mocking, fantastic shapes – at first frightening but then strangely reassuring because they seem to affirm the presence of another, non-material world. This construction of the mirage as a Romantic symbol for transcendent reality appears to be unique to Watson and to have arisen directly from his own mystical experience.

> The surface is twisted and torn by faint, hot gusts of wind into wisps of shining vapour, which are in shape like the bodies of fantastic creatures, which run over the vibrating sheen of water beneath. And now in recurring lines, beyond the horizon, there appear images of the desert, trees and low scrub, salt-bush, and here and there cattle, large beyond all natural proportion . . .
>
> As Martin watches, his fear slowly leaves him . . . To his boy's heart comes the first knowledge of illusion. . . . He tastes an unexpected freedom; the world is changed into unsubstantial air and vapour.[28]

During his time near Kalgoorlie, Watson himself recorded similar experiences of 'something, sensed but unseen, behind phenomena' when 'the veil of time seemed drawn aside, and eternity gazed in the sun's glare or in the cracking of a seed-pod'.[29]

In the acting out of this psychodrama in the desert Watson's characters display a strongly gendered response. Near the end of *Daimon* a doctor and an engineer discuss how the desert affects people differently. The doctor distinguishes three groups: those who come to make money and leave as soon as they have done so; those who 'see a little and the sight frightens them so that they go out of their minds and blow out their brains'; and some who 'see it, and having seen it, [find that] all other things lose their value'.[30] The majority of the first kind are prospectors and miners, hoping to make their fortune and spend it elsewhere. They hold little interest for Watson, although, as we saw in Chapter 8, he is not derogatory about the search for gold per se. The third group are his heroic protagonists, prepared to accept the desert's epiphany of a mystery beyond the material world. But those who have suffered mental affliction from living in the desert are his female characters. Lacking both rational and practical outlets for their energies, and the spiritual capacity to seek a transcendent vision, they become victims of their unfulfilled desire to possess their men. Thus, despite his interest in Jungian psychology, Watson clung to a Platonic binary view of man as spiritual principle and woman as earthly vessel to whom the mystery of the desert remains obscure. Demented by their perceived imprisonment in the desert, they leave, die prematurely, commit suicide, or become insanely malevolent. Maggie tells her father: '"Nobody can stand against it. The isolation, the strange, awful feeling. There's something. . . . Nobody is just happy and normal. They all get changed; it's a sort of madness."' This female discontent is judged as a moral deficiency – an intractable materialism, an unworthy fear that renders women unable to participate in the numinous dimension of the desert.

199

On the other hand, Watson's male protagonist, Martin, experiences a close spiritual communion with the desert. Appropriately, Martin's physical form takes on aspects of the landscape until, like Wordsworth's leech-gatherer, he becomes almost indistinguishable from his environment. 'A dust-stained fragment of a man he looked: hardly a man: a piece of earth detached from it and imbued with movement . . . a piece of dust propelled in circles and spirals, in a tangle of interpenetrating figures, attracted to that one spot by some mystical affinity.' The vision of transcendence that the desert imparts is essentially pagan and amoral, echoing Watson's own affirmation of Jung's belief in the inseparable nature of good and evil: 'I believe, with Dr. Jung, that it is impossible and undesirable to separate the good from the evil. Only by becoming familiar with the Shadow side of our natures, will we be able to know how to deal with the evil in the world.'[31]

'A futile heart'

We saw in Chapter 8 that travel books, documentary films and the magazine *Walkabout* set out to de-mystify the Centre and proclaim a gospel of progress whereby the desert would be settled, mined, grazed and cultivated into prosperity. But the arrival of artists such as Drysdale and Nolan in Central Australia during the 1930s, and their revolutionary symbolic representations of a vast existential emptiness peopled by strange, emaciated figures, prompted writers to see the potential of the desert as a metaphor for psychological and spiritual barrenness and, by extension, the emptiness and futility of a nation with no soul. Even before this nudge from the art world, however, two important poems had drawn on the symbolism of the arid centre to comment on the Australian character.

Erupting upon the optimistic nationalism of the interwar years, A.D. Hope's poem 'Australia' (1939) appeared as a shocking and savage betrayal. Throughout the first five stanzas, Australia is presented as a sequence of absences: 'She is the last of lands, the emptiest'; 'within the womb is dry'; 'Without songs, architecture, history', 'Her rivers of water drown among inland sands,/The river of her immense stupidity'. 'Australia' typifies to the point of parody the view of this former convict settlement that was espoused both at the imperial Centre and by the 'second-hand Europeans' who immigrated and then spent the rest of their lives complaining about the lack of culture in Australia. But, the reversal that comes in Hope's last two stanzas, though partial, is unambiguous. It is Europe, not Australia, that is spiritually exhausted; as in the days of the prophets, a seemingly barren land is the site of spiritual rebirth. Significantly, the 'periphery' has become the focal point for renewal and the former Centre (Europe) is dismissively 'over there'.

200

> Yet there are some like me turn gladly home
> From the lush jungle of modern thought, to find
> The Arabian desert of the human mind,
> Hoping, if still from the deserts the prophets come,
>
> Such scarlet and savage as no green hills dare
> Springs in that waste, some spirit which escapes
> The learned doubt, the chatter of cultured apes
> Which is called civilisation over there.[32]

Thus Hope signals the beginning of a new approach to the desert as a source of spiritual strength, not confidently but merely as a possibility.

This image of a barren 'dead heart', from which may come a revelation of spiritual and poetic value, was echoed, though with less confidence, in James McAuley's short poem of the following year, 'Envoi for a Book of Poems' (1940). Whereas the nationalist writers had seen the men and women of the outback metonymically, as an extension of the strength and toughness of the land, McAuley identifies them as Australia's 'Hollow Men', emotionally stunted by the barrenness of their surroundings, reflecting only the blank, the absence at the heart of the continent:

> Where once was sea is now a salty sunken desert,
> A futile heart within a fair periphery;
> The people are hard-eyed, kindly, with nothing inside them,
> The men are independent but you could not call them free.[33]

Where Hope was concerned with spiritual barrenness, McAuley's focus is on poetic inspiration; his fervent wish is less that prophets will emerge from the desert than that like-minded poets in the classical (pre-Modernist) mode will do so. This leads McAuley to the paradoxical conclusion that the land's beauty could indeed flourish despite our obstruction, while at the same time the land itself rejects attempts to initiate fertility. The invoking of the 'artesian heart' is offset by the land's resentment of the 'gush of waters' and the 'fretful seed' that has imbibed the bitterness of the farmer-settlers. As in Hope's poem, the reversal is potential rather than actual, hoped-for but with only qualified confidence in its eventuality. There is no suggestion that the desert is intrinsically good, beautiful or productive. On the contrary: its flowering, if ever it occurs, will be a miracle.

Although inclusive of, even dependent on, a psychological correlative, these images are grounded in the basic notion of the desert as unrelieved barrenness. The immediate catalyst for recognition of its greater complexity and apocalyptic potential came, in the first instance, not from literature but from art, and involved a revisionist reading of the explorer figure that is discussed in detail in Chapter 12.

'The land and the Tao are one': Randolph Stow's desert

While it might be thought that Western Australians would have more reason than the citizens of other states to resent the central desert, which isolates them physically and psychologically from the continent's larger centres of culture, it is remarkable that two of the very few novelists who have affirmed the spiritual qualities of the desert have written out of a Western Australian experience – Grant Watson and Randolph Stow. Like Watson, Stow was interested in anthropology,[34] but whereas for Watson the fascination exerted by the desert was a profoundly disturbing experience, subversive of his European heritage, for Stow, a fifth-generation Australian, it represented, at one stage of his career, a surer identity than its European counterpart. His novels *To the Islands* (1958) and *Tourmaline* (1963) and some of his poems are concerned to explore the dynamic relationship between the inner and the outer landscape. In an article entitled 'Raw Material: Some ideas for a new, epic art in an Australian setting', published in the year in which he drafted the first chapter of *Tourmaline*, Stow wrote: 'The boundary between an individual and his environment is not his skin. It is the point where mind verges on the pure essence of him, that unchanging observer that, for want of a better term, we must call the soul. ... The environment of a writer is as much inside him as in what he observes.'[35] Stow found this union of landscape and mindscape best represented in the work of Drysdale and Nolan, 'the external forms filtered back through the conscious and unconscious mind; that is what these artists convey, and what I would hope to convey if I were capable of executing all I can conceive'.

201

In this same article Stow singled out as particular attributes of the Australian environment its vastness and the sense of the ancient past, features most prominently identified with the desert. He concluded:

> what, in the end, I see in Australia . . . is an enormous symbol: a symbol for the whole earth, at all times, both before and during the history of man, and because of its bareness, its absolute simplicity, a truer, broader symbol of the human environment than, I believe, any European writer could create from the complex material of Europe.

These signifiers are especially evident in *Tourmaline* which opens with a manifesto of seemingly universal and eternal inclusiveness:

> I say we have a bitter heritage, but that is not to run it down. Tourmaline is the estate, and if I call it a heritage I do not mean that we are free in it. More truly we are tenants; tenants of shanties rented from the wind, tenants of the sunstruck miles.[36]

To erase particularity yet further, the novel carries a note, 'The action of this novel is to be imagined as taking place in the future'. The introductory description tells us very little about the town of Tourmaline itself[37] but much about the desert which continually dominates it and periodically overwhelms it, literally, through sandstorms that obliterate the town. The town is so cut off from the rest of the world as to be allegorical, even surreal. '"Just keep on going through the broken fence, and keep an eye open for Leichardt [*sic*]"', jokes one of the characters.

Stow has been greatly influenced by the *Tao Teh Ching*, the central text of Taoism, as he made clear in the twelve poems published as '*From* The Testament of Tourmaline: Variations on Themes of the *Tao Teh Ching*' corresponding to the twelve verses of the *Tao*.[38] He called the sequence 'something of a key to the novel. It could be considered as written by the people of Tourmaline'.[39] In 'Poem VII' he writes: 'The loved land will not pass away./ World has no life but transformation. . . . Body is land in permutation.' Throughout *Tourmaline*, there are recurrent instances of such symbolic transmutation between body and land. The novel opens with a death, 'not one of importance'. Billy Bogoda is consigned to the earth ('dust to dust') in a packing case on the day Michael Random, the self-styled Diviner, arrives, apparently resurrected from virtual death, in a truck which heralds its arrival in advance by 'a cloud of dust'. When the truck driver departs the narrator remarks, 'his tyre marks would remain with us, to remind us of his reality; but as soon as the first wind erased them he became insubstantial, and our memories could not recreate him'. Like the tracks, the town itself is constantly threatened with burial, Ozymandias-like, by the desert at its doorstep. Byrne tells the Diviner that a nearby town, Lacey's Find, has disappeared: 'The sand blew up and buried it', and the narrator reflects, 'I imagined the gentle tidal encroachment of the dunes, the soft red sand, wind-ribbed and untrodden, mounting, mounting. . . . and the sand would lie unbroken and printless over all the places that knew me. In my terrible loneliness I grow elegiac'. This prefigures the powerful description of the closing scene in which a dust storm threatens to engulf Tourmaline:

> Everything was flowing, insubstantial. The obelisk and the hotel would appear through the dust and then, in an instant, melt away. . . .
>
> I walked out, into the thick red wind.
> It was like swimming under water, in a flooding river. . . .
> There was no town, no hill, no landscape. There was nothing. Only myself swimming through the red flood that had covered the world and spared me only, of all those who had been there. . . . Caught in the current, drowning, I ceased to struggle, and let it bear me up the road. . . . What could this be if not the end of the world?
> Then the wind dropped for half a minute. And I saw my tower, the boundary of Tourmaline, waiting.

This evocative description of insubstantiality and flux, as the dust obliterates every external marker as well as the narrator's sense of identity, symbolises a central tenet of Taoism. But another important point is also made here in relation to the landscape: only when the narrator ceases to struggle and surrenders to the dust storm does he relocate himself. This incident dramatises Stow's acceptance of the Taoist view of passivity.

203

In 'Poem I' of '*From* The Testament of Tourmaline', Stow writes:

> Nevertheless, the land and the Tao are one.
> In the love of the land, I worship the manifest Tao.
>
> To move from love into lovelessness is wisdom.
> The land's roots lie in emptiness. There is Tao.

Through this attempt to marry the self-emptying principle of Taoism with the emptiness of the desert, Stow characterises both by an absence, a lack, which is, paradoxically, the precondition for spiritual fulfilment.

Another aspect of this surrender is the acceptance of the land as it is in the present, without any attempt to 'improve' it. In *Tourmaline* this involves a rejection of the Diviner's project to find more water. Although Tourmaline is situated in the desert, it has some water – sufficient for people's basic needs. The frantic search for super-abundant water in order to grow exotic fruits and vines arises from a dream of domination over nature, a desire to turn the desert into a Garden of Eden, whereas, we are told from the beginning, 'The sky is the garden of Tourmaline'. Predictably the search fails. The Diviner finds no water, only gold – another superfluity since there is already a stockpile of it in the town. Excess gold brings subjection as Kestrel, the publican, a more sinister Diviner, returns with the implements of mechanisation and mass-production to enslave the town's inhabitants.

Depite the strong Taoist influence on Stow, *Tourmaline* is starkly at odds with one principle of Taoism: the desired balance of yin and yang. As in the majority of literature of the desert, women, if they are present at all, play no significant role; the feminine yin is entirely dominated by the masculine yang. The two female characters, Mary Spring and Deborah, function only as servants, entirely subservient to their men.

Robert Drewe's recent novel *The Drowner* (1996) also draws on a counterpointing of desert sand and water, introducing a variation on the notion of divining in *Tourmaline*. According to Drewe a drowner, in Wiltshire tradition, is one who can empathically control the flow of water, diverting it across meadows when required and later returning it to its river channel. This tradition is translated into observable fact when Drewe's protagonist, former drowner William Dance, becomes the site engineer on a project to lay a pipeline from Perth to the Great Victoria Desert (some 560 kilometres) in order to pump water uphill to the goldfields. However, the Australian desert provides its own macabre version of drowning. While the aqueduct is still incomplete the Western Australian Government finally responds to the desperate plight of the drought-stricken goldfields by sending a water train with 10,000 gallons (45,500 litres) of fresh water from the coast. With the savage irony so frequently attributed to the Australian desert, the train encounters a freak flood: 'Halfway to the goldfields the water express was stranded by the leading edge of a tropical cyclone ... flooding the track and the flat western desert for a hundred square miles.'[40] The longed-for rains flood the town, filling the mines, sweeping away the Cobb & Co. mail coach and drowning its horses. Nevertheless, in the cycle of nature the flooded desert, like the drowned English meadows, provides a window of opportunity for non-human forms of life.

204

> Two weeks after the deluge began the sun burst over the sheet of clotted red water spreading to the horizon and turned it purple. ... Flocks of swans and ducks, egrets and herons and ibises appeared in the crisp sky. The birds gorged themselves in the receding waters while glistening succulents and crimson creeping pea-flowers spread over the red shores.

Drewe's novel provides some of the most keenly observed descriptions of the desert, pointing to the minute variations within the seeming monotony of the landscape. In a passage reminiscent of the details observable through the traditional Aboriginal planar perspective, one of Drewe's characters notes:

> the elliptical way the desert's surface expressed the fundamentals. Sand, wind, sun. On its crust, living things sketched their lives. Sinuous snake trails, traceries of spinifex bush, windblown grass stems drawing geometry theorems in the sand. And scratchers of unknown origin, their claw marks crisply shaped in the dampness risen overnight in the surface of the sand.

If Drewe has been influenced by Aboriginal art, Stow acknowledged his debt to Nolan. His poem 'The Land's Meaning' (1962) was dedicated to Nolan who, in turn, provided the painting published with the poem in *Australian Letters*.[41] As in *Tourmaline* the overwhelming mood is of absence. There are no figures, human or animal; the only movement indicated is of the heat haze rising from the sand and partly obscuring the cloudless blue sky. The poem firmly locates the source of morality in the desert. Without sojourning there, it suggests, we cannot truly know what love, in the sense of *caritas*, is. Its opening lines, 'The love of man is a weed of the waste places./One may think of it as the spinifex of dry souls', are clearly intended to be read in parallel, thereby linking not only 'weed' and 'spinifex' but 'waste places' and 'dry souls'. Thus from the start the desert is standing in for the soul, indicating how terrifying is the journey. To discover *caritas* we must explore the inland of the self, in isolation and in silence, those characteristic attributes of the desert. In this exploration there can be no deputies: the journey must be made alone. The men in the tin barroom, seeking safety in numbers and the shield of 'mateship', unwillingly know this and feel challenged as others depart on the journey: 'the footprints of the recently departed/march to the mind's horizons, and endure'.

The reports that come back from the interior are not reassuring; they merely assert:

> that the mastery of silence
> alone is empire. What is God, they say,
> but a man unwounded in his loneliness?

205

After being 'bushed for forty years' a traveller returns, as unsuccessful as the inland explorers, 'his eyes blurred maps/of landscape still unmapped', just as, in 'The Singing Bones', the charts of the interior are 'gapped,/unreachable, unmapped, and mainly in the mind'. His impressionistic description recalls details from earlier Nolan paintings: 'cockatoos dropped dead in the air' (*Pretty Polly Mine*, 1948), 'the camels knelt down and stayed there' (*Burke and Wills Expedition*, 1948), 'and a skin-coloured surf of sand-hills jumped the horizon' (*Burke and Wills at the Gulf*, 1961). His minimal reward, and we are not sure whether he receives it, or whether he is indeed blind or mad, is some limited shade from the merciless sun:

> And I came to a bloke all alone like a kurrajong tree.
> And I said to him: 'Mate – I don't need to know your name –
> Let me camp in your shade, let me sleep, till the sun goes down.'

'The Singing Bones' (1968) carries as its epigraph a phrase from Barcroft Boake's poem of the same name, 'Out where the dead men lie'. It epitomises the notion of the dead heart of the continent which has claimed the lives of its most gallant men, 'sand-enshrined lay saints', martyrs 'who died of landscape' in the cause of exploration. Leichhardt and Gibson disappeared, their remains inhabiting some unknown place, undefinable other than as '*out there*', but their names have entered into the nation's psyche, not only determining how the Centre will be understood ('My country's heart is ash in the market-place,/is aftermath of martyrdom'), but becoming an obsession with poets who internalised the journey to the Centre and the explorers' deaths: 'who kept their end in mind in all they wrote'. Finally, in the case of Adam Lindsay Gordon and Barcroft Boake, the poets succumbed to what has been called 'an inherent *mal du pays*, a geography of sentiments and attitudes which have their root in separation and alienation'.[42] For Stow that influence still emanates from the Centre, alluring though terrible, a recurrent death-wish calling for successors:

> Time, time and time again, when the inland wind
> beats over myall from the dunes, I hear
> the singing bones, their glum Victorian strain.
> A ritual manliness, embracing pain
> to know; to taste terrain their heirs need not draw near.[43]

Desert cults

Janette Turner Hospital's recent Gothic novel *Oyster* (1996) focusses on the psychological violence, desperation and imprisonment that may flourish in an isolated community. Set in the town of Outer Maroo, which, like Astley's Allbut, is located in the desert areas of western Queensland, *Oyster* draws on literary traditions as diverse as the ripping yarn and the spiritual pilgrimage. Hospital plots the connections between obsession with wealth (opals have succeeded Lasseter's gold and Wafer's sapphire but the violence engendered is the same), the desire of 1990s hippies to believe in a desert community of simplicity and self-denial, and the religious mythology attaching to a desert-generated saviour. Even devout members of the Living Word Gospel Hall are lured to the cult of Oyster, evangelist of an Armageddon programmed to occur on 1 January 2000. *Oyster* draws together numerous strands of the history of human interaction with the Australian desert. It contrasts the local Aborigines' relationship with the land as a mother[44] to the violent attack on the land by white settlers who instinctively hate it. A red-neck farmer tells Miss Rover, the teacher imported from Brisbane:

> 'As for forage-dusting and shooting 'roos and mining on the so-called sacred sites, she's a real bugger, the land. If you don't slap her round a bit, the land gives too much damn cheek. . . . She's a tough old bitch, is the land. We respect her, and that's why we give her no quarter. . . . You don't understand our way of loving.'
> 'No,' Miss Rover agrees . . . 'Sounds more like rape to me,' Miss Rover says.[45]

In the character of Jess, a former government surveyor, Hospital pours post-colonial ridicule on the naive belief in maps and charts as representations of the actual. Official maps give credence to what is not there (rivers, borders)

206

and, conversely, in a parody of the notion of *terra nullius*, they omit what *is* there: a town of eighty-seven people, the sudden disappearance of all outsiders, the traffic in arms and opals. 'By cunning intention, and sometimes by discreet bribery (or other dispatch) of government surveyors, Outer Maroo has kept itself off maps'. This anomalous deception of maps, and the futility of all attempts to find the truth by surveying, culminate in the paradox: 'All those who find the place [Outer Maroo] are lost'. *Oyster* virtually paraphrases one of the tenets of the revisionist, feminist geography: 'The translation of these markings from map to landscape is a psychic skill . . .' The subjectivity of maps and the history of colonialism are equally encapsulated in the observation: 'The arrival of any foreigner changes the map, and foreigners spell the beginning of the end'.

Like the nineteenth-century explorers, Hospital is intrigued by the metaphorical possibilities of mirages but it is typical of her fascination with post-Newtonian physics that, rather than dismissing them as deception, she introduces the classic scientific explanation in order to demonstrate its inadequacy, while simultaneously invoking a moral dimension.

> Time is a trickster, and so is space, but the air above an ocean or a desert is more devious than either of these. The air in such places is bent . . . the shimmering outback air can present on the track ahead a man who passed behind you a day ago. . . . Questions that interest me: What would constitute a true mirage?

207

In the course of the novel mirages are subtly aligned with both the mesmerism exerted by Oyster, who can induce his hearers to see what he wishes, and the 'hysteria that sits on the edge of sunstroke and dehydration'.

Hospital imports her chief villain from outside, but the willing collusion of the inhabitants of Outer Maroo is necessary for the execution of Oyster's plans and, with few exceptions, they are ready followers, asking no questions. Their evil derives partly from their greed for the riches to be had from the opal trade, but equally from their perspective as farmers in a drought-ridden land. They harbour a paranoid hatred of all outsiders and all Australian institutions that might be suspected of attempting to take away their land – the Federal and State governments, the ABC, newspapers, Aborigines, ecologists and permaculture farmers. Against such evil forces the 'cow cockies' stockpile armaments: '"It's for when the government or the Aborigines, or whoever, comes to take their land."' Thus the explosives engineer, Major Miner, cannot be sure whether it was Oyster who detonated his Reef and all his followers: '"You see," he says, "almost everyone wanted them gone."'

Oyster's dupes are the idealistic youth, recruited from the east coast, who are seeking the perfect spiritual community. For them the desert offers the acceptable setting, the traditional wilderness, and they drink in Oyster's words, '"We are the last of God's free people in the wilderness"'. One writes on a postcard fated never to leave Outer Maroo, '"We live out in the desert like shamans used to do, in tunnels and caves and tents. . . . It's incredibly beautiful out here, and we're like a family, all one in the mystical Body of Christ . . . all the things we believed in in college, they're here.'" In this sense *Oyster* both examines and subverts the attitudes of willed belief in a supernatural experience promoted by the desert factors that will be discussed in Chapter 14.

The climactic obliteration of Oyster's opal mine and the innocents that live there in a labyrinth of tunnels under the earth re-enacts the attempted genocide of Aborigines but Hospital plays on a series of ironic parallels and inversions that universalise the outrage. In this case, the innocents are out-siders; the Murris have departed the scene long before the explosion, though, as Ethel later affirms, "'My mob'll come home now, any day now, you'll see.'" When Sarah and Nick[46] go to the underground cavern where their respective children, along with Oyster's other followers, have been incinerated, they find the creamy white rock walls coated with carbon dust and soot from the cremated bodies. For Sarah it is a re-enactment of the Nazi holocaust and, in an action that is both profoundly pathetic and macabre, they scrape the carbon off a section of the wall with dinner knives.

Traditional Gothic took as its focus the endangered heroine, imprisoned in an ancient castle/home that was designed originally to protect the inhabi-tants against an external enemy. The sublime scenery outside the castle terri-fied as well as fascinated; the male guardians whom society had taught her to trust proved the most sinister and malevolent. The focus on attempted rape of the heroine also symbolised the broader attack on her identity.

The Australian desert has provided writers with counterparts to all this classic Gothic machinery. The desert itself imprisons characters through isola-tion and cannot protect them from the evil within themselves. Rather the very monotony of the scene drives them to consider the interior prospect of the subconscious. The immensity and antiquity of the desert both repel and fasci-nate. Like other forms of the sublime the desert lures people towards the eroti-cism of death. And like the Gothic obsession with attempted rape it threatens the identity of the individual.

ABOVE
Albert Tucker, *Death of an Explorer, 1978*, gouache and watercolour on paper, 51 × 66 cm, Tolarno Galleries.

BELOW
Brett Whiteley, *Fellow Countryman: Gibson and Compass*, 1986, illustration from *Native Rose*, Michael Driscoll and Brett Whiteley (Cammeray, NSW: Richard Griffin, 1986). Courtesy Whiteley Estate.

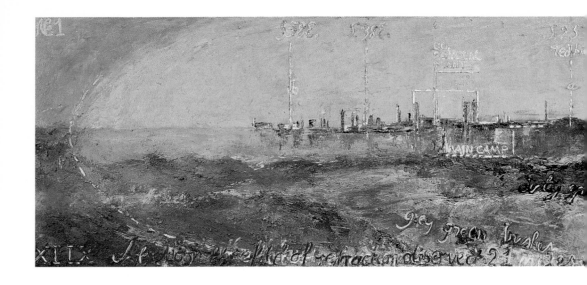

ABOVE
Mandy Martin,
Reconstructed Narrative,
Strzelecki Desert No. 8,
1991, oil on linen,
100 × 244 cm. Courtesy
the artist.

BELOW
Sidney Nolan, *Drought,*
1962, oil on masonite,
120 × 90 cm, private
collection.

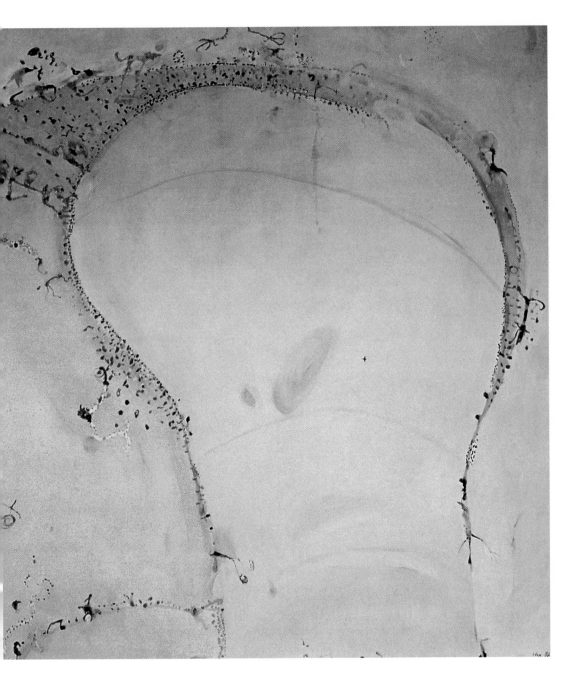

John Olsen, *Lake Eyre*,
1975, oil on canvas,
216 × 198 cm. Courtesy
the artist.

John Wolseley (England, born 1938), *A Journey Near Ormiston Gorge in Search of Rare Grasshoppers*, 1978–80, watercolour on pencil on gouache on paper on canvas, 183.0 × 294.5 cm, collection National Gallery of Australia, Canberra.

Chapter 11

Revisioning the Explorers

In Australian landscape painting, as in all great landscape painting,
the scenery is not painted for its own sake, but as the background of
a legend and a reflection of human values.

KENNETH CLARK[1]

In the growth and transformation of its myths a society achieves its own
sense of identity.

CHARLES BLACKMAN, ARTHUR BOYD,
DAVID BOYD, JOHN BRACK,
BOB DICKERSON, JOHN PERCEVAL,
CLIFTON PUGH, BERNARD SMITH,
'Antipodean Manifesto'

During the decade following World War I the Anzacs temporarily eclipsed the
inland explorers as the nation's heroes. But in the long term the collective
identity of Anzac could not compete with the individual personalities of Eyre,
Sturt, Leichhardt, Burke and Wills in providing the nation with prototypes of
heroism. Sidney Nolan, whose Burke and Wills series represents the most
important and sustained revisiting of the inland explorers in art, explained his
fascination in similar terms:

> Our culture has its roots in our boyhood and the nineteenth century, because
> we heard stories of Livingstone, Stanley, the Congo and Burke and Wills.
> Schoolrooms had those sepia reproductions of drawings of our explorers. That
> was our visual culture. . . . I take a tribal view of our landscape and culture.[2]

Equally important was the sense of place. The cliffs at Gallipoli, while
dramatic, were not a scene with which Australians could identify, but the archetypal lone figure lost in the desert became, in the national consciousness, an
icon not only for the inland explorers but also for the nation's view of its
history, its battle for survival, and, increasingly in the twentieth century, for the
individual soul marooned in an existential void. It is in this latter sense that the

explorers re-emerged in twentieth-century art. Their attraction lies not in themselves but in their situation; it is the desert context that makes them perennially relevant.

One of the first modern artists to revisit the inland explorers was Ivor Hele. His painting of *Sturt's Reluctant Decision to Return, 1937* (1937) is based on the anti-climactic moment when the agonised leader, plagued by loss of sight, illness and the imminent death of yet more of his men, finally decides to abandon his quest for an inland sea. Hele still casts the explorer as leader and decision-maker: heroic in defeat, Sturt stands with telescope and map in hand, gazing into the distance, his hands hanging helplessly by his side. His lieutenant, Dr John Harris Browne, seated on his horse, cranes forward in an endeavour to see some sign of hope. The rest of the men busy themselves with the horses, having no part in the decision. The brown, barren landscape is echoed in the colours of the horses and the men's clothes, but to a modern viewer the most striking aspect is the soldierly impression of the men, and particularly of Sturt.[3] The explorer's riding breeches, boots, despatch pouch and even his hat suggest the uniform of the Light Horse Brigade so closely

Ivor Hele (Australia 1912–33), *Sturt's Reluctant Decision to Return, 1937*, 1937, oil on canvas, 46.0×61.4 cm, Art Gallery of South Australia, Adelaide. Mrs M.C. Dunstan Bequest 1954.

210

associated with Anzac, while the slope and colours of the hill on which they stand recall Lambert's *Anzac, the Landing* (1915). Despite these resonances of Anzac, Hele's painting is still firmly within the tradition of nineteenth-century historical genre painting – a great man caught at a critical moment in the history of the nation. In this sense it was already an anachronism. By the 1930s the explorers were no longer regarded as great men but rather as flawed individuals, representatives of an inimical imperial past. The catalyst for their transformation from history to myth must be attributed to the vision of one person, Sidney Nolan. Wrenching Burke and Wills from their historical context and repositioning them as universalised figures, solitary and often naked, in an archetypal, featureless desert, he recast them as figures of dream or nightmare, emerging from the subconscious as images of the individual soul lost in an existential void.

Nolan's Burke and Wills series

Although most of Nolan's Central Australian landscapes have no trace of human presence, that very absence continually emphasised for him the land's implacable hostility to human habitation. He wrote, 'I doubt that I will ever forget my emotions when first flying over Central Australia and realizing how much we painters and poets owe to *our predecessors the explorers,* with their frail bodies and superb will power'.[4] (my emphasis) This suggests that even at this preliminary stage explorers were less important to Nolan as individuals than as representatives of determination, of 'will power' with whom painters and poets could align themselves.[5] During the 1940s Nolan wrote two poems suggesting the links in his thinking between the hostility of the terrain, the ambiguity of the explorers' character and their national relevance for all who inhabit 'this extraordinary continent'. One was entitled 'Cooper's Creek':

211

> As crystals descend through the evening
> so the camels descend and men descend
> in this extraordinary continent.
>
> As drought destroys through the earth
> so the throat destroys and thirst destroys
> in this extraordinary continent.
>
> As heat discards through a heart
> so the heart discards and skin discards
> in this extraordinary continent.
>
> As men vanish through their eyes
> so the bones vanish transparent
> in this extraordinary continent.[6]

The other, 'Explorer Poem', focusses on Leichhardt and may have provided Patrick White with the powerful image at the end of the novel *Voss* where the explorer's name carved in trees represents both his colonial inscription on the land and the sign that his spirit has been subsumed by the land.[7]

> This is
> Leichhardt country,
> from the fall of the
> Meteor and Dawson;
> this is the man
> they hated, the earth hated
> right up to this mountain,
> the trees his name, carved
> in the name of Paradise, Purgatory.
>
> Here he watched, with
> the white cloud and
> stars, calling himself
> lover, eater of dingoes.[8]

Seeing from the air the terrain in which Burke and Wills perished gave Nolan the idea for the first of his explorer paintings. He researched his subject meticulously, reading the explorers' diaries and *Dig*, Frank Clune's fictional account of the expedition, studying sepia photographs and engravings of nineteenth-century Melbourne and contemporary portraits of Burke and Wills. However, Nolan's figures are strikingly dissimilar to those produced by nineteenth-century iconography. His revisionist treatment demotes them from the rank of noble men while elevating them to the status of legendary heroes. The first painting of this series, *Burke and Wills Expedition* (1948)[9] (see illustration following page 176), was later reproduced on the dust jacket of Alan Moorehead's *Cooper's Creek* (1963), a book written at Nolan's urging. The two explorers, their too-large heads mimicking the stiff, formal portraits painted by William Strutt before the expedition departed from Melbourne, seem pasted onto the brilliant orange landscape they traverse, like figures on a felt board. Burke's head is improbably turned through 180 degrees to face us as he rides away, implicitly drawing us into this archetypal journey. Ignoring the historical reality of the large expedition, Nolan, with few exceptions, depicts his explorers as solitary. In *Burke and Wills Expedition, Gray Sick* (1949), Charles Gray, the least senior member of the expedition and the one conspicuously absent from the nineteenth-century artistic record, is shown lashed to his camel. This was factually correct: Gray's legs became paralysed with cramps caused by severe malnutrition and he was tied to the saddle to prevent him from falling. But in Nolan's painting the visual focus on Gray's bound form emphasises that the real agent of bondage is not the ropes but the desert. Gray's hat dangles down behind him, exposing him to the fierce sun; his camel stands like a cardboard cut-out figure on a red-ochre landscape beneath a bright blue enamel sky. There is no other living thing in sight.

Nolan's next Burke and Wills series, of 1949–50, focusses on well-known historical incidents but, as in the case of the earlier Ned Kelly series, Nolan is not interested in a faithful re-creation of events; he virtually parodies the nineteenth-century historical paintings that had attempted to do that. Instead he reflects on the significance of the explorers in this century. As the basis for *Perished* (1949) Nolan used William Strutt's melodramatic drawing, *Burke's Death*, well known from the engraving in Edwin Hodder's *Heroes of Britain* (1884) and later in William Pyke's *Australian Heroes and Adventurers* (1889).[10] However, while preserving faithfully the posture of Burke, who lies with the famous pistol in his right hand, left arm stretched by his side, hat and mug

Sidney Nolan, *Burke and Wills Expedition, Gray Sick,* 1949, ripolin enamel and red ochre oil paint on hardboard, 92.0×120.0 cm, private collection. Courtesy Lady Nolan.

discarded at his right elbow, Nolan has introduced several critical changes which subvert the mood of Strutt's hagiography. Burke's eyes are not decorously closed but open, glaring balefully at heaven; there is no weeping figure of King as our mourning representative; and the event has been removed from the fertile surroundings of Cooper's Creek to a stereotyped desert landscape. Burke's body lies technically unburied, as he had requested, but the surrounding desert appears to be gradually incorporating him into itself, as though he is sinking into quicksand. The painting is no longer one of homage to the noble hero but a critique of colonial arrogance and incomprehension, as epitomised by this ill-devised expedition which made no attempt to accommodate itself to the continent it set out to dominate.

The following year Nolan's twin portraits *Robert O'Hara Burke* (1950) and *William John Wills* (1950) further undermined the heroic legend. Burke's wild blue eyes cast him as obsessive to the point of paranoia and monomania, while Wills appears merely ineffectual. *Departing from Melbourne* (1950) represents a yet more radical reworking of the myth. In stark contrast to the familiar contemporary paintings by Nicholas Chevalier and Strutt, depicting the departure from Royal Park amidst a huge crowd of cheering citizens, Nolan's Burke sets out on a camel (rather than on his horse), from a virtually deserted Melbourne. The city itself is reduced to a cluster of makeshift, two-dimensional buildings in the middle of a desert, like the stage set for a Western, a parody of the nineteenth-century topographical style. By this means Nolan not only links the setting out to Burke's lonely death at the end of the journey but suggests the long traverse of the continent and Burke's fall from favour by the time Nolan is painting.

214

Stimulated by his discussions with Alan Moorehead during the writing of *Cooper's Creek*, Nolan became almost obsessed with the multiple possibilities of the theme. By 1965 he had produced a third series of Burke and Wills paintings in which the explorers are even more frankly mythologised. Symbolically naked, they sit precariously on their unsaddled camels, seemingly always on the point of sliding off these agents of their survival. An early work in the series, *Burke and Wills at the Gulf* (1961), is an almost lyrical fantasy of the two mounted explorers frolicking on a wide beach (Burke's party failed to reach the coast because of the mangrove swamps), but the majority of the paintings locate Burke and Wills squarely in the desert, symbolic of their helplessness and a reminder of Europeans' inability to relate to the continent. This mismatch is emphasised by Nolan's juxtaposition of almost ethereal explorers with the rough-textured landscape.

In *Burke* (1962) (see illustration following page 176), the figure of Burke, naked and alone on an unharnessed camel in a landscape of barren rock faces, offers a powerful symbol of man ill-at-ease in Nature. On one level Burke's nakedness refers to the plight of the returning party whose torn clothes gave them no protection from the Central Australian winter, but Nolan's painting is more symbolic than historical. Neither the conquering heroic leader nor yet the pathetic dying victim, but welded to his camel like a centaur, Burke gazes about him with interest and some perplexity. Camel and man, both painted in

tones of brown that blend with the rocks, and both depicted in an exaggeratedly angular way that mimics the angles of the cliffs, at first seem part of this barren nature. But there is a distinction between man and camel. While Burke
looks surprised and awkward perched on his unsaddled camel, his head jutting
above the horizon, the camel merges easily with the jigsaw planes of the rocks.
The curve of its neck as it nibbles opportunistically – ever a survivor – at a few
leaves on a wispy branch, is identical with that of the rock below. Unlike Burke's
contemporaries who were struck by the exotic nature of the camels on this
expedition, Nolan depicts them as supremely at home in the desert. Overhead
some of Nolan's characteristic birds inhabit the sky. He later summed up the
essentials of his Burke and Wills series as: 'the actuality of the landscape, which
for Australians is intensified to the point of a dream; the strange conjunction of
a man on a camel, from which he surveys the landscape as if he were walking on
giant stilts; and always the birds, which make everything vivid.'[11]

A scene from the Hoyts–Edgley film *Burke and Wills*, 1985, Burke (Jack Thompson) and
Wills (Nigel Havers) at the Dig Tree. Courtesy Michael Edgley International/Hoyts Ltd.

In 1985 Hoyts–Edgley made a $10 million epic film, *Burke and Wills*, starring Jack Thompson and Nigel Havers. Nolan was appointed 'official artist', in which role he finally visited Cooper's Creek. His response to the film and the trip was another Burke and Wills series, a set of five triptychs, including *Burial of Burke* (1985). This particular painting deliberately references Strutt's 1911 painting of the same name, but subverts the formerly sentimental rendition of the solemn wrapping of Burke's remains in a Union Jack by members of Howitt's rescue party. In Nolan's version there are no mourners. Burke's

A scene from Bob Weis's film *Wills and Burke: the Untold Story*, 1985, the explorers being farewelled in Royal Park. On the stage are Macadam (Jonathon Hardy), Burke (Garry McDonald) and Landells (Rod Williams). Courtesy Generation Films.

remains are literally that: a diagrammatic head surmounted by a black tricorn, skeleton rib cage and two unattached feet lie squarely on the flag, as though an integral part of its design, suggesting both Burke's intimate identification with British imperialism and the simultaneous burial by the desert of the empire together with its hapless representative. Ironically the tone of Nolan's *Burial of Burke* is closer to Bob Weis's comedy *Wills and Burke: the Untold Story*, filmed in the same year as the Edgley blockbuster and starring comic actor Garry McDonald as Burke.

Nolan's mythographic Burke and Wills series prompted other artists to revisit the explorers, reclaiming a historical subject for contemporary art by subverting the sentiment in which it had been shrouded, and reinterpreting the character of the explorers in the light of modern psychology.

David Boyd's parodies

Unlike Nolan, David Boyd was interested in the explorers less for the Australian desert context than for the human characteristics exposed when individuals failed to come to terms with their environment. In her introduction to the catalogue of Boyd's exhibition, *The Explorers*, Jessie MacLeod, a history teacher whose conversation about the explorers had sparked Boyd's interest in this topic, explicitly made this connection:

> Burke and Wills . . . represent in the popular mind the heroic qualities of courage, endurance and defiance in the face of insuperable difficulties. In these pictures, using as his symbols the men who have become part of our folk-lore and history, the artist has conveyed the struggle of man to come to terms with his environment and with himself. The bonds of custom and belief are cast off until, even in loneliness and death, he becomes strong, wise and part of all that is around him. . . . The shadowy people [Aborigines] saw with curiosity and wonder the white man's magic; they felt compassion for his suffering, but they were struck with fear and anger at his savagery and desecration. . . . More is needed than courage; man must first accept his environment, then only can he move forward to wisdom and enlightenment.[12]

217

For Boyd the exploring expeditions were not just historical events but a warning for the present. Each painting in his *Explorers* series (1957–58) has a strong, if humorous, moral. *The Journey into the Desert* shows four men's faces and hands, expressive of their fear and helplessness in the face of an environment with which they make no attempt to compromise. *Burke and Wills Bed Down for the Night* (see illustration following page 176), hilariously satirising the inappropriate impedimenta of the Victorian Exploring Expedition, shows Burke and Wills tucked up in an outsize Victorian brass bed in the middle of the desert, oblivious of the precipice on which they are poised, while Aborigines look on in amazement. *Burke and Wills in the Desert II* again expresses the fear and credulity of the explorers. Burke turns Wills's head to show him a stylised, parodic crow with huge curved beak, which mocks their predicament. *Death of Burke* expresses the arrogance of a man refusing to come to terms with his own failure. Clutching the insubstantial trunk of a diminutive ghost gum, Burke, grinding his teeth and with right hand raised in imprecation, rails at heaven, blaming others for his misfortunes. *King Found* records the compassion of the Aborigines at Cooper's Creek who succoured the desperate explorer until the rescue party arrived. *In Search of Leichhardt* depicts the flurry of ill-advised expeditions to the desert to locate the lost explorer. A white bird flies above them, seeming to lead but equally possibly mocking their efforts – perhaps in reference to Sturt's misplaced faith in the flight of birds to guide him to an inland sea. In *Edward John Eyre* the explorer, hands outstretched in wonder, gazes at the mirage of the inland sea he obsessively seeks. In all these paintings the scene is of minimal importance; it is the universalised explorers,

David Boyd, *Death of Burke*, 1957–58, oil on board, 122.0×183.0 cm, private collection. Courtesy the artist.

depicted almost entirely by their exaggerated heads and enlarged, expressive hands, who dominate the paintings, expressing Western man's predicament in a world he has failed to understand but tried to dominate on his own terms. For David Boyd we are all, still, the explorers.

Albert Tucker's Antipodean heads

In 1954, in self-imposed exile in Rome,[13] Australian artist Albert Tucker met up with Sidney Nolan who showed him some photos of the Australian outback, presumably including those he had taken for the *Courier-Mail* assignment to record the Queensland drought. The impression on Tucker, who had never been to the outback and whose work had, until then, been almost exclusively urban and international in focus, was profound; they were the inspiration for *Ayers Rock* (1955), *Drought* (1956), and *Desiccated Horse* (1956) as well as several paintings that drew on Nolan's Ned Kelly theme.[14]

Ayers Rock, an almost monochromatic landscape in red ochre, shows the monolith set on red sand under a red sky, with a row of stunted dead trees in the foreground like a picket fence. The most striking aspect of the painting is the deeply folded, fissured and pock-marked surface of the Rock, previously (and still most frequently) depicted as a distant, smooth shape. *Ayers Rock* is the predecessor of Tucker's Ned Kelly paintings in which the heavily cratered landscape provides a shield and protection for the outlaws[15] and of his later series of Antipodean heads in which the craters have become the deep eye sockets and pock marks on the face of Australia – and of Australians.

Subsequently, during his years in London, 1956–58, Tucker began to fuse more closely and consciously these originally disparate notions of lunar-like landscape, the explorers who ventured there and the icon of what he called an Antipodean head,[16] a pun on the derivation of 'Antipodean' as 'opposed feet'.

Not satisfied with creating an illusion of craters and crevices on a flat canvas, Tucker had begun to model his 'paintings' in three dimensions, incorporating sand, grit, cement and PVA into a viscous paste that protruded from the canvas like a sculpture. In 1957 this experimentation produced, as critic Robert Hughes has described it, 'a small purplish–brown head, silhouetted against a flat plain of Australian saltbush, [...] a projection of the scarred, inhuman landscape.'[17] Tucker had discovered the rich field of metonymic imagery: the head was itself the landscape and, conversely, in this intriguing metaphor of geographical phrenology, the barren landscape reflects what is inside the 'mind' of the continent. In Tucker's own words, 'I finished up with this semi-human shape – half woman, half landscape – with some kind of emerging Australian physiognomy. It parallels the human involvement with the Australian landscape. The Australian mind has a kind of vast unknown hinterland feeling behind it.'[18] In *Antipodean Head II* (1959) the cratered, craggy surface looms threateningly from the canvas, like the wrinkled crust of the Central Australian desert, symbolic of both the interior wasteland of the

219

continent and the depths of the subconscious. Thus the interior of the head expresses itself in the bumps of this bleak, outward configuration. In these reciprocal statements, whereby the land stands in for the nation's collective unconscious and the Antipodean head stands in for the landscape of a continent, Tucker comes closest of all contemporary artists to delivering the painterly equivalent of that popular theme in mid-twentieth-century Australian literature that was examined in Chapter 10: the symbolic use of the dead centre as interior landscape for the barren soul of a people.

The figures of Albert Tucker's Explorer series clearly developed from his Antipodean heads but the emphasis falls on the incongruity and fragility of their situation. *The Last Days of Leichhardt* (1964) (see illustration following page 176) typifies the earlier series of Tucker's explorer paintings before the thick pastiches of sand and concrete intervened. Leichhardt is dressed circumspectly and inappropriately in black suit, dazzling white shirt and black hat suggestive of a missionary, but carrying a gun behind him. Wearing mirror sunglasses, his angular face is gaunt rather than cadaverous, though his protruding mouth resembles the physiognomy of a chimpanzee and behind his sunglasses the blood vessels of the eyeball parody tributaries of the river that exists only in his mind's eye. The barren land around him offers no sign of other living creature or plant.

When he returned to Australia in 1960 Tucker renewed his two-pronged attack on the desert and its explorers. In the *Arrival at Cooper's Creek* triptych (1958) the despairing explorer, squatting or sitting, is harassed by a pincer-beaked bird that homes in on his neck and heart. *Desert* (1961–62) depicts a craggy mountain (possibly Uluru) and a barren foreground as suggested by the title, but the painting shocks us with its dominant colour – green. Mountain and cloud-like foreground are painted in shades of jade and viridian, while a flight of birds is etched against an orange sky. A green desert is more disturbing than a brown or red one because it mocks our stereotype and parodies the initial hopes of the settlers.

Like Nolan and David Boyd, Tucker was interested exclusively in the unsuccessful explorers – Leichhardt, Burke and Wills – but his figures are intrinsically different from those of the other artists. *Leichhardt* (1967) projects a gaunt image, with prominent ribs and collarbones, hawk-ridged nose and cadaverous eyes, while in *Explorer and his Camel* (1979) a skeletonised figure trudges across a cracked desert, leading his camel. The death's-head with empty eye sockets beneath a battered hat recalls images of war, helmeted dead soldiers, victims of concentration camps. Deeply influenced by German Expressionist images of war, Tucker used his explorer myth to create a peculiarly Australian counterpart to European images of suffering.

In *Death of an Explorer* (1978) (see illustration following page 208, on the other hand, the eyes, so far from being cavernous, protrude exaggeratedly. The figure is buried up to the neck in sand, and from his upturned face the eyes project, quite literally on stalks, like twin lollipops. Behind him a riot of rounded hills in garish tones of crimson, purple and orange (Kata Tjuta – the

Olgas?) are starred with four white-ringed black holes like other eyeballs staring straight back at the dead explorer's staring but unseeing eyes. The correspondence between head and landscape is the dominant feature.

Tucker's later paintings abandoned this heavily symbolic mode, reverting to something more approximating to realism. *Camel in the Desert* (1979), for example, depicts a camel running across a golden desert as a red ball of sun sets amidst mauve clouds. The animal is natural, even joyful, in its non-threatening element where the watercolour effects suggest subtle rock formations and shadowy clumps of spinifex.

Through the eyes of Ernest Giles

After Nolan and Tucker's revisioning of Burke and Wills as symbolic figures, enthusiasm for the explorers as historical individuals waned, even though artists of the 1980s and 90s have increasingly been attracted to the desert as a subject. Instead, there has been a new wave of interest focussing on the explorers' diaries. English-born Australian artist John Wolseley, for example, has no interest in depicting the explorers as individuals:

> I'm conscious of them, but I'm more conscious of all the curious people who did amazing things in the early days: the bushmen, for instance, and people who carted loads of strange materials. Quite often one's interest in the explorers is how extraordinarily silly they were. I've been through all the country where Burke and Wills were, and I'm fascinated by their inability to survive. I mean, I've eaten nardoo.[19]

221

But Wolseley has no hesitation in appropriating the style, language and methods of explorer artists such as Ludwig Becker.

In one case at least the explorers' diaries have proved a fertile source of collaboration between an artist (Brett Whiteley) and a poet (Michael Driscoll). The 1986 publication *Native Rose* represents a combined response to Uluru and Kata Tjuta, mediated through Ernest Giles's account of the area in *Australia Twice Traversed: The Romance of Exploration* (1889). The book brings together maps and quotations from Giles regarding specific locations and incidents, Driscoll's poems written in response to those quotations, photographs, and Whiteley's sketches, paintings and collages of Uluru, Kata Tjuta, Giles and Gibson. Whiteley found Kata Tjuta, in particular, a fertile source of shape and form. They emerge in *Native Rose* as Byzantine domes, as fingers of a hand, as phallic forms, and as female torsos and buttocks, 'peaks, breasts and thighs of stone'. Most of the paintings have seemingly incongruous inserts that refer to Giles's experiences – a leaking tap to recall his leaking waterbags in the Gibson Desert, a compass which Gibson took and which was lost with him, tracks, skeletons. An aerial photograph of Uluru with Kata Tjuta in the distance shows Giles's eyes peering through a slit in the Rock like Ned Kelly's helmet in a

Nolan painting, a humorous reminder that we are seeing Uluru through Giles's eyes, and Giles through Uluru.

Whiteley's art, though it engages with the terrible – the death of Gibson and the near-death of Giles in the desert – conveys a sense of exhilaration in the desert that is not found in the work of any other artist. The paintings and collages shout at us with their intense colours and their witty and parodic suggestions, undercutting the seriousness of both realist landscape composition and history's estimate of the explorers. Many of the seemingly extravagant images involve visual puns on images actually used or implied by Giles. In *Fellow Countryman* (see illustration following page 208), the feckless Gibson riding off into the desert with his head full of a compass he could not read, but was obsessed with having, is depicted by Whiteley with the compass totally replacing his head. In particular, Whiteley's characteristic delight in 'improper' chameleon suggestions meshes with Giles's exuberant prose and irreverent comparison of Mount Olga to 'several rotund or rather elliptical shapes of rouge mange which have been placed beside one another by some extraordinary natural convulsion'. Perhaps more than any other artist, Whiteley has contrived to suggest the vast and terrible extent of the Gibson Desert in relation to a solitary individual, whether riding or on foot. The large-scale photograph of an endless expanse of stony desert, and the painting of a red sand waste across which Gibson, unable to see for his compass-head, plunges blindly with no knowledge of direction, have an immediacy which shocks us into realisation.

222

Antony Hamilton's bare necessities

Describing himself as 'Artist as Explorer', Antony Hamilton has entered into the experience of the explorers Burke and Wills in yet another way. Having lived and travelled extensively around the Oodnadatta area, the Strzelecki Desert and Cooper's Creek, and having personally traced the route of the Victorian Exploring Expedition, Hamilton has a respect for the elements of basic survival that is different from that of most modern travellers, well equipped with supplies and comprehensive safety devices. Nothing emphasises this more than his installation or 'situation' with the cumbersome title, *I can only look out, like Mr Micawber, 'for something to turn up'. A view of the melancholy situation of the party Burke, Wills and King of the Victorian Exploring Expedition of 1860* (1989). As Hamilton's title allows itself to be determined by the words of William Wills's last entry in his journal, so the work allows itself to be determined solely by the objects remaining at the explorers' last campsite – oil-cloth, string, camel hair, camel meat and a camel's nose peg, feathers from a crow (one of the few sources of meat), tobacco, a wirha brush, two small coolamons, nardoo seed which the Aborigines showed them how to collect and grind into a paste as a minimal food source, and faeces derived from the diet they subsisted on.

This work, apparently simple, is extraordinarily dense and complex in its implicit commentary on both this particular event and, by extension, on desert exploration in general. At one level it expresses the pathos of the situation more confrontingly than any of the sentimental epic paintings of the nineteenth century. Following the last journal entries of the explorers, Hamilton insists that the basic urge to survive overrides any heroic aspirations. At another level the installation can be seen as a secular reliquary: these are the sacred objects of Australian religion, like the hair or nails of a saint or the medals of Anzac. Such a view can, in turn, be read either at face value or satirically. While it seems at first to present us merely with facts, leaving us, like archaeologists presented with a dig, to form our own interpretation, this professed 'objectivity' is actually as contrived and manipulative as the heroic depictions of the past. Its philosophy is as relentlessly reductionist as the analytic procedures of scientific materialism, since its implicit statement is that the explorers and their expedition are *nothing more than* these fragments. On the other hand Hamilton introduces, by inference, an element minimalised, or even excluded, from most artistic representations of the expedition, namely the role of the Aborigines in attempting to save the party.[20] Burke died because of his arrogant attitude towards them; King survived because he accepted their help. This statement, hinted at by the nardoo and the coolamons, is a statement for today as much as of the past. Art critic Timothy Morrell, explaining the origin of the crescent-moon shaped wad of tobacco, concludes: 'This suggests that the natural and social worlds which the explorers entered were potentially benign rather than hostile, and provides a sadly ironic memorial to an enterprise which took the image of conquest as a model.'[21]

223

Mandy Martin's reconstructed narratives

Equally complex is Mandy Martin's response to the inland explorers. It combines her personal engagement with the historical figures, contemporary representations of their journeys by the artists who accompanied the expeditions, and reference to the way the national culture has apotheosised them. Her series of paintings titled *Trip to Cooper's Creek* (1996) record her impressions of areas located on the site of Australia's ancient inland sea. They not only explore the appearance of the landscape but also draw on Sturt's journals, on the archetypal wanderer epitomised in Coleridge's 'Rime of the Ancient Mariner', and the emotional and metaphorical significance that the national culture has invested in this area. Within this series the large painting *Littoral* (1995), meaning sea shore, plays on both Sturt's notion of an inland sea and the actual inland sea of the Cretaceous Period. Painted with ochred beach sand it depicts a vast wave breaking on the desert. In *Apotheosis* (1995), a landscape of the rocky plateau above Cooper's Creek near the site of Burke's death, the words 'transcendent failure' are inscribed in the landscape as Australian culture mentally inscribed Burke's death on this area, transforming his failure into a quasi-divine event.

It is in the form of their diaries and the natural-history drawings produced during the expeditions that the explorers enter the work of Mandy Martin. In her studies of the Lake Mungo area (1992–93) phrases from the explorers' diaries are transcribed onto the landscape, partly as a reference to the work of Ludwig Becker, but also to emphasise the post-colonial reading of these texts as imperial inscriptions on the land, and to acknowledge that we cannot now see the land without them. However, Martin suggests that, through this process, an interesting reciprocal appropriation takes place: the diaries are themselves subsumed in the land's ongoing speaking history which extends back and forward through time. This complex interaction between past, present and eternal provides one of the most intriguing aspects of Martin's desert landscapes. Her overwriting on the landscapes of place names, directions ('due west'), and explanatory phrases such as 'native grasses', 'Burrstick seed and black blue bush clay' and 'effect of refraction' allows us to see what has interested her most in the scene, but it also acts as a post-modern reminder that we are seeing not reality but one person's perception, modified by ulterior motives, and that landscape is a way of seeing.

Martin's heroic explorer is not the high-profile Sturt, Leichhardt, Burke or Wills, but Ludwig Becker, the German artist who accompanied the Victorian Exploring Expedition and died in the field.[22] Her series *Reconstructed Narrative, Strzelecki Desert No. 8*, subtitled 'Homage to Ludwig Becker' (see illustration following page 208), resulted from a trip in 1991 to the Moomba Gas Fields located in the Strzelecki Desert. From the beginning of her career, Martin has been committed to the expression of socio–political problems in her art and this journey provided the opportunity to juxtapose the landscape traversed by Becker with a controversial industrial development. *The Effect of Refraction, Fata Morgana*, and *The Effect of Refraction at Noon, Cooper's Basin* are reworkings of Becker's paintings, especially his *Border of the Mud-desert near Desolation Camp* (1861) where the refractive effects at noon created a ghostly image of Burke's party riding out of the heat haze. Martin's recent diptych *Crossing the Bulloo Overflow* (1996), in the *Tracts: Back O' Bourke* series, implicitly commemorates the place where Becker died in April 1861. In an innovative rewriting of Becker's art, Martin substitutes the domes and towers of the gas refinery, looming up so incongruously in the desert, for the conventional mirage of water, suggesting the dependence of Western society on fuel as though it were a basic necessity of life. Commenting on her own work, she writes, 'I imagined Becker struggling over the interminable sand dunes and seeing in the mirage on the horizon a castle; the stainless steel gas refinery with its sci-fi chimneys. "Fata morgana", more commonly known in European folk tales, is the Queen of the Fairies, the queen of trick and illusion. ... In recent work this has been simplified to "F-A-T-A"'.[23]

Following Becker's practice, Martin frequently engraves the title of her paintings in the paint, and overlaid on many of her desert landscapes are phrases from Becker's writings, diagrams of the Santos Oil refinery or notes from her own sketchbook. *Crossing the Bulloo Overflow* has 'Due West' inscribed above a distant hill, as in one of Becker's paintings. By inscribing her own written comments on her paintings Martin claims the status of discoverer, creating her own journey narrative in parallel with those of the explorers. As well as being descriptive and factually informative, these comments on (literally *on*) the landscape also serve to critique the ongoing colonisation of Australia – geographical, cultural and industrial. In this way Martin has appropriated the texts of exploration to comment on a multiplicity of concerns, from art history to socio–political involvement, while consciously positioning herself in the tradition of the explorer/artist. Although recalling Nolan's acknowledgment, quoted earlier, of 'how much we painters and poets owe to our predecessors the explorers', Martin's stance in fact marks a new phase in Australians' changing relationship to the nineteenth-century explorers. Revered at first as the great men of the nation's history, they moved through a period of denigration and satire to become a critique of imperialism or, in Nolan's treatment, mythological figures outside history, representing the individual soul in an existential void. In Martin's work, the artist–explorer is revived as contiguous with the contemporary artist embarked on a quest to discover both the land's meaning and the techniques to express it in art. In all these modes of relating to the explorers the desert is the primary factor; it is what endows the explorers with their interest, their allure, and their perennial relevance.

Transforming Myths

Are all these dead men in our literature, then, a kind of ritual sacrifice?
And just what is being sacrificed? Is it perhaps the European
consciousness – dominating, puritanical, analytical (Richard Mahony
was a doctor, Voss a botanist), that Lawrence saw as negated by this
landscape? ... Reconciliation, then, is a matter of death – the death of
the European mind, its absorption into the soil it has struggled against.

JUDITH WRIGHT[1]

No pilgrims leave, no holy-days are kept
for those who died of landscape. Who can find,
even, the camp-sites where the saints last slept?
Out there their place is, where the charts are gapped,
unreachable, unmapped, and mainly in the mind.

RANDOLPH STOW[2]

Each generation reinvents its myths in response to its particular needs. In
Australia this has been particularly evident in the recasting of the explorers.
The heroic figures of nineteenth-century literature and art who carried with
them the hopes of the colony for expansion were constructs of desire – desire
not only for more pastoral land but for inspiring models of valour and
resourcefulness. In the twentieth century the requirements were different. At
first the new nation needed internationally acknowledged heroes to establish
and adorn its identity. Subsequently it needed to demote these role models
because they were not Australian but European. By the 1950s the notion of any
kind of heroism was regarded with cynicism, and psychoanalysis of these
figures, to unearth their unacknowledged motives and their existential despair,
was more intellectually respectable. Later still, towards the turn of the twentieth century, in a materialist culture where it is nevertheless fashionable to
bemoan materialism and search for a new spirituality, the explorers have again
been pressed into service by writers and artists as our representatives. What
they are now shown as seeking in the desert is not land or colonial power but
spiritual enlightenment and wholeness, a purging of wrong priorities and the
discovery of cosmic meaning.

The figure of the explorer has particular potency in literature, accounting for the continuing interest in reworking the model. In part this fascination has a technical basis: the very process of exploration provided an important organising metaphor for the novel or the long poem – the linear order, both spatial and temporal, implicit in the notion of the journey, and particularly the mapped journey. Ironically, although the physical trek has become progressively less important, so that in many recent treatments the significance of the journey is not primarily external but rather psychological or spiritual, the figure of the explorer retains a central role re-enacting a mythic journey in the tradition of Dante, Melmoth or the Ancient Mariner.

Not only does the desert journey offer a peculiarly Australian version of the Romantic quest for self-discovery but the perceived monotony of the terrain through which it occurs, the very absence of varied external features, drives the attention inwards to focus on the interior landscape. Such few external objects as there are assume enhanced significance as projections of, or pointers to, the traveller's interior world. Thus the apparent emptiness of the desert invites continuity between geographical and psychological isolation. The mirage provides an especially important connection here, symbolising the failure of reason to empower us with explanations of the universe and parodying our dream experiences of inhabiting a place that is familiar, yet strange, realistic but fantastic. Similarly, the commonly recorded sense of entrapment by the fears and contingencies of the desert mirrors the imprisonment of the personality by internal fears and psychological determinants.

227

The desert journey also provides an obvious metaphor for spiritual pilgrimage, suggested in part by the tradition of seeking enlightenment in the wilderness, but greatly enhanced by the nature of the desert, its vastness and sense of antiquity combining to suggest the closeness of the infinite and the eternal. In this sense the explorer also functions as trenchant critic of the community he leaves behind. At the literal level this is the colonial society but many of the works featuring exploration in these terms also carry a more contemporary condemnation of mid-twentieth-century Australia.

Reassessing heroism

As we have seen, with remarkably few exceptions, the nineteenth-century literature of inland exploration, whether generated by the explorers themselves in their published reports, or in fictional treatments, was adulatory, even fulsome. There was no doubt in the minds of these writers that such exploration was necessary or that those who undertook it were heroic in direct proportion to the hardships they encountered. However, even before the end of the century such simple notions of heroism were already being questioned on several counts. One of these was nationalism. Historian Manning Clark wrote:

> At the end of the nineteenth century, one section of Australian society swung
> against veneration of the explorers as national heroes. . . . Inferiority had

become offensive: grovelling to the English must cease. . . . Those brave men who had endured the hardships of the Australian wilderness were put up for examination and found wanting. Many of the explorers were not democratic. Some of them, such as Thomas Mitchell and Charles Sturt, were army officers: some, like Edward Eyre and Ludwig Leichhardt, believed that their mission was to protect the culture of the few from the barbarizing influence of the masses. . . . In the eyes of the nationalists, some of the explorers had committed the sin against the Holy Ghost. They had modelled themselves on the English governing classes. . . . The Australian must find heroes from his own people.[3]

But there were other grounds for disaffection. Sturt's obsession with finding an inland sea, and the heavy wooden whaleboat he had carted at such cost across the dunes and the gibber plains, provided a powerful trope of the ineffectual plans and misguided determination of this explorer. Longstanding unease concerning the gross mismanagement of the Victorian Exploring Expedition tarnished the reputation of Burke himself. Favenc's stringent comments on this fiasco were echoed in fiction in the words of such characters as Mosey and Thompson, bullock drivers in Joseph Furphy's *Such is Life* (1903). Mosey asserts: 'there ain't a drover, nor yet a bullock driver, not yet a stock-keeper, from 'ere to 'ell that could n't 'a bossed that expegition [*sic*] straight through to the Gulf, an' back agen, an' never turned a hair – with sich a season as Burke had. Don't sicken a man with yer Burke. He burked that expegition, right enough'. Thompson's opinion is equally direct: 'You'll never read a word against him . . . [but] in conversation, you'll always learn that Burke never did a thing worth doing or said a thing worth saying; and that his management of that expedition would have disgraced a new-chum schoolboy; and old Victorian policemen will tell you that he left the force with the name of a bully and a snob, and a man of the smallest brains.'[4]

Nevertheless, as already mentioned, the nationalism associated with World War I, and particularly the celebration of the Anzacs as heroic victims of British ineptitude, temporarily restored the Burke and Wills story to contemporary relevance and led to its being embraced by early Australian film-makers. First in the field was Francis Birtles, whose six-month journey following the expedition's route in a Ford motorcar resulted in the film *Across Australia on the Track of Burke and Wills* (1915), the publicity for which claimed: 'By the aid of the cinematograph he [Birtles] has been able to bring to the very doors of the city dweller, the scenes, the people, the habits, the customs of the great Out-back – the Land of the Never-Never!' The film posters made a far-fetched bid for topical relevance by alluding to the war: 'peace hath her victories as well as war'. Three years later Charles Byer Coates's film *A Romance of the Burke and Wills Expedition of 1860* was billed as both a national event, 'made by Australians for Australians, about Australians' (the support of which was clearly a public duty: 'Advance Australia by Supporting Local Industry', advised the poster) and a contemporary issue since 'the indomitable spirit of 1860' was being replayed 'on the Battlefields of Europe'. The opening scene of this 1918 film showed a child praying for both the brave explorers and for 'dear daddy fighting in France', while anti-German feeling was exploited through the vilification of William Brahe. His 'betrayal' of the main party is traced to his rejection by an actress, Mina Doyle, in favour of Burke,[5] leading to the substitution of a German villain for the desert as the drama's main antagonist.

Although C.E.W. Bean's immensely popular *Anzac Book* (1916), which sold 100,000 copies within the year, identified the heroes of Gallipoli not with the explorers but with the outback bushman,[6] the Anzacs suffered a major disadvantage from a literary point of view: their historical anonymity. With the exception of Simpson the Donkey Man, no one hero's name was widely known. Moreover, it was difficult for Australians to resist the judgement of Sir Henry Newbolt who accorded Burke and Wills hero status in his influential *Book of the Long Trail* (1919). Disenchanted with the war, in which his son had been killed, Newbolt collected stories of gallantry in peacetime in order to relocate the components of heroism, which he defined as emanating from 'first the contest, the struggle against odds and obstacles, second the moments of special daring or success'. In company with the more famous explorers (Franklin, Burton, Livingstone, Stanley and Scott), Burke and Wills could be seen as raising Australia's international profile. Newbolt's argument for their inclusion was based on the premise that, although 'ordinary men', Burke and Wills had provided a 'shining example of how men play the game to the last, faithful to each other and to their purpose, even when others have failed them. Best of all, they suffered and died without leaving one word of bitterness behind them.'[7]

Newbolt aside, the interwar period was no time for cultivating failed inland explorers. The urgent optimism involved in encouraging soldier settlement on the land discouraged reminders of a hostile interior that was the necessary counterpart of the explorers' heroism. It was another twenty years before any writer sprang to Burke's defence but, by dint of resorting to a host of inaccuracies, Frank Clune's *Dig* (1937) contrived to cast Burke as hero. Clune had become interested in the expedition when he arrived at Cooper's Creek during the process of writing his popular travel book, *Roaming Around the Darling* (1936).

Scenting a ready-made plot that could enhance his hoped-for reputation as an intrepid travel writer, Clune decided to disinter Burke and Wills from limbo and restore them to heroic status. *Dig* outraged most serious critics with its indiscriminate mingling of documentary quotation and fictional reconstruction, both equally dignified with quotation marks, freely invented conversations, cliché-ridden soliloquies and outbursts of polemic.[8] Clune's Burke pleads melodramatically with opera singer, Julia Matthews:

> 'I want to do something great,' said Burke '. . . do not let me go into this maelstrom of mystery, to dream of you, with this dreadful uncertainty in my mind!' . . . I ask only that you will give me a keepsake of yourself, and a lock of your beautiful hair, that I shall carry across Australia, and through the deserts where no man has trod before.'[9]

229

Clune seems oblivious to the incongruity of the enticement proposed by his hero to the stage-struck young Julia – namely that, on his return with the reward of £2000, 'we could buy a sheep station, and find peace after so many wanderings'!

Given Clune's prior career as a travel writer, his novel is remarkable for its dearth of description of the desert, which is merely a dreary backdrop for a plot featuring stereotyped characters: Burke is a 'Nelson of the Desert' and his party 'starving Spartans', murdered by the manifest villains 'Deserter Brahe and Racketeer Wright'.[10] The following year, Clune produced an article for *Walkabout*, 'With O'Hara Burke to the Gulf', reiterating his celebration of Burke's heroism and, by implication, his own in following the explorer's track, albeit by plane and car rather than by camel. Arriving at Burke's northern-most camp, he exclaims, 'I could not help taking off my hat to a bold and brave man, whose memory has been senselessly slandered.'[11] Throughout, Clune's stated aim is to rescue Burke's reputation from detractors, allegedly on evidence freshly collected by himself, though it would seem that a shared Irish ancestry was a not-insignificant factor in his spirited defence of Burke. The article is peppered with references to Burke's Irish background: 'a wild, romantic Irishman', 'the wild Irishman from Galway', 'the Irishman and the callow Englishman'. Clune bases his case on the fact that Burke did, in fact, accomplish what he set out to do – the first crossing of the continent from south to north. Moreover, argues Clune, his dash to the Gulf was,

> directly or indirectly, the means of opening up Australia's vast hinterland in Western Queensland and on the borders of the Northern Territory. . . . Honour where honour is due! In the annals of Australian exploration, Burke and Wills are entitled to an undying place. Their endurance and their fortitude, *and their success*, should be remembered, rather than what is termed their 'failure'.

Complementary to the celebration of Burke and Wills was the vilification of Brahe, a stance that was as politically popular in the climate of World War II as it had been during World War I. Clune's condemnation of Brahe in *Dig* can hardly count here, as Clune calls him a Swede throughout, but M. Barnard Eldershaw's story, 'The Man Who Knew the Truth About Leichhardt' (1938), which cast the explorer as a poseur – even, by extension, a spy – is unambiguous in linking Leichhardt's moral faults with his nationality:

> He knew he wasn't a bushman and never would be, so he trusted to luck. He talked a lot about his star – like Napoleon. He had all sorts of poses. Sometimes he liked to think of himself as a simple, unworldly scientist, sometimes he was Don Quixote, the leader of lost causes, or he was a great leader, a Bismarck, or a martyred exile. He could never make up his mind.[12]

It was swiftly followed by Alec Chisholm's demolition of Leichhardt's reputation in *Strange New World* (1941), which undertook to prove that the explorer was not only incompetent, vindictive, greedy and dishonest but a 'constitutional psychopath'.[13] Chisholm's book, carrying the imprimatur of a contribution by a medical doctor, achieved such credibility in the anti-German climate of the time that most writers thereafter have felt it necessary to acknowledge its views, even if more mildly. Horst Priessnitz has commented, 'It was as if Leichhardt must pay the penalty for the global aspirations, the power politics of the German *Reich*'.[14] Chisholm's book came to infect not only subsequent treatments of Leichhardt but, by a kind of osmosis, other explorers in the pantheon as well.

The centenary of the Burke and Wills expedition in 1960 tempted a number of writers to revisit the theme. Most portrayed the whole expedition as a tragedy, though where the blame lay was generally left vague.[15] The best known and longest surviving of these was the international bestseller, *Cooper's Creek* (1963), written by the expatriate Alan Moorehead at the suggestion of Sidney Nolan who provided the dust cover illustration for the first edition and two plates from among his own first series of Burke and Wills paintings. Hurriedly researched and written to captivate an overseas readership eager for recognisable Australian 'colour', *Cooper's Creek* featured camels, kangaroos, snakes and dingoes in great abundance, but failed to pose any new or significant questions about the expedition. Its depiction of the desert remained firmly rooted in the cliché of 'weird melancholy', for Moorehead believed that '[t]heir story perfectly expresses the early settlers' deeply felt idea that life was not so much a struggle against other men as against the wilderness'. As Geoffrey Dutton remarked, he kept 'hammering away at the frustrating, enigmatic emptiness of Australia',[16] attempting to mythologise the landscape. Suspense is generated by an atmosphere of mysterious heavy breathing emanating from a land ready to pounce on these interlopers, a transparent reworking of Lawrence's more evocative passages in *Kangaroo*. This mystique is more appropriate to the Bush, the context in which Lawrence invoked it, than to the desert and it is not surprising that Moorehead is more comfortable with the word *bush*: 'The silent unrevealing bush enfolded them, the dingoes loped away as they approached, the kangaroos stared meaninglessly at the strange procession, and nothing was communicated.'[17]

Since *Cooper's Creek*, the revisitings of the Burke and Wills expedition have been more focussed, more contentious and more thoroughly researched. The 1968 play *Burke's Company*, by Bill Reed, reaffirmed the accusation of Brahe as deserter but for more complex reasons than the simplistic, nationalist insinuations of Clune,[18] and remains the only dramatic attempt to subject all the members of this expedition to psychological inquiry. Tom Bergin, a biologist, set out in 1977 with a film crew to re-enact the north-bound part of the expedition, and made interesting dietary deductions from the failure of nardoo to sustain Burke, Wills and King at Cooper's Creek.[19] But two films of the 1980s appear to have exhausted the cinematic potential of the episode. The high-budget Hoyts–Edgley production, *Burke and Wills* (1985), on which Sidney Nolan was official artist and which included music by Peter Sculthorpe, was a glossy epic

231

of heroism, delivering an unambiguous conclusion: the explorers were victims of circumstance and unfortunate coincidence. No one was blamed for their tragedy, not even the desert, and certainly not the two leaders who play their heroic roles impeccably. This view is consistent with that of historian Manning Clark, who insisted on Burke's 'mighty spirit', albeit 'destroyed by a "fatal flaw"'. Appearing in the same year, and in keeping with the reversal implied in its title, Bob Weis's Monty Pythonesque comedy, *Wills and Burke* (1985), treats the expedition as a theatrical farce, but does so with semi-serious intent. Tim Bonyhady has pointed out that this film, which depicts the Exploration Committee appointing the otherwise hopeless Burke solely because he can act, shows a much clearer grasp of the political issues involved. The whole expedition is presented as a burlesque, one of Marvellous Melbourne's most successful theatrical performances.[20]

Psychoanalysing the explorers

After *Cooper's Creek* there is a distinct break in the focus of literature dealing with the explorers. Simple heroism is no longer just suspect; it is irrelevant. We saw in Chapter 10 that there was increasing interest in a reciprocal relationship between geography and psychology, each reflecting, informing and determining the perception of the other. We have also seen, in Chapter 11, that Sidney Nolan's paintings of Burke and Wills, along with Albert Tucker's explorer paintings, provided a new symbolism for investigating the psychological terrain by linking it to the journey of exploration.[21] At first this analytical process involved no more than a re-examination of the explorers' motives for undertaking what seemed a masochistic exercise. Whereas it had been assumed at the time that expeditions were undertaken in response to the land, specifically 'undiscovered' land, fictional treatments of exploration in the second half of the twentieth century virtually ignore the land as motive, or even as objective reality, locating the impetus almost wholly within the explorer's own psyche.

The explorer in fiction is often ill at ease in his complacent, materialistic society and therefore driven to search for a transcendent ideal or to seek absolution for his past: Patrick White's Voss despises Sydney society; Randolph Stow's Heriot is driven both by his conviction that he has killed an Aborigine and by a need to expiate his attempts to 'civilise' the Aborigines at his mission. Increasingly through this century, writers have disregarded the social imperative in order to focus on the individual soul confronting itself in a timeless desert. As a result, the explorer's ultimate vindication is divorced entirely from the material 'success' of the expedition, being dependent only on his achieving personal enlightenment.

Douglas Stewart's *Voyager Poems*, written in 1931 although not anthologised until 1960, are a conscious attempt to create a glorious history for Australia through the remembrance of the nation's heroes. In his foreword to the volume Stewart writes:

> ... there seems to come a time in the history of nations when whatever it is that moves the production of poetry ... demands that the poets should sing the nation itself into shape. How did it come to be? What kind of men made it? What are its ideas and ideals? ... if the poets can tell us what our tribal ancestors were like, and why and how they brought us here, we shall have a better chance of understanding ourselves.[22]

The essential mission of Stewart's explorers is not geographical discovery but self-discovery, for which the significant factors are not worldly success but solitude and humility. Thus all his voyagers are cast alone into a wilderness, whether at sea or in a desert.

Leichhardt, Stewart's representative inland explorer, is one of the last such figures to be conceived as unambiguously heroic. Notions of altruism, desire for fame, and even the pragmatism of exploration, as the motives for inland expeditions are replaced by self-seeking and arrogance. Keith Harrison's poem 'Leichhardt in the Desert' (1966) begins by assigning to the explorer a compelling sense of vocation, even against his will:

> I did not choose to make this westward journey
> Into the dry rock country of the dead ...
> I did not choose; say rather I was called,
> By a voice that ...
> Grew louder, more insistent – till I came.[23]

233

But this potentially heroic beginning leads not to a noble enterprise but to a 'sullen band ... bound in a hate that has no symbol'. Leichhardt is no saintly or compassionate leader: rather he retains a distance from his men. 'That way, control./Hate, sorrow, fear; these three unite us.' The poem ends with an invocation to 'You mad saints who claim to know this place', but whether those saints are Leichhardt and his men, or whether the exclamation comes from Leichhardt, remains ambiguous. In either case, the 'mad saints' are exhorted to 'Make prayers for those on a dry journey:/Pray that our arrogance does not fail', suggesting that only intense pride can keep men going in such a place. Similarly, Max Harris's poem 'Sturt at Depot Glen' not only derides Sturt's vision of an inland sea but shows him as a failed hero, arrogant, mad, believing all things are known to him:

> Sturt wasn't sure, didn't care, if he were mad or not,
> Like the thirst-crazed abo who stumbled in from the desert
> Blazing with recognition. To him all things were known. ...[24]

Harris also insists on the explorer's ordinariness and the farcical and inflexible pretensions of British regimen: 'Where Poole's black body sweltered in its porous grave./Sturt rubbed his scabby chin. "I suppose I'd better shave."'[25]

These poems examined the explorers' claims of heroism in terms of their achievement and found them severely deficient. But meanwhile other writers, having accepted this failure as self-evident, moved on to interpret exploration as a metaphor for a spiritual journey in which success and failure were assessed quite differently.

Exploring the soul

With Francis Webb's *Explorer Poems* we reach a new stage in the re-reading of the nineteenth-century explorers. Judith Wright has observed of Webb's poetry, 'there was, from the first, something that related less to the man who was the ostensible subject, than to the poet's own problems and, by extension, the problems of the human soul. . . . Leichhardt is set to act the pantomime-part of a man mazed in guilt and memory; Eyre . . . is a man returning from a nightmare to common day'.[26] Webb moves beyond preoccupation with histori-cal sources, physical hardships and psychological probing of character to focus on a spiritual journey through pride to humility, from the profane to the sacred. It was important for Webb's purpose that his chosen explorers, Sturt, Eyre and Leichhardt, all journeyed through the desert, designated throughout his work as the place of spiritual search and vision. Webb's 'Poet' begins:

> I'm from the desert country – O, it's a holy land
> With a thousand warm humming stinging virtues.
> Masters, my words have edged their way obediently
> Through the vast heat and the mystical cold of our evenings.[27]

234

We have seen in earlier chapters that Leichhardt had been the contro-versial subject of numerous biographical accounts, beginning with the criti-cisms of members of his own expeditions, and of contemporary poems celebrating the success of his first expedition or mourning his loss during his third. It was his unexplained disappearance that continued to intrigue both his contemporaries and subsequent generations so that even in the twentieth cen-tury there were recurrent, often costly, attempts to locate the remains of the lost expedition.[28] However, Webb's poem sequence 'Leichhardt in Theatre' (1952) bypasses the expedition itself to consider the motivation of the explorer and the process of exploration within the social context. As such, it almost cer-tainly influenced Patrick White's treatment of Leichhardt in *Voss* five years later.[29] Both writers chart the spiritual growth of a vainglorious protagonist through suffering and humiliation in the desert; both suggest that the contemporary social pressures to open up the interior for settlement were at least partly responsible for inducing his monstrous arrogance; both endow Nature with a spiritual presence, presenting it as an active protagonist in the drama of exploration. In addition, as we shall see in more detail later, both were using the figure of the explorer to express their frustrated condemnation of Australian society in the 1950s – its crass materialism, bourgeois ethics and self-complacency.

Webb's sequence, beginning with 'Advertisement', immediately sets the expeditions within the context of public spectacle and economic expectation. The trek from Brisbane to Port Essington is intended not only to seek out grazing land but to provide a highway for trade with the rest of the world. Interestingly at this point Webb introduces Sturt. To some extent Sturt was Leichhardt's implicit rival, the one who posed the problem, the predecessor he had to surpass. Yet Sturt, too, was the victim of influential colonial interests that demanded rich pastures, an inland sea. A shrivelled, broken man, 'fused-out, brittle',[30] blinded by the intense light of the interior, he is described in terms strongly reminiscent of Joseph Conrad's Kurtz: 'Light has rapped at his skull, flooded into his heart,/Shrivelled, consumed him'.[31] The only report he can deliver on the inland sea will turn their 'ambitions and trafficking' to 'ash in his crucible', the crucible of the burning desert. His only recourse is to ironic metaphors playing on the visual similarities between the desert and the sea.[32] In Webb's account Sturt has created the 'Impasse at the Centre' which lures Leichhardt to resolve it. Moreover, the burnt-out figure of Sturt is a tragic forewarning, unheeded, of Leichhardt's own end.

When Webb's curtain rises on Leichhardt, he is still on board ship to Australia, supremely confident that his European knowledge and conventional heroic virtues of 'honour, ambition, courage' will suffice to conquer this visionary land 'where man becomes a myth'. His purpose is to achieve fame through exploration and, in the traditional gendered language of conquest, the land is a virginal female awaiting his devouring gaze, his sexual possession: 'No famished eyes save his/Shall know her radiant body' (significantly, the Aborigines are dismissed as 'eyeless and incurious as death'). This inflated imagery is immediately punctured by 'the funny old leader of the pantomime' who ridicules Leichhardt's appearance and pretensions, invoking stereotyped racial differences. When the audience disapproves of such levity being turned on one of its heroes, the clown berates them for not tearing this burlesque figure to pieces.

During his first expedition Leichhardt is incorrigible. Even the death of the naturalist Gilbert, speared to death by Aborigines, fails to humble him. Returning to the extravagant lionising of Sydney, he colludes in the adulation, envisaging a towering bronze statue to match his self-admiration:

Wise for the Doctor so to steep himself
In this sweet Lethe: hear fat city voices
Follow in his path with accents thoroughly seasoned
To after-dinner feats, hear other voices
Already cradling spiritual flecks of gold
From his alluvial march that has gushed through
The channels of a continent parched for news.
. . . In the faces of women,
Their gracious sidelong eyes, he reads his own
Transfiguration, his solar permanence;

235

And their narcotic murmurs connote bronze:
Leichhardt, enormous, seen from passing coaches,
Striding above tree-level.[33]

This pinnacle of his worldly success coincides with the nadir of Leichhardt's spiritual career. 'This leading man we shall not see again. . . . In a sense he died . . .'. Webb suggests that the farcical disasters of Leichhardt's second journey are the consequences of his pride. The 'honour, ambition, courage' of his original setting out have dwindled to 'Courage, Ambition' in the second, honour being lost on the way. Poor leadership, ignorance of animals, stealing of supplies, bad decisions and inappropriate rhetoric (indicated by the repetition of the pompous announcement, 'The Doctor makes a speech') speedily reduce the expedition to farce. 'He makes another speech./ The expedition sinks to a watery grave'.[34]

Before setting out on his third expedition, Webb's Leichhardt appears in 'The Room', the cramped space of introspection, where, forced to consider his motives, he achieves some self-knowledge, while in 'The Third Expedition', he is seen as of a humbled spirit, beyond materialism and rhetoric. In the light of Leichhardt's spiritual redemption, his physical end is unimportant; in place of the monstrous inflated egotism, the supersize bronze statue, he is now 'life-sized and breathing':

236

In such clean space the man and his shadow ride.
See them upon the hills, life-sized and breathing,
Where they will go, how perish – this is nothing.

We are thus encouraged to see beyond both history-book rhetoric and mean-spirited denunciation to celebrate Leichhardt's real achievement. As the critic Michael Griffith remarks, 'It is because he has failed as a grandiose promethean hero that he has achieved his humanity'.[35]

Webb turned next to the figure of Edward Eyre, but in 'Eyre All Alone' (1961) his frame of reference widened. Here the psychoanalysis of the protagonist, while undoubtedly an important factor, is subsumed in Webb's conscious mythologising of the process of exploration as an example of the solitary individual embarked on a lonely, archetypal quest. A note on the poem affirms this: 'My insistence on Eyre's aloneness is not an overlooking of Wylie, but comes from my seeing such a journey of discovery as suggestive of another which is common to us all.'[36] The crossing of the desert is both a journey into the self and a universal myth about the progress of the soul, through the wilderness of solitude and despair. There are obvious and insistent parallels with *Heart of Darkness*, but where Conrad's myth is informed by the anthropology of his day, notably Frazer's *The Golden Bough*, Webb's is grounded firmly in Catholic tradition, largely biblical but also drawing on the mystics' experience of a dark night of the soul and, as Patricia Excell has shown, on Spenser, Milton and Eliot.[37]

The poem's first words, 'East to west', introduce all three levels of meaning – the geographical plane of Eyre's actual journal, described in his *Journals*; the passage of the individual life from birth to death, conventionally symbolised in the Sun's passage across the sky; and the spread of Christianity from the East to Western tradition. Like a meditation on the fourteen Stations of the Cross the poem's fourteen units focus on incidents in Eyre's journey from Fowler's Bay to King George's Sound. A chorus of eight lines draws attention to the biblical parallels implicit in the intervening stanzas, demanding a closer reading of the images and their original context. As an example of such density of reference we can consider the following lines:

Walk, walk. From dubious footfall one
At Fowler's Bay the chosen must push on
Towards promised fondlings, dancings of the Sound.
Fourth plague, of flies, harries this bloodless ground.
Cliff and salt balance-wheel of heathen planet
Tick, twinkle in concert to devise our minute.
But something on foot, and burning, nudges us
Past bitter waters, sands of Exodus.

'Walk, walk' suggests a traditional pilgrimage, in particular the Exodus from Egypt to Canaan: 'the chosen must push on/Towards promised fondlings', for Eyre, although dubious of God's providence, sees himself as singled out for this task, as Moses was chosen to lead the Israelites to the Promised Land. A series of biblical references and verbal puns cements this connection: flies, the fourth plague of Egypt; the water turning to blood on the land; the burning bush which seals Moses's vocation and the pillar of fire that leads the Israelites by night; the bitter waters of Marah.[38] The metre of the opening line, with its resonances of Tennyson's 'Break, break, break,/On thy cold gray stones O Sea!', prompts us to expect another repetition of 'walk', engendering a sense of indefinable sadness that subverts in advance the optimism of the subsequent setting out: 'So we dream of the strock-route east to homely west ...' Yet Eyre, of all people, knew how unlikely this was: he had already publicly rejected the idea in favour of another foray to seek for pasture north from Adelaide.[39] It was only his signal failure to find a passage past Lake Torrens that drove him westward, determined not to return home in defeat but to clutch at heroic status in the annals of exploration.[40]

The third poem, 'April 29th', introduces the murder of Baxter, Eyre's only white companion, by two of the three Aborigines. In terror Eyre realises he must complete the journey with only Wylie, the third Aborigine, whom he still mistrusts. Although Webb is aware of the falseness of Eyre's melodramatic claim, made in his *Journal*, that he is 'alone in the desert', he retains it as having symbolic truth. It functions as a reminder that we should see Eyre's expedition as an enactment of the long and hazardous journey of life, the individual alone before God, 'Transfixed in fear and loneliness'. Eyre's great discovery was not the stock route he attempted (and failed) to find, but himself.

Section 6, 'From the Centre', is the one poem in the series that refers to the abortive northern trek before the journey west to the Sound. This, the lowest emotional point of the journey, is precipitated by the murder of Baxter and Eyre's humbled recollection of his vulnerability crossing Aboriginal land: 'Through their territory I grovel on hands and knees'. In contrast to his earlier flag-planting rhetoric of conquest, he finally comes to realise that *he* is the interloper: it is *their* territory. His subsequent journey of self-examination is conducted through the metaphor of the desert. Each stanza of this section ends in 'pride'.

> Desert, big stick, or inland sea
> Were all the Promised land to me.
> Horses with a gross family tree
> Carried my pride.

This stanza is followed by two that detail, in repulsive imagery, the physical horror of Lake Torrens, Eyre's obsession and *bête noir*. 'Hag Torrens ... Glassnaked the lake-bed sprawled in muck,/Loutish bogs would belch and suck'. Through the frustration, pain and failure of this experience, his pride is at least partially humbled.

> The Centre has rolled me a dice
> Into the hot air above tableland, face.
> Remains substantial (by God's grace)
> Some narrow pride.

In Section 8, 'Aborigines', Eyre continually fears attacks ('All my days and all my nights/You haunt me') and, hampered by a rifle with a stuck breech, he finds that 'Innumerable times the great Expedition of my thought/Has gone to pieces,/Frightened horses, galloping in all directions'. Eyre's partial humbling and realisation of his need for help are rewarded by an epiphany in the form of a banksia which, he reasons, must indicate continuity with the western settlement since he had not found such plants on the eastern side of the Bight. Like Moses's Burning Bush it embodies a spiritual revelation. 'Banksia, carry fire, like the thurifer/Over my sandy tongue-tied barren ground' and, purified by this floral flame he and Wylie seem to hear 'the sound, the Sound'.

As in any pilgrimage, there are recurrent dangers. Fear of the Aborigines is replaced by extreme thirst but, again, Providence rescues them through the extraordinary, coincidental arrival of a French whaling boat, *Mississippi*, whose English captain Rossiter takes them aboard, feeds and clothes them, and sends them forth with generous provisions. Eyre is overcome by this Good Samaritan: 'Lord, who is my neighbour/On the long road to the Sound?'

The final section, 'The Sound', opens with the two travellers struggling through heavy rain, an image that is both ironical after their desperate search for water through long stretches of desert, and a traditional sign of grace. Soon

Eyre, as befits the heroic leader, is 'truly alone', Wylie having been borne off in triumph by his fellow tribesmen and the inhabitants of the town being still indoors. Looking down on the Sound from a hill, Eyre reflects on the multiple significance of his journey: 'One year on the march, an epoch, all of my life. ... the long knotted absurd beard/That is my conscience grown in the desert country'. The end of the journey is marked by an apotheosis: 'On the main road Someone moves'. The 'Someone' (Webb insisted on the upper case) is Christ glimpsed on the Road to Emmaeus, a promise of resurrection and rebirth. This realisation is the sole and sufficient vindication of a journey that, in terms of its alleged purpose to reveal a viable stock route to the west, was a manifest disaster. But for Webb the vision negates and transforms the failure.

Voss

The philosopher Fredric Jameson has argued that the historical novel 'can only "represent" our ideas and stereotypes about that [historical] past',[41] but in *Voss* (1957) Patrick White created a protagonist and imagery[42] that for subsequent generations of Australians *became* history. Although the novel itself appealed mainly to a relatively small group of literati at home and abroad, its ideas percolated far more widely than this, influencing writers and artists whose work did infiltrate into the popular culture of successive generations. In this extended sense *Voss* did more than any other single literary work to transform the Australian desert from dead heart to arena for psychological struggle and spiritual quest. As well, White produced a revisioning of the notion and purpose of exploration. As the critic Andrew Taylor remarks, although *Voss* 'is not itself history in any verifiable sense ... it has become a powerful influence on the way many Australians of the present see their country's past and, therefore, on the way they inhabit its present'.[43]

239

White described the genesis of *Voss* as emanating from the combined experiences of war and the desert. World War II, which had at first seemed to offer fulfilment, produced only disenchantment with the goals sanctioned by Western society. 'What had seemed a brilliant, intellectual, highly desirable existence, became distressingly parasitic and pointless'.

> Afterwards I wrote *Voss*, possibly conceived during the early days of the Blitz, when I sat reading Eyre's *Journal* in a London bed-sitting room. Nourished by months spent trapesing backwards and forwards across the Egyptian and Cyrenaican deserts, influenced by the arch-megalomaniac of the day, the idea finally matured after reading contemporary accounts of Leichhardt's expeditions and A.H. Chisholm's *Strange New World* on returning to Australia.[44]

White also acknowledged Drysdale and Nolan's visions of the desert as powerful influences. In asking Nolan to design the jacket for the English edition, he confessed, 'I often felt in writing *Voss* that certain scenes were, visually, in the Sidney Nolan Manner'.[45] White's own experience of desert terrain in the Middle East during the war was also a factor in transforming a novel about explorers into one about a spiritual quest. 'For some of that time in the desert I had a posting in which I was free to wander, and I covered a lot of ground. It was then that I began to realise the possibilities of the desert, and that the Voss character really had a chance to develop.'[46]

As a returning expatriate after the war, White was also expressing, in his analysis of nineteenth-century colonial society, a more contemporary criticism: his own bitter reaction to what he saw as the narrow, censorious society of Australia in the 1950s, with its cult of conformity and mediocrity.[47] The 'possibilities of the desert' thus derive from its multiple aspects and, in particular, the variable interpretations ascribed to it, ranging from the material and historical to the symbolic, from a God-forsaken place to a site of spiritual renewal.[48] Not only are these diverse views identified with particular characters in the novel, but the development of Voss himself, as of Laura Trevelyan, is indicated by a changing attitude to the desert.

In post-colonial terms, *Voss* retraces European attitudes to the land, from desire for conquest, whether scientific or geographic, and ownership of the land, to appreciation of the Aboriginal understanding of being owned by the land. Voss's patron, Edmund Bonner Esq., represents the first stage of the colonial appropriation of the land. To this wealthy drapery merchant (and hence literally a dealer in the material) the underwriting of this desert expedition 'in hard cash, and not in sufferings of spirit'[49] offers not only the immediate 'power of patron over protégé' but pre-eminently the chance to open up new land for the colony and to buy a place in history. Yet the notion of this fussy, frightened man inscribing his name on a vast expanse of timeless desert implicitly debunks not only such procedures but the associated view of history as the narrative of 'great men'.

Like the European colonisers Voss thinks of Australia as 'this country of which he had become possessed by implicit right'.[50] The implicit 'right' to domination is based on a claim to divine intention (Voss regards himself as being 'reserved for a peculiar destiny'), superiority of race and what Laura calls his 'right of vision'. Voss's journey recapitulates the underlying intentions of exploration history, beginning with the familiar trope of the rape of a virgin land. This is clearly suggested in the extended metaphor of sexual conquest, 'as he entered in advance that vast, expectant country, whether of stone deserts, veiled mountains, or voluptuous, fleshy forests. But his. His soul must experience first, as by some spiritual *droit de seigneur*, the excruciating passage into its interior.'

The other members of Voss's party also exemplify various forms of the European will to conquest. Albert Judd, the ex-convict, superior to most of the group morally as well as in practical terms, but essentially a humanist, embarks on the expedition as a trial of will, determined, like Voss, to prove his ability to conquer. As befits the most practical member, he alone survives the ordeal, but only to become deranged on finding his wife and children dead. Frank Le

ABOVE
Landcruiser 'UFO'
advertisement. Courtesy
Saatchi & Saatchi.
Copywriter: Mike
Newman. Art Director:
Jonathon Teo.

BELOW
Wunala Dreaming –
Qantas plane. Courtesy
Qantas Airways Limited.

Uta Uta Jangala (left)
directing the painting of
Yumari, assisted by (left to
right) Anatari Jampijinpa,
Dinny Jampijinpa,
John Jakamarra,
Kania Japangardi,
Charlie Japangardi and
Yala Yala Jungarrayi Gibson
(back to camera), Papunya,
Central Australia, 1981.
Courtesy J.V.S. Megaw,
Flinders University Art
Museum.

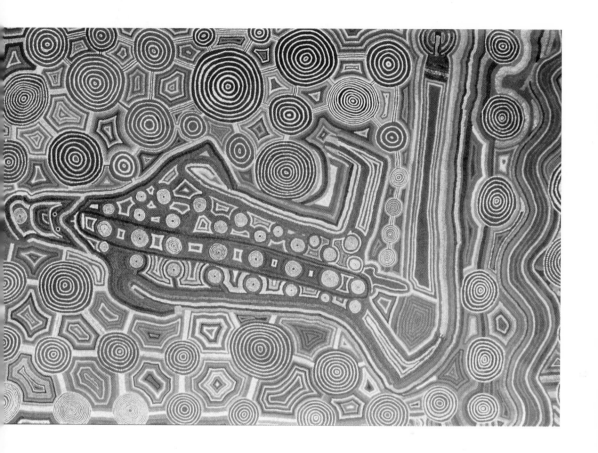

Uta Uta Jangala, *Yumari*,
Papunya, Central
Australia, 1981, acrylic on
canvas, 244 × 366 cm.
Courtesy J.V.S. Megaw,
Flinders University Art
Museum.

Yam and Bush Tomato
Dreaming on Yuendumu
school door, Yuendumu,
Central Australia, 1983,
acrylic on metal door,
200.6×102 cm, South
Australian Museum,
Adelaide.

Mesurier, amateur artist and poet, seeks truth in the form of the poetic word, itself an extension of the divine word, Logos. This is why he embraces the vision of extreme suffering that Voss holds out to him.

Voss's own desire for conquest re-enacts the ambition of Western culture to colonise the continent intellectually by locating it within an explanatory scientific ideology: 'in the infinite distances of that dun country of which he was taking possession, all, finally, would be resolved.' (This aspect is neatly satirised in Randolph Stow's children's novel, *Midnite: The Story of a Wild Colonial Boy* (1967), when the seventeen-year-old Midnite-turned-bushranger encounters an eccentric explorer named Johann Ludwig Ulrich von Leichardt [*sic*] zu Voss, who goes by the name of Mr Smith. Accompanied by two camels called Sturm and Drang, Smith has written in his Diary, '"Today I have this desert the Cosmic Symbolical Desert named."')[51] As an essential part of his attempt to conquer the continent intellectually Voss proclaims himself the map-maker of the continent: '"The map?" repeated the German. "I will first make it."'

However, during the expedition such simplistic notions of owning and mapping territory are subverted. White insists on a more complex arena of exploration that encompasses the internal, the spiritual. In this sense *Voss* can be seen as a precursor of revisionist and particularly feminist geographies with their insistence on the inadequacy of the grid map as an explanation of the land.[52] Voss's assertion 'I will cross the continent from one end to the other. I have every intention to know it with my heart' ironically recalls the quotation from the great German mystic Meister Eckhart[53] that White later used as the epigraph to *The Solid Mandala* (1966): 'It is all within, not outside, but wholly within.' Thus Voss's boast 'The map? ... I will first make it' is progressively annulled, notably by his contact with the Aborigines who have already 'mapped' the land in a different, more meaningful sense. He realises that the two black guides walk with authority on the land: 'Their bare feet made upon the earth only a slight, but very particular sound, which, to the German's ears, at once established their ownership.'[54] Laura's remark in the final scene of the novel encapsulates this view: 'Knowledge was never a matter of geography. Quite the reverse, it overflows all maps that exist. Perhaps true knowledge only comes of death by torture in the country of the mind.' To the fatuous Mr Ludlow who has inquired playfully about the identity of 'this familiar spirit whose name is on everybody's lips, the German fellow who died', Laura replies in all seriousness: '"Voss did not die. .... He is there still, it is said, in the country, and always will be. His legend will be written down eventually, by those who have been troubled by it."' The final 'it', deliberately ambiguous in its reference to both legend and landscape ('the country'), links these two concepts, a liaison reinforced by the counterpointing of scientific 'facts' with the 'spoken legend ... the stubborn music that was waiting for release.' To Ludlow's more practical question, '"Come, come. If we are not certain of the facts, how is it possible to give the answers?"' Laura affirms, '"The air will tell us"'.

Through the interior journey that parallels his geographical progress Voss re-enacts and prefigures the changing attitudes to the land culminating in his

241

ability to understand the Aboriginal boy's explanation of the X-ray cave paintings:

> 'Men gone away all dead, . . . All over . . . By rock. By tree. No more men. . . .
> Wind blow big, night him white, this time these feller dead men. They come
> out. Usfeller no see. They everywhere.' . . .
> 'Now I understand,' said Voss gravely.
> He did. To his fingertips. He felt immensely happy.

More explicitly Judd, the demented survivor of the expedition, insists that Voss participated in both the European act of dominating the country by marking/naming it, and the Aboriginal process of entering spiritually into the landscape, being possessed by it.[55]

> 'Voss left his mark on the country,' he said.
> 'How?' asked Miss Trevelyan, cautiously.
> 'Well, the trees, of course. He was cutting his initials in the trees. He was a
> queer beggar, Voss. The blacks talk about him to this day. He is still there – that
> is the honest opinion of many of them – he is there in the country . . . you see,
> if you live and suffer long enough in a place, you do not leave it altogether. Your
> spirit is still there.'

Yet the analysis of colonial attitudes to the land, with their intended reference to those of the 1950s, and the gradual acceptance of Aboriginal values were not White's main purpose in *Voss*. They are counterpointed against, and in White's view secondary to, the spiritual journey undertaken by Voss and Laura from egocentric pride, scepticism, even atheism, to acceptance of the Christian virtues of humility and service.[56]

When Voss sets out he is a monster of pride and arrogance. In a letter to Nolan, White described Voss as 'a megalomaniac German explorer' and there are clear resonances of Hitler in his Messianic pretensions. At her first meeting with him Laura immediately characterises him as 'this enclosed man . . . one of the superior ones'.[57] His obsession with crossing the desert is grounded in the desire for conquest, for knowledge and for self-aggrandisement. It represents a means of conquering his own weaknesses and hence demonstrating his superiority over others. Later Laura identifies the attraction the desert holds for him as an extension of himself: 'You are so isolated. That is why you are fascinated by the prospect of desert places, in which you will find your own situation taken for granted or, more than that, exalted. . . . Everything is for yourself.'

While rejecting the humility of Christ, Voss nevertheless makes his preparations in almost parodic reference to Jesus choosing his disciples, offering his men a cross and a martyr's crown if they will leave their former ways to follow him. Indeed, Voss is unable to resist the temptations relating to power. Unlike Jesus, who refused to test his power by flinging himself down from the temple, Voss is only too ready to attempt a miracle, declaring that if he had his way he would set out alone and barefooted. Where Jesus rejected the offer of all the world's kingdoms, Voss, as we have seen, casts himself as the map-maker of the continent. For Voss, the spiritual message of the Gospel is translated into self-transcendence through will, rather than through grace. He expects and intends to emerge from this desert as an acknowledged saviour, 'the apotheosis for which he was reserved': '. . . in this disturbing country, so far as I have become acquainted with it already, it is possible more easily to discard the inessential and to attempt the infinite.' Voss sets out despising Palfreyman, the only convinced Christian of the party, satirising him when, '"in his capacity of Jesus Christ [he] lances the boils"', but he is well aware of the superiority this confers on Palfreyman and when Le Mesurier falls ill with diarrhoea, Voss insists on appropriating the moral power by acting as his nurse. At first his motive is pride: 'So he set about it, woodenly. Prospective saints, he decided, would have fought over such an opportunity . . .'; but in performing these acts he discovers the redemptive power of suffering. At the moment of his decapitation by Jackie, the Aborigine of his own party, he believes himself to be speared in the side like the figure in the Aboriginal cave drawing and like the crucified Christ, a belief which Judd, who had not witnessed the event, also endorses. Awaiting death, Voss is 'finally dragged from his golden throne, humbled in the dust':[58]

> Now, at least, reduced to the bones of manhood, he could admit to all this [his fear] and listen to his teeth rattling in the darkness.
> 'O Jesus,' he cried, '*rette mich nur! Du lieber!*'

243

Laura Trevelyan, whom Voss met only briefly in Sydney, but whom he enjoins to accompany him 'in thought, and exercise of will, daily, hourly', also receives enlightenment in a spiritual journey parallel to his physical one. At the beginning Laura, too, is proud, self-sufficient and contemptuous of others: an atheist, she thinks, and keen to test her will through self-humiliation. In one of their few actual encounters she tells him, '*You* are *my* desert'. Although she does not physically leave Sydney, she joins Voss metaphorically in his journey to the interior. Suffering in parallel with his hardships, even to the point of a symbolic death through brain fever and the cutting of her hair on the night of the explorer's decapitation, Laura achieves a mystical union with her bridegroom, symbolically 'giving birth' to the servant's child, Mercy, whom she adopts as an indication that she, like Voss, has attained to compassion, humility and love.

In *Voss*, then, the Australian desert exists on two planes, the temporal and the apocalyptic. It functions as the terrain for Voss's literal journey as he re-enacts the nineteenth-century exploration narrative; as a metaphor for the whole continent it allows White to critique the processes of imperialism and colonisation as well as carrying resonances of the 1950s; and it provides the imagery for the individual's spiritual journey of transformation from arrogance to humility.

Accepting the explorers

Once it was realised that Australian history could be immeasurably extended
to include tens of thousands of years of Aboriginal occupation, the importance
of the explorers, even as psychological studies, diminished rapidly. They were
no longer called upon to bear the full weight of responsibility for the country's
legends, for this role was increasingly being invested in stories from the
Dreaming. The vindictiveness directed against them as inadequate heroes was
replaced by a level of low-key, post-colonial irony – even fondness, as though
for a socially inept but well-meaning relative.

This mood is epitomised in 'Sturt's Dreaming', a poem by Bruce
Lundgren, which counterpoints the 'topographical dream' that Sturt projects
'on this mysterious and unknown land with Aboriginal dreamings'. The second
stanza exposes the ineffectual nature of Sturt's plans, based on his premise of
an inland sea, erroneously derived from the triangulation of birds' flight paths.
Sturt's dream is compared to the Dreaming, a comparison that both mocks
and dignifies it:

> Aborigines, immersed in their own dreaming,
> watch this ancestral canoe
> toil up the sliding sides of dunes
> bobble, insect-like, through spinifex,
> on its way to a legendary ocean,
> charted only
> by the false trigonometry of birds.[59]

244

Although Ernest Giles was one of the most prolific writers among the
inland explorers and probably the most interesting stylistically, he has rarely
been the chosen subject of other writers. The only fictional work in which he
appears is Dal Stivens's novel *A Horse of Air* (1970). Ostensibly this is the autobiography of one Harry Craddock, eccentric millionaire, passionate ornitholo-
gist and inmate of an asylum, describing his expedition to the Gibson Desert
in search of the allegedly extinct night parrot, *Geopsittacus occidentalis*.[60] Half the
novel is taken up with preparations for the expedition; but once out in the
desert with his motley party Craddock is in his element. His wife Joanna
records, 'He invents himself daily. He'd like to be like Ernest Giles exploring
this region for the first time and with death his companion.' Intrigued by the
story of Giles and Gibson, the expedition members determine to search for the
compass with which Gibson, unable to use the instrument but greatly desirous
of such a status symbol, had ridden off on Giles's mare. Ironically, despite the
compass, Gibson lost his bearings and headed south to the Rawlinson Range to
die in the desert that bears his name.[61] Stivens's descriptions of the desert, indicating the diversity of the landscape and often incorporating quotations from
a range of explorers, are among the most accurate in fiction. 'A great undulating desert of gravel' gives way to 'undulating sand-ridges and plains of
yellow seeding spinifex' with 'a wide belt of desert oaks evoking, paradoxically,

water until I realized why: their shawl-like, drooping foliage reminded me of weeping willows. We drove the Land-Rovers over the crackling carpet of fallen needles, suddenly pungent'.

Finally Craddock, cheated by his scientific colleague, abandoned by most of his party, and marooned when his vehicle is smashed by an unknown agent, does indeed relive Giles's experience as, without food or water and with a sprained ankle, he sets out for the Rawlinson Range. Like Giles, he loses consciousness and, when he regains it, is mysteriously saved from death by what appears to be Giles's mare.

> I had gone painfully only a few yards when I saw the small bay mare trotting towards me with flirting tosses of her finely moulded head. I could scarcely believe my eyes as she continued to approach me until she was only a few feet away. There she stopped, waiting. She bore a saddle and the wild hope sprang up, 'If I could get into the saddle, she'd bear me to safety'. . . . Immediately I was settled in the seat, swaying slightly she set off at a gentle but swift walking pace, due east for the Rawlinsons. . . . when I awoke she was entering a narrow, rocky defile which, astonishingly, opened out into a green valley through which ran a wide stream. . . . If it was a hallucination, how did I survive for eight days without water or food? The tracks of a horse did lead into the defile.

The intention here is complex. The 'rational explanation' is that Craddock suffered a hallucination, resulting from his ordeal, though, as he says, it does not account for the 'facts'.[62] Rather Stivens, like Grant Watson, implies a benign and therapeutic influence in the desert itself, nurturing those who respect and love it. The desert changes Craddock's personality: 'I recall that in Central Australia I gave up the critical self-examination of every action and thought. I was relaxed and tried to live by my sense . . . at a joyous fever-heat of emotion.' *A Horse of Air* is probably the first Australian novel since Grant Watson's to suggest a positive, therapeutic role for the desert.

Another admirer of Giles is Michael Driscoll, whose poems in *Native Rose*, the joint publication with Brett Whiteley, are linked to extracts from Giles's *Australia Twice Traversed*. In 'Chambers' Pillar' Driscoll writes:

> The continent is falling away
> as the night falls away,
> with all I've left behind me.
> . . .
> Dawn's first ray strikes the pillar
> and like slow light
> through an opening door before me,
> the sky and the desert grow luminous.

Visited, as Giles had been, by a party of Aborigines, Driscoll in 'Incursion' reflects on both the nineteenth-century imperialist conquest and the equally invasive appropriation of the desert by twentieth-century Western culture:

245

> There are rock-paintings in the caves here
> and we are constantly being watched.
> . . .

> This morning, three of the natives approached the camp.
> Covered in dust and white clay,
> they were like part of the landscape
> moving towards us
> and as I watched them draw near,
> the tragedy of our incursion was suddenly brought home to me:
> they are one and the same,
> these people
> and the deserts we've come to conquer.

In 'Fellow Countryman', Driscoll, like Stivens, describes Gibson's fatal fascination with the compass, giving his own version of Giles's temporary unconsciousness as a sense of timelessness and, despite the blinding nature of the intense light, vision beyond the material world. In 'Heart of Light', he, like Stivens, plays on the idea of the mirage as more real than its material surroundings.

> The desert revolves
> its shoulder into day
> and I am borne out upon it.
> The range collapses in mirage,
> sky and stones blow white.
> . . .
> Beyond the scrub, flares
> illumine vistas of lakes and cities,
> the light infusing substance
> into everything I see.

Ironically, now that Australians feel comfortable with, even proud of, an adopted Aboriginal heritage and history, there is a more complacent attitude to the once-maligned explorers. Geoff Page's poem 'Nullarbor' (1994) describes how, to his own surprise, he comes to feel respect for Eyre and Wylie walking the route that he drives in airconditioned four-wheel comfort. His poem recapitulates the changing attitudes of twentieth-century Australians towards the previous century's heroes, from amused post-colonial denigration of these pillars of the Empire to grudging respect for the ordeal if not for the purpose, and a recognition that the same spirit of adventure that drove the explorers has underpinned the great conquest myths of the twentieth century.

> Those gentlemen with khaki leggings
> strolling through the 'empty land'
> observing the 'salsolaceous plants'

taking their bearings, writing up notes,
complete with their horses, wagons and camels
and longboat for the inland sea

bequeathed their names
to roads and highways
and stepped off into bronze at last.

I used to see them there in etchings
striding through my schoolboy texts
preceded by their 'native guide'. . .

Cruising the bitumen some years later
airconditioned 'round the Bight
maintaining a steady hundred and ten

somewhere there just short of Eucla
I saw two figures on the left,
Edward Eyre and 'faithful Wylie'

between the highway and the cliffs
forward-tilting, sweating on foot,
slogging it out through the calf-length scrub

247

with only certain nouns to help them –
Empire, Duty, strange devotion
(or Wylie's need for getting home)

the land already known and named
by shadows at a distance.
Perversely now, against the grain,

the airy boredom of the drive
supplies an edge of quiet respect
for gentlemen in khaki leggings

who in their mute
enduring madness
might later stare from Everest
or step out on the moon.[63]

Geographical exploration was intimately linked to its most important outcome and credential, the map. Above all else, it was the map that the explorer
was required to deliver up to his patron, whether state or individual, as representing the treasure with which he had returned. During the twentieth century
there was a gradual rejection of the conventional notion of the map as an

objective grid, derived from linear measurement and determining for all time the landscape on which it is imposed. Instead there emerges a counter-discourse grounded in the notion of a complex, multi-layered map that includes many facets of experience not defined by measurement. Through the literature of this time we see the progressive qualification of the grid map to include the psychological map and, with *Voss*, an awakening to the significance of Aboriginal map-art in which a journey is depicted in terms of the experiences encountered, not only in the chronological present but also in the mythical, eternal dimension of the Dreaming.

D.H. Lawrence had sensed this cultural dichotomy during his brief stay in Australia, and *Kangaroo* (1923), although written about the bush, expresses his sense of combined fascination and terror at the immensity of space and time, concepts equally relevant to the desert: 'The vast uninhabited land frightened him. It seemed so hoary and lost, so unapproachable.'[64] For Lawrence, as for most writers, the spirit of the land demanded too great a sacrifice, the subsuming of the individual into a pre-human consciousness: 'What was the good of trying to be an alert conscious man here? You couldn't. Drift, drift into a sort of obscurity, backwards into a nameless past, hoary as the country is hoary. Strange old feelings wake in the soul: old, non-human feelings. And an old, old indifference, like a torpor, invades the spirit.' Lawrence sees only two possibilities, both undesirable: 'Would the people awaken this ancient land, or would the land put them to sleep, drift them back into the torpid semi-consciousness of the world of the twilight?' But half a century later, writers, artists and film-makers were proposing a different, essentially neo-Romantic, alternative. This concept has been difficult for those of European descent to accept, since it demands assent to processes of knowing other than the rational. Some of the attempts, genuine and spurious, by writers to engage with a spiritual understanding of the desert will be discussed in Chapter 14. Some artists, too, have sought to express more about the desert than can be deduced from physical observation. While it might be thought that such a rejection of rationalism is opposed to the procedures of Science, we shall see in Chapter 13 that the insights of biology have been particularly important in producing new artistic insights.

248

'Landscape' is a way of looking at a terrain: it is a perceptual term, not
an objective reality.

GEORGE SEDDON[1]

Freed from the constrictions of perspective we can see the range and
lack of subordination – there is a sense of mystical reciprocity, of all
things residing in the one, one in all.

IVOR INDYK[2]

We pay too much attention to the surface of the earth.

JOHN WOLSELEY[3]

The desert environment offers a ready-made theatre in which to observe the
competitive struggle for existence among a vast diversity of life forms, yet for
nearly a century after the publication of Charles Darwin's *The Origin of Species*
(1859) it was associated only with the struggle of settlers against the land or the
narrow preoccupations of Social Darwinism focussed specifically on the
Aboriginal question.

The first explicitly Darwinian paintings of the desert were those of Clifton
Pugh, whose journey across the Nullarbor Plain in 1954 led him to revise his
style radically. As well as responding to the sense of immensity in land and sky,
'as if one had cut back through time into the old deserted vastnesses',[4] Pugh was
struck by the appropriateness of the desert as a setting and a rationale for his
cyclic view of life and death. His birds are distinctly predators. In *Flight of Birds*
(1957) the sky is black with the wings of kites whose pointed beaks are poised
over the blood-red land beneath. Art critic James Gleeson commented that:

> Pugh's vision of nature, red in tooth and claw, has made him the outstanding
> Australian exponent of the post-Darwinian approach to landscape and animal
> painting. Predators, as stark and angular as death, attack their prey, which dies
> on earth as red as blood. . . . Pugh sees this terrible, inevitable pageant of life
> and death with clear, unsentimental eyes.[5]

Despite this vision of the predatory cycle, Pugh was far from being fatalistic or reductionist. He was outraged at the cruelty perpetrated against native animals, and *Dingo Trap* (1975) expresses his anger at the poisoning and lingering death of dingoes caught in traps by 'doggers' for a bounty. In *Depredations of a Wild Dog* (1956) and *On the Edge of the Salt Pans* (1960), both paintings of savage animals devouring weaker ones, small delicate flowers insist that life continues to spring from the blood-soaked earth. His overall intention was to see each part in relation to a whole that was more than just material. In the copy of Sheldon Cheyney's *The Story of Modern Art* that Pugh carried with him through his time as a soldier in New Guinea and Japan, he marked a quotation from Goethe: 'Man's intellect alone cannot compass the creation of art, it must act in union with the heart', and an extended one from the Expressionist painter Kandinsky, including the injunction: 'He [the artist]

Clifton Pugh, *Dingo Trap*, 1975, oil on canvas, 90 × 120 cm, private collection. Courtesy the Artist.

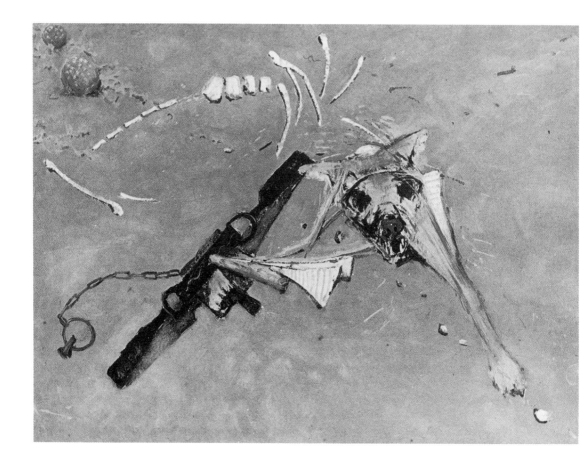

must heed above all else the total spiritual rhythm, and the harmonies and tensions, the spiritual weight of each part.'[6]

Man-made deserts

Settler Australians have rarely been willing to accept in practice the extent of the continent's aridity or their own part in contributing to it. Following European precedent, they saw the years of plenty as the norm and the drought years as the aberration, when the converse was true. The enthusiastic spread of pastoralists into rangeland areas, overstocking in the 'good' years, erosion from clear felling and the drying out of waterholes that had served the Aborigines for millennia had the effect of extending the 'desert' far beyond its pre-settlement area. Consequently, memories of drought and fear of its recurrence have stalked the collective memory for two hundred years. But only in the 1940s was drought accepted as a subject for art. Unlike the stereotypical desert, drought-affected pastures offered a clear focus for composition: the tortured frames of recognisable beasts dying in agony offered diverse possibilities for representation as abstract sculptures, or as signifiers of the unequal struggle between pastoralist and Nature. Yet in the evocative pictures that resulted, the drought is invariably presented as the 'act of God' that insurance companies designate it. Artists, like farmers, failed to see the intimate causal connection between the two elements of their pictures – livestock and drought.

251

We saw in Chapter 9 that Russell Drysdale's images of the 1940 drought in the Riverina and western New South Wales were the first paintings to introduce human figures as an integral part of the desert. These paintings also broke new ground with their desiccated forms and skeletons of animals, which were an immense and confronting symbol of the spectre that had haunted the country since European settlement. When, in 1944, drought again struck inland New South Wales the *Sydney Morning Herald* commissioned Drysdale to tour the outback with a journalist and make sketches to accompany the paper's articles. Although disappointed with these sketches, Drysdale later worked many of them into oil paintings that were starkly confronting in their colours, size and power. He had been struck by the sense of seeing the naked structure of the earth. 'The landscape', he remarked, 'looks like dinosaur bones',[7] and a number of his paintings pun on the relationship between the land and the literal bones of dead animals. In *The Walls of China, Gol-Gol* (1945), for example, the exposed roots of fallen trees mimic the pelvic bones of a cow or horse. *Landscape with Figures* (1945) parodies *Dead Horse* (1945), with its own further internal pun on the similarities between the horse skeleton and the uprooted tree behind it. Similarly, the outlines of birds in the middle distance of *Emus in a Landscape* (1950) are reflected in the curved shapes of the assortment of junk iron piled up in the foreground. That drought should now be considered a suitable subject for art showed a remarkable change in public opinion since the 1920s when such images were rigorously censored.

In 1952 another severe drought struck, in which one-and-a-quarter million cattle died in Queensland and the Northern Territory. In August of that year Sidney Nolan was commissioned by the Brisbane *Courier-Mail* to travel to the drought-stricken areas and record the images of destruction, as Drysdale had done for the *Sydney Morning Herald*. Following the Murranji cattle route from the Victoria River to Newcastle Waters and then the Barkly stock route eastward into Queensland, he sketched and photographed the carcasses of thirst-tortured cattle. The next year Nolan travelled the Birdsville Track from Marree to Birdsville, assailed with yet more piles of carcasses and skeletons. For a decade these images continued to emerge as powerful paintings such as *Burnt Carcass* (1952) and *Carcass* (1953), in which the ribs, whether exposed or outlined through the shrunken hide, form their own architecture, and the staring eyes of the dead cattle capture our own gaze. These are striking and peculiarly Australian works, yet at the same time they are suggestive of a universalised post-holocaust world. In *Drought* (1962) (see illustration following page 192) the carcass is being absorbed into sand of the same colour, recalling Nolan's painting of Burke's body melting into the land in *Perished* (1949). In *Drought* the effect is heightened by the dark hollow in the foreground, as though another carcass had recently sunk down there. Both works are singularly lacking in immediate horror; instead they carry a gentleness, even tenderness, a fatalistic suggestion of the cycle of life and death, a connection made wryly in a poem Nolan wrote in 1971 entitled 'Carcass':

252

> Screwed up by the sun, held together
> by maggots, dehorned and castrated anyway
> it stands like a rotting ship struck by lightning.
>
> The eye is a window to unmoving space, the
> brain inside defrauded. Any birthmarks
> are made by a whip.
>
> And yet nothing is forever, this universal
> victim will not be knocked, it was not
> mummified in the belief that God is a drover.[8]

In all Nolan's desert paintings, whether aerial panoramas, the Burke and Wills series, or the drought paintings, there is consistent emphasis on the interior parallel with the external representation – correlations between a harsh and hostile Nature and human nature. It is a starkly modernist vision. Commenting on Nolan's retrospective of 1987, critic Barrett Reid concluded:

> We now see that, like Boyd's, Nolan's vision is a tragic one. It is mocking, . . .
> it is cruel, . . . and it occupies a vast and arid inner space as lonely as the surface
> of the moon. It is the peculiar triumph of this painter that when all the time we

thought he was painting our landscape, our inland, our drought, he was at the same time painting a private interior space, reflecting, floating, dying. It is the silence after Auschwitz. It is a central fact of contemporary experience which we cannot avoid, even though our humanity turns away to seek other answers, other spaces.[9]

A few years later Nolan's near-contemporary, Jon Molvig, was also attracted to the subject. In *Carcass No. I* and *Carcass No. II* (both, 1959) he exploits the emotional, formal and symbolic potential of these terrible reminders of drought, but his Expressionist style obscures many of the facets notable in the earlier works. His massive skeletons fill the canvases to the exclusion of landscape, so their desert origin can only be inferred. Unlike those in the work of Drysdale and Nolan, these carcasses do not clearly denote the animals from which they are derived, incorporating instead composite suggestions of cattle, sheep, prehistoric animals and even human forms; nor are they fallen on the ground but seem to be in the process of walking. They represent death personified, stalking the land and recalling Yeats's 'rough beast [that] slouches towards Jerusalem to be born', rather than any actual drought victim.

The ecological web

Biologists have played a notable part in Australian art from the first fruitful collaboration between Joseph Banks and Sydney Parkinson aboard *Endeavour*, but they have been particularly influential in rescuing the desert from the stereotype of a 'Dead Heart' by teaching artists to see the great diversity of flora and fauna in a terrain popularly supposed to be devoid of life forms. Where writers have been prone to regard biologists with suspicion, as scientific materialists bent on reducing life to sub-cellular components, artists have discovered, in their company, a new perspective on the desert. For numerous desert painters the appreciation of minute details otherwise obliterated by the desert's immensity and the sensation of void has derived from accompanying biologists on their field trips. Russell Drysdale accompanied Alan John ('Jock') Marshall's zoological expedition to the Kimberley and the central desert areas of Western Australia in 1958[10] and Marshall's close friendship with Clifton Pugh encouraged him to pursue his environmental crusade in both art and children's literature.[11] Drysdale was also influenced by Dom Serventy of the CSIRO Wildlife Division. The trek by conservationist–naturalist C. Warren Bonython and artist–naturalist Charles McCubbin across the Simpson Desert in 1973 will be described in detail in Chapter 14 but it is worth quoting here part of McCubbin's comment about the flowering of the desert. Formerly, any such aberrations from the stereotypical picture of the desert as necessarily stark and barren, authentic only when it complied with this image, had been strictly edited out of the artistic narrative; but McCubbin is fascinated by the detail and the contrast:

253

> We saw flowers from the beginning, but nothing prepared us for the vast
> exuberant flower garden that filled the middle desert. Mile after mile of blooms
> – great incredible sea of flowers that flowed between the dunes and splashed
> their slopes in yellow, white, pink and gold. Rain had followed rain and the
> desert bloomed as never before.[12]

JOHN OLSEN

John Olsen's perspective on Nature was transformed under the influence of
three visits to Lake Eyre with the conservationist Vincent Serventy,[13] the first of
these being in 1974, only the second occasion in recorded history when it was
filled with water. He found the normally dry, salt-crusted basin swarming with
fish, bird and animal life – the whole food chain seemingly created *ex nihilo*.
Through this experience he not only developed a new interest and delight in
minute biological details but became intensely aware of the kinetic aspect of
the desert where before the prevailing image had been one of stasis. The Lake
Eyre experience had a profound effect on Olsen. 'To come in contact with a
person like Serventy is to see the landscape in another way. To see it as
"process" seems to me to have a parallel with my interest in Chinese art and
philosophy – the sense of the immovable, the eternal.'[14] The sense of a ferment
of life, often depicted with a quiet humour, enters into Olsen's paintings of the
Lake as tiny dots and squiggles erupting everywhere so that *Life Approaching
Lake Eyre* (1978), emphasising the role of the lake as the centre of life, resembles a picture of sperm racing to fertilise an ovum. Olsen also became acutely
aware of a tissue of interconnections, not only biological but cultural, philosophical and aesthetic:

> As if the visual qualities were not in themselves quite staggering, the lake had
> other layers of meaning to contemplate. There were metaphysical, historic and
> mythical overtones to deepen its colours and enrich the general atmosphere.
> The Aborigines believed that Kuddimurka, a great evil snake spirit with the
> head of a kangaroo, inhabited the lake.[15]

The poet Ken Taylor celebrated Olsen's search for connections in his poem
'John Olsen at Lake Eyre 1977':

> Beneath that sun
>   he could paint the dry rivers and
>   occasional waterholes,
> flick across the membrane
>   of the earth
>   (thin,
>   drawn as rabbit gut),
> colours matched to the memory
>   of a Ming dynasty vase

254

(a light blue, white
    and brown),
search for seeds and speckled eggs
        and other patterns so long hidden
        on the reedless, thick-papered surface
of that salt
flat and
faded
place.[16]

Always intrigued by edges, Olsen was particularly fascinated by the aerial perspective of Lake Eyre, emphasising, as it did, the overall shape of the lake and relative sizes of areas. His *Lake Eyre* (1975) (see illustration following page 208) shows an almost circular lake, not because the lake is actually this shape but because this is a semiotic reference to Chinese art. 'The + represents conflict and the West, the O peace and the East. While I do not try to emulate Chinese art, I try to utilize the things I know and like about it; its minimalism, its attention to detail, its shapes and spaces.'[17] Fringed with yellow sand and with a broad channel running out of it from 'below', Olsen's Lake Eyre might equally well suggest, at first glance, a yellow-haired round head drawn by a child. To Olsen it symbolised a fertile womb giving birth to a multitude of life forms in a festival of life – a complete reversal of the common image of the desert as a barren woman past her time.

255

Though intrigued by the visual possibilities of this shape, Olsen was also aware of the Lake's geographical significance as the lowest level in the continent, the drainage point, the wished-for and never-found inland sea which parodied the explorers' desire with its mirage effects of waves frozen in the hard salt surface. For Olsen, with his long-term interest in Taoism, in the reconciliation of Yin and Yang and a prevailing interest in process rather than stasis, the full Lake Eyre simultaneously suggested the ghost of the empty lake that preceded it and, much further back in time, the prehistoric inland sea.

> When I am out there there's empty fullness. I found parallels with it in Taoism: if you have a drinking vessel its function is not in its walls but its emptiness – and this brings in another notion, that in emptiness there is fullness. And I think this has a great mystic parallel with Australia . . .[18]

Thus, even while the full lake supports a sudden incursion of teeming species, it recalls the empty lake, past and to come, which represents the death of that life. These binarisms of lake/desert, life/death, fullness/emptiness are not only prompts to each other but mutually illuminating. 'There is a feeling of an abyss, a void between oneself and everything, and one has the impulse to bridge it. The thing I always endeavour to express is an animistic quality, a certain mystical throbbing throughout nature.'[19] Olsen's concrete poem about the paradoxical connections of void and creativity affirms in another medium this sought-for fusion of opposites discovered pre-eminently in the desert:

The Void
In emptiness lies
Creative possibility.
A place for the imagination
To ponder and wonder
A place of finality.[20]

Consistent with this construction of the land as source of creativity, Olsen rejects models of domination in art, inclining towards an aesthetic that is receptive rather than prescriptive. 'The landscape,' he says, 'has its own writing. My quest is to decipher this. Aborigines understood the language of landscape.'[21]

JOHN WOLSELEY

Like Olsen's, John Wolseley's vision of the outback, and particularly of the desert, draws heavily on his interest in natural history and the detailed notes he makes of his observations. Since coming to Australia from England as a mature artist in 1976, he has made numerous extended forays into the wilderness, mostly in the Northern Territory, discovering it minutely at ground level and recording it equally minutely in words and pictures. In *Study for Gosse Bluff, Tnorula, NT* (1985) two lizards lie curled together, every scale drawn with care, their mauve shadows on the brown earth emphasising the delicacy of their claws. Several shared expeditions with Peter Latz, nature photographer and ethno-botanist with the Northern Territory Conservation Commission, have been mutually illuminating. Indeed, the apparent monotony of the desert landscape is a powerful incentive to look more closely than one does when the visual interest is obvious. Since the early 1980s Wolseley has been visiting and studying Gosse Bluff (Tnorula) west of Alice Springs, an ancient crater six kilometres in diameter, formed when a comet exploded on the surface of the Earth 130 million years ago. There he has discovered not just detail but ecological interconnections and correlations, some occurring over great distances:

256

> It is fascinating to take a piece of ground and explore what is happening in it, how every plant and creature interrelates in some beautiful mosaic. The more you look, the more interconnections you see. Roots run enormous distances under soil to find water, pollen lines travel from tree to tree, a moth can smell another moth a great distance away, a mole cricket can chirp out of his trumpet-shaped mud hole to attract another cricket half a kilometre away.
>
> The circular shape of Gosse is an obvious metaphor for our search for circularity, completeness, equilibrium in life . . . the circular image repeats itself inside Gosse Bluff. Spinifex grows in circular shapes, trees grow in rings, large bare patches of ground are perfect circles.[22]

When he left school, Wolseley was fascinated with the writings of the Desert Fathers and he has never lost the belief that deserts offer a path to spiritual perception. Since arriving in Australia he has also been influenced by Aboriginal beliefs.[23] One entry in his diary reads: 'We pay too much attention to the surface of the earth. It presents itself so obviously to our eyes. We forget the layers above and below, the interweaving lines that connect; paths of energy and moving particles, and the traces of long past events.'[24] This view has striking parallels with the relation to the land expressed in Aboriginal art. Wolseley believes that the unique combination of immensity, space, silence and ever-changing colours in the desert makes the sense of the spiritual in the land more immediate, the Dreamtime stories more credible, the landforms more alive. Also influential on Wolseley's perception of the desert is Zen Buddhism, from which he derives his belief that his art 'is a form of involved contemplation. If you live in nature for a time you have almost mystical experiences'.[25]

Involvement takes on a new level of meaning in Wolseley's art. He is opposed to the magisterial European attitude to landscape as something awaiting composition by the artist for his own aesthetic purposes, on the grounds that it implies possession and domination of Nature. He therefore rejects the term 'landscape artist' with its implications of aesthetic and ideological theories, referring to himself instead as a 'land artist' who seeks to 'de-claim the desert, to find out what the desert does to me rather than what I can do to it'.[26] For this reason he is wary of the Western emphasis on perspective which is about ordering and ranking the landscape in terms of a pre-determined importance relative to the viewer. 'Any of my paintings you can enter from any area.'[27] This suggests a visual equivalent of Roland Barthes' 'writerly text' as one which 'has no beginning; ... we gain access to it by several entrances, none of which can be authoritatively declared to be the main one.'[28]

So, in *48 Days in Tnorula, Gosse Bluff, NT* (1980), there is no unambiguous path through the painting. Tracks meander in various directions, and the artist's notes recall us to his sense of wonder at each incident recorded, each micro-ecological system unravelled. In a real sense Wolseley has evolved a new, biological impressionism in which the elements are not dots but minute and intricate details of the landscape on which his attention falls. 'I find by drawing this detail that you get more of a feeling of vastness than if you sat down and tried to paint a straight landscape picture.'[29] He describes his project to examine the Simpson Desert as a process of wandering/wondering rather than exploring. 'Wandering and finding things and systems which have not been thought of as being significant, wondering about the idea that the connection between things is more important than the things themselves'.[30]

Wolseley's land paintings are not just about what we see, but about the process of seeing and its relation to thinking and memory – even, perhaps, race memory. Many of his large paintings are a mosaic assemblage of small sheets of paper, each presenting a topographical sketch of the view in one direction from a particular point in the terrain. On his return to the studio, Wolseley collects

257

all the sheets and pastes them on a base, a wallpaper pattern of his own design, forming a 360-degree panorama of the area and detailing contour lines, tracks of animals, flight paths of birds. So in *A Journey Near Ormiston Gorge in Search of Rare Grasshoppers* (1978–80) (see illustration following page 208) the search, indicated by a faint wandering pencil line, provides the organising principle. It seems likely that novelist Robert Drewe had Wolseley's work in mind when writing *The Drowner* (1996). He describes the character Felix Locke, undertaker at a goldfields camp in the Great Victoria Desert, in these terms:

> Locke prided himself on seeing abstracts as well as tangibles. Of course he saw the distant clouds of red dust . . . But on the cracked skin of a salt flat beneath his camel's feet, mired in the pink mud and preserved by the sun and salt, he also saw the iconic outline of a scorpion and the dotted tracery of a dragonfly.[31]

Critical of the way in which Europeans colonised Australia artistically as well as politically, Wolseley invites Nature to contribute to its portrait. He frequently tears his paintings in half and buries the pieces for one to ten years before digging them up and allowing the rain marks, sun bleaching, etc to speak for themselves in mosaic, marbling patterns – provided the paper has not been eaten by termites, as frequently happens! In any one painting there will be multiple constructs: an ecological interest (tracks of animals), a cultural interest (scientific diagrams, geological maps), as well as an aesthetic interest. Striving for completeness, his finished paintings record incidents, far perspectives and microscopic details, charts of bird migration paths, lizard and ant tracks, extracts from his diaries recording thoughts that occurred to him at the time, abandoned camp fires, plastic bags and other rubbish. 'I love charts, graphs, grids, I love the irony of how we use such methodologies to try to understand what the hell has happened to the world. I enjoy taking these logical paradigms of our ingenious minds, and juxtaposing them with images of the mad, teeming, generous flow of the natural world.'[32]

Wolseley therefore aims for a mobile, rather than a static, perspective, mobile in both space and time, to convey the sense of what it's like really to be there. 'I realised that a description of how you move and explore things is going to say far more about that place than any static things. . . . I'm always trying to make a connection between the serial thing that happens in a space and my occupation of that space. . . . I've put *dasein* there [in *Concerning the First Rains, Simpson Desert*], which is one of the words Heidegger employs to describe an intensity of being.'[33] *The Napier Range* (1985–86) has a drawing of a fossil fish, representing a microcosm within the macrocosm. *19 Days by a Dry Creek-bed, 'Meda Station', Kimberleys, W.A.* (1984) appropriates the viewpoints of Wolseley's travelling predecessors, thereby commenting obliquely on changing ideologies and cultural expectations of landscape – eighteenth-century topographical art, detailed natural-history drawings of insects and seed pods, explorers' maps, nineteenth-century view paintings and the legacy of tourism (as represented by a pair of abandoned plastic thongs). Thus the line of acces-

258

sibility travels through time as well as through space. This relates also to Aboriginal legends and song lines.

Wolseley is intensely concerned about the environment. Many of his paintings include an environmental message about human destruction and the way the colonists have affected the land. In his collages he includes pieces of rubbish left behind by travellers – a cigarette packet, a plastic thong,[34] but he refrains from sermonising. 'I'm a naturalist and I paint what I love, what concerns me, what I think is endangered, but I don't go for overkill ecological preaching. I'm always searching to show a bigger metaphor about life's mysteries, and at the core is the wondrous balance that exists in nature. Everything relies on everything else, and if we severely damage some elements in the ecosystem, the unity will collapse.'[35]

MANDY MARTIN

We have seen in Chapter 11, Mandy Martin's interest in the nineteenth-century explorer–artists and the ways she positions herself in the tradition of the topographical artists. But her desert paintings are also influenced by her knowledge of biology and her concerns about environmental degradation. Because she has engaged with the question of spirituality in the Australian landscape Martin has explored the dual influence of Darwinism and the tradition of the Romantic sublime on the naturalist–artists.[36] Like Ludwig Becker she finds a 259 fascination in Australia's arid land spaces for their paradoxical vision of beauty within the inconceivably ugly, the delicacy within the rugged, the picturesque within the melancholy. Peter Haynes remarks of her exhibition *Tracts: Back O'Bourke* (1997):

> Through a process of active astonishment Martin poetically transforms the harsh attritions of nature into beautiful images which evoke the essential play back and forth between the natural and the human, reading the human into nature and the natural into humanity.[37]

Throughout her career Martin has been strongly committed to expressing socio–political concerns through her art and recently these have included environmental issues. She affirms that 'The motivating drive behind my work then, in previous industrial series, and now has been and still is the urgency to address the major issues of land-use and exploitation in Australia'.[38] Her almost-five-metre-long desertscape *The Great Land Can Only Hope that It Will Defeat Man Yet by Being So Great that it Can Never be Found* (1996), representing a landscape near Tibooburra in Sturt National Park, comments on the Anglo–Australian perception of an ongoing battle with the land while *Tracts: Back O'Bourke* (1997) focusses on the environmental experience of the Murray–Darling basin and in particular the cultural and practical links between the communities and the land use in this area. In the *Tracts* series

Martin is committed to raising our awareness of the land itself, not just as an external entity but in a relational sense.

Seeing the desert through the window of biology has doubly empowered artists. It has alerted them to details hidden to the casual observer, the presence of many species hiding underground during the day, or lurking beneath the clumps of spinifex. Perhaps more importantly it has made them aware of the kinetic processes occurring in the desert milieu where previously Europeans had observed only stasis. The cliché of an eternal, timeless land, unchanged since antiquity, can now be seen as a self-indulgent fiction, an act of ideological imperialism on the part of settlers who, to legitimise their claim to the continent, conveniently pictured it as a land where for millennia nothing had occurred, pending their arrival. The corollary of an unchanging land was the belief in an unchanging indigenous people. The most common label applied to the Aborigines was 'stone-age', with its clear implications of a primitive, possibly pre-human, race inevitably headed for evolutionary extinction, and the impossibility of their adaptation to a changing environment. The notion of a timeless land also carried the environmentally dangerous connotation that nothing could affect or change the desert, blinding settlers to the effects of imported pastoral practice and leading to a fatalistic acceptance of increasing desertification. By reaffirming notions of change and process occurring in the desert, artists such as Mandy Martin and John Wolseley have not only allowed us to see the desert through their unique vision but have contributed to the environmental awareness of this fragile ecological system.

Self-Image, Environmentalism and Renewal

> The Centre ... is pre-eminently the zone of the sacred, the zone of
> absolute reality ... The road leading to the centre is a 'difficult
> road' ... arduous, fraught with perils, because it is, in fact, a rite of the
> passage from the profane to the sacred, from the ephemeral and
> illusory to reality and eternity, from death to life, from man to the
> divinity. Attaining the centre is equivalent to a consecration, an
> initiation; yesterday's profane and illusory existence gives place to a
> new, to a life that is real, enduring, effective.
>
> MIRCEA ELIADE[1]

> Yet there are some like me turn gladly home
> From the lush jungle of modern thought, to find
> The Arabian desert of the human mind,
> Hoping, if still from the deserts the prophets come.
>
> A.D. HOPE[2]

We have seen that the mid-century re-reading of Australia's desert areas, triggered by the work of Sidney Nolan and Patrick White, was the spearhead of a
high cultural re-appraisal. Both visually and psychologically the Centre was
seen to offer something more than the 'hideous blank', even to stand in judgement on the materialistic society huddling at the margins of the continent.
Since the 1980s, however, there has been another stage of reconstruction. The
Red Centre has been embraced so warmly by popular culture that it has
become the most exported Australian landscape, the new advertising short-
hand to market almost anything. European travel agencies characteristically
advertise Australia with posters showing a red desert while Uluru has not only
achieved international iconographic status but become a site of modern pilgrimage – magnificent, pure, even mystical. The attributes with which the
desert is now credited are often inconsistent, partly because of the many
incongruous causes for which it is appropriated and partly because of the
diverse influences that have been involved in constructing the concept of 'the

desert' in the so-called Age of Aquarius. These factors range from neo-Romanticism to modern technology, from the politics of nationalism to New Age cults, from the economics of tourism to environmentalism and interest in Aboriginal beliefs.

Technology and terror: tourism and the sublime

Before the mid-eighteenth century only those embarked on a heroic quest, or seeking spiritual enlightenment, voluntarily sought out the wilderness. But in Europe in the latter half of the eighteenth century the desire to experience wild landscapes became so fashionable that the philosopher Edmund Burke was prompted to analyse the psychological motivation for this cult of the 'sublime'. As we saw in Chapter 2, in the natural world the sublime was associated with immensity, usually of the ocean or of mountains. Writing in 1995, another philosopher, Kate Soper, has convincingly argued that only a society already experiencing alienation from nature, as a result of industrialisation, hankers to return to the wilderness and preserve its wild places against further curtailment.[3] Such cavalier self-confidence in voluntarily seeking out places of wildness and terror is also contingent on the ability to return, equally voluntarily, to safety and comfort so that transitory physical hardship is transformed into a lasting intellectual pleasure. Such an experience is an aesthetic luxury reserved only for those already in a position of dominance over the very 'nature' they profess to desire in its untamed state, and their power is, in turn, the result of the very technology they affect to decry. In England, these pre-conditions of receding wilderness and technological power came together after the industrial revolution, leading to the cult of mountain scenery, the popularity of Turner's stormy seascapes and the boom in tourism to the Lake District. In Australia only the desert offered an equivalent sense of immensity, but for the nineteenth-century European settlers, confronted with a vast inimical expanse that threatened their survival unless they 'conquered' and tamed it for their economic purposes, there was no question of a 'sublime' experience. For the white settlers the immediate dangers of the Australian desert were all too alarmingly real to be an aesthetic experience. Immensity, isolation from civilisation, the danger of being lost and dying of thirst were not options to be played with. Now, except for rare misadventure, technology has overcome all of these terrors so that going to the desert is in one sense like seeing a horror film: playing with fear while knowing we are safe.

The technological breakthrough that recast the cultural perception of the desert was the four-wheel-drive vehicle, which became readily available to a mass market in the 1980s. Thus equipped, armed with the added safety precautions of Codan radio or global positioning system (GPS) and with reasonable expectation of fuel stops at appropriate intervals, the traveller can readily negotiate the terrors and monotony of the desert, transforming them into a safe, an aesthetic and, perhaps most importantly, a *limited* engagement with the sublime. Although organised tours to the Centre are advertised as offering an experience of physical hardship in the tracks of the explorers, they actually provide the opposite: a wholly visual acquaintance with the desert (with the heat and flies screened out) in the airconditioned comfort of buses and plush hotels, with Western-style meals and drinks. In particular, the duration of the tour is carefully prescribed, for, however much they may enjoy this flirtation with the desert, few visitors would willingly remain there. Continuation of the experience is limited to that offered by another technological phenomenon – colour photography. Indeed it was the advent of cheap, high-quality colour film that educated Australians to appreciate the redness of the desert and close-up studies of beetle and lizard tracks across sand.[4]

Tourism, the new above-ground goldmine of the desert, has not been slow to exploit and create further demand for such experiences. The main tourist circuit from Alice Springs is determined by the spectacular red rock formations of Standley Chasm, Ormiston Gorge, Simpsons Gap, Glen Helen Gorge and King's Canyon, while the high points of the tour are, necessarily, Uluru and Kata Tjuta (the Olgas), with their brilliant and varying colours intensified at sunset and sunrise. There is no complaint of monotony here. Tourists who, whether through respect for the wishes of the Aborigines or for other reasons, decline to 'conquer' Uluru by climbing it, are encouraged to develop a different interest and learn about the traditional A̱nangu beliefs associated with the features of its walls, thereby creating a burgeoning demand for guided tours and a profitable industry in Aboriginal artefacts. So-called 'eco-tours' market the desert as an ecological system, although most operate at the superficial level of providing tourists with the botanical names of various flora and the opportunity to take less usual photos of, say, Chambers Pillar, or a perentie lizard.[5] Ironically, the demand for such eco-tours to lesser travelled areas is one of the greatest hazards to the preservation of this fragile ecological environment.

Travellers desiring to escape from the organised tourist industry can now safely traverse the Birdsville Track from Marree to Birdsville, once legendary for its difficulties and dangers, while the Simpson Desert, the last to be crossed by white Australians, holds a special charm for modern tourists schooled to admire the classic geometry of its deep-red parallel dunes. The Leyland Brothers' television documentary of their 1966 crossing of the Simpson from west to east assisted the boom in recreation tourism that has continued to expand, boosted by the coverage given to public figures such as C. Warren Bonython, Charles McCubbin and Derek Walker who have crossed the desert on foot. The prevalence of caps and tee-shirts proclaiming 'I crossed the Simpson' and the hundreds of business cards pinned to the ceiling of the Birdsville pub attest to the numbers still attracted to this particular package of the sublime. As historian Ann McGrath writes:

> In their imaginations, the outback is where white Australians negotiate their present. As a highly flexible mythological site and signifier, it easily incorporates new historical traditions. . . . By going there and 'seeing it', by witnessing living

263

Aborigines in their own country, by breathing in the unpolluted air of the outback, such travellers enact rituals of colonial sanctification.[6]

Despite the relative comfort of such journeys, travellers are often struck with a new sense of admiration for the nineteenth-century explorers. Jenny Stanton's response to Chambers Pillar would not be atypical:

> I sat gazing at the pillar until well after dark, imagining I was seeing it exactly as Stuart and Giles had done more than 100 years earlier. We were travellers of different eras: they were on horseback; I was in an air-conditioned 4WD. They relied on compass bearings; I had maps and a global positioning system. But I liked to think that despite our differences, we shared a similar sense of adventure and regarded the pillar with similar awe.[7]

National symbol

Incredible as it would have seemed half a century ago, the desert is now accepted as Australia's most appropriate national symbol. While the Sydney Opera House and the Great Barrier Reef offer superb visual examples, respectively, of cultural and natural beauty, for Australians they are too localised, being closely identified with specific states. By contrast, because of its geographical centrality, some part of 'the desert' can be validly claimed by the citizens of all states except Tasmania.

The historical and psychological importance of the Centre as national symbol operates on two temporal levels – the two centuries of settler history and the 'timeless' frame of the Dreaming. For many Australians, the journey to the Centre is inevitably linked with the exploring expeditions of last century, and they see their journey as a form of pilgrimage, preserving the nation's history by participating in a ritual celebration of its heroes. On the other hand, a strong message is conveyed to tourists that the 'authentic' Australia exists at the Centre because that is where the 'real' Australian is to be found – a stereotypical Aboriginal figure, culturally identical with his or her pre-contact ancestors.

Despite these advantages, the desert is not intrinsically marketable in terms of the visual criteria that govern publicity. It requires a specific icon, an explicit and instantly recognisable signifier, a counterpart to the Sydney Opera House, the Pyramids, the Kremlin or St Peter's Cathedral. And of course there is one – Uluru – sufficiently close to the centre of Australia to symbolise its heart. Uluru has impressed Europeans from the first glimpse of it by Ernest Giles, who also jokingly referred to it as the 'Rock of Ages':

> Its appearance and outline is most imposing, for it is simply a mammoth monolith that rises out of the sandy desert soil around, and stands with a perpendicular and totally inaccessible face at all points, except one slope near

the north-west end ... Down its furrowed and corrugated sides the trickling of
water for untold ages has descended in times of rain ... Mount Olga is the more
wonderful and grotesque; Mount Ayers [*sic*] the more ancient and sublime.[8]

The term 'sublime' fell out of fashion soon after Giles's visit but the monolith
has continued to evoke a strong emotional response. The 27-year-old anthropologist, Ted Strehlow, brought up at the Hermannsburg Mission some five
hundred kilometres away, also had recourse to absolutes to describe his first
sight of the outcrop:

> The Rock was reached at last, the goal of my boyhood dreams – the shadow of a
> great rock in a weary land, and how welcome it was. All hushed tonight, only
> the moon is shining down upon the great black walls of the rock – and one feels
> that the Land of God is indeed near. It is like the great silence of eternity.[9]

As we have seen, the mystique associated with Uluru has not always been
benign. In the myths that sprouted after the disappearance of baby Azaria
Chamberlain in 1980 'Nature', formerly associated with the Bush, was jointly
represented by a wild animal and a mysterious monolith, and Uluru was suddenly recast as a place riddled with arcane pagan rituals.

More recently still, New Age cults have attempted to appropriate Uluru,
transforming it into a substitute cathedral, mosque or temple,[10] its ambience
the expected scene of spiritual revelation and renewal. There are moves to
extend the aura associated with 'The Rock' to the nearby but formerly less well
known Olgas, now also increasingly called by their Aboriginal name, Kata
Tjuta. Sociologist Julie Marcus identifies 'at least four sets of cosmologies [*sic*]
circulating around Ayers Rock and the Olgas': the partly secret Aboriginal one
wherein Uluru is the location of both men's and women's sacred sites while
Kata Tjuta is predominantly a male place; the international mystical tradition,
which situates them at a key point on a terrestrial magnetic grid; the claims of
some feminists that the rounded forms and vulval crevices of Kata Tjuta are the
women's counterpart of the masculinist monolith; and the nationalist appropriation, particularly of Uluru, by settler Australians, leaving Aboriginal
Australians with no unique cultural focus.[11] There is no convincing evidence
that Uluru was, at any time in the past, a traditional focus for Aborigines
throughout Australia but, as Ann McGrath has pointed out, cultural transfer
may operate bi-directionally:

> Pan-Australian myths are growing, with many northern Aborigines subscribing
> to a belief that all the dreaming tracks around Australia meet up at Uluru. It is
> unlikely that this belief existed prior to white contact, with bitumen roads now
> said to be ancestral paths, but the Dreaming has never been a static story; it has
> always evolved, and been informed by the present. Uluru as pan-Aboriginal
> sacred site is, therefore, an important example of cultural convergence between
> Aborigines and white Australians.[12]

265

The desert in advertising

The advertising industry, while clutching at the coat tails of tourism, also evolves its own pervasive symbolism which is speedily incorporated into popular culture. Although the desert's associations with spiritual pilgrimage and renunciation might seem to work against the materialism and consumerism implicit in advertising, images of a red sandy desert, usually with Uluru in the distance, are widely exploited to market a diverse range of products, most of which have no intrinsic connection with the desert. In the semiotics of advertising the desert pre-eminently represents immense size and hence signifies Australia as the Big Country. The implication is that such vastness requires unusual ability to cope and, happily, the product being promoted confers, or is somehow connected with, just such competence. Often this dubious conjunction is presented in the form of humorous exaggeration as in the 'BP On the Move' advertisement in which a motorist, filling up at a petrol bowser in a flat expanse of desert, looks up to see a train, several semi-trailers, a helicopter, a jet and a road train all bearing down on the BP pump. A clever Landcruiser advertisement shows a flying saucer abandoned in the middle of a red sand desert with a sign, 'For Sale' after its former passengers have taken off in a more appropriate four-wheel-drive vehicle – 'the best way to explore earth' (see illustration following page 240). Here again exaggeration can risk self-parody, because the desert remains the one essential element of the picture.

Like the Bush, the desert also signifies the conquest of difficulties, and the national characteristics formerly supposed to be embodied in the nineteenth-century bushman have been relocated to the desert milieu. But whereas survival was formerly seen as dependent on innate abilities – toughness, endurance, physical skills, capacity to withstand loneliness and privation – at the end of the twentieth century survival is more frequently associated, at least in the logic of advertising, with having the right equipment, the right products. These may vary from the right kind of car or the right kind of tour company, through the right kind of boots and tents to the right kind of coffee or margarine, but the message is the same. The mere pictorial association of these products with the experience is assumed to confer moral status on the purchaser. Ironically, the rationale of the association is now almost completely the inverse of that obtaining in the case of the bushman: by having these products you can now cleverly experience the desert without the hardships. Thus an advertisement for International Roast coffee combines the image of the bushman/swaggie, complete with broad-brimmed felt hat, billy, swag (sleeping bag) and faithful dog, with red sand, spinifex and the inevitable Uluru as specific landmark; but it also includes comforts unknown to the bushman/swaggie but familiar to the prospective consumer: the land cruiser, the folding chair, the car fridge, and of course the instant coffee.[13]

Again, because the desert has come to represent, iconographically, the unique Australian location, products associated with it acquire nationalist prestige, even though more than ninety per cent of Australians live on the coastal fringe and even though the products in question are frequently those of a multi-national company based outside Australia. A 1996 advertisement for the Range Rover situates the object of desire on a plain of sun-baked red earth, with the caption 'To a Range Rover it's just another red carpet'. The connection between the outback experience and the comfort expected by urban Land Rover buyers is made explicit in the opening paragraph: 'Quite simply, this is the only luxury vehicle capable of transporting you from the theatre steps on opening night to almost anywhere in this wide, red land.' This connection clearly succeeds in advertising. The majority of four-wheel-drive vehicles sold are exclusively for city use, yet their owners enjoy displaying the image of the outback, the tough, the genuine Australia.

The brilliantly decorated Qantas Boeing 747 (see illustration following page 240), 'Wunala Dreaming', unveiled in 1994, provided one of the largest national statements of this kind. The whole fuselage is painted in a red which suggestively links the conventional colour of Qantas aircraft tails with the Red Centre. On this background are overlaid Aboriginal-inspired depictions of kangaroos and their footprints, and diagrammatic waterholes to represent the Wunala Dreaming of the Yanyuwa people from Borroloola on the Gulf of Carpentaria (certainly not the Red Centre, but the kangaroo symbol was presumably more important). The Yanyuwa story tells of Spirit Ancestors who, in the form of kangaroos, led the people to water and food and thus conveniently carries assurance of safe carriage, guaranteed by a timeless tradition of powerful, caring and uniquely Australian beings.

Commercial iconography of the desert is now so familiar that it can be used in a self-deprecating, playful mode, as in one of the Coca-Cola 'You Can't Beat the Feeling!' advertisements (1991), which features a surfboard rider apparently twisting in mid-air above an aerial view of desert country, ready to land at the door of a solitary shanty displaying the Coca-Cola logo on its tin roof.

267

The mantle of nationalism: the Jindyworobaks

The first attempt to introduce the desert as a national image was initiated by the Jindyworobak Club.[14] Founded by poet Rex Ingamells in Adelaide in 1938, this movement can, in many ways, be seen both as the tardy literary counterpart of the Heidelberg School's appropriation of the Bush and as forerunner of the metaphysical environmentalism of the 1990s. Like the *plein air* painters, the Jindyworobak writers, the majority of them poets, determined to forge a unique 'Australian myth of place and time and destiny',[15] derived from the spirit of place, and, more controversially, to assimilate Aboriginal myths of the Dreamtime or *Alcheringa*[16] as an integral part of such a synthesis. Ingamells's manifesto included 'A clear recognition of environmental values' and an 'understanding of Australia's history and traditions, primeval, colonial and modern'. It was this conjunction of environmental values and Aboriginal traditions that both distinguished the Jindyworobak movement and led to its marginalisation. In his introduction to the Portable Australian Authors edition Brian Elliott compares the Jindyworobaks to the English Romantic poets in their focus on the spirit of place:

> Every location, every feature of the visible landscape was inhabited with mystical, mythical and totemistic presences – places where mythical events had occurred, where the wandering ancestors had rested . . . Naturally in these circumstances there was a profound suggestiveness in all places, ritually important to the natives, imaginatively so (in a more or less Wordsworthian sense) to the poets; a mystical experience, in fact, which may be designated for both the white and the black, though with different implications, as Australian site-magic.[17]

Although in theory this mystique of place could be experienced anywhere, the most characteristic Jindyworobak poems are situated in the desert which, as the place of last and least European contact, was identified as the particular preserve of Aborigines. Many of the Jindyworobak poems describe some form of secular conversion which transforms their psychological state.

In Roland Robinson's 'The Wanderer' (1962), for example, the train traveller begins by seeing the desert as 'a symbol of his mind's despair' where 'a yellow/whirlwind writhed through trembling air' and 'red sand ridges beneath a merciless/sky shut in the halted train'. While this seems at first to intensify the traveller's despair, it actually focusses and circumscribes it: 'His mental hell looked out upon/this other hell at last made known'. Therefore, when the beauty of the desert dawn breaks, he is able to accept the revelation that 'heaven/or hell were regions of the mind'. Ian Mudie's poem 'On Reaching the Summit of Horrocks Pass' also describes the acceptance of the desert on its own terms as a transforming experience. In 'Uluru, An Apostrophe to Ayers Rock', Ingamells, one of the first to use the Aboriginal name, celebrates his empowerment at 'Uluru of the eagles':

> It would not be enough to walk
> footsore, a thousand miles to you, Uluru,
> Rock, Uluru, over the dry and harsh
> expanses of sand and gibber, ridge and valley,
> saltbush, bluebush, spinifex, mulga,
> casuarina,
> beneath the unblinking blue.
>
> Arrival is more than physical: it is
> the dreaming at the inner shrine,
> with sun and star, sun and star,
> moon after moon,
> message-stick and tjurunga,
> rock-hole and dune. . . .

Approach must be naked of Knowledge, except
what is relevant. . . .

As I stepped out from one of your Caves of Paintings,
I knew myself forever part of you,
inspirited through ochre, charcoal and pipeclay,
through aeons of ochre, charcoal and pipeclay,
into your colourful darkness of timeless Being –
yesterday, today and ever after
eternal Dreaming in your heart, Uluru.

As I stepped out from one of your Caves of Paintings,
you and the wedge-tailed eagle soared together
high in the battering blue;
and I, in your vibrant shade, Uluru, knew
life-strength that wells alone
from your stupendous quietness of stone.

Despite his statement that 'Approach must be naked of Knowledge', Ingamells falls into the Western mode of attempting to account for this vision-ary experience through the stereotyped notions of the immensity, antiquity and changelessness of the desert, citing the 'magnificent beauty' of Uluru, its immense age, its 'timeless Being', 'a Past so distant/that Man is but a perilous dream of Nature'. These notions became articles of faith with the Jindyworobaks. Ingamells's poem 'Australia' begins: 'This is the oldest Land,/ wisest, most stoic,/where rock-hearted ranges stand,/Archeozoic' and in Ken Barratt's poem 'Burke and Wills', the scientist Wills remarks, 269

These rocks
are so old, they have forgotten the singing
and the shouting of the sea, the violence
of the earth in the making.

The success of the Jindyworobak experiments was limited, partly because there was no single 'Aboriginal' culture or language to use, and partly because Aboriginal words did not work well in metric verse developed for English words. Moreover, because the Aboriginal lifestyle was not that of their readers, there was inevitably a sense of observing a 'primitive' 'other' from a safe dis-tance, even of erasing that 'other'. From a post-colonial perspective it seems now that the Jindyworobaks were more like Egyptian archaeologists, far less interested in existing Aborigines than in exhuming a dead Aboriginal culture from the distant past and claiming expert knowledge. Decontextualising its narratives, as Margaret Preston appropriated its symbols for decorative purposes, they rigorously divorced these from living Aborigines, tacitly sub-scribing to the view that Aborigines were extinct. A notable exception was

William Hart-Smith's poem 'Nullarbor' (1946) in which an experience of revelation on the Nullarbor Plain is mediated through the priest-like figure of an Aborigine, who appears and disappears with the suddenness of a vision (or mirage?) as though from the burning bush.

Confronted by the presence of the Aborigine, with his 'earth smell, a special earth smell', the white speaker begins to see himself from the outside, as the 'other':

> I changed. Slowly I changed. I became a grotesque thing.
> I became white-skinned, a human being with a white skin . . .
> A thin being with a sharp nose and a strong reek,
> Huddled into myself, covered up, cowering away from life,
> A distorted thing with my senses only half awake,

The Aborigine, however, accepts him: 'You came and sat down beyond the limits of my camp,/The camp of my personality' until the rapport is broken: 'my own world broke in . . . roared down on me and shrieked . . . [and] shattered something in my head', leaving the poet's voice diminished. 'Only the desert remained itself, remained unchanged.' The poem identifies spiritual wisdom with the Aborigine, implying that, until we can step outside our complacent self-image and accept identification with the people of the desert, we cannot know ourselves, nature or truth. Yet the poem also indicates how easily the will to identify with Aboriginal values is overpowered by the dominant concerns of Western culture.

Despite the demise of the Jindyworobak movement, the notion of a spiritual encounter, pre-eminently accessible in the desert, was to re-emerge in a popular vein in the 1980s when it tied in with the international reassessment of indigenous cultures.

270

Making tracks to self-discovery

The wealth and materialism of the 1980s in Australia generated a general if vague desire for something more spiritually and psychologically satisfying than the ease and luxury that money could provide. In a secular approximation to monastic regimen, physical hardships, voluntarily undertaken and combined with solitude, were popularly regarded as the path to psychological self-discovery. Travel to the outback was believed to offer life-changing potential by realigning priorities.

TRACKS

The first extended autobiographical account of such a pilgrimage was Robyn Davidson's *Tracks* (1980),[18] which described her 2700-kilometre solo journey in

1977 from Alice Springs across the Western Desert to the Indian Ocean, accompanied by four camels and her dog Diggity. Written in the aggressive feminist political climate of the 1970s, the book begins by castigating the chauvinist male hegemony prevailing in Alice Springs, but more enduringly it presents the closest feminine counterpart of the nineteenth-century explorers' engagement with the Australian desert, providing a perspective that was almost wholly absent from reports of expeditions to the Centre.

The alleged purpose of Davidson's journey, which launched the myth of the 'camel lady', was multiple; it included a desire to test her own asceticism and endurance in a serious challenge for survival. There is an implicit suggestion of Davidson's need to prove herself to her father on his own terms. She writes, 'He had spent twenty years in Africa, walking across it in the 1920s and 1930s, living the life of a Victorian explorer. He could now refer to me as a chip off the old block.'[19] This thought is attributed to the father but it can hardly have been absent from Davidson's personal motivation. There is also the clear suggestion of a parallel inner journey in the tradition of Joseph Conrad's *Heart of Darkness,* and an eventual victory, in some unspecified way, for all women. Rocketing to the international bestseller list and selected by Patrick White as one of his 'Books of the Year', *Tracks* overtly contradicted the 'camel lady' myth while covertly perpetuating it. In the process it proved a significant factor in the emergence of a neo-Romantic cult of the desert as a place of enlightenment and self-discovery.

Although retaining the asceticism associated with the biblical sojourn in the 'wilderness', Davidson, unlike the nineteenth-century explorers, makes no pretence of altruism. Indeed, she is less interested in the desert as such, or even as an ecological location, than in coming to terms with it as personal space. This is immediately evident in the introductory epigraph from Doris Lessing's powerful expression of feminist politics in *The Golden Notebook* (1962):

> Anna knew she had to cross the desert. Over it, on the far side, were mountains – purple and orange and grey. The colours of the dream were extraordinarily beautiful and vivid. .... The dream marked a change in Anna, in her knowledge of herself. In the desert she was alone, and there was no water, and she was a long way from the springs. She woke knowing that if she was to cross the desert she must shed burdens.

This passage stands as a summary of the main elements that Davidson elaborates in her book, foreshadowing a sense of inner compulsion about the need to undertake this task rather than a concern for externally generated goals: the importance of colours rather than the economic potential and functional deployment of the land; the sense of solitude and material privation as a prerequisite for self-knowledge; the traditional trope of the journey as initiation into enlightenment; and, most significantly, the emphasis on the dream as the immediate path to understanding and Truth. Davidson also stresses the irrational and non-quantifiable aspects of discovery, the meaninglessness of the

271

Western focus on clock time, and a growing awareness of overall pattern that makes sense of experiences. All these factors stand in sharp opposition to the foci of the nineteenth-century expeditions with their emphasis on discrete, measurable entities, rationality and material goals.

At times Davidson's response to the vastness of the desert is one of fear:

> I could feel the enormity of the desert in my belly and on the back of my neck. I was not in any real danger – I could easily have set a compass course for Areyonga. But I kept thinking, what if this happens when I'm two hundred miles from anywhere? What if, What if. And I felt very small and very alone suddenly in this great emptiness.

But more often her reaction is exhilaration: 'I had built something intangible but magical for myself.' The high points of her journey are those of quasi-spiritual empowerment through a sense of oneness with the world. Of the day when she has finally left behind her family and well-wishers from Alice Springs, she writes in Blakean terms of a new transcendent vision:

> All around me was magnificence. Light, power, space and sun. And I was walking into it. I was going to let it make me or break me. A great weight lifted off my back. I felt like dancing and calling to the great spirit. . . . I wanted to fly in the unlimited blue of the morning. I was seeing it all as if for the first time, all fresh and bathed in an effulgence of light and joy, as if a smoke had cleared, or my eyes had been peeled, so that I wanted to shout into the vastness, 'I love you, I love you, sky, bird, wind, precipice, space, sun, desert, desert, desert.'

In contrast to the male explorers' prescriptive gaze, which imposed on the landscape a rationally grounded description and definition, Davidson seeks to foreground the inner experience. Hence her anger and dissatisfaction with Rick Smolan's photographic record of her trek (as required by *National Geographic*), on the grounds that it recorded only the external manifestation of events. She affirms that her most rewarding insights emerged from her subconscious mind, in dreams, in non-premeditated insights. 'I was becoming involved with [the country] in a most intense and yet not fully conscious way. . . . My environment began to teach me about itself without my full aware-ness of the process. It became an animate being of which I was a part.' During the journey she frequently characterises herself as mad – talking to herself, stripping off her clothes, and speculating how she must appear to others. But throughout this process there is an ambivalent subtext affirmation that these practices are more sound and valuable than the socially accepted norms.

Davidson links the ability to be changed by the environment to the Darwinian notion of evolutionary advantage: 'Capacity for survival may be the ability to be changed by environment. . . . The self in a desert becomes more and more like the desert. It has to to survive. . . . But as is its nature, it desper-ately wants to assimilate and make sense of the information it receives, which

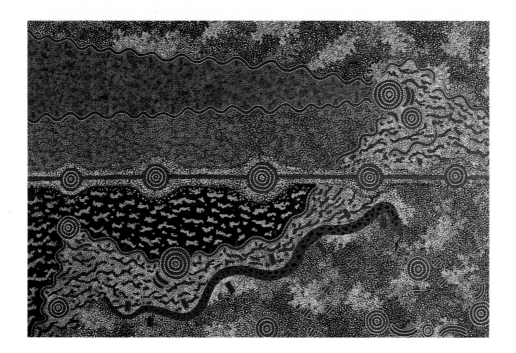

ABOVE
Michael Nelson
Tjakamarra assisted by
Marjorie Napaljarri,
Five Dreamings, 1984,
Papunya, Central
Australia, acrylic on
canvas, 122 × 182 cm.
Courtesy Gallery
Gabrielle Pizzi,
Melbourne.

BELOW
Kimberley artists at work
on a collective canvas at
Pirnini, Northern Territory,
1996, Photo Elke Wiesmann.

Tim Leura Tjapaltjarri,
Anmatyerre c. 1939–84
with Clifford Possum
Tjapaltjarri, Anmatyerre
born c. 1939, *Napperby
death spirit Dreaming*, 1980
synthetic polymer paint on
canvas 207.7 × 670.8 cm
Felton Bequest, 1988
National Gallery of
Victoria, Melbourne.

in a desert is almost always going to be translated into the language of mysticism.' This provides an interesting gloss on the response of the nineteenth-century explorers who, with few exceptions, named and categorised with ease but refused to be drawn into the admission or terminology of mysticism. Davidson's frequent description of the landscape in terms of the dreams it invoked is explicitly associated with a female mode of knowing. She comments on an interchange with a Marxist friend who 'could use the traditionally masculine language of the political intelligentsia to win any argument, and to produce an impenetrable aura of dominance and power around him. He saw any entry into the morbid internal landscape as, traditionally at least, the realm of the female.'

Another distinctive feature of Davidson's desert experience is her growing perception of a universal pattern, a further point of contrast with the colonial discourse of exploration. 'The motions and patterns and connections of things became apparent on a gut level. I didn't just see the animal tracks, I knew them. I didn't just see the bird, I knew it in relationship to its actions and effects.' The importance of such a relational understanding of the world as a unified whole, of which the observer is an integral part, stands in stark contrast to the traditional scientific model of reified perception and knowledge acquisition, derived from Newtonian physics. Davidson associates relational knowing with the Aboriginal vision of reality, a connection which is now well understood but which was still novel when *Tracks* was published. Davidson also relishes the freedom from social restrictions: '. . . when there is no one to remind you what society's rules are, and nothing to keep you linked to that society, you had better be prepared for some startling changes'.

273

Despite setbacks and misconceptions,[20] the book is clear in its affirmation that, overall, Davidson did gain insight and this, of course, is the reason for its impact and popularity and for the belief it fostered that spiritual perception can be attained with greater immediacy in the desert. The aspects of this enlightenment, both individual and universal, are closely connected to the contemporary rhetoric of empowerment: 'I had discovered capabilities and strengths that I would not have imagined possible. . . . I had learnt to use my fears as stepping stones rather than stumbling blocks, and best of all I had learnt to laugh. I felt invincible, untouchable, I had extended myself . . .'[21] This passage contains clear echoes of hippie and New Age discourse, but Davidson's particular contribution is in anchoring them to the wilderness tradition and locating that in the specific context of the Australian desert.

Overall, there is explicit rejection of individual heroism of the kind associated with the inland explorers. Davidson repudiates the media's construction of her as extraordinary.[22] On the contrary, her message is: 'That anyone could do anything. If I could bumble my way across a desert, then anyone could do anything. And that was especially true for women, who have used cowardice for so long to protect themselves that it has become a habit.' She bemoans the fact that 'a myth was being created where I would appear different, exceptional. Because society needed it to be so.' This was the same myth, the same need that prompted the lionising of the inland explorers, but in Davidson's case there is the added impetus to provide a feminine role model. The particular combination of a single woman, alone in a vast desert with camels, chimed in well with an age seeking a paradoxical fusion of empowerment and self-denial, individualism and cosmic pattern, and in the process promoted the Australian desert as the favoured and specific locus of spiritual renewal.

DESERT WALKER

Perhaps surprisingly there have been no comparable successors to *Tracks*. The closest parallel has been the film, *Desert Walker* (1985), an account of Denis Bartell's 2500-kilometre trek across the Simpson Desert from Burketown on the Gulf of Carpentaria to Glenelg.[23] Bartell had already completed four crossings of the Simpson Desert, three vehicle crossings and a solo walk from west to east the preceding year. While one of Bartell's alleged purposes was to raise money for the Royal Flying Doctor Service, and he did in fact raise $80,000 through sponsorship of his walk, his personal philosophy, as enunciated in the film, focusses on the notion of challenge: 'I have a burning desire to succeed in whatever challenge I give myself ... I am for the individual who dares to challenge, and our strength as a nation can only be enhanced by them.' The symbolic gesture of filling a bottle of water at the Gulf of Carpentaria to be emptied into Gulf St Vincent emphasised this need to make a statement of having united, through his feat, two gulfs separated by a continent. The action symbolises, in effect, his having cancelled out, through conquest, the intervening land. Where Davidson focussed on the fertility of the desert, Bartell emphasised its aridity. The film opens with the cliché: 'If Australia has a dead heart, it must lie here ... salt lakes, sand ridges ... one of the most desolate and forbidding places on earth.' Bartell began by dragging his water supply on a light-weight trolley but was forced to abandon this device which was repeatedly bogged in the sand dunes, and to rely instead on food drops and Aboriginal wells located from information in David Lindsay's journal of his 1886 expedition.

As well as the physical endurance test involved in his trek Bartell was also seeking a mystical experience. His clairvoyant had prophesied that he would be changed by this episode, and recommended that he wear a red headband to assist in maintaining links with Aboriginal spirits respecting their land. He, too, affirms in the film the importance of meditation to 'feel and be with the desert ... a part of it. ... To come back to nature, to meander at a slow pace through wilderness areas, to simply sit by a shady stream, or on a desert sandhill, seeing life far away from a concrete jungle of noise and pollution, can only enrich the soul and mind.' In the main, though, Bartell represents the desert as harsh and desolate, vast and dangerous. This, of course, magnifies his heroism in attempting the journey and his achievement in completing it. Yet he also desires to indicate something of its beauty and spiritual potential. The result is

274

a confusion similar to what we have seen in the published accounts of the nine-teenth-century explorers who desired to validate their journey in economic terms while emphasising their heroism in enduring a harsh environment. Bartell's film already contained a number of the viewpoints and symbols that were to burgeon in the 1990s: respect for the Aboriginal culture and religious values, and belief in the mystical presence of the desert and its potential for offering an experience of unity with its power. Yet a comparison with *Tracks* highlights Bartell's emphasis on personal physical endurance, conquest and the development of character, rather than as an opportunity to be significantly changed.

The desert as spiritual experience

Ernest Giles was probably the first European to record, albeit tentatively, an incident in the Australian desert whereby physical reality merged into spiritual revelation, when 'the imagination can revel only in the marvellous, the myste-rious and the mythical';[24] but a century later there has been virtually a flood of such experiences. In the 1990s desert spirituality throughout the world has taken diverse forms. Among the most publicised are the New Age pilgrimages centring on the pyramids of Egypt which, according to their devotees, possess an energy point and can be used to create a vibrational power. Uluru has achieved a similar status with some believers. In his study of the stories attached to Uluru, Barry Hill records that, in 1985, two years after the Rock was handed back to its traditional owners, the Mutitjulu received a request from a group of cosmic believers calling themselves Harmonic Convergence, who were intent on staging an international event on 16 August 1987, with a scenario not dis-similar to the revelations presented in Steven Spielberg's *Close Encounters of the Third Kind* (1977):

275

> They would lay down their bodies in circular formation, heads towards a fire, feet outward, gazing skyward. They would surrender control to the Earth, allowing the forces of Life to use them as channels for the purification of the planet. . . . This would happen at key planetary points such as the Kings Chamber of the Great Pyramid, Diamond Head in Hawaii, as well as, they hoped, Ayers Rock.[25]

A second cosmic gathering was planned for Easter, 1990, when 'their mental activity would activate the crystal fire image at the centre of the Rock, and the activation of these pathways would help heal the earth and its peoples.' A large number of those who have tried to appropriate some of this power for them-selves by removing a piece of the Rock appear to have suffered extraordinary sequences of unpleasant occurrences and have hastened to return their sou-venirs with remorseful notes and explicit instructions for their return to the exact spot from which they had been removed.[26]

Kevin Roberts's poem 'I do not climb the Rock' (1992) sets out consciously to engineer a moment of spiritual insight of the kind outlined in Bruce Chatwin's *Songlines*. The essential ingredients of this prescription are: acceptance of the physical self (the natural smell of sweat from which society recoils), the sense of touch-communication with the Rock, openness to the elements (the Sun), and the expectation that transcendent, synaesthetic communication will be granted to the pilgrim:

> I shove my hands
> under my armpits
> to get my scent, place
> both hands palm down
> on the shiny red scale
> of Uluru, say hello
> my country, this is me,
> can you sing me straight?
> Or have I come out of this earth, white, without
> the land dancing within?
>
> I lie back on Uluru
> and the sun points its white
> bone at my belly, my palms
> flat on the rock, not expecting
> instant revelation, burning
> saltbush or voices from the sky
> but to feel a touch of
> what might be known
> might be sensed, after years
> of the songlines folded
> one into another until
> the chorus unifies, strikes one
> harmonic chord.[27]

In an age of rapid change, it can be a short mental step from antique to eternal, from the central desert to its indigenous inhabitants. The Aborigines, who a few decades ago were regarded as too primitive to subscribe to anything more than the vaguest animism, have now been categorised as the guardians of the eternal spiritual values that Western culture has allegedly lost in its pursuit of materialism. This belief, though not accepted by everyone, has permeated popular culture through the media of film and music, as well as literature. Whereas, during the 1960s and 70s, the models were American – the freedom songs, the hippie cult and 'flower power' – in the 1980s Australians began to discover that they, too, had a ready-made source of transcendental values at the heart of the continent. Tony Leach's video for the rock band Midnight Oil's *Beds are Burning* (1989) showed the group against a background of an otherwise empty desert landscape en route to Redfern. Here the desert is directly implicated in the cause of Aboriginal land rights but, as Kathleen Phillips points out, 'the images of the band alone in the desert do raise some questions. Is *Beds are Burning* primarily a land rights statement or a means to sell records? Or, less cynically, is the song exploiting nationalist mythology for a political purpose?'[28] Other bands using desert imagery are Icehouse (*Great Southern Land*, which has lyrics about primitive man and 'ghosts of time'), INXS (*Kiss the Dirt* and *Burn for You*), Warumpi Band and Blekbela Mujik.

Even outside Australia there is now strong acceptance of the claim that Aboriginal culture offers unique spiritual insights into the meaning of the land, often with unfortunate results. The now wholly discredited hoax fiction *Mutant Message Down Under: A Woman's Journey into Dreamtime Australia* (1991),[29] by American author Marlo Morgan, has been a bestseller in several editions. Morgan professes to be relaying a true account of her spiritual odyssey among a tribe of nomadic Aborigines who modestly call themselves the 'Divine Oneness Real People', all other people being mutants. During a four-month journey with them she apparently learns to live without possessions in harmony with the desert, and is transformed in the process. She also finds that the Real People are about to leave the Earth and have commissioned her, like the Ancient Mariner, to return and teach other mutants to regain their 'true being-ness' before it is too late to save the planet. They tell her: 'We are the direct descendants of first beings. We have passed the test of surviving since the beginning of time, holding steadfast to the original values and laws. It is our group consciousness that has held the earth together.'[30]

277

Few authors make such transparently ludicrous claims as Morgan for divine knowledge, but a number of Australian novels have focussed on a spiritual journey of the kind described by Bruce Chatwin in *Songlines* (1987), where the messianic agent who brings about the epiphanic experience of self-discovery is Aboriginal. Bruce Pascoe's *Fox* (1988) and Brad Collis's *The Soul Stone* (1993) are among these, all strongly didactic in their claims for Aboriginal spirituality.

FOX

In Bruce Pascoe's novel *Fox* the desert provides the site and the means for Fox, on the run from the police, to discover his Aboriginality and reclaim the spiritual illumination available to his people. The 'true' desert, as opposed to the regions that have been made barren by white settlers, is typically characterised as ancient, immense and unchanging, as expressed in the patterns of bird life and the rituals of those who share the desert with its native fauna.

> Further and further he walked into the desert and he came to a large open plain and in its centre was a single red gum. The closer he came to it the greater was his realization of its size. . . . when Fox lay beneath he felt its aspiration, the upward reaching limbs, the slow clamour of an ageless tree reaching to celebrate the sun. The aspirant direction of the soul. Up.[31]

Fox receives his final epiphany by following a lowan or mallee fowl, the totemic bird of the Mallee tribes. The bird leads him through a maze of mallee scrub in a ritual dance which effectively initiates Fox into the traditional spirit knowledge of life and continuity, this knowledge being presented as uniquely associated with the spirit of the desert. '[T]he bird's image seemed as insubstantial and wavering as a haze of smoke, a plume from a cooling fire. . . . Fox followed the maze deeper into the persistent pattern of the trees, a three-dimensional mosaic of clutching limbs and smokey blue foliage. . . . Bird and man in an ancient processional of the desert. . . .'[32]

This identification with Nature cannot be made through an act of will. Aboriginal knowledge is conceptual rather than perceptual, derived not from observation but from initiation into tribal values that are intimately linked with the idea of the sacredness of the land. Mircea Eliade, a religious history scholar, has argued that a fundamental aspect of the sacredness of place is that it represents the axis, the centre of the world.[33] Hence the building of a sanctuary, or even the house of a believer, requires that the profane spot be transformed to a sacred one. Similarly, the geographer Yi-Fu Tuan, whose ideas were discussed in Chapter 2, affirms that 'in every instance the spot was sanctified by some outside power, whether it be a semidivine person, a dazzling hierophany, or cosmic forces that undergird astrology and geomancy.'[34]

However, Aboriginal concepts of the numinous represent an enormous expansion of such confined sacred places. When the whole land is sacred because it is the site of creation by the ancestral beings of the Dreaming, to know the meaning of the stories, and in particular to re-enact them in ritual dance and song, is to partake of the sacred character of the land. In existential terms this involves exchanging the I–it relation with nature, the basis of scientific rationalism and reductionism, for the I–Thou relationship of religious experience. This is the doctrine implicit in Brad Collis's novel, *The Soul Stone* (1993),[35] its title designed to startle by yoking together terms representative of these antithetical extremes.

278

THE SOUL STONE

Collis's hero, Simon Bradbury, is a Catholic priest at a desert mission who learns from the local Aboriginal elders the spiritual meaning present in the land – not merely in sacred sites but in the whole land. In *The Soul Stone*, characters are authorially judged by their response to the desert. Nearly all the Euro-Australians hate and fear the desert because it threatens their acquisitiveness – its droughts destroy their crops and its goldmines are soon depleted. The bishop, in particular, is unnerved by it. To him, 'It was empty and lifeless, a terrain fit only for savages'. By contrast, to a handful of socially marginalised characters – 'the goat lady', old Karl the German immigrant fleeing from a Nazi past, the Aborigines and, increasingly, Simon – it is a place to find the truth. During a personal retreat in the Great Victoria Desert, Simon experiences through the process of initiation 'wonderful mysteries ... a tangible spiritual dimension; a dimension that was a product of this land'. His sermon in the cathedral on his return to Perth outrages his bishop and bewilders the white congregation as he speaks of his pilgrimage in the desert:

> 'I discovered a wonderful truth and beauty; a knowledge that we here are blessed to dwell in such an ancient land that is suffused with spiritual presence. ...
> '[God] comes from the land ... this ancient unspoiled land. And he watches ... not from the heavens ... but from the red earth beneath your feet, from the tall white gums.
> 'Listen to the land and its people ... seek out the songlines that only they can teach.'

The threat this Aborigine-channelled spirituality poses to Catholic orthodoxy as represented by the bishop resides in the competing similarities of the two – in particular the emphasis on sacrificial blood and on the initiation cicatrices that Simon eventually bears on his chest like stigmata. Although Simon points out that 'The world's three great faiths, Christianity, Judaism and Islam, were born of the desert', the bishop can see before him only a demonised priest.

An interesting and unusual feature of Collis's novel is the reciprocal relationship of responsibility between people and land. Not only are the accepting characters renewed and spiritualised by the desert, but, as we saw in Chapter 1, the desert itself is believed to need their active ceremonial participation for its regeneration. Early in the novel Isaac, an Aboriginal elder, tells Simon that when the old people who know the tribal secrets of their land die, 'The spirit that holds the people and the land together will be gone ... and then I think the land here will die.' This is later confirmed by one of the few enlightened white Australians, Ada the old 'goat lady' camped outside Cumalong near Kalgoorlie, who tells Simon, 'We took this place ... from the only people who understood it. Well, it died right under our feet didn't it?' The reversal of that process occurs only when the Aboriginal people are free to sing the land and engage with its spirits in the prescribed way. Simon's ability to experience this spiritual power is contingent on the physical and mental ordeal of initiation and acceptance of the responsibilities it entails, a more thorough-going version of the pilgrimage in the desert and salvation through self-denial and suffering.

This elevation of Aboriginal culture is far removed from the early colonial attitudes of denigration of Aborigines as the lowest form of humanity and complacent acceptance of their allegedly imminent extinction when confronted with a superior race. However it has not gone unchallenged. It can also be seen as an appropriation of Aboriginal culture to supply a deficiency in settler history, or as the exploitation of a highly marketable commodity which, in post-colonial times, is promoted as the one authentic Australian civilisation. In *Edge of the Sacred* (1995) David Tacey points out that, while allotting to the Aborigines the priestly 'duty' of responsibility for the sacred may seem a mark

279

of honour, in practice it perpetuates the existing racist hegemony, not only disempowering white Australians spiritually but precluding Aborigines from secular status and material wealth, and thus keeping them in a position of socio–economic subjection. 'The split is convenient but it is also fatal.'[36]

Given the prevailingly secular, even anti-religious, ethos of Australian culture, it is perhaps not surprising that Aboriginal sacred values, which require little or no personal religious commitment from white Australians, have been embraced with more enthusiasm than the Judaeo–Christian tradition.[37] It is relatively easy for white Australians to attribute shaman-like powers to Aborigines in theory, without any serious desire to acquire them. Catholic poet Les Murray suggests that this acknowledgment of Aboriginal spiritual superiority is a facile and temporary way of absolving white Australians of the guilt of settlement and will soon be retracted:

> but fairytale is a reserve, for those rich only
> in that and fifty thousand years here.
> The newcomers will acquire those fifty thousand
> years too, though. Thousands of anything
> draw them. They discovered thousands,
> even these. Which they offer now for settlement.[38]

On the other hand Catholic philosopher Max Charlesworth argues that revelations of the divine and the development of authentic religious values have often occurred outside the edifice of Christianity and urges the need for open dialogue and interchange with other religious traditions, including that of the Aborigines. His goal is not a lowest-common-denominator amalgam of religious truisms but the hope 'that there is a possibility of a creative religious explosion occurring early in the next millennium with the ancient land of Australia at the centre of it, and that the Holy Spirit may come home at last to *Terra Australis*'.[39]

Chapter 15

The Art of Cultural Encounter

The [Papunya] painting movement articulated once more with
immense brilliance the relationship of these people to their land.
It gave them pride of self and let them once more become men and
women speaking in their own right and their own traditions. ... The
great aphorisms of space which the paintings so luminously set forth
have already transformed our understanding of the continent.

GEOFFREY BARDON[1]

My work is an involved form of contemplation. If you live in nature for
a time, you have almost mystical experiences. You get into a state of
lyrical excitement and become part of the things that are happening
around you: the grass quivering, the birds singing. On a sunny day there
is an extraordinary feeling of energy, as light dazzles, bees buzz, birds
dart, lizards slither. Nature moves through your veins in a spiritual way,
and then the work of art flows out like birdsong.

JOHN WOLSELEY[2]

Traditional Aboriginal art as described in Chapter 1 interrogates the assumptions and prejudices of the European art canon in almost every detail.

Western society accepts criteria of originality and authenticity as self-
evidently valuable. Ideally, therefore, each piece of art should be unique since,
by analogy with natural resources and so-called precious metals, rarity is an
important component of value. Thus, whatever its aesthetic merit, a painting
that is once established to be a copy of another becomes virtually valueless
from that moment. Secondly, both art dealers and the public wish to be able to
attribute a particular work to an identifiable, individual artist. Even when there
have been assistants, one artist is credited with the work. Thirdly, there is a
strong belief that the best art is non-aligned and that art created for the sake
of propaganda is inherently less worthy. Again, paintings are assumed to be
merely objects that can be bought and sold, taken away, exhibited or kept in a
bank vault without any change in their value since this is determined by the
market place, not by their location. In the case of a landscape, the painting

presents a scene from the outside, as a grouping of natural objects depicted to conform to a given style of composition, using conventions of perspective and gradations of size and shading to determine the importance of the objects within the scene relative to the viewer.

For traditional Aboriginal communities, on the other hand, all these criteria are either meaningless or in need of major qualification. Originality and authenticity are properties only of the Dreaming Ancestors. They not only created the land; they devised the songs and ceremonies and the associated art forms, giving them in trust to the rightful people to perform. The artists, like the performers in a ceremony, are creating not of themselves but because of the power operating through them. Hence the notion that an individual might change these forms is unthinkable. Even if it appears new, the idea of a painting or a dance is believed to have been given to the artist, perhaps in a dream. The value of the art cannot be expressed materially since it is a spiritual offering; in the case of the ground and body painting it is meaningful only on the occasion for which it was created and it is destroyed during the ceremony. Taken away from its spiritual context, the land, it is nothing. The value of the art resides not in the material object but in the power inherent in it, a power that was sung into it at the time of its creation. Thus those taking part in the singing were as much the creators of the painting as the person or persons applying the pigments. Ultimately that power comes from the Ancestral Spirits, not from the people. The art is always created for a purpose other than itself. Traditionally this was a religious purpose; now it might also be a political statement. The land is depicted not only externally but, primarily, as though looking down through it to the powerful spirits dwelling within it.

282

Bridge or take-over?

Given these antithetical parameters, it is not surprising that at first contact these two traditions were mutually unintelligible. For more than a century it was inconceivable to the white settlers that the Aborigines had any art at all. At the Paris exhibition of 1919 which included works from Africa, North America and Oceania, there were no works from Australia because the organisers considered the Australian Aborigines to be a people without art.[3] However, with the rise of interest in anthropology, there was a growing market for Aboriginal artefacts, which were collected not for their aesthetic value (this was considered negligible), but as curios.

The opening of the Trans-Australian Railway in 1915 facilitated the movement of white settlers and missionaries into the desert area and, in the normal processes associated with intercultural boundaries, trade occurred. The missions at Ernabella and Hermannsburg encouraged Aboriginal people to produce carvings for sale in the mission shop. All such art was classified, technically, as 'primitive' – a term that is, of course, loaded with Eurocentric resonances. As Anne-Marie Willis reminds us, primitivism is 'a label used to designate culture that is non-European; "primitive" never describes how the cultures would see themselves. Similarly the "appreciation" of "primitive" art only occurs within the parameters of European aesthetics; it is to be appropriated for its "simplicity", "bold designs", "strong colours".[4]

The first white person to think of Aboriginal culture in terms of art was Margaret Preston who, as early as 1925, became committed to developing a new, specifically Australian Modernism. She believed passionately that the patterns and motifs of indigenous art could be removed from their original cultural purpose and re-embedded in a Western context to furnish a new nationalist art form. Her article in *Art in Australia* delivered a manifesto to this effect:

> In wishing to rid myself of the mannerisms of a country other than my own,
> I have gone to the art of a people who had never seen or known anything
> different from themselves. . . . These are the Australian Aboriginals, and it is
> only from the art of such people in any land that a national art can spring.
> Later come the individual or individuals who with conscious knowledge
> (education) use these symbols that are their heritage, and thus a great
> national art is founded.[5]

Preston followed this with a seminal article on the application of Aboriginal designs. Viewed in post-colonial terms Preston's program involved an arrogant and insensitive appropriation of Aboriginal art, totally ignoring its cultural context and religious purpose. But at the time it was assumed that only through this process of removal was value conferred; the designs achieved significance only when integrated into the Western art canon. Whether destined for museums or the primitive/ethnic section of art galleries they were invariably seen as the inferior 'other', a curiosity to be compared unfavourably with civilised art, lacking a history or meaningful context. Yet Preston's energetic program to familiarise white Australians with these designs was, in another sense, extremely successful. Disseminated on tea towels, writing paper and fabrics, they necessarily lost their cultural meaning but they initiated white Australians into other ways of seeing and appreciation. Preston's campaign gained force through the interest sparked by the career of Albert Namatjira (see Chapter 9). Namatjira was bridging the divide from the other side, producing art using the perspective and the technology of the West but painting out of his passionate identification with his land, his Dreaming. The glowing colours of his pictures were his innovative way of expressing the radiant power within the land, as the white pigments of traditional painting had done. His was genuinely assimilationist art, combining two messages, two traditions.

Also important in educating white society in Aboriginal art were the major exhibitions mounted in Sydney and Melbourne during the 1940s and 50s. All these art works were in the traditional style: anything else would have been considered garish and non-authentic. The doyens of the Western art world had no trouble deciding on what was authentic: that which perpetuated the oldest

283

known works and was produced using the traditional designs, colours and surfaces. This was consistent with the belief that genuine Aboriginal culture, like the desert landscape it came from, was changeless. Indeed, it was a necessary ideology: it justified the Australian Government's 'assimilation' program which was based on the premise that Aborigines, especially children, must be removed from their 'stone age' culture in order to give them a chance of surviving in the twentieth century.

Papunya – and beyond

The realisation that Aboriginal art could be as vibrant and innovative as anything in the West, if not more so, is dated back to the famous Papunya painting movement. Some 250 kilometres from Alice Springs, and traditionally the site of the Honey Ant Dreaming, Papunya was chosen by the Government in the 1960s as an assimilation site. Accordingly, about one thousand Aborigines from surrounding areas were transplanted to this Western Desert settlement without any regard for their restrictions on relationships with other language groups. This was a totally disempowering experience for these formerly free-moving but closely knit people and there was little incentive for creativity or the preservation of their inherited culture. However, Geoffrey Bardon, a social studies and art teacher who arrived at the Papunya school in 1971, encouraged some of the older men to participate in producing a mural on the walls of the school using the customary patterns and designs of their community. This proved controversial because some of the images were regarded as secret–sacred, but eventually the owner of the Honey Ant Dreaming gave permission for the designs to be used and there was a sense of achievement as well as pleasure at sharing these traditional images. When the mural was finished Bardon provided acrylic paints and boards for a continuing expression of this artistic talent which was further encouraged and inspired by Kaapa Tjampitjinpa, the prime mover in setting up the Papunya Tula Artists' Cooperative.

Since the 1970s the Papunya artists have developed several different styles, though their art is best recognised by its characteristic dot and circle designs. However, the use and functions of these dots have evolved over time. Having their most likely origin in the white dots of down integral to body and ground painting (described in Chapter 1), they were used at first in the acrylic paintings only to outline important components of the overall design, giving a sense of a pulsating energy to shapes and forms. In particular, the dazzling effect of white dots on a darker ground indicated the brilliance of the supernatural power associated with a sacred site. Some artists then extended the use of the dots to fill in formerly plain background areas, indicating, in the swirls or concentric circles of dots, the topography of a landscape or the circular growth of spinifex clumps. The subtle depiction of different features within a surface covered by dots, through use of colour shading of the dots, gives a vivid impression of animals camouflaged within a landscape and caught only in the peripheral vision. The dots were also used to conceal from the eyes of the uninitiated the most sacred aspects of the picture.

The Papunya Tula school of Western Desert acrylic dot paintings is widely regarded as the one great Aboriginal success story, a means of acquiring new dignity and economic empowerment for the artists' communities. Not surprisingly it has inspired other groups to develop their own particular artistic styles. The Yuendumu community, also produced by an assimilationist program but comprising mostly Warlpiri people, began in a small way when the women started to paint boards with acrylics to earn the money for a four-wheel-drive vehicle in which to visit their sacred sites. In 1984 the school principal invited five of the elders to paint their Dreamings on thirty-six school doors. Seeing this as an opportunity to ensure that the children did not grow up in ignorance of their culture's rich stories and images, they agreed. One of the artists has said: 'We painted these Dreamings on the school doors because the children should learn about our law. The children do not know them and they might become like white people, which we don't want to happen.'[6] Unlike the murals at Papunya – which were painted over after Bardon left, in order to clean up the school – the Yuendumu doors were fully documented from the start and many of them have been preserved to be exhibited in isolation from their school context. The publicity given to the doors led to a flourishing of art at Yuendumu. Characterised by brilliant colours, it was very different from the Papunya style and this was important because it indicated that the artists themselves had control over what they produced; it was not entirely consumer determined.

Since these two early cooperative ventures, indigenous communities have continued to evolve different styles, though a common theme of many acrylic paintings designed for the art market is the visual equivalent of the epic song cycles: the depiction of the Dreaming tracks of the Ancestors, linking the sacred sites on their journeys. Like the ground paintings, they have as their basic elements circles representing the static and eternal entities – such as waterholes, sites, fires, women and sources of fertility – and lines, representing movement – journeys, tracks, spears and the male activation of fertility. The meeting of lines with circles represents the release of creative power. Because of their diverse social, gender or geographical backgrounds, various artists may have the right to represent only certain segments of a Dreaming track and will thus map different events, though by the use of similar designs they may demonstrate their shared inheritance of the one basic Dreaming.[7] Some geographic locations are intersected by many Dreaming tracks. The Yuendumu region, for example, testifies to the journeys of the Flying Ant, the Wild Yam, the Blue-tongue Lizard, the Initiated Youths and the Emu. Mount Nicker, west of Alice Springs, is the meeting place of at least six Dreamings – Witchetty Grub, Snake, Wallaby, Spider, Wild Yam, and Vine. Sometimes an artist may have permission to include several Dreamings in one painting. A fine example of this is *Five Dreamings* (1984) (see illustration following page 272) by Michael

285

Nelson Jakamarra, assisted by Marjorie Napaljarri. In such cases a painting may be a statement not only of the artist's particular Dreaming affiliation but of his or her place in a network of intersecting social groups owning different Dreamings.

As well as this social component, the paintings may include specific indications of the topographical features associated with the Dreaming – for example, Tim Leura Tjapaltjarri's *Napperby Death Spirit Dreaming* (1980) (see illustration following page 272), which depicts the artist's country on Napperby Station. The journey of *Warnayarra*, the Rainbow Snake, between Papunya and Yuendumu is depicted by artists of these two areas as the body of the Snake itself and also as Mijilyparnta Creek which today represents both the Snake body and its track.

Such paintings have captivated buyers internationally, particularly since the striking success of the Aboriginal components of the Paris Autumn Festival of 1983 where it was observed that 'without the Aboriginal participation – the dance spectacular at the Bouffes du Nord, the Aboriginal video programme and the acrylic paintings at the Australian Embassy – the Australian contribution ... would have been a non-event.'[8] Certainly art by favoured Aboriginal artists now fetches unprecedented prices. In June 1997 Sotheby's sold $2.73 million of Aboriginal art works, with the top price of $206,000 being paid for Johnny Warangkula Tjupurrula's *Water Dreaming at Kalipinypa* (1972).

It would be naive, as well as inappropriate, to judge these apparent success stories wholly on their economic returns. Although willingly undertaken by the artists in order to earn money, the process can be regarded as a form of cultural colonisation. Anne-Marie Willis has cynically characterised successful modern Aboriginal paintings as 'the aestheticised anthropological (re-)invention of "Aboriginal art"'.[9] Furthermore, the new style of art production has had a subversive effect on the social systems of some communities. Traditionally the creation of paintings was a communal activity, while the Western world requires a single artist's name on the painting. But who is the artist? The person whose family owns the Dreaming? The person(s) who conceive(s) of the design and colours? The person(s) who paint(s) the canvas? The person(s) with whom the dealer negotiates? In many communities young artists may be more successful in the market place than the elders, thereby threatening the social hierarchy. This destabilisation is exacerbated by the financial aspect of art, an element newly imported from the West. The new source of income which comes to specific artists may be no longer distributed across the community but used to purchase luxury items such as cars, thereby overturning the traditional social order. It is also arguable that the unprecedented interest in Aboriginal art within Australia is at least partly guilt-driven. Enthusiasm for Aboriginal art (the least threatening aspect of indigenous culture) tacitly declares a wish to erase memories of previous racist treatment of Aboriginal communities and proclaims our credentials as card-carrying liberal internationalists.

Conversely, however, it could be argued that Aboriginal artists have colonised the Western art world. They have skilfully exploited the potential offered by Western materials, especially acrylics and canvas, to develop an industry that is burgeoning financially while offering at least some artists the potential for economic autonomy. In addition they retain a level of power that is largely unsuspected by those who buy their work. The purchaser of *Water Dreaming* will never know the inner secret–sacred meaning of the painting. From the Aboriginal perspective, the works produced for sale are merely that – a commodity produced to capture a market niche. They provide a useful, even necessary, form of income but they have no real meaning in the sense that art traditionally had in an Aboriginal community. Even when they carry a tag or document 'explaining' the story behind the painting, they must be sung into existence by the appropriate people before they can acquire spiritual power and become alive. In other words, the art world gets what it pays for: so much paint on a canvas or board, so many dots to the centimetre, in the colours that the market decides are 'authentic'. To the quantitative eye of the West, more dots, like more pixels on your screen, means better quality. White viewers are mostly unaware that the dots are there partly because the potential buyers now expect them, and partly because they conceal the secret designs from uninitiated eyes. In one sense, then, the more dots the more obscure the meaning.

Painting land rights

287

Possibly the most important outcome of European intervention in Aboriginal art production is that the artists have played a vital role in educating white Australians about their culture. Just as the religious influence of traditional Aboriginal art was not confined to the painted object but pervaded the whole ceremony, empowering all participants, modern Aboriginal art spills over from the canvas to make a mission statement that is strongly political but also inherently religious. Much of the art produced for widespread dissemination as tee-shirts and prints carries the unmistakable message of the claim for land rights, often in a witty parodic form. Indeed, paintings may now be a serious and integral part of the claim for land rights on the grounds that they are evidence of traditional ownership. The Warlpiri women produced diagrammatic picture maps as part of their evidence for the Mount Allen Land Claim, a bid to regain the legal right to enter their traditional land.[10]

In June 1997 a group of almost sixty Kimberley men and women determined to establish their native title claim over a vast area of the Great Sandy Desert (see illustration following page 272). Gathering on the northern edge of the Desert at the out-station of internationally known artist Jimmy Pike, they represented four major language groups of the area. Their huge canvas, eight metres by ten metres, was produced not for aesthetic or economic purposes but as cultural evidence of their traditional ownership of the land in question. It is a map in Aboriginal terms. A broad stripe across the canvas indicates the Canning Stock Route, a marker recognised by both black and white Australians. The artists then depicted their own traditional territories in relation to this line using designs that incorporate both physical and spiritual sites on their land. Those actually painting were advised by others whose knowledge of the land was more detailed – usually elders whose physical sight prohibited them from painting but whose insight into the land was second to none. The resulting canvas incorporates many different techniques and styles of painting, from the dot and circle style of the Wangkajungka artists to the more Western style of the landscapes by Walmajarri artists from Fitzroy Crossing. The colours, which vibrate on the canvas, are not confined to the subtle earth and sky colours that the art world has selected for acclaim, but use the whole dazzling range of the acrylic palette. For these artists it is not the colours that determine authenticity (that is an irrational, Western, restriction) but the inherited right of the artist to paint his or her land. To them it is self-evident proof that if they have painted it so precisely, then it is indeed their land. In the words of Tommy May, Director of the Association of Northern Kimberley and Arnhem Land Artists and a contributor to the canvas, 'If [non-Aboriginal] people can't understand our word they can see our painting. They say the same thing.'[11]

Whatever the immediate outcome of the Land Rights Claims, such paintings may achieve their aim in the long term because of their educative influence on the nation. However superficially they may be understood relative to the knowledge of the artists, Aboriginal paintings have led many white Australians not just to an appreciation of the aesthetic value of indigenous art but to a new awareness of the depth of Aboriginal culture and, as a result, to a new understanding of the land. In this book we have seen that an increasingly spiritual relation to the land has informed the art of several contemporary desert artists, including John Coburn, John Olsen, John Wolseley and Mandy Martin. The concept of the Dreaming is increasingly understood, at least at a basic level, and valued by non-indigenous Australians. The eminent anthropologist Derek Mulvaney affirms that the Aboriginal artists at Papunya 'have illuminated the mythological interactions between people and nature, for white viewers, in a more deeply humanised manner than those landscapes offered by the European myth-making painters and authors'[12].

Geoffrey Bardon, who played such an important role as catalyst in the process of education and reconciliation, had just such a vision:

> The [Papunya] painting movement points for all of us toward a great resurgence of the human spirit in this country. The Western Desert painters have, by their insight of artistic form and towering compassion towards their land, provided for us all, and for all time, a re-perception of the continent.[13]

Epilogue

Geographically this book has followed the progressive attempts of the inland explorers to reach the middle of the continent and the frustrated efforts of white Australians to survive in these desert regions. A major focus of the book has therefore been the range of changing responses to the desert – from the bewilderment and abhorrence of the nineteenth-century settlers faced with a terrain that mocked their hopes of agricultural and pastoral development, through the frantic search for gold, to the pride with which their descendants now acknowledge its stark beauty captured in the glowing images on posters, calendars and movie screens. But equally I have been concerned to trace the particular mystique associated with 'the Centre' and its gradual substitution for the older, imperial notion of Europe as the centre of education, of knowledge, of identity.

In the coda to his book of essays, *Landprints: Reflections on Place and Landscape* (1997), earth scientist and cultural studies scholar George Seddon cites an excerpt from E.M. Forster's novel *Passage to India* (1924) to show that Forster, steeped in the culture of Cambridge, was both 'immensely enriched by that imaginative possession of a human past that begins with the Greeks and embraced the Italian Renaissance; [and] crippled by a limiting Eurocentrism, fully apprehending one world only by rejecting another'.[1] Until recently white Australians found the centre of their own continent and the associated indigenous culture even more strange than India and it has taken two centuries for them to overcome their own Eurocentric limitations and embrace a different kind of cultural enrichment.

For two centuries the desert has been commandeered in Australian literature to provide 'atmosphere', whether as a plausible venue for adventure, a source of Gothic terror, a psychological symbol for a nation dismissed as barren and empty, or a springboard for a spiritual rebirth, for 'finding oneself'. In art the desert has been the site for an even more remarkable renaissance in perception. Once, it was regarded as a terrain of absences that defied the parameters of classical landscape art, with its tightly preserved conventions of framing, perspective and shadow designed to simulate a vertical confrontation with Nature – a scene brought into being, composed and dominated by the spectator; now it generates its own images, demanding and inspiring other ways of seeing.

Underlying these conceptual changes have been the gradual re-evaluation and acceptance of Aboriginal culture, associated most strongly, if eclectically, with the central deserts. The original belief of Europeans that the Aborigines possessed no civilisation at all has yielded to a celebration of indigenous art, oral tradition, social values and the profound spiritual relationship that Aboriginal peoples have with their land. These are now seen as revitalising and inspirational elements of a broader Australian culture.

The otherness of the desert has come to epitomise a new perspective, an unsuspected beauty, a suggestion of dissenting values, a context that demands a modification of economic rationalism and Western materialism. The central deserts have forced Australian writers and artists to discover new possibilities and new meanings, and to create new myths:

> Whether as they, we explore a continent, or are content
> to explore ourselves, we find that mysterious centre,
> that vast and utter loneliness, which is the heart of being[.][2]

Where a bibliographical reference is shortened, the complete information is given in the bibliography. Where there are several sequential quotations from the same text, page references are grouped together in the note to the first quotation.

Preface
1 In Lindsay's 1967 novel one of the girls is subsequently found but is psychologically changed by the experience. The story was well known through Peter Weir's 1975 film based on the novel.
2 Les Murray, 'Equanimity', *Collected Poems*, p. 180.
3 See page ii for a brief outline of some of the main geographical and biological features of the Australian deserts.

Introduction
1 William Blake, *Complete Writings of Blake*, ed. Geoffrey Keynes (Oxford: The Clarendon Press, 1913, repr. 1952), p. 456.
2 Schama, *Landscape*, pp. 6–7.
3 Bachelard, *Space*, p. 188.
4 Gibson, 'Middle Distance', p. 31.
5 Vernon, *The Garden and the Map*, pp. 35–6.
6 Giles, *Australia Twice Traversed*, vol. II, book III, p. 202.
7 The first occurrence of this phrase in print appears to have been in the Melbourne newspaper, the *Argus*, 3 September 1858.
8 This notion is developed at length in Sellick, 'The Explorer as Hero'.
9 See, for example, Richard Kimber, 'The Dynamic Century before the Horn Expedition: a Speculative History' in Morton and Mulvaney (eds), *Exploring Central Australia*, pp. 91–102.
10 Jameson, *The Political Unconscious*.
11 On 3 June 1992 the High Court of Australia decided that Eddie Mabo and the Meriam People he represented had property rights in the Murray Islands, off the north coast of Queensland. Their rights to live there derived from their traditional ties to the land rather than from title deeds. In coming to this decision, the High Court rejected the idea of *terra nullius* and recognised Aboriginal native title rights.
12 In 1996 Justice Drummond in the Federal Court decided that the claim of the Wik and Thayorre Peoples to native title of their traditional lands in Queensland could not succeed, as the lands were subject to pastoral leases. In response to an appeal, the High Court ruled against Justice Drummond's decision, leaving the way open for the Wik and Thayorre Peoples to return to the Federal Court and present evidence of their native title rights.

Chapter 1
1 Tinamin, 'One Land . . .'.
2 Silas Roberts, Chairman of the Northern Land Council, submission to the Ranger Inquiry in 1977. Quoted by Djon Mundine OAM, 'Without land we are nothing. Without land we are a lost people' in Mellick (ed.), *Spirit + Place*, p. 48.

3 Davis, 'From the Plane Window' in *Black Life*, p. 73.
4 See Strehlow, 'Personal Monototemism'. Strehlow's account is based on his intimate knowledge of Aranda religion. However, Robert Layton found no such 'emergence' narratives among the peoples of the Western Desert. See Layton, 'Relating to the Country in the Western Desert', p. 217.
5 See Lowe with Pike, *Jilji*, p. 6.
6 See Ronald M. Berndt, 'Territoriality', p. 137.
7 See, for example, Munn, 'Excluded Spaces'.
8 Strehlow, *Central Australian Religion*, p. 16.
9 For a detailed discussion of this issue see Hiatt and Jones, 'Workings of Nature'.
10 F.J. Gillen, 'Notes on some Manners and Customs of the Aborigines of the MacDonnell Ranges belonging to the Arunta Tribe', in Spencer (ed.), *Horn Expedition*, vol. IV. It should be acknowledged that even the most well-meaning attempts to interpret Aboriginal ideology in Western terms will inevitably involve reductionism.
11 This belief matches closely what philosopher Maurice Merleau-Ponty describes as the mythical situation expressed in the Garden of Eden before the Fall: 'Things are taken for the incarnation of what they express, because their human significance is compressed into them and presents itself literally as what they mean.' (Merleau-Ponty, *Perception*, p. 290.)
12 Langford, *Love*, p. 234.
13 In most Aboriginal groups, this place is determined by the mother at time she first feels her child move within her. She calls the Elders who, knowing the Dreaming history of the area, determine the sacred natural feature and totem appropriate for a child.
14 Levi-Strauss, *Totemism*.
15 The great armchair anthropologist Sir James Frazer, author of the monolithic *The Golden Bough*, assumed that such a simplistic connection existed. See Frazer, 'Totemism'. Compare Hiatt and Jones, p. 17.
16 Ronald and Catherine Berndt, *Speaking Land*, p. 6.
17 See, for example, T. Griffith and M. McCaskill (eds), *The Atlas of South Australia* (Adelaide: SA Government Printing Division and Wakefield Press, 1986).
18 Layton, 'Relating . . .', p. 224.
19 Andrew Taylor, p. 140.
20 Sally Morgan, *My Place*, epigraph.
21 Ronald and Catherine Berndt, *Speaking Land*, p. 3.
22 The well-known *Wandjina* figures on rock walls in north-west coastal regions are closely associated with the Rainbow Snake.
23 Ronald and Catherine Berndt, *Speaking Land*, p. 125.
24 Peter Sutton, 'Dreamings', in Sutton, *Dreamings*, p. 19. Howard Morphy's study of the artistic system of North-East Arnhem Land found no simple relationship between the painters as members of clans, the Dreaming sites of the clan lands, and the clan designs. The art does encode relations between the people and the land, but not in the same form as other systems in the culture. (PhD dissertation, ANU, 1977.)
25 See Djon Mundine OAM, quoted in Mellick (ed.), *Spirit + Place*, p. 48.
26 See also Sutton, *Dreamings*, p. 61.
27 Judith Wright, 'Landscape and Dreaming' in Stephen R. Graubard (ed.), *Australia: The Daedalus Symposium* (Sydney: Angus & Robertson, 1985), p. 32.
28 Sutton, *Dreamings*, p. 16.
29 See Caruana, *Aboriginal Art*, pp. 99, 103.
30 See Sutton, *Dreamings*, p. 61.
31 Kimber, 'Mosaics', 5.
32 Red ochre is considered particularly efficacious, representing the 'blood' and life force of mythological men and animals. Kimber, 'Mosaics', 6.
33 Strehlow, *Religion*, p. 27.

34 See Caruana, *Aboriginal Art*, p. 14.
35 See Anthony Forge, 'The Desert: Tradition in the Present', in Caruana, *Windows*, p. 153.
36 Stanner, *Aboriginal Religion*, p. 63.
37 See Judith Ryan with Kim Akerman, 'Figurative Art of the North-west and Central Kimberley', in Ryan, *Power*, p. 14. For a discussion of both views, see Murray Hogarth and Leigh Dayton, 'By Whose Hand?', *Sydney Morning Herald Good Weekend*, 21 June 1997, 30–35.
38 The OSL (optically stimulated luminescence) technique involves exposing the quartz grains to laser light to free electrons trapped in imperfections in the quartz. The freed electrons release energy as light and the more light emitted, the greater the age of the crystals. For a full description see Richard Roberts et al., 'Luminescence Dating'.
39 The first European to describe the figures was George Grey who first saw them in March 1838 in two caves near the Glenelg River. Believing the figures 'far superior to what a savage race could be supposed capable of', Grey sought explanations from other cultures and found parallels with European art for what he described as their haloes, head-dress, their long robes and their script. Grey, *Journals*, vol. 2, pp. 202–6. See also Elkin, 'Grey's Cave Paintings'.
40 See Ryan, *Power*, p. 12.
41 *ibid.*, p. 13.

Chapter 2
1 Edward Said, *Culture*, p. 6.
2 Ludwig Wittgenstein, *Philosophical Investigations*, para. 115.
3 Gerald Murnane, *The Plains* (Ringwood, Vic.: McPhee Gribble/Penguin, 1982), p. 92.
4 Although Spanish rule in Florida and the south-west predated the landing of the various Protestant groups in the seventeenth century and continued to exert an influence locally, it had far less impact on the self-image of the emerging nation as a whole.
5 For explanations of these theories, see, for example, Oldroyd, *Geology*.
6 Stafford, *Voyage into Substance*, p. 29.
7 For a detailed account of such preconceptions, see Eisler and Smith (eds), *Terra Australis*.
8 The very name 'Australia' carries in its construction two Eurocentric assumptions: 'south' is tacitly defined in relation to Europe, while the use of a derivation from the Latin word for 'south' signified a statement universally understood.
9 As we shall see in Chapter 7, by the last decades of the nineteenth century, there was growing concern that Australia might be invaded by the oriental races to its north, if not militarily then, perhaps more abhorrently, by miscegenation.
10 Fairies' Glen, Glen Edith, Glen Helen and Glen of Palms are but four of the many 'glens' named by Giles. Along with Titania's Spring, the Vale of Tempe, the Gorge of Tarns and the Tarn of Auber (the last named after Edgar Allan Poe's poem) they indicate Giles's penchant for a Romantic view of the desert when any opportunity offered.
11 See also Healy, 'The Lemurian Nineties'.
12 Paul Wenz, quoted in Friedrich, *Australia . . .*, p. 202.
13 Brock, *To the Desert with Sturt*, p. 137.
14 Giles, book v, chs 1 & 2, pp. 265–6, 269.
15 Short, *Imagined Country*, p. 5. In Hebrew, ancient Greek and Latin the words for wilderness were associated with lack of cultivation, while in old English the likely root, *wildeoren*, meant 'wild beasts'.
16 In *Two Treatises of Government* (1690) the British philosopher, John Locke, had conveniently proposed that wild country, not previously owned, could be legally enclosed for use by anyone desirous of doing so.

293

17 See Jennings, *Invasion of America*, p. 73.

18 Tuan, 'Desert and Ice', pp. 146–7.

19 Promulgating this myth was convenient for several groups of people – from Australian farmers in need of labour to shipping agents keen to promote immigration.

20 John Locke, *Second Treatise on Government* [London, 1689], Section 35, in Peter Laslett (ed.), *John Locke: Two Treatises on Government*, p. 310.

21 The apparent exception is the Ord River scheme in north-west Australia, but this project, too, while technically successful, has proved to have unfortunate side effects.

22 William Ramson, 'Wasteland to Wilderness: Changing Perceptions of the Environment' in D.J. Mulvaney (ed.), *The Humanities and the Australian Environment* (Canberra: Australian Academy of the Humanities, 1991), p. 9.

23 Heseltine, 'Literary Heritage'.

24 Ironically Clarke goes on to explain the fascination of the wilderness, but this part of the passage is usually ignored. Marcus Clarke, Preface to *Poems*, p. vi [1880].

25 Judith Wright, *Preoccupations*, p. xiii.

26 Quoted in Robert Paynes, *Jerome: the Hermit* (New York: Viking, 1951), p. 99.

27 See Sano di Pietro (1406–81), *Penitence of St Jerome*; Jacopo di Arcangelo (1441–93), *St Jerome in the Desert*; Joachim Patenier (1480–1524), *St Jerome in the Desert*.

28 I am indebted for this connection to Brown ('Landscape', p. 32).

29 R.B. Blakney, *Meister Eckhart: A Modern Translation* (New York: Harper Torchbooks, 1941), pp. 200–201.

30 Williams, *Wilderness*, pp. 4–5.

31 Edmund Burke, *Philosophical Enquiry into the Origin of our Ideas of the Sublime and Beautiful* [1757], ed. James Boulton (Oxford: Blackwell, 1987), p. 39. The notion of the sublime dates back to a Greek treatise 'On the Sublime', written in the first century A.D. and ascribed to Longinus. Longinus correlated poetic excellence with deep emotion on the part of the author, an idea that was revived in force by Nicholas Despreaux-Boileau's French translation of the work in 1674.

32 James Cook described New Caledonia as 'very barren and desert'; to Alexander von Humboldt the Andes were 'desert solitudes'. See Barbara Maria Stafford, pp. 152–4.

33 Bachelard, pp. 204–5, 184. Here Bachelard is referring to Philippe Diolé's book, *Le plus beau désert du monde!*

34 *ibid.*, p. 196.

35 Said, *Orientalism*, pp. 54–5.

36 Pratt, 'Scratches'. Compare also Pratt, *Imperial Eyes*, p. 7.

37 Rhys Jones, 'Ordering the Landscape', in Donaldson and Donaldson, pp. 205, 207.

38 The fact that most of the exploring expeditions included Aboriginal guides to find water and paths through the scrub was suppressed or made light of. The kidnapping of Aboriginal women who were tied up in the midday sun until prepared to lead their captors to water was taken as evidence of the intellectual superiority of the whites.

39 Stanner, 'Caliban Discovered' in *Essays, 1938–73*, p. 145. Patrick Brantlinger ('Victorians and Africans', 166) notes a parallel deterioration in Africa 'from the altruism of antislavery to the cynicism of empire building'. *Bringing Them Home* (1997), the report of the Human Rights and Equal Opportunity Commission into the separation of Aboriginal and Torres Strait Island children from their families, details the genocidal results of the national assimilation program for Aborigines. Its underlying rationale was the assumption that the indigenous races would be rendered extinct by the arrival of a superior race and the only chance for survival was to 'breed out the blackness'.

40 D.J. Mulvaney, 'The Darwinian Perspective' in Donaldson and Donaldson, p. 72.

41 Giles, book II, ch. 2, p. 184.

42 Thomas Henry Huxley in Charles Lyell, *The Geological Evidences of the Antiquity of Man* (London: Murray, 1863), pp. 86–9. For a detailed account of the way Aborigines were slotted into Darwinian theory, see D.J. Mulvaney, 'The Darwinian Perspective' in Donaldson and Donaldson, pp. 68–75.

43 Giles, book v, ch. 4, p. 320.
44 *ibid.*, ch. 3, p. 228.
45 Charles Darwin, *The Descent of Man and Selection in Relation to Sex*, 2nd edn (New York and London: Merrill & Baker, 1874), p. 613. See also Patrick Brantlinger, 'Victorians and Africans', 166–203.

Chapter 3

1 Christopher Marlowe, *Tamburlaine*, part II (v. iii. 123–4).
2 Charles Sturt, public lecture delivered at the Adelaide Mechanics' Institute, 28 May 1840.
3 Giles, book III, ch. 2, p. 126.
4 Conrad, *Darkness*, p. 11.
5 Ericksen, 'Conflict', 38.
6 Sir Joseph Banks, Letter to the Colonial Secretary, 15 May 1778.
7 For a detailed discussion of exploration of the American desert see Hollon, *American Desert*.
8 This belief, like the notion of the Australian inland sea, was based on a mistake. In 1771–76, Father Hermenegildo Garcés discovered what is now known as the Kern River, and understood from the local Indians that it was part of a more extensive river system. Thus was born the belief in an inland sea, drained by numerous rivers that were navigable to the Pacific. A map to this effect was quickly produced and soon assumed the status of fact. Later cartographers optimistically added the desired river systems connecting the putative inland sea to the Pacific Ocean.
9 The myth was finally laid to rest in 1844 when John Charles Frémont at last showed that the area between the Rockies and the Sierra Nevada comprised 'deserts and oases' and that 'no river from the interior does, or can, cross the Sierra Nevada – itself more lofty than the Rockies'. For a detailed discussion of the role of imagination in exploration see John L. Allen, 'Lands . . . Waters'.
10 R.L. Heathcote, 'Visions', pp. 82–3. On the basis of such suppositions, in 1838 Captain Vetch 'calculated the future Australian population by dividing the continent into nine convenient units and awarding each the population of the European nation nearest in size, assuming of course an analogous land productivity potential'. (Quoted by Heathcote, p. 83.)
11 Sturt, *Narrative*, vol. I, p. 272. c.f. 'It struck me then, and calmer reflection confirms the impression, that the whole of the low interior I have traversed was formerly a sea-bed, since raised from its sub-marine position by natural though hidden causes' (p. 381).
12 See *ibid.*, pp. 33–4.
13 As early as 1820, while tracing the eastern river system, John Oxley wrote, 'For all practical purposes the nature of the country precluded me from indulging the hope, that even if the river should terminate in an inland sea, it could be of the smallest use to the colony. The knowledge of its actual termination, if at all attainable, was, however, a matter of deep importance, and would tend to throw some light on the obscurity in which the interior of this vast country is still involved.' (Oxley, *Journals*, p. 241.) Captain John Lort Stokes who, during his five years in Australia as commander of the *Beagle*, had charted much of the coastline and met all the major inland explorers of the period – King, Grey, Sturt, Frome, Eyre, Strzelecki, Mitchell and Cunningham – concluded that the centre of the continent was a vast desert, the area around Lake Torrens being not more than 300 feet above sea level. (Stokes, *Discoveries*.)
14 Mitchell, *Three Expeditions*, vol. I, p. 5. The fabled River Kindur was the brain-child of an escaped convict, Clarke, who knew as well as the explorers what governments wished to hear. He sought pardon for his escape in return for information about an alleged great inland river system which, according to Clarke, the Aborigines called the Kindur.

295

15 Sturt had served as military secretary to Sir Ralph Darling, 1827–28.
16 Letter to Sir Ralph Darling, 5.3.1844. *Sturt Papers*, Rhodes House Library, Oxford. Robert Sellick has argued that as 'the possibilities of material rewards, and hence of recognition, receded as explorers penetrated towards the centre of the continent . . . the idea of exploration is already, as early as the 1840s, undergoing a profound change. . . . Since the material discoveries are denied the explorer, he insists on recognition for the difficulties he has had to surmount . . . the focus shifts from the results achieved to the hazards of the journey itself.' (Robert Sellick, 'From the Outside In: European Ideas of Exploration and the Australian Experience', in Donaldson, *Australia*, p. 179.) However, Sturt continued to focus his belief in an inland sea and the fame such a discovery would confer.
17 Letter to Lady Darling from Moorundi at the start of his journey to Central Australia, 22.8.1844. *Sturt Papers*, Rhodes House Library, Oxford. Brock also records this incident, *op. cit.*, pp. 49, 55–6. Interestingly, at the time Sturt wrote this, Alexander von Humboldt (1769–1859) was very much alive, so the comparison presumably rested on Sturt's desire for scientific and geographical credibility, two areas which he explicitly mentioned in the *Narrative*.
18 Queen Victoria, wearing a halo-like tiara, holds the scantily clad Prince Arthur, who, like many an infant Jesus figure in art, clutches a spray of lily-of-the-valley, as the kneeling Duke of Wellington, a modern Magus in military braid, offers a gold casket as a birthday gift to his god-child. Prince Albert stands, Joseph-like, behind the Queen and celestial rays illuminate the scene, which includes a representation of the newly completed Crystal Palace, secular temple of the British Jerusalem. This iconography clearly links the royal family with the Holy Family and casts Victoria as the Queen of Heaven, validating her right to receive homage from her subjects.
19 Giles, vol. II, book III, p. 201.
20 For the popularity of African exploration accounts see Brantlinger, 'Victorians and Africans', 166–203.
21 Giles, vol. II, book III, p. 202. David Livingstone's *Narrative of an Expedition to the Zambesi and its Tributaries and the Discovery of Lakes Shirwa and Nyasa* was published in 1865.
22 Forrest, *Explorations*, p. 311.
23 The *Empire*, 7 October 1860.
24 Sturt, *Narrative*, vol. I, Preface, p. ii.
25 *ibid.*, vol. III, Appendix, p. iii.
26 Sturt, letter to Grey, 12.7.1845. Quoted by Beale in *Chipped Idol*, p. 222.
27 Jill Waterhouse, in Sturt, *Journal*, Introduction, p. 6. Waterhouse argues that alternative reasons advanced by Sturt do not bear scrutiny. Sturt did not really need the money, as he claimed, for his sons' education, for his wife had expectations of an adequate inheritance; nor, although he had fallen out with Sir George Grey, the governor, would he have been refused promotion permanently.
28 For contemporary comments on the Burke and Wills expedition's failure to deliver any worthwhile information, see, for example, Bonyhady, *Burke & Wills*, p. 202.
29 Quoted by Ericksen, 42.
30 For example, Anon., 'Review', *Athenaeum Journal* 1845, p. 868; Anon., 'Australia', *North British Review* 4 (1846), 312.
31 Giles, vol. II, book V, p. 341. Compare the concluding remark of his Introduction (*ibid.*, p. li): 'During my first and second expeditions I had been fortunate in the discovery of large areas of mountain country, permanently watered and beautifully grassed, and, as spaces of enormous extent still remained to be explored, I decided to continue in the field . . .'.
32 Stuart, *Explorations in Australia*, pp. 149, 400–401.
33 Eyre, *Journals*, p. vi.
34 The official purpose of Sturt's expedition was to establish the existence of an alleged mountain range running NE to SW near latitude 28°S and to report on any rivers rising from it.

35 *Sydney Morning Herald* editorial quoted in Cotton, *Leichhardt*, p. 244. Michael Griffith ('Webb's Challenge', 452) remarks that Leichhardt 'was the man who, in the wake of Sturt's failure to discover the inland sea, had literally saved the nation from a sense that it existed on the fringes of a desolate country.' Georg von Neumayer, in his biography of Leichhardt, also compared the reception of the two expedition reports: 'Considering that Sturt has just returned from his unfortunate experience in the "Stone Desert", whilst Leichhardt's expedition brought back from the north such great achievements, one can understand the rejoicing which took place at that event.' (Dr G. Neumayer, 'Dr. Ludwig Leichhardt as Naturalist and Explorer', republished in *Dr. Ludwig Leichhardt's Letters from Australia during the years March 23, 1842, to April 3, 1848*, [1881] ed. Alec C. Chisholm (Melbourne: Pan, 1944), pp. 82–3).

36 Giles, *Australia Twice Traversed*, vol. I, Introduction, pp. xxv–xxvi.

37 The many idiocies perpetrated by Burke have provided abundant raw materials for revisionist readings of the whole Northern Exploring Expedition, stressing the anti-heroic qualities of the leader as well as the bungling of the expedition organisers and backers. The first detailed account of these was given by Kathleen Fitzpatrick, 'The Burke and Wills Expedition and the Royal Society of Victoria', *Historical Studies of Australia and New Zealand* 10:4 (1963), 470–78.

38 Thomas Mitchell, George Grey, Charles Sturt and Augustus Charles Gregory all received knighthoods for their achievements in exploration.

39 See Simon Ryan, '"Like a Map at our Feet"'. As we shall see, however, in the desert this topographical triumph has proved, in most cases, to be temporary and illusionary.

40 Ryan has argued that their enemy status was frequently exaggerated in the explorers' narratives to conform to the tradition of the explorer confronting murderous savages. See Simon Ryan, 'Discovering Myths', 4.

41 Smith, *European Vision*, pp. 5, 317–32.

42 W.A. Dampier, *A New Voyage Round the World* [1697], ed. N.M. Penzer (London: 1927), p. 453.

43 A number of such instances are quoted, with disapproval, by J.W. Gregory, in *Dead Heart*, pp. 165–7. They are not unknown in the 1990s.

44 Sturt, *Journal*, p. 255.

45 Giles, *Australia Twice Traversed*, vol. I, p. 161.

46 Eyre, *Journals*, vol. I, p. x.

47 Giles, *Australia Twice Traversed*, vol. I, p. 184.

48 Stuart, *Journals*, p. 219.

49 Giles, *Australia Twice Traversed*, vol. II, p. 332.

50 See, for example, Eyre, 'Manners and Customs of the Aborigines of Australia and the State of their Relations with Europeans', in *Journals*, vol. II, pp. 147–512; Grey, 'Observations on the Moral and Physical Condition of the Aboriginal Inhabitants', in *Journals*, vol. II, pp. 207–390; Sturt, *Journal*, pp. 252–64, where he advocates removing Aboriginal children from their parents.

51 This discussion is not concerned with the smaller private expeditions mounted by settlers hoping to extend their holdings if the land further afield should prove fertile. It is possible that these men produced some written accounts of the terrain, but such reports were not disseminated and hence had little if any influence on public perceptions of the desert.

52 The exploring parties comprised a leader, one or two officers, a surveyor, in the case of a large party, a botanist or zoologist and artist/naturalist, and 'the men'. It was expected that the leader would keep the formal log of the expedition and that the scientists would keep a detailed record of specimens found. In many cases the officers and scientists also kept journals or diaries, and wrote letters home. Occasionally some of the better-educated 'men' (Daniel Brock on Sturt's expedition to Central Australia is an outstanding example) would do so. A surprising number of these narratives have survived.

53 For an account of these see Melman, *Women's Orients*. Several women explored difficult Australian wilderness areas, but none of them entered what could technically be called the desert. Possibly the only exceptions were the wives of the German missionaries at the Hermannsburg Mission south-west of what is now Alice Springs, and unfortunately we have no written records of their impressions of the land. Of the famous women travellers studied by Dea Birkett, the only Australian, Mary Elizabeth Bakewell Bruce (b. 1861), did not travel until 1908 when she went to East Africa. See Birkett, *Spinsters Abroad*.

54 Pratt, *Imperial Eyes*.

55 See Bohls, *Women Travel Writers*, and Lewis, *Gendering Orientalism*, ch. 3.

56 See, for example, Lloyd, *Man of Reason*; MacCormack and Strathern, *Nature, Culture and Gender*.

57 Giles, *Australia Twice Traversed*, vol. II, book II, p. 52.

58 Simon Ryan ('Voyeurs in Space', 43) has pointed to several instances where the explorers write of their commanding position vis-à-vis the land and deduces that 'This visual command has an object that is not simply a neutral land, but a feminized space which invites vision.'

59 See, for example, Jacques Lacan, *The Four Fundamental Concepts of Psycho-Analysis*, ed. Jacques-Alain Miller, transl. Alan Sheridan (Harmondsworth: Penguin Books, 1977), pp. 67–116.

60 Sturt, *Two Expeditions*, vol. I, p. 151. However, when Sturt and his party sail triumphantly down the Murray to Lake Alexandrina, the capricious female nature is construed as yielding to male determination: 'It almost appeared as if nature had resisted us in order to try our perseverance, and that she had yielded in pity to our efforts.' Sturt, *ibid.*, vol. II, p. 162.

61 Giles, *Australia Twice Traversed*, vol. II, book IV, p. 247.

62 Sturt, *Journal*, p. 22. c.f. 'the desolate and heated region, into which we had penetrated . . .' (*Narrative*, p. 265.)

63 Charles Sturt, Letter to John Morphett Esq. M.C., 14.10.1844, quoted in Eyre, *Journals*, vol. II, p. 130.

64 Eyre, *Journals*, vol. I, p. 23.

65 Thompson, 'Romance Australia', 165.

66 Derek Gregory, *Geographical Imaginations*, p. 129. See also, Ella Shohat, 'Imagining *terra incognita*: The Disciplinary Gaze of Empire', *Public Culture 3* (1991), 41–70.

67 Dixson, *Matilda*, p. 23.

68 Edward John Eyre and Ernest Giles were among the few who began their careers as 'overlanders', driving sheep and cattle into new territory, before entering into public exploration where both the risks and the rewards were potentially much higher.

69 Simmons, *Pilgrims*, p. 327.

70 Simon Ryan, *Cartographic Eye*.

71 Alan Ramsay's 'Ode to the memory of Sir Isaac Newton: Inscribed to the Royal Society' (1727) began with a flourish not atypical of the fulsome verse occasioned by Newton's death: 'The god-like man now mounts the sky'. For a discussion of the influence of Newton on contemporary thought see my *Faust to Strangelove*, ch. 4.

72 Australian explorers who received Royal Geographical Society gold medals were: A.C. and F.T. Gregory, John Forrest, John McDouall Stuart, Peter Warburton, Ernest Giles, Ludwig Leichhardt, Paul Strzelecki, John Eyre, Charles Sturt, and Robert O'Hara Burke. All were associated with desert exploration.

73 Oxley, *Journals*, p. 91. In 1852 the poet Tennyson wrote to his brother Frederick, 'Captain Inglefield has called an arctic promontory Cape Tennyson after me which makes me as proud as Lucifer.' Alfred Tennyson, Letter to Frederick Tennyson, 9 December 1852.

74 See, for example, Slemon, 'Post-Colonial Allegory'.

75 For a more detailed discussion of this point, see also David Carter, 'Modernity'. The recent recognition of, and discomfort with, this implication are apparent in the moves

298

to restore Aboriginal names to Australian places, though it should be noted that an impressive number of Aboriginal names were retained as town and street names by the early town surveyors.

76 For a discussion of links between surveying and commanding see Simon Ryan, '"Like a Map at our Feet"'.

77 Paul Carter, *Road to Botany Bay*, p. 56.

78 Giles, *Australia Twice Traversed*, vol. I, Preface, pp. liv and li.

79 Sturt, *Narrative*, vol. I, p. 20.

80 Eyre, *Journals*, vol. I, p. 100. He continued: 'From my present elevation, the lake was seen bending round to the N.E., and I became aware that it would be a barrier to all efforts to the north.' Eyre's lack of training in surveying led him into several geographical blunders.

81 Sturt, letter to Sir Ralph Darling, 5.3.1844, quoted in Mrs Napier G. Sturt, *The Life of Charles Sturt* (London, 1899), Notes, p. 39.

82 Sturt, letter to Sir Ralph Darling, 5.3.1844, in Mrs Napier G. Sturt, *ibid.*, Notes, p. 48.

83 See Sturt, letter to Miss Cooper, 7.8.1844, SAA, A594.

84 Sturt, *Narrative*, vol. I, p. 35.

85 Stuart presumably decided on this spot as the centre of the continent by estimating the intersection between the longitude mid-way between the extreme east and west points and the latitude mid-way between the extreme north and south points of the mainland. Using this method, modern calculations set the centre slightly to the north of Central Mount Stuart. In 1895 C.H. Barton proposed that the centre of the continent should be defined as the point farthest removed from the sea in all directions. Barton's centre is located some 60 miles north of Charlotte Waters, and 225 miles south from Stuart's centre. Yet another method was proposed by the explorer and geologist, Cecil Thomas Madigan. Madigan's calculation of the central point, which involved determining the centre of gravity of the continental land mass, set the centre close to Crown Point, near where Stuart reached the Finke River. 299

86 Sturt was deeply stirred by the thought of the British flag flying in far places. His account of his earlier journey down the Murrumbidgee to the mouth of the Murray in 1829–30 dramatised the scene when his party realised the tributary they had reached was the Darling. For Sturt the importance of this incident is the theatrical moment when the Aborigines fall silent out of instinctive respect, as he believed, for the British flag. Sturt, *Two Expeditions*, vol. II, pp. 109–10.

87 Stuart, *Journals*, p. 165.

Chapter 4

1 John L. Allen, 'Lands . . . Waters', p. 42.

2 Slemon, 'Post-Colonial Allegory', 164–5.

3 Giles, Preface, p. xxx.

4 Michel Foucault, quoted in Mark Poster, 'Foucault and History', *Social Research* 49 (1982), 118–19.

5 For a discussion of such changes see Smith, *European Vision*, pp. 36–40, 46–9.

6 Bernard Smith quotes Alan Frost's information that it was the most popular title in the Bristol Library from 1773 to 1784. Smith, *European Vision*, p. 343, n. 109.

7 See, for example, Harley, 'Maps'.

8 Paul Carter comments of the explorers' maps: 'Only rarely did even the competent surveyor succeed in locating his position on the earth's surface accurately. The most he could usually hope for was to preserve the spatial relationship between whatever geographical objects crossed his path. The internal logic of his chart might be impeccable, but its relationship to other maps remained approximate . . . it would be enough to assume, as most historians do, that any discrepancies between journal and maps represent nothing more than personal incompetence or idiosyncrasy.' Carter, *Road to Botany Bay*, pp. 71–2.

9 This was not an isolated phenomenon. For 16 October, the *Narrative* states that the party was 90 miles from a creek; the 'Account' sets it at 100 miles, while the map scales it at 60 miles. Similar instances abound, always in the direction of increasing overstatement with time lapse from the event. Beale points out that similar confusion characterised Sturt's accounts of his earlier journey to the mouth of the Murray. (Beale, *Chipped Idol*, p. 180.) Beale also gives sundry other instances, from the later journey, of what he interprets as self-aggrandisement at the expense of accuracy.

10 Sturt, *Narrative*, vol. I, p. 406.

11 The variations in latitude of the most northerly point Sturt claimed to have reached are considerable: –24° 30' on Arrowsmith's map, –24° 40' in the *Narrative*, and –24° 50' 23" in the *Journal*; while in a letter to Macleay, Sturt claimed it was 24° 35'. (Quoted in Beale, *Chipped Idol*, p. 182.)

12 Simon Ryan, 'The Cartographic Eye: Mapping and Ideology' in Caroline Guerin, Philip Butterss and Amanda Nettelbeck (eds), *Crossing Lines: Formations of Australian Culture*, Proceedings of the Seventeenth Annual Conference of the Association for the Study of Australian Literature, 1995 (Adelaide: ASAL, 1996), 13.

13 Giles, vol. II, book IV, ch. 2, pp. 186–7.

14 Eyre, *Journals*, vol. I, p. 448 and vol. II, pp. 1–2.

15 Perhaps the most notorious was Thomas Mitchell who triumphantly announced his discovery in 1836 of Australia Felix, an area which not only proved to be considerably less than felix (fortunate) but which, as J.H.L. Cumpston has pointed out, had already been settled in 1834–35 by 'a great migration from Tasmania to Victoria, as a result of which . . . there were two hundred persons with 30,000 sheep and numerous cattle and horses' in the area west of Geelong, where Mitchell mentioned only one settler. See Cumpston, *Inland Sea*, p. 112. c.f. Carter, *Road to Botany Bay*, pp. 109–11. Ross Gibson has pointed out that the diction used by Mitchell to describe Australia Felix is drawn directly from the book of Genesis: 'The land is another Eden, and Mitchell is a new Adam.' (Gibson, *Diminishing Paradise*, p. 122.)

16 Jill Waterhouse has discussed in some detail the lengthy passages of self-justification that Sturt included to assuage his guilt at leaving his family on an expedition which he had drummed up in the face of apathy from the South Australian Government. See Sturt, *Journal*, pp. 6–7. Part of this is quoted in Chapter 3.

17 Brock, *Desert*, p. 199.

18 *ibid.*, p. 22.

19 *ibid.*, p. 14. The account of the 'memorable expedition' was Sturt's *Two Expeditions into the Interior of Southern Australia, 1828–31*.

20 John Harris Browne in Finnis, 'Dr. John Harris Browne's Journal', 45.

21 Sturt, *Journal*, p. 94.

22 For example, Stuart's published *Journals*, compared with his diary written in the field; P.E. Warburton's *Journey Across the Western Interior of Australia*, relative to his diary of the same expedition; and Giles's *Australia Twice Traversed* compared with his earlier, less embellished accounts of his expeditions. From Ludwig Leichhardt's second journey, an abortive attempt to cross the continent from east to west, we have Leichhardt's own diary, notebook, sketchbook and letters, but no published account to set beside his earlier, triumphant *Journal of an Overland Expedition in Australia from Moreton Bay to Port Essington*. No doubt Leichhardt had no wish to broadcast a failure. However, we do have an account of the expedition written by Daniel Bunce, a botanist. Several other members of the expedition also kept short journals (some far from complimentary to their leader) which have survived, for example Henry Turnbull, *Leichhardt's Second Journey: A First-Hand Account*. Similarly, from the Burke and Wills expedition, we have the journal of William Wills, the diaries of William Brahe, Alfred Howitt and Hermann Beckler, a portion of a diary kept by John King, as well as letters, scientific reports and superb watercolours from Ludwig Becker.

23 Compare John McDouall Stuart, *Explorations*, his account in *South Australian*

Parliamentary Papers 169 of 1861 and 21 of 1863 and his published *Exploration of the Interior*. Compare also Peter Egerton Warburton's *Journey* and *Diary*, and Ernest Giles, *Diary of Mr. Ernest Giles's Explorations in Central Australia, 1872* (Adelaide: 1875), *Geographic Travels in Central Australia, 1872–4* (Melbourne, 1875), *The Journey of a Forgotten Expedition* (Adelaide, 1880) and *Australia Twice Traversed* (London, 1889).

24 Gregory, *Dead Heart*, pp. 155, 156.

25 Sturt, letter to Governor Sir George Gibbs 15.7.1843, Gibbs Papers, ML, A2025; Sturt, Letter to Capt. Phillip Parker King, 5.12.1843, ML, Doc. 684, transcript in King papers, ML, A3599; Sturt to John Gould, 19.1.1843, ML, Doc. 1802. See also *Narrative*, vol. I, pp. 62–3. For Sturt's optimistic view of the River Darling see Sturt, *Two Expeditions*, vol. I, p. 100: 'the river [Darling] itself had increased in size, and stretched away to the westward, with all the uniformity of a magnificent canal, and gave every promise of increasing importance.'

26 Sturt, *Narrative*, vol. I, pp. 63–4.

27 Sturt, letters to Gipps, 24.6.1840 and 15.7.1843, Gipps papers, ML, A2025. c.f. *Journal*, p. 49.

28 Sturt, *Journal*, p. 46.

29 Letter of Mr E.J. Eyre to Lord Stanley, 22 August 1844. *Historical Records of Australia*, series I, vol. XXIV, p. 51. Quoted by Jill Waterhouse in Sturt, *Journal*, p. 104. n. 34. Sturt records that Eyre showed him the letter, asking whether he had any objection to it, and that he had replied, 'None whatever. All men are free to think what their experience dictates to them. I can only say, as regards the opinions you have expressed that I would not have expressed them so confidently.' (Sturt, *Journal*, p. 22.)

30 Sturt, *Narrative*, vol. I, p. 51.

31 Eyre, *Journals*, vol. II, p. 134.

32 Sturt, *Journal*, p. 45. For a discussion of dune formation in the Simpson Desert see, e.g. Shepherd, *The Simpson Desert*, pp. 2, 7–9, 11, 14.

33 Sturt, *Journal*, pp. 64, 68, 71; *Narrative*, vol. I, p. 397.

34 Sturt, *Narrative*, vol. I, p. 375.

35 Sturt, *Journal*, pp. 86–7

36 Sturt, *Journal*, p. 94. Sturt's Stony Desert is actually only a part of the much more extensive gibber plains of the Lake Eyre basin. Sturt crossed this area in a time of drought and was therefore unaware that, after rain, the Diamantina River flows from central Queensland to Lake Eyre across his route.

37 Sturt, *Narrative*, vol. I, p. 176.

38 James Hutton, 'Theory of the Earth; or an investigation of the laws observable in the composition, dissolution, and restoration of land upon the globe', *Transactions of the Royal Society of Edinburgh*, 1 (1788), 209–304.

39 Sturt, *Narrative*, vol. I, p. 381.

40 *ibid.*, vol. I, pp. 24–5, 34. Long after it had been demonstrated that there was no extant inland sea of the kind originally postulated, the desire for one continued to emerge. In 1883, and again in response to the severe drought of 1901–2, there was a proposal to flood Lake Eyre by means of a channel from Port Augusta. (See Gregory, *Dead Heart*, pp. 342–50.) The many schemes of Sir Sidney Kidman and others for irrigating the central desert with artesian water from an underground 'inland sea' indicate the tenacity of the desire.

41 According to today's standard explanation, the draining of the sea resulted from sea levels falling (due to an ice age) rather than the land mass rising. Sturt's view, however, was consistent with the neptunist and cataclysmic theories current in his day.

42 Stuart, *Explorations*, Preface by William Hardman, p. viii. Thomas Mitchell's account of a Lake Salvator, which he allegedly discovered and named on 7 July 1846, cannot, however, be explained so conveniently. The geological evidence 'clearly show[s] that there never was a lake on this site'! Brian Finlayson, quoted in Paul Carter, *Road to Botany Bay*, p. 107.

301

43 Sturt, *Narrative*, vol. I, p. 332.

44 *ibid.*, p. 319; c.f. pp. 328–9.

45 Sturt, *Narrative*, vol. I, p. 329.

46 Giles, *Australia Twice Traversed*, Introduction, p. xxv.

47 *ibid.*, p. xxxiii. Otherwise, Giles argues, 'it is impossible, if such things were above ground, that they could escape the lynx-like glances of Australian aboriginals, whose wonderful visual powers are unsurpassed among mankind'.

48 Eyre, *Journals*, vol. I, pp. 111–12.

49 Sturt, letter to John Morphett, Esq. M.C., 14.10.1844, published in the *Adelaide Observer*, 9 November 1844. The letter is quoted by Eyre in *Journals*, vol. II, pp. 130–33. The passage quoted here occurs on pp. 132–3.

50 Letter to the Colonial Secretary, 16.10.1844, in *Proc. Royal Geographic Soc. SA*, vol. 4, pp. 137–41.

51 Sturt, *Narrative*, vol. I, p. 142 and vol. II, p. 17.

52 Brock, *Desert*, p. 52 (17.10.1844).

53 'Goyder's Northern Exploration', *Parliamentary Papers of South Australia*, No. 72 (1857), pp. 2, 4.

54 'The extensive bays described in that [Goyder's] report, the bluff headlands, the several islands between the north and south shores, the vegetation covering them and their perpendicular cliffs, have all been the result of mirage, and do not, in point of fact, exist as represented.' Freeling's 'Report on Lake Torrens and Country Adjacent', *Parliamentary Papers of South Australia*, No. 174 (1857), p. 1.

55 Stuart, *Journals*, p. 20.

56 Sturt, *Journal*, p. 15.

57 For example, Sturt, *Journal*, p. 85; *Narrative*, vol. I, pp. 290, 406.

58 Sturt, *Journal*, vol. I, pp. 45–6. c.f. *ibid.*, p. 97: 'aid from Providence' and 'the bounty of heaven'.

59 *ibid.*, vol. I, p. 265.

60 *ibid.*, p. 86.

61 *ibid.*, p. 100 (14.12.1845).

62 Sturt, *Narrative*, vol. I, pp. 404, 406.

63 Brock, *Desert*, p. 192.

64 Sturt, *Journal*, p. 220; c.f. *ibid.*, p. 454. Gibson contrasts Sturt and Thomas Mitchell in their approach to the desert: 'They both interpret the Australian experience as purgatorial, but their presentations of the manner in which redemption might be obtained are markedly dissimilar. . . . In Sturt's writing the landscape regulates all human action; Mitchell's narrative becomes a sequence of *events* which the author himself instigates and controls.' Gibson, *Diminishing Paradise*, p. 120.

65 Sturt, letter to Grey, 22.6.1844, SAA, GRG. 24/1, No. 1844/77. Capt. (later Sir) George Grey, governor of SA.

66 Brock, *Desert*, p. 197.

67 *ibid.*, p. 2.

68 *ibid.*, pp. 11, 102, 167, 172 (4.7.1845).

69 *ibid.*, p. 179 (26.8.1845).

70 *ibid.*, p.15.

71 *ibid.*, p. 19.

72 *ibid.*, pp. 29 (22.9.1844), 36 (28.9.1844), 37–8 (29.9.1844).

73 Giles, *Australia Twice Traversed*, vol. II, book IV, ch. 1, p. 257.

74 *ibid.*, vol. II, book V, ch. 4, p. 320. c.f. *Hamlet* V. ii. 10.

75 *ibid.*, vol. II, book II, ch. 10, p. 41.

76 *ibid.*, vol. II, book V, ch. 4, p. 319.

77 Sturt, *Narrative*, vol. I, pp. 321, 328.

78 When James Poole, Sturt's second-in-command, died of scurvy, Daniel Brock described his grave as a 'wild, wild tomb'. Brock, *Desert*, p. 165.

79 The fear of becoming lost in the Bush was a very real one until well into the twentieth century. The 'lost child' image, in particular, became a powerful visual symbol of this condition in both literature and art.

80 Sturt, *Journal,* 14 September 1845, pp. 74–5.

81 'At this point the open spaces at the bottom of the valleys had all closed in.' Sturt, *Narrative,* vol. I, p. 413.

82 Sturt's party arrived here on 27 January 1845. They could not leave until the next rains fell in mid-July.

83 Browne, 'Journal of the Sturt Expedition', entry for 12 March 1845, p. 44; entry for 31 May 1845, *ibid.,* p. 48.

84 Sturt, *Narrative,* vol. I, p. 265.

85 *ibid.,* vol. I, pp. 290, 319.

86 Sturt, letter to Grey, 16.7.1845, Grey Papers. c.f. '... the ground was now so completely saturated that I no longer doubted the moment of our liberation had come' (*Narrative,* vol. I, p. 331); and '... our release from the spot ...' (*ibid.,* p. 332).

87 Sturt, *Narrative,* vol. II, p. 99.

88 P.E. Warburton, *Diary.* Entry for 12 November 1873.

89 The most quoted but by no means the only example of such an emotional response is Marcus Clarke's comments on two paintings, Louis Buvelot's 'Waterpool near Coleraine' and Nicholas Chevalier's 'The Buffalo Ranges'. His text was later printed as the Preface to the 1876 edition of Adam Lindsay Gordon's *Sea Spray and Smoke Drift.*

90 Sturt, *Two Expeditions,* vol. I, p. 73.

91 *ibid.,* vol. II, p. 59.

92 Sturt, *Narrative,* vol. I, pp. 277–8.

93 *ibid.,* vol. I, p. 269. This is particularly ironic because Sturt had premised his inland sea on the 'evidence' of the birds and had portrayed himself as saved from death by Providence in the form of a pigeon.

94 *ibid.,* vol. I, pp. 34, 278, 280; *Journal,* pp. 75, 86; *Narrative,* vol. I, p. 389.

95 Brock, *Desert,* pp. 65, 72.

96 Giles, *Australia Twice Traversed,* vol. II, book III, p. 108 and vol. II, book IV, p. 191.

97 Stuart, *Journals,* pp. 35–7.

98 Not the least of Burke's many misjudgements was his order to off-load his lime juice supply in order to save weight and therefore travel faster. Four of his men subsequently died from scurvy.

99 Brock's early entries constitute a picturesque eulogy of the 'stirring bush life'. Like a traveller in Europe armed with a Claude glass, he frames up for us vivid visual images, the detail giving the composition the interest of a Constable painting.

100 Brock, *Desert,* pp. 64–5. Rejecting both the perfunctory Anglicanism, as he judged it, of the officers (even the religiously inclined Sturt did not measure up to Brock's requirements as he sometimes performed work on Sundays) and the ribald atheism of the other men, Brock was as isolated in religious affiliation as he was in social status.

101 Although, after the death of his only white companion, Baxter, Eyre made much of being alone on his journey west from Port Lincoln along the South Australian coast to Albany in 1841, he was in fact accompanied to the end of his journey by a loyal Aborigine, Wylie.

102 Giles, *Australia Twice Traversed,* vol. I, book II, p. 166.

103 *ibid.,* vol. I, book II, pp. 263–4.

104 *ibid.,* vol. I, book II, p. 264.

105 Cecil T. Madigan, *Crossing,* pp. 151–2.

106 Foucault has remarked: 'A whole history remains to be written of *spaces* – which would at the same time be the history of *powers* (both of those terms in the plural) – from the great strategies of geopolitics to the little tactics of the habitat.' 'The Eye of

Power' in Colin Gordon (ed.), *Power/Knowledge: Selected Interviews and Other Writings* (New York: Pantheon, 1980), p. 149.

107 Slemon, 'Post-Colonial Allegory', 164–5.

Chapter 5

1 Crandell, *Nature Pictorialized*, p. 13.

2 Novak, *Nature and Culture*, p. 47.

3 Bernard Smith has shown that the impact of Pacific exploration, and its resistance to existing ideas of cosmology, precipitated the Darwinian revolution. See Smith, *European Vision*, pp. 4–7.

4 Quoted in W. Blunt, 'Sydney Parkinson and his Fellow Artists', in Carr, *Sydney Parkinson*, p. 25.

5 Thomas Watling, *Letters from an Exile at Botany Bay, to his Aunt in Dumfries*, Penrith (Scotland): Bell, 1794, DL79/91, p. 10.

6 Crandell, *Nature Pictorialized*, p. 13.

7 Ironically, the only remaining panorama in Australia (one of 33 in the world) is Panorama Guth in Alice Springs, the work of Dutch artist Henk Guth. Its thirty-three 6-metre-high linen panels displayed in a circle of 60 metres circumference depict all the landmarks of the surrounding desert landscape. Visited by some 90,000 tourists annually, its popularity offers further confirmation of Crandell's contention.

8 Cole's series of five large paintings, collectively named *The Course of Empire* (1836), plots the movement of a civilisation based on Rome from *Savage State*, through *Pastoral State, Consummation, Destruction* to *Desolation*. The series is clearly intended as a moral lesson to the developing American nation.

9 Oxley could write of western New South Wales, 'One tree, one soil, one water, and one description of bird, fish, or animal prevails alike for ten miles and for one hundred' (Oxley, *Journals*, p. 115), thereby conveying his own frustration; but how could such an experience be depicted visually? And how much less interesting still was the central desert?

10 For a more detailed discussion of this term see Bruce, 'Landscape of Longing', 17.

11 Adam Sedgwick, 'A Discourse of the Studies of the University' [London, 1833] (Leicester: Leicester University Press, 1969), p. 18.

12 Embarrassingly, before his appointment was known in the colony, the governor, Lt.-Gen. George Gawler, had induced Charles Sturt to give up his property in New South Wales for appointment to the same position of surveyor-general of South Australia. For a detailed account of Frome's life see Newland, 'Edward Charles Frome'.

13 Henderson (1827–1918) later migrated to the gold diggings in Ballarat where he produced a watercolour of troops storming the barricade at the Eureka Stockade in 1854.

14 It was not until 1858 that the Western Australian explorers, Augustus and Francis Gregory, passed between Lake Blanche and Lake Callabonna, finally disproving the horseshoe theory.

15 Facing pp. 71 and 143 respectively. The former was based on a watercolour of similar title by S.T. Gill in the South Australian Museum. See John Tregenza, *George French Angas*, p. 17. In Angas's *South Australia Illustrated* Gill is acknowledged to be the original artist.

16 Angas, *Savage Life*, vol. I, p. 145. c.f. p. 177.

17 Angas, *South Australia Illustrated*, plate xx.

18 From 1864 to 1884, after his return to England, he published numerous illustrated papers on conchology in the *Proceedings of the Zoological Society*.

19 Smith, *European Vision*, p. 303.

20 Sturt, *Journal*, p. 48.

21 *ibid.*, p. 58 (27 July 1845).

22 The drawing was reproduced, with minor changes, as an engraving in the *Narrative of an Expedition into Central Australia* (1849), facing p. 266. In the engraving there is no human figure and without the soft sepia wash of the watercolour, the area appears more starkly Gothic.

23 Sturt, *Narrative*, vol. I, pp. 265–6.

24 The same is true of his 1844 untitled watercolour of a mob of cattle by a bush pond, now in the National Library of Australia.

25 'Opossum hunting near Gawler Plains', vol. 1, facing p. 68, 'Mode of disposing of the dead at the Lower Murray', vol. 2, facing p. 344.

26 In the *South Australian Register* of 15 July 1846 (one week before the expedition departed) Gill was reported as saying that 'he would, he felt assured, be a great acquisition to the expedition, and was destined, ultimately, he hoped, to receive deserved remuneration for his voluntary exertions and the indefatigable exercises of his talents in localities hitherto unvisited by human art'.

27 Quoted in Alan McCulloch, *Artists of the Australian Goldrush*, p. 74.

28 *First Interview with Hostile Blacks North-west of Spencer's Gulf* almost certainly refers to the incident described in Gill's diary for 22 August 1846. The extreme example of Gill's racist commentary is his satirical *Native Dignity* (c.1865) depicting an almost grotesque black couple, idiotically proud of their ragged and incomplete European finery, contrasted with a well-dressed white couple. However, in a lithographic version of this composition, the tone is changed to suggest that the black couple are more attractive in their honest sensuality and good humour than the supercilious white couple behind them.

29 Queen Elizabeth II has now returned them to the National Library.

30 See Grandison, 'The Relocation of Fifteen Sites', 17.

31 The paintings, purchased at two guineas each, were hung in the directors' room.

32 The forty drawings and watercolours held by the La Trobe Library of the State Library of Victoria were sent to Melbourne from Swan Hill, Balranald or Menindee. Others were begun and finished at a later date, or remained unfinished at his death. The forty in the La Trobe collection are reproduced in Tipping, *Ludwig Becker*.

33 For a full description of Becker's life and scientific activities, see Tipping, *Ludwig Becker*.

34 Tim Bonyhady points out that a similar unwillingness to offer a place to a naturalist obtained in South Australia where James Chambers, the patron of Stuart's fifth expedition, refused a place to F.G. Waterhouse, Curator of the South Australian Museum. It took the action of the South Australian governor, Sir Richard McDonnell, to obtain a place for Waterhouse on Stuart's final expedition in 1861–62. See Bonyhady, *Burke and Wills*, p. 54.

35 Burke's report dated 4 October 1860. Both statements are quoted in Tipping, *Ludwig Becker*, p. 26. For Becker's account of the hardships he endured, see Tipping, *ibid.*, pp. 201–2.

36 Beckler, *Journey to Cooper's Creek*, p. 145.

37 Letter to Dr Macadam, 25 December 1860, reprinted in Tipping, *Ludwig Becker*, p. 190.

38 Tipping, *Ludwig Becker*, p. 202.

39 *ibid.*, p. 204.

40 Darwin's *Origin of the Species* was published in London in November 1859 but there is no suggestion that Becker had seen or heard of it when he left Melbourne in August 1860. Kathleen Dugan has argued that Becker's views on adaptation of organisms to their environment 'remained consistent with the theory of special creation'. Kathleen Dugan, Dissertation, quoted in Tipping, *op. cit.*, p. 39, n. 2.

41 Hermann Beckler, Letter 4 and Letter 13, both in the La Trobe Collection of the State Library of Victoria. Quoted by Stephen Jeffries, Introduction to Beckler, *Journey to Cooper's Creek*, pp. xx, xxi.

42 *ibid.*, pp. 116–17.

43 *ibid.*, pp. 118, 122.

44 These figures are taken from Bonyhady, *Burke and Wills*, p. 77.
45 *Melbourne Punch* (8 November 1860), 124. See illustration 3.5.
46 S.T. Gill also produced a watercolour of the event (now held in the Dixon Library).
47 For more details of the various versions of Summers' conception see Bonyhady, *Burke and Wills*, pp. 246–54.

Chapter 6
1 Kendall, 'The Fate of Burke and Wills'.
2 Lewin, 'Australia's Heroes'.
3 Myers, *Bleeding Battlers*, p. ii.
4 Carter, *Road to Botany Bay*, p. 90.
5 Kingsley, 'Eyre', 502.
6 *ibid.*, 502.
7 Sellick, *Epic Confrontation*, p. 401.
8 In the twentieth century Eyre and Sturt have joined the pantheon of those deemed worthy subjects of literature, but they received no special treatment by their contemporaries.
9 See Bonyhady, *Burke and Wills*, pp. 124–5.
10 *The Burke and Wills Exploring Expedition*, p. 16.
11 *ibid.*, p. 19.
12 Margaret Thomas, 'Death in the Bush'.
13 H.P. Heseltine, 'Australian Image I', 45, 49.
14 E.K.S., 'Stanzas', pp. 3–4. Robert Sellick comments, 'These are not the dangers and privations as they are recorded in Leichhardt's journal; indeed the expedition had a relatively easy, if protracted, time of it. However, ease and cautious progress are inappropriate to legend, and so they are set aside.' ('The Explorer as Hero', 6.)
15 Ironside, 'Death of Leichhardt'.
16 Henry Halloran, 'Leichhardt', *Empire* (28 April 1853).
17 S.H. Wintle, 'Leichhardt', republished in Sellick, *Epic Confrontation*, Appendix, p. 514.
18 Anon. 'Not Too Late', *Australasian*, 12 May 1865.
19 Kendall, 'Leichhardt', *Leaves*, pp. 189–93.
20 Horst Priessnitz points out that this is one of the few nineteenth-century poems to acknowledge Leichhardt's German background and, even here, Kendall is more interested in establishing the explorer's affinity to the Australian Romantic poets, of whom Kendall considered himself one, than in emphasising national difference. Horst Priessnitz, 'The "Vossification" of Ludwig Leichhardt' in Walker and Tampke, *Berlin to the Burdekin*, p. 206. By the end of the 1930s, Germanic origins were definitely a liability in an explorer.
21 Kendall, 'Mooni', *Leaves*, pp. 149–53.
22 Judith Wright, *Preoccupations*, p. 37.
23 Henry Kendall, 'Christmas Creek', *Leaves*, pp. 194–7.
24 Judith Wright, *Preoccupations*, p. 38.
25 E.K.S., 'Stanzas', pp. 3–4.
26 *ibid.*
27 Sellick, *Epic Confrontation*, p. 372.
28 For a full discussion of the funeral of Burke and Wills, see Bonyhady, *Burke and Wills*, pp. 231–54, to which I am indebted for these details.
29 *Argus*, 3 November 1861.
30 Henry Wadsworth Longfellow's *The Song of Hiawatha*, published in 1855, was immediately popular and well known, though the hypnotic effect of its metre, based on that of the Finnish epic, *The Kalevala*, elicited as many parodies as imitations.
31 Horne, 'Australian Explorers' (December 1963), 126–33, ll. 68–71.
32 'Another lay/Prostrate in body, with a teeming brain,/Wandering between Science and Delirium, /With Art to weep his epitaph. So passed/Thy spirit, Ludwig Becker,

– cast away/By the "ignorant present", – scarcely named – and soon/Forgotten, like a common clod. O shame!' (ll. 130–6).

33 Horne, 'Australian Explorers', 133.

34 Gordon, 'Gone', *Poetical Works*, p. 14, st. 1.

35 Catherine Martin, *The Explorers: A Chronicle of the Burke and Wills Expedition* in *Explorers and Other Poems*. The three quotations that follow are from pp. 8, 69 and 119 respectively.

36 For a detailed discussion of this and other aspects of *The Explorers* see Roslynn D. Haynes, 'Ambivalent Eulogy'.

37 Catherine Martin, *Explorers*. The two quotations that follow are from pp. 127 and 129 respectively.

38 Laura Wilson, 'Burke and Wills'.

39 Loyau, 'Tales in Verse'.

40 Favenc, *Voices of the Desert*, Introduction, pp. xii–xiii.

41 Ernest Favenc, 'In the Desert', the *Queenslander* (3 May 1879), p. 553.

42 'Mulga', 'On a Dry Plain', *Bulletin* (23 September 1893), p. 20.

43 Ernest Favenc, 'The Ghosts of the Desert', *Bulletin* (15 September 1894), 24.

44 C. Holdsworth Allen, 'How Long'.

Chapter 7

1 Bean, *Dreadnought*, pp. 317–18.

2 Martin Green, *Dreams*, p. 3.

3 The founding of the Boys' Brigade in Glasgow in 1884 and the Boy Scout Movement in 1908 were parallel responses to the same perceived problem.

4 Robert Dixon, *Writing the Colonial Adventure*, p. 1.

5 Dawe, *Golden Lake*, p. 104

6 For a discussion of the de Rougemont hoax see, for example, Keay, *Explorers*, pp. 125–50.

7 Hogan, p. 2. The quotation that follows is from p. 65.

8 This man is clearly intended to be the fictional counterpart of Andrew Hume, a prisoner who professed to have received Leichhardt's papers from Classen, allegedly a survivor of the lost expedition.

9 Favenc, *Secret*, p. 1. This romance was first published as a serial, *The Burning Mountain of the Interior*, in the *Queenslander*, 1890. The quotations that follow are from pp. 34 and 208–9 respectively.

10 Haggard, 'Henry Rider Haggard'.

11 Sometimes titled *Moondyne Joe*, the story was published several times, both as serials and in novel form, in Boston and in Australia.

12 Fox, *Expedition*. Lady Mary Fox may have read Barron Field's description of the Bathurst Plains as eminently suitable for settlement, or may even have heard about them from him in person in London.

13 Anon. 'Oo-a-deen', p. 17. The story was first published in the *Corio Chronicle and Western Districts Advertiser* (October 1847). The quotation that follows is from p. 27.

14 See Spence, *Lemuria*, p. 137. For a more detailed discussion of literary responses to Lemuria, see Healy, 'Lemurian Nineties'.

15 Grey, *Journals*, vol. I, p. 207.

16 Hogan, *Lost Explorer*, p. 140.

17 Favenc, *Secret*, p. 99. The two quotations that follow are from pp. 98 and 99 respectively.

18 Dixon, *Colonial Adventure*, p. 63.

19 Scott, *The Last Lemurian*, p. 253.

20 Macdonald, *Lost Explorers*, p. 46. The five quotations that follow are from pp. 12, 211, 287, 294 and 308 respectively.

21 Quoted in Christensen, *Edward Bulwer Lytton*, p. 177.

Chapter 8

1 Ernestine Hill, *Loneliness*, p. 340.
2 Finlayson, *Red Centre*, p. 8.
3 Watson, *Daimon*, pp. 291–2.
4 James Walter, 'Defining Australia: A Case Study' in Walter, *Australian Studies*, p. 21. Walter points out that, paradoxically, this was a case of using European concepts to proclaim difference from Europe.
5 See Anderson, *Imagined Communities*, pp. 11–16.
6 David Carter and Gillian Whitlock point out that realism was 'seen to be the appropriate art form for a new society – vigorous, egalitarian and actual. Thus realism came to be associated with nationalist and democratic politics'. David Carter with Gillian Whitlock, 'Institutions of Australian Literature' in Walter, *Australian Studies*, p. 127.
7 Crawford, 'Australian National Character'.
8 Edwin J. Brady, *Australia Unlimited*, p. 630.
9 *ibid.*, p. 628. In 1883 Wells, a South Australian Government surveyor, re-surveyed the western part of the South Australian–Queensland border and then, with Augustus Poeppel, marked the Queensland–Northern Territory border from Poeppel Corner to the Gulf of Carpentaria.
10 *ibid.*, p. 1023. Kidman became known as the 'Cattle King'. Ion Idriess's *The Cattle King* (1936) kept the legend alive and was filmed as a television documentary of the same name in 1984.
11 W.E. ('Bill') Harney, 'West of Alice', in Leonie Kramer (ed.), *My Country: Australian Poetry and Short Stories, Two Hundred Years* (Sydney: Ure Smith, 1992), vol. II, pp. 186–7.
12 From its inception in 1945 the Australian Government's film unit, known since 1973 as Film Australia, concentrated overwhelmingly on the ideology of developmentalism. See, e.g. Moran, *Projecting Australia*, pp. 60–80.
13 For an account of Griffith Taylor's 'crusade' and the acrimony he suffered see J.M. Powell, 'An Australian Geographer', in Whitlock and Reekie, *Uncertain Beginnings*, pp. 180–98.
14 Quoted by D.J. Mulvaney, '"A splendid lot of fellows": achievements and consequences of the Horn Expedition', in Morton and Mulvaney, *Exploring Central Australia*, p. 8.
15 Review in the Melbourne *Argus*, 6 August 1904, p. 4. Quoted by Mulvaney, *ibid.*, p. 8.
16 Tom Griffiths, 'The social and intellectual context of the 1890s', in Morton and Mulvaney, *Exploring Central Australia*, p. 17.
17 Griffiths, *Hunters and Collectors*, p. 68.
18 Lawson, *Archibald Paradox*, p. 172.
19 Gregory, *Dead Heart*, p. 171. The quotation that follows is from p. 207.
20 Finlayson, *Red Centre*, pp. 8, 16–17. The quotation that follows is from p. 26.
21 'After this visit no one will be able to suggest to me that Central Australia is a dead heart. From now on I shall always look upon it as a living heart, beating with confident energy. . . .' From the reply made by Queen Elizabeth II to an address of welcome during the Royal visit to Alice Springs, 1963.
22 Ernestine Hill, *Loneliness*, p. 247.
23 The first of fifteen novels *A Little Bush Maid* was serialised in the *Leader*, 1905–7. The Billabong series, which ran until 1942, was extremely popular and influential in creating an acceptable image of the native-born Australian girl as brave, strong, and resourceful in the bush, an honorary 'male' in a masculine world.
24 Ernestine Hill, *Loneliness*, p. 247.
25 *ibid.*, p. 248. The two quotations that follow are from pp. 250 and 340 respectively.
26 *ibid.*, p. 293. c.f. 'For scenic magnificence and sunburnt colour, there is nothing in Australia to approach the Finke River. If you would at one and the same time, glimpse the awakening of the world, and gasp at the age written in the wrinkles of the face of earth, follow the Finke' (p. 300).

27 *ibid.*, p. 252. Hill later wrote a book about Daisy Bates, *Kabbarli: A Personal Memoir of Daisy Bates*, published posthumously in 1973, in which she claimed that she had ghost-written Bates's most famous book, *The Passing of the Aborigines*. Julia Blackburn, in *Daisy Bates in the Desert* (1994), suggests that Bates despised Hill and found her arrogant and overbearing.

28 Bates, *Passing of the Aborigines*, p. 207. The Prologue is entitled 'A Vanished People'.

29 Ernestine Hill, *Loneliness*, pp. 254–5.

30 'The race on the fringe of the continent has been there for about a hundred years, and stands for Civilization; the race in the interior has been there for no man knows how long, and stands for Barbarism. Between them a woman has lived in a little white tent for more than twenty years, watching over these people for the sake of the Flag, a woman alone, the solitary spectator of a vanishing race. She is Daisy Bates, one of the least known and one of the most romantic figures in the British Empire.' Arthur Mee, 'Kabbarli', Introduction to Bates, *Passing of the Aborigines*, pp. xiv, xi.

31 Ernestine Hill, *Loneliness*, pp. 224–9.

32 *ibid.*, p. 336.

33 Groom, *I Saw a Strange Land*, pp. 14–15, 203.

34 Farwell, *Land of Mirage*, p. 1. Many travellers have singled out for comment the exceptionally vivid mirages around Marree. The film-makers Charles and Elsa Chauvel wrote of their experience: 'There is one mirage that often occurs out here, and that is the "Mirage of Marree". It appears in the sky as a shimmering lake and upon the waters of this lake there appears a settlement with palms and a mosque and islands of green trees. Many travellers and people who live in this country have seen this strange mirage of Mohammedan mosque and bleached, galvanised-iron buildings and clumps of large pepperina trees – the whole conglomeration of township is metamorphosed by the desert air and sunlight into a mirage of phantasy.' Chauvel, *Walkabout*, p. 99. The two quotations that follow are from pp. 2 and 119–20 respectively.

35 Beadell, *Too Long in the Bush*, p. 43. The two quotations that follow are from pp. 128–9 and 44 respectively.

36 Mountford, *Brown Men and Red Sand*, p. 75. The three-volume official report of the expedition was also publicly available.

37 Simpson describes an incident when the Aborigines at Oenpelli refused to perform a 'fake' rain ceremony to the rain pole, since that would have been sacrilegious to the Rainbow Serpent, but were happy to perform it before the ABC microphone. Simpson, *Adam in Ochre*, pp. 75–6.

38 A.T. Bolton, Preface to *Walkabout's Australia*, p. 5.

39 Doggers were employed to catch dingoes, being paid one pound per scalp. Pastoralists were desperate to exterminate dingoes, which killed their sheep. Dingo-proof fences were introduced and by 1950 a complete barrier had been erected over 10,000 km from Ceduna across South Australia to the New South Wales border and through Queensland to Winton. Although it is now shortened to 4850 km, it remains the longest man-made barrier in the world, three times the length of the Great Wall of China.

40 Stewart, 'The Fierce Country' from *The Birdsville Track* in *Selected Poems*, p. 129.

41 *Lasseter's Last Ride* had been reprinted 35 times by 1991.

42 So spelt by Idriess but more usually *kadaicha*, the word signifies a magic power associated with revenge. The kadaicha man is empowered to avenge a wrong by casting a magic influence on the wrongdoer and causing him to die. In performing the appropriate magic he may wear kadaicha shoes, made of emu feathers stuck together with blood, to prevent his tracks being followed.

43 Pike and Cooper, *Australian Film*, p. 234. Since the film included lengthy interviews with those who had met or worked with Lasseter, the threatened lawsuit provides an interesting example of a case where a fictional reconstruction assumes rights over historical facts.

44 *Lasseter* poem sequence in Kinsella, *Night Parrots*, pp. 34–5, 45–8, 51, 56.
45 O'Connor, 'Interview'.
46 E.L. Grant Watson, *Journey under the Southern Stars* (London, New York, Toronto: Abelard-Schuman, 1968), p. 17. c.f. also Watson, *But to What Purpose*, pp. 98–104.
47 Watson, *The Mainland*, p. 243.
48 Watson, *Daimon*, pp. 291–2.

Chapter 9
1 Fred Williams, quoted in McGrath and Olsen, *The Artist and the Desert*, p. 110.
2 Gleeson, 'Painting in Australia', 4.
3 For a comprehensive discussion of this issue see Burn, *National Life and Landscapes*, chapter 1.
4 Letter from Mr A.O. Barrett to the Minister for Home and Territories, Australian Archives, A.C.T. CRSA458 Item A.B.37015. Quoted in Burn, *National Life and Landscapes*, p. 206, n. 1.
5 *ibid.*, pp. 62–7. Burn remarks that 'No other nation so meticulously documented its participation – or chose to remember its soldiers on the day its fighting began rather than on the day it ended.' (*ibid.*, p. 62.)
6 *ibid.*, pp. 77, 79.
7 See Tulloch, *Legends of the Screen*, p. 395.
8 As Ian Burn points out, the most popular and widely disseminated painting of a war subject was Will Longstaff's semi-mystical *Menin Gate at Midnight* (1927) (on permanent exhibition in the National War Memorial), in which the ghosts of the fallen soldiers rise up like poppies from the fields of Belgium to march across the landscape.
9 Eagle, *Australian Modern Painting*, p. 74.
10 George Lambert, letter 12 February 1918, quoted in Lambert, *G.W. Lambert*, pp. 82–3.
11 *Mystic Morning* (1904), *Summer* (1909), *Hauling Timber* (1911), *Red Gold* (1913), *Gums under Mist* (1917), *Afternoon in Autumn* (1924) are probably the best known from these years. All but *Red Gold* were winners of the Wynne Prize for Landscape in their respective years of execution.
12 Thiele, *Heysen*, p. 95.
13 Hans Heysen, letter to Lionel Lindsay, quoted in Thiele, *Heysen*, p. 202.
14 Heysen, 'Some Notes on Art', *Art in Australia* Series 3, no. 44 (June 1932), 20.
15 Hans Heysen, letter to Lionel Lindsay, 25.4.1927, quoted in Thiele, *Heysen*, p. 196.
16 Heysen, 'Some Notes on Art'.
17 Hans Heysen, letter to Sydney Ure Smith, 1926, quoted in *Hans Heysen Centenary Retrospective 1877–1977* (Adelaide: Art Gallery of South Australia, 1977).
18 Bonython, *Walking the Flinders Ranges*, p. 88.
19 Hans Heysen, letter to Lionel Lindsay, 23.8.1928, quoted in Thiele, *Heysen*, p. 205.
20 Moore, *Story of Australian Art*, vol. I, p. xx.
21 Lionel Lindsay, 'Heysen's Recent Watercolours'.
22 Hancock, *Australia*, p. 255.
23 Moore, *Story of Australian Art*, vol. II, p. 226.
24 See Caruana, *Aboriginal Art*, p. 106.
25 Burn, *National Life and Landscapes*, p. 196.
26 Ian Burn and Ann Stephen, 'Namatjira's White Mask: A Partial Interpretation' in Hardy, Megaw and Megaw, *The Heritage of Namatjira*, p. 278.
27 See, for example, Nicolas Peterson, 'The Popular Image' in Donaldson and Donaldson, *Seeing the First Australians*, pp. 164–80.
28 Smith, *Australian Painting*, p. 251. Yet arguably Drysdale's models were English painters. Neville Weston believes that the misshapen forms of Drysdale's works are 'very reminiscent of the tree forms to be found in English painters such as Nash, Ayrton, Sutherland, Vaughan and Minton, whose works rejected the homely view of nature in favour of an uneasy and cruel landscape'. See Weston, 'Provincialism, Regionalism and Nationalism', p. 66.

29 The critic John Reed wrote, 'I find his interpretation of the Australian landscape essentially banal and insignificant, having an appeal which is superficial only, and that his lanky figures and gaunt stock – derived as they seem to me from American sources – do not satisfy one beyond their first impression.' (*Angry Penguins* (Autumn 1944).)

30 Gleeson, 'Painting in Australia', 4.

31 Dutton, *Drysdale*, p. 190.

32 Lou Klepac notes that the low horizon and the monumental figures – in the *Drover's Wife*, for example – are attributable to this practice for his camera was of the kind held at chest level while the photographer looked down into the viewfinder. Many of his figures stand stiffly posed, gazing back at us, confronting the camera lens as equals. Klepac, *Drysdale*.

33 The landscapes that resulted from that visit include *Ayers Rock after Rain* (1958), *Centralian Landscape No. I* (1958), *The Brumbies* (1959), *Centralian Nocturne* (1959), *Carcass No. I* (1959) and *Carcass No. II* (1959).

34 Churcher, *Molvig*, p. 73.

35 Cynthia Nolan, *Outback*, p. 31. She added that the paintings resulting from this experience, which were 'executed with fiery speed, savage scrubbing, tender delicacy and penetrating wit would eventually confront entranced or outraged spectators'. (*ibid.*, p. 57.)

36 Sidney Nolan, 14 July 1947, from Brisbane. Quoted in Jane Clark, *Sidney Nolan*, p. 110. As a boy Nolan had been intrigued by the historic flights of Cobham, Amy Johnson and Kingsford Smith. The idea of following these hero-figures would certainly have been an added attraction. (*ibid.*, p. 110, n. 4.)

37 Mary Cecil Allen, 'Notes on Central Australia', p. 192.

38 Sidney Nolan, letter to Sunday Reed, January 1944, Reed papers. Quoted by Reid, 'A Landscape of a Painter', 180. Nolan's delight in brilliance, combined with the seeming child-art style of his paintings, burst upon the Australian art world of the 1940s like the outrageous behaviour of a delinquent adolescent. The Ned Kelly series was virtually ignored when first shown in Melbourne in 1948. It was not until the paintings received the imprimatur of a warm reception in Paris the following year that they elicited any positive interest in Australia.

39 Norman Bartlett, *Daily Telegraph*, 7 April 1950, p. 8.

40 James Gleeson, 'Landscapes Triumph for Australian Artist', the *Sun*, Sydney, 31 March 1950.

41 Sidney Nolan, from the film *Nolan at Sixty* (1977). Quoted in McGrath and Olsen, *The Artist and the Desert*, p. 60.

42 Sidney Nolan, in Lynn and Nolan, *Sidney Nolan – Australia*, p. 13.

43 Fred Williams, in the film *Patterns of Landscape: Fred Williams 1927–1982*, directed by Christina Wilcox, 1989.

44 Fred Williams, quoted in McGrath and Olsen, *The Artist and the Desert*, p. 110.

45 Fred Williams, diary entry, 16 October 1967. Quoted in Mollison, *A Singular Vision*, p. 123. The two quotations that follow are both from p. 133.

46 Tim Storrier in McCullough, *Each Man's Wilderness*, p. 96. The quotation that follows is from the same page.

47 McGrath and Olsen, *The Artist and the Desert*, p. 172.

48 John Coburn, quoted in Dodd, 'John Coburn', 10.

49 As in *The Tree of Life* (1968), *Summer Garden* (1968), *Spring* (1986) and *Spring* (1987) and, most famously, in the curtains Coburn designed for the Sydney Opera House, *Curtain of the Sun* (1971) and *Curtain of the Moon* (1971).

50 John Coburn, quoted in Dodd, 'John Coburn', 13–14. The quotation that follows is from p. 14.

51 Robert Juniper, interviewed by Bianca McCullough in McCullough, *Each Man's Wilderness*, p. 49. The quotation that follows is from p. 49.

52 Like Aboriginal artists, he characteristically paints flat with his canvases on work tables, standing over them to gain this vertical perspective.

53 Robert Juniper, quoted in O'Brien, *Robert Juniper*, p. 45. The three quotations that follow are from pp. 48, 53 and 55 respectively.

54 Grazia Gunn has traced this image to Boyd's memory of a woman on St Kilda beach walking her dog wheelbarrow-like, holding its paralysed back legs. Quoted in Pearce, *Arthur Boyd Retrospective*, p. 15.

55 Patrick McCaughey has interpreted this painting and *Kneeling Figure with Canvas and Black Can* as part of a series showing the deterioration of the artist who, forsaking the world of nature, succumbs to the tyranny of the imagination. McCaughey, 'The Artist in Extremis', pp. 210–20.

56 Compare Boyd's etching and aquatint, *Narcissus*, 1983–84, showing a figure gazing at his reflection in a pool with an enormous animal skull poised above him.

57 He later commented, 'I had expected Alice Springs to be more or less an oasis in a desert-like landscape, instead of which I found these beautiful sagey greens and lovely colours.' (Lloyd Rees, the *Australian* (29 June 1977), 3.)

58 Lloyd Rees, quoted in McCullough, *Each Man's Wilderness*, p. 76.

59 For a discussion of the fourth dimension in Aboriginal art, see Bardon, *Papunya Tula*, pp. 130–32.

60 Jörg Schmeisser, quoted in Susan McCulloch, 'The Printmaker Propelled by Voyages'. The quotation that follows is also from p. 49.

61 Gates, 'Journeyman in Purnululu', in *Jörg Schmeisser*, p. 28.

Chapter 10

1 William Faulkner, *Go Down Moses*.

2 Heseltine, 'Australian Image I', 46.

3 Patrick White, *Voss*, p. 446

4 Chris Baldick (ed.), *The Oxford Book of Gothic Tales* (Oxford: Oxford University Press, 1993), p. xix.

5 Spurr, *The Rhetoric of Empire*, p. 94.

6 Schaffer, *Women and the Bush*, pp. 106–7.

7 Margaret Allen, Introduction to Catherine Martin, *Incredible Journey*.

8 An anthropological term referring to an attempt to understand and portray the social norms of an alien culture through its own eyes rather than from an outside perspective.

9 Katharine Susannah Prichard visited a cattle station in the north-west of Western Australia in 1926. The novel was serialised in the *Bulletin*, which carried as its motto 'Australia for the White Man', but only after the author acceded to the editor's request to remove any explicit mention of physical touch between races.

10 Katharine Susannah Prichard, *Coonardoo*, p. 100.

11 Abdul R. JanMohamed calls this the Manichean allegory of colonialism. See JanMohamed, 'The Economy of Manichean Allegory'.

12 See also Sue Thomas, 'Interracial Encounters'.

13 Quoted by Cunningham, *Featuring Australia*, p. 157.

14 Rattigan, *Images of Australia*, p. 309.

15 Ruhen, *Naked Under Capricorn*, pp. 242, 252. c.f. the passage from *Coonardoo*: 'Generous, kindly their relationship had been, in an overlordship imposed gradually, imperceptibly, until the blacks recognized and accepted it, by conditions of work for food and clothing' (p. 100.)

16 J.K.P., 'Revenge of Charterhouse', 7.

17 Cook, *Wake in Fright*, p. 7. The three quotations that follow are from pp. 6, 7 and 190 respectively.

18 Ross Gibson, 'Formative Landscapes' in Scott Murray, *Back of Beyond*, p. 29.

19 George Miller referred to the nation's 'car culture' as a major reference in *Mad Max*. Quoted by Adrian Martin, '*Mad Max*' in Scott Murray, *Australian Film 1978–1992*, p. 41.

20 'Why he blew our way . . . when every other karma bum was mumbling mantras

through lush coast nirvanas, no one could imagine unless he was a desert father, a brutal self-purger who wanted a landscape skinned to the bone.' Astley, *Late News*, p. 3.

21 Dorothy Johnston, *Maralinga*, p. 13. The two quotations that follow are from pp. 173 and 222 respectively.

22 Jackson, *Fantasy*, p. 42.

23 Hélène Cixous, 'La fiction et ses fantômes: une lecture de l'*Unheimliche* de Freud', *Poétique* 10 (1973), 199–216, transl. in Jackson, *Fantasy*, p. 208.

24 *Where Bonds are Loosed* (1914), *The Mainland* (1917), *The Desert Horizon* (1923), *Daimon* (1925), *The Partners* under the pseudonym 'John Lovegood' (1933), and *The Nun and the Bandit* (1935).

25 Watson, *But to What Purpose*, p. 252. The quotation that follows is from p. 108.

26 In *Where Bonds are Loosed* Sherwin and Hicksey fight to the death for Alice Desmond who, seemingly against all sensibilities, capitulates to the formerly repulsive Sherwin; in *The Mainland* John Sherwin, infatuated with an older, married woman, Mrs Cray, enters into competition with her husband; in *Daimon* Maggie encourages a relationship with the jackaroo Bob Carey as rival to her husband Martin; and in *The Partners* Sam Lawson and Tim Kennedy compete for Sam's wife Vera.

27 Watson, *Daimon*, p. 331. The two quotations that follow are from pp. 256–7 and 282–3 respectively.

28 Watson, *Desert Horizon*, pp. 53–4.

29 Watson, *But to What Purpose*, pp. 63, 100.

30 Watson, *Daimon*, p. 315. The two quotations that follow are from pp. 75 and 316 respectively.

31 Watson, *But to What Purpose*, p. 211.

32 Hope, 'Australia', in *Collected Poems*, p. 13.

33 McAuley, 'Envoi for a Book of Poems' [1940] in *Selected Poems*, p. 2.

34 Stow studied Anthropology and Linguistics at the University of Sydney in 1958 and the following year worked in Papua New Guinea as assistant to Dr Charles Julius, the government anthropologist.

35 Stow, 'Raw Material', 3, 4. The two quotations that follow are from pp. 4 and 5 respectively.

36 Stow, *Tourmaline*, p. 7.

37 Stow has said, 'What stimulated me most was the ghost townships of the eastern goldfields of Western Australia.' Beston, 'Interview with Randolph Stow', 223.

38 '*From* the Testament of Tourmaline: Variations on Themes of the *Tao Teh Ching*' was published in Stow, *A Counterfeit Silence*, pp. 71–5. In an interview in 1976 Stow said, 'I tend to adhere to Taoism, which is a very pragmatic religion concerned mostly with time and change, action and inaction. That warped kind of Christianity which the Diviner brings into Tourmaline is the absolute opposite of this.' (Xavier Pons and Neil Keeble, 'A Colonist with Words: An Interview with Randolph Stow', *Commonwealth (Rodez): Essays and Studies Mélanges 2* (1976), 77.) For the most comprehensive discussion of the centrality of the Tao Teh Ching in Stow's novel see Tiffin, '*Tourmaline* and the *Tao Teh Ching*'.

39 Beston, 'Interview with Randolph Stow', 228.

40 Drewe, *The Drowner*, p. 229. The two quotations that follow are from pp. 229–30 and 93 respectively.

41 Nolan later did a series of illustrations for *Outrider* (1962), Stow's second book of poems.

42 Leer, '*Mal du pays . . .*', p. 20.

43 Stow, 'The Singing Bones', in *Counterfeit Silence*, p. 52.

44 Hospital, *Oyster*, pp. 310–12. This relationship parallels the Taoist avoidance of force in favour of persuasion as the way to survive. One of the characters, Major Miner, relates a story told by Chuang-tzu of Prince Wen Hui's butcher who has used the same cleaver for nineteen years because, following the Tao, he lets the blade follow its instinct. 'It

finds the secret openings and the fine spaces between joints. . . . The ox falls apart.'
(*Oyster*, p. 213.)

45 Hospital, *Oyster*, p. 346. This is echoed by Junior Godwin, the only progressive farmer
in the district. (*ibid.* p. 246.) The quotations that follow are from pp. 4, 5, 5, 10, 7, 30,
223, 380, 327, 334 and 397 respectively.

46 Sarah Cohen, a lapsed Jewess and Nick, a Greek-Australian who wants to forget his
Greek heritage, exemplify the biblical verse 'There is neither Jew nor Greek'
(Galatians 3:28).

Chapter 11

1 The source of this quotation is unknown.

2 Sidney Nolan in conversation with Elwynn Lynn, quoted in Lynn, *Sidney Nolan's Ned
Kelly*, pp. 10–11.

3 Hele later became the official Australian war artist of World War II, and it is no
coincidence that the central figure of his painting *Tobruk* (1944) bears a strong
similarity to his image of Sturt.

4 Sidney Nolan, letter to Geoffrey Dutton, quoted in Dutton, 'Sidney Nolan's Burke and
Wills Series', 459. Cynthia Nolan wrote of their Central Australian flight, 'This was the
land of some of the most heroic explorers, of John Eyre who came here in 1840
expecting to find good pasture land, only to escape narrowly with his life; of Sturt
whose eyesight failed through the privations of his several journeys.' (Cynthia Nolan,
Outback, p. 22.)

5 In this Nolan is closer to the nineteenth-century heroic view of the explorers than to
the attitudes of his contemporaries, ranging from lack of interest to cynicism. He was,
indeed, always in need of heroes, as is suggested by the Ned Kelly paintings of which
Nolan said: 'I'm reluctant to drop the concept of a hero figure. If I lost this I would be
discarding something very Australian. Without a hero you end up with anonymity.'
Quoted by Splatt, *Australian Landscape Painting*, p. 196.

6 Sidney Nolan, 'Cooper's Creek', unpublished poem, quoted in Jane Clark, *Sidney
Nolan: Landscapes and Legends*, p. 107.

7 This is discussed in Chapter 12.

8 Sidney Nolan, unpublished poem, quoted in Clark, *Sidney Nolan* p. 159.

9 There is an earlier painting of two explorers and a camel in a sunset-coloured desert,
dated 1945. See *ibid.*, p. 96, n. 7.

10 Tim Bonyhady points out that the engraving in Pyke's edition was wrongly titled 'They
found the Remains under a Box Tree', implying that the weeping figure is Howitt or
another member of his rescue party, whereas in Strutt's original, titled 'Burke's Death',
the kneeling figure is clearly intended to be King. Bonyhady, *Burke and Wills*, p. 298.

11 Sidney Nolan, quoted in Dutton, 'Sidney Nolan's Burke and Wills Series', p. 459.
Cynthia wrote that 'Sidney became increasingly obsessed by the camels and spent
hours watching them and planning big, delicate and detailed paintings'. (Cynthia
Nolan, *Outback*, p. 152.) Certainly in *Camels in the Desert* (1951) the beasts have finally
taken over, the explorers are dispensed with. Unlike their erstwhile riders, the camels
belong in their surroundings. Their humps mimic the distant hills, their colour blends
with the landscape.

12 Jessie MacLeod, 'Introduction' to *The Explorers* (catalogue), 1958, quoted in Benko, *Art
of David Boyd*, p. 19.

13 In 1938 Tucker, like Nolan, joined the Contemporary Art Society of Australia and
proceeded to shock Eurocentric Australian society from its complacent artistic cocoon.
However, the cocoon proved more impenetrable than expected and Tucker stormed
off to Europe.

14 *The Kellys – Dead or Alive* (1956) and *King Kelly and His Legions* (1957).

15 *Ned and Dan Kelly* (1958), also titled *Desert with Armoured Bushrangers*, is characterised
by the same craters in the landscape and Nolan's slit-like openings in Ned Kelly's
helmet have already become two round socket shapes in Tucker's version.

314

16 Two paintings titled *Lunar Landscape* (both 1957), *Explorer* (1957), *Antipodean Figure* (1958), *Explorer* (1958), *Cratered Landscape* (?1958), *Explorer* (?1958), *Antipodean Head* (1958–61), *Explorer 1* (?1958), *Explorer 2* (?1958), *Explorer 3* (?1958), *Antipodean Head* (1958) and two more paintings titled *Explorer* (1958) show both the fanatic intensity with which Tucker embraced this theme and the increasing coalescence of figure, landscape and the notion of the Antipodean. It is interesting that Tucker's first Antipodean figure predates, by a year, the Antipodean Manifesto of 1959. See Blackman, 'The Antipodean Affair'.

17 Hughes, *Art of Australia*, p. 229.

18 Albert Tucker, quoted in Laurie Thomas, *The Most Noble Art of them All: the Selected Writings of Laurie Thomas* (St Lucia: University of Queensland Press, 1976), p. 297.

19 John Wolseley, quoted in Catalano, 'The Source of Things', 20.

20 Among the few were Montagu Scott's painting, *Natives Discovering the Body of William John Wills, the Explorer* (1865), and the wood engraving, *The Finding of King* (1891) by F.A. Sleap, after J. Macfarlane, for *Illustrated Australian News*, supplement, 1 January 1891, pp. 8–9.

21 Morrell, 'Antony Hamilton', p. 46.

22 Becker's work was discussed in Chapter 5.

23 Mandy Martin, personal communication, notes from 'On the Line Conference', June 1994.

Chapter 12

1 Judith Wright, 'The Upside Down Hut' [1961] in *The Writer in Australia*, ed. John Barnes (Melbourne: Oxford University Press, 1969), p. 335.

2 Stow, 'The Singing Bones', in *Counterfeit Silence*, p. 52.

3 Manning Clark, 'Heroes', p. 63. Originally published in *Daedalus* (Winter 1985).

4 Joseph Furphy, *Such is Life*, pp. 32–3, 34.

5 In the film the crime of Brahe's dastardly departure from Cooper's Creek is compounded by his attempt to seduce King's fiancée, Stella, but happily King returns in time to reclaim Stella and denounce the villain.

6 C.E.W. Bean's *Official History of Australia in the War of 1914–1918* created a new class of national hero, the Anzac soldier. It has generally been assumed that his account was impartial, based on his personal experience in visiting the trenches, but, as Adrian Mitchell points out, Bean 'approved of the men not so much for what they were, but for the ideals he believed they confirmed. . . . these ideals derive from himself as much as from the bush tradition. . . . his nationalism included a sense of continuity and congruity with Britain. . . . he articulated the accepted values of the British public school at the end of the nineteenth century – ideals of conduct rather than of belief.' Adrian Mitchell, 'The Ambivalence of C.E.W. Bean', pp. 104–6.

7 Newbolt, *The Book of the Long Trail*, 1919 p. 175. The book sold eight editions in as many years.

8 Tim Bonyhady has given a detailed account of the reception accorded *Dig* in *Burke and Wills*, pp. 294–6. Clune's alleged research, conducted with P.R. Stephensen, ignored the State Library of Victoria, the main repository of the material relating to the expedition. As well as describing the German William Brahe throughout as a Swede (p. 53) Clune designated von Mueller 'hereditary Baron of Württemberg [*sic*], known as the "Wandering Dane"' (p. 116).

9 Clune, *Dig*, p. 32. The four quotations that follow are from pp. 33, 52, 111 and 117 respectively. Clune also wrote 'With O'Hara Burke to the Gulf', a brief outline of the north-bound part of the expedition for *Walkabout* (1 March 1938, 13–19). It ends with a plea to revive Burke's memory.

10 Brahe's guilt is established beyond doubt, in Clune's treatment, by his response to the accusation of the dying Paton: ' "You are a murderer, Wright! You have murdered Burke and Wills, and now you want to murder me. You are more than a murderer, you are a torturer . . ." ' . . . 'Wright's face paled, as he burst into explosive blasphemy' (p. 111).

11 Clune, 'With O'Hara Burke to the Gulf', 18. The quotation that follows is from p. 14.

12 Eldershaw, 'The Man Who Knew the Truth'.

13 Chisholm, *Strange New World*, p. 270.

14 Priessnitz, 'Vossification', p. 214.

15 For example, Oakley, 'O'Hara 1861'; Gary Hogg, *With Burke and Wills Across Australia* (London: Ferdinand Muller, 1961); John McKellar, *Tree by the Creek* (Sydney: Cheshire, 1961); and Southall, *Journey into Mystery*. Oakley's short story is unique among the fictional reconstructions in suggesting that Burke, Wills and King almost came to physical blows in their last days at Cooper's Creek. The most impeccably researched offering was Kathleen Fitzpatrick's lecture to the Royal Society of Victoria, later printed in *Historical Studies*. Few parties involved escaped criticism in Fitzpatrick's treatment, though her strongest censure was reserved for the Exploration Committee. (Fitzpatrick, 'The Burke and Wills Expedition'.)

16 Geoffrey Dutton, 'Burke's Will and Testament', *Australian Book Review* (March 1964), 96.

17 Moorehead, *Cooper's Creek*, p. 136.

18 Reed, *Burke's Company*. Reed's careful analysis of the transcript of evidence given before the Commission of Inquiry led him to conclude that Brahe and Wright had, in fact, noticed signs of Burke and Wills's return to Cooper's Creek and deliberately ignored them.

19 Tom Bergin, *In the Steps of Burke and Wills* (Sydney: Australian Broadcasting Commission, 1981). The film was shown as the 200th episode of the ABC series, *A Big Country*.

20 Bonyhady, *Burke and Wills*, p. 310.

21 Conrad had, of course, pioneered this internalisation of the epic of discovery in *Heart of Darkness* but it was half a century before the symbolism was applied in the Australian context.

22 Douglas Stewart, Foreword to *Voyager Poems*, pp. 11–12. Stewart's earlier verse play, *Fire on the Snow* (1939), based on Scott's Antarctic expedition of 1912 and later popular as a radio play, also examines the nature of heroism in relation to the explorer.

23 Harrison, 'Leichhardt in the Desert'.

24 Harris, 'Sturt at Depot Glen', p. 41.

25 Compare also Francis Berry's radio play, *Eyre Remembers* (1982), a retrospective on Eyre's life, which includes the segment relating his journey along the Great Australian Bight with Wylie. The focus of the section is on the overpowering thirst of man and horses, and the actions to which they are driven in order to survive, but Berry's intermittent chorus also allows questioning of Eyre's motives in the light of his later arraignment for the murder of Jamaicans. (Francis Berry, ' "Eyre Remembers": An Extract' in Joost Daalder and Michèle Fryar (eds), *Aspects of Australian Culture*. (Adelaide: Abel Tasman Press, 1982), pp. 16–17, 20.)

26 Judith Wright, *Preoccupations in Australian Poetry*, pp. 214, 216.

27 Webb, 'Poet', *Collected Poems*, p. 152.

28 As late as 1938 Dr Archibald Grenfell Price led a South Australian Government expedition to Ritchie's Ridge, in the southern part of the Simpson Desert, following reports of seven to eight skeletons thought to be the remains of Leichhardt's party. The 'skeletons' proved to be calcified tree roots but the incidental discovery in the area of human bones and teeth, leather, iron and several coins, notably a rare English Maundy threepence of 1841, a year when Leichhardt was in England, suggested that it might be a possible site. (Price, 'The Mystery of Leichhardt'.)

29 Michael Griffith mentions, as an example of similarities between the two works, Leichhardt's fear of eyes in 'Two on the Map' and 'Introduction in a Wax-works' (the original title of the 'Advertisement' section). See Griffith, 'Francis Webb's Challenge', p. 459. Patrick White, on the other hand, acknowledged as sources only 'contemporary accounts of Leichhardt's expeditions and A.H. Chisholm's *Strange New World*'. Patrick White, 'Prodigal Son', p. 39.

30 This and all further quotations from Webb's poetry are from Webb, *Collected Poems*.
31 Compare: 'The wilderness had patted him on the head, and, behold, it was like a ball – an ivory ball; it had caressed him, and – lo! – he had withered; it had taken him, loved him, and embraced him, got into his veins, consumed his flesh.' Conrad, *Darkness*, p. 69.
32 As we have seen in Chapter 4, Sturt's published accounts repeatedly use such similes. Leichhardt's first expedition was favourably contrasted with Sturt's in a contemporary *Sydney Herald* editorial, quoted in C.D. Cotton, *Ludwig Leichhardt and the Great South Land* (1938) which Webb had read very thoroughly.
33 Webb, *Collected Poems*, p. 41. Henry Turnbull, a member of Leichhardt's second expedition, gave a public lecture in Launceston in 1855, seven years after the explorer set out on his ill-fated third journey. Turnbull ended his speech with the following exhortation to his audience: 'Here is a real hero, a truly great man. His shrine alone is wanting! ... Let it be a monument of some sort or other – a statue if you will – not of bronze, however, but of marble – pure marble – pure as the unsullied reputation of the man whose memory it would perpetuate.' (Turnbull, *Leichhardt's Second Journey*, p. 57.)
34 This section of the poem appears at first to concur with the fierce demolition of Leichhardt's reputation mounted by Alec Chisholm in his book, *Strange New World* (1941), but Webb does not leave his protagonist unredeemed, thereby suggesting that Chisholm is one of the crass audience that judges by its own prejudices.
35 Michael Griffith, 'Francis Webb's Challenge to Mid-Century Mythmaking', 459. Webb's poem shares a striking image, 'the death's-head continent', with Albert Tucker's *Antipodean Head* series and his five Leichhardt paintings executed between 1959 and 1967, though all may have been derived independently from Conrad's *Heart of Darkness*.
36 Webb, *Collected Poems*, p. 251.
37 See Excell, *Dancings*.
38 For a detailed exposition of these and numerous other references see Excell, *Dancings*.
39 Eyre had written an article for the *South Australian Register* of 23 May 1840, explaining his reasons for scepticism about an overland stock route west to the Swan River, and why it was preferable to look to the north.
40 Webb, *Collected Poems*, p. 184. The four quotations that follow are from pp. 185, 186, 190 and 192 respectively.
41 Jameson, 'Postmodernism', 71.
42 The obvious comparison is Conrad's complex use of the Congo in *Heart of Darkness* but White denied any influence from Conrad, saying that he 'read several books [of Conrad's] in my teens, when I could not understand what all his conflicts were about, and consequently did not like him. (The one Conrad I do like, and which I read just at the end of the War ... is *Under Western Eyes*.)'. (Letter to The Moores, 8.ii.58. *Patrick White Letters*, p. 129.)
43 Andrew Taylor, *Reading Australian Poetry*, p. 8.
44 Patrick White, 'The Prodigal Son', p. 157. Although the similarities between Voss and Leichhardt as depicted by Chisholm are obvious, there are also significant parallels with Edward John Eyre's expedition. For Chisholm's probable motives in denigrating Leichhardt, see Burrows, '"Voss" and the Explorers', 238–9, and Marcel Arousseau, 'The Identity of Voss', *Meanjin* 17:1 (1958), 86.
45 Patrick White, letter to Sidney Nolan, 7.iii.57, in *Letters*, p. 113. He later wrote of the Nolan retrospective 1947–67, 'It was staggering to see all the imaginative and painting genius that has poured out of one man. ... To me this has been the greatest event – not just in painting – in Australia in my lifetime.' (Letter to Luciana Arrighi, 16.x.67, in *Letters*, p. 318.)
46 John Hetherington, 'Patrick White: Life at Castle Hill', in *Forty-Two Faces* (Melbourne: Cheshire, 1962), p. 144. c.f White's outline of *Voss* to Ben Huebsch of Viking Press. (See letter to Ben Huebsch, 11.ix.56, in *Letters*, pp. 107–8.)

317

47 This view, most aggressively expounded in his diatribe 'The Prodigal Son' (1958), was shared by many of his contemporaries, particularly the poets Kenneth Slessor, Douglas Stewart and Francis Webb.

48 As Cavan Brown points out, these conflicting concepts are already present in the Old Testament where the prophets confer on the desert imagery of both judgement and renewal. Brown, *Pilgrim*, p. 169.

49 White, *Voss*, p. 155. The six quotations that follow are from pp. 19, 27, 15, 29, 137 and 190 respectively.

50 The ambiguity is deliberate; Voss assumes he is possessed *of* it, in the sense of possessing it; ultimately he is possessed *by* it.

51 Stow, *Midnite*, p. 93.

52 See, for example, Gillian Rose, *Feminism and Geography*, and Howells, 'Disruptive Geographies'.

53 White, *Voss*, p. 53. Johannes Eckhart (1260?–1327?). White had also been impressed by the religious meditations of Simone Weil, the French mystic and philosopher (1909–43), particularly in reference to her insistence on the role of personal affliction. See *Letters*, pp. 89, 401. Voss's statement is parodied in Stow's *Midnite*, where the stereotypical German explorer, Johann Ludwig Ulrich von Leichardt zu Voss, tells Midnite, '"I too am exploring. . . . I am exploring me." "How can you explore you?", asked Midnite. "I will not explain," said Mr Smith. "You would have to be me to understand."' Stow, *Midnite*, p. 92.

54 White, *Voss*, p. 169. The four quotations that follow are from pp. 446, 448, 446 and 275 respectively.

55 This dual understanding also enacts White's stated intention for the novel: 'Always something of a frustrated painter, and a composer *manqué*, I wanted to give my book the textures of music, the sensuousness of paint, to convey through the theme and characters of *Voss* what Delacroix and Blake might have seen, what Mahler and Liszt might have heard. Above all I was determined to prove that the Australian novel is not necessarily the dreary, dun-coloured offspring of journalistic realism.' Patrick White, 'The Prodigal Son', p. 157. The quotation that follows is from *Voss*, p. 443.

56 White's intentional focus on a spiritual dimension may be gauged from his remark to Ben Huebsch of Viking Press about his pleasure with the cover of the American edition. 'Incidentally, I read last night that the colours blue and yellow are the colours of introverted and extrovert spiritual perception. I wonder whether the designer was conscious that he had hit the nail so subtly on the head!' (Patrick White, letter to Ben Huebsch, 19.viii.57, in *Letters*, p. 120.) David Marr comments (p. 120) that George Salter's design for the cover of the Viking edition 'had shreds of Voss's letter to Laura floating in a golden haze over blue distance'.

57 Patrick White, *Voss*, p. 15. The four quotations that follow are from pp. 87–8, 35, 270 and 283–4 respectively.

58 Patrick White, letter to Ben Huebsch, 11.ix.56, *Letters*, p. 108. The quotation that follows is from *Voss*, p. 390.

59 Lundgren, 'Sturt's Dreaming'.

60 This appears to be the one biological inaccuracy in the novel. *Geopsittacus occidentalis*, though difficult to flush, is not an endangered species.

61 Stivens, *Horse of Air*, p. 116. The four quotations that folllow are from pp. 179–80, 217, 219 and 162–3 respectively.

62 Giles recorded a similar experience in that, 'while lying down there, I thought I heard the sound of the foot-falls of a galloping horse going campwards, and vague ideas of Gibson on the Fair Maid – or she without him – entered my head. I stood up and listened, but the sound had died away upon the midnight air.' Giles, *Australia Twice Traversed*, vol. 2, book II, ch. 10, pp. 42–3.

63 Page, 'Nullarbor'.

64 D.H. Lawrence, *Kangaroo* [1923] (Sydney: Angus & Robertson, 1992), p. 9. Lawrence wrote to Katharine Susannah Prichard, 'For some things too I love Australia: its weird, far-away natural beauty and its remote, almost coal-age pristine quality. Only it's too far for me. I can't reach so awfully far. Further than Egypt. I feel I slither on the edge of a gulf, reaching to grasp its atmosphere and spirit. It eludes me, and always would. It is too far back . . .' (D.H. Lawrence, letter to Katharine Throssel [1922] in *The Letters of D.H. Lawrence*, ed. Roberts et al. (Cambridge: Cambridge University Press, 1987), vol. IV, letter 2550.

Chapter 13

 1 Seddon, *Landprints.*
 2 Ivor Indyk, 'Some Versions of Pastoral', *Southerly* (1988) 2, 127.
 3 John Wolseley, quoted in Hawley, *Encounters*, p. 146.
 4 Clifton Pugh, *Sunday Times*, Perth, 26 January, 1955.
 5 Gleeson, *Modern Painters.*
 6 Quoted in Macainsh, *Clifton Pugh*, pp. 2, 3.
 7 Quoted in McGrath and Olsen, *The Artist and the Desert*, p. 44.
 8 Sidney Nolan, 'Carcass', in Lynn and Nolan, *Sidney Nolan – Australia*, p. 88.
 9 Reid, 'A Landscape of a Painter', 181
10 This collaboration resulted in the jointly written, illustrated book, Marshall and Drysdale, *Journey Among Men.*
11 *Death of a Wombat* and *Dingo King.*
12 McCubbin, 'Desert Diary'.
13 In November 1974, October 1975 and August 1976. Even before his journey with Serventy to Lake Eyre, Olsen had been exercised by the process of observation which art and science have in common.
14 Quoted in Sandra McGrath, 'A Remote Eden', 147.
15 *ibid.*, 146–7.
16 Ken Taylor, 'John Olsen at Lake Eyre 1977' in *A Secret Australia*, p. 71.
17 Quoted in Sandra McGrath, 'A Remote Eden', 150.
18 John Olsen, from a conversation with Christopher Leonard, July 1986. Quoted in Leonard, 'Art and Memory', 372–3.
19 Quoted in Sandra McGrath, 'A Remote Eden', 147.
20 John Olsen, 'Lake Eyre, Aug. 23' [1976], quoted in Sandra McGrath, 'A Remote Eden', 151.
21 Quoted *ibid.*, 151.
22 John Wolseley, quoted in Hawley, *Encounters*, p. 142.
23 Catalano, 'Source of Things', 18.
24 John Wolseley, quoted in Hawley, *Encounters*, p. 146.
25 *ibid.*, p. 146.
26 John Wolseley, quoted in Ferguson, 'Land and Identity', 41.
27 John Wolseley in conversation with Peter Ross, ABC Radio, 1996.
28 Quoted in Raman Selden, *A Reader's Guide to Contemporary Literary Theory* (Brighton: Harvester Press, 1988), p. 77.
29 John Wolseley, quoted in McGrath and Olsen, *The Artist and the Desert*, p. 166.
30 John Wolseley, *The Simpson Desert Survey 1991–1993*, artist's statement.
31 Drewe, *Drowner*, pp. 91–2.
32 John Wolseley, quoted in Hawley, *Encounters*, p. 140.
33 John Wolseley, in Catalano, 'Source of Things', 21.
34 Wolseley's exhibition *Tasmania to Patagonia: Origin, Movement, Species, Tracing the Southern Continents* (1996) included a forthright attack on woodchipping in the Tasmanian forests.
35 John Wolseley, quoted in Hawley, *Encounters*, pp. 141–2.

319

36 Martin sees the Romantic sublime and its antipodean manifestations as the 'possible origin and site for a European-Australian point of spiritual contact with our landscape'. Mandy Martin, Notes for a Workshop on Windorah Ecological Perspectives, Cooper's Creek, September 1996. Personal communication.

37 Peter Haynes, 'Mandy Martin: the Continuing Narrative', in Martin and Sinclair, *Tracts*, p. 8.

38 Martin, Notes for a Workshop on Windorah Ecological Perspectives, Cooper's Creek, September 1996. Personal communication.

Chapter 14

1 Eliade, *Myth of the Eternal Return*.

2 Hope, 'Australia', in *Collected Poems*, p. 13.

3 Soper, *What is Nature?*, p. 227.

4 It is significant that none of the nineteenth-century explorers expatiates on the colours of the desert. Their admiration, where it surfaces at all, is reserved for the green areas around waterholes, indeed for the areas which represent a temporary denial of the surrounding desert.

5 Chambers Pillar is a spectacular sandstone column on a small hill, rising in total 50 metres above the plain on the north-west edge of the Simpson Desert. It was named in 1860 by the explorer John McDouall Stuart in honour of James Chambers of Adelaide, one of the sponsors of his expedition. The perentie (*Varanus giganteus*), Australia's largest lizard, grows up to 2 metres in length.

6 Ann McGrath, 'Travels to a Distant Past', 123.

7 Jenny Stanton, *Book of the Red Centre*, p. 154.

8 Giles, *Australia Twice Traversed*, vol. 2, book II, ch. 11, pp. 61–2.

9 T.G.H. Strehlow, Diary entry for 11 June 1935. Quoted in Barry Hill, *The Rock*, pp. 120–21.

10 'I felt like an ant at the door of a cathedral', wrote Arthur Groom in *I Saw a Strange Land* (1950). Quoted by Barry Hill, *The Rock*, p. 88.

11 Marcus, 'The Journey out to the Centre', 270–71.

12 Ann McGrath, 'Travels to a Distant Past', 116.

13 See Willis, *Illusions of Identity*, p. 182, fig. 59.

14 The name 'Jindyworobak' was derived by Ingamells from the word 'Jindy-worabak' meaning 'to annex, to join' which he found in the glossary of James Devaney's *Vanished Tribes* (1929)

15 Elliott, *Jindyworobaks*, p. 270.

16 *Alchera* or *Alcheringa* (the adjective) is the Aranda word for what is most often known as the 'Dreamtime'. Ingamells came across it when reading Spencer and Gillen's seminal work, *The Arunta* (1927). See Elliott, *Jindyworobaks*, Introduction, p. xxiii.

17 Elliott, *Jindyworobaks*, Introduction p. xxx. The quotations that follow are from pp. 132 ('The Wanderer'), 33–5 ('Uluru'), 22 ('Australia'), 178 ('Burke and Wills') and 112 ('Nullarbor').

18 Robyn Davidson, *Tracks*. The first account of Davidson's journey appeared in an article 'Alone Across the Outback' in *National Geographic* 153:5 (May 1978). The National Geographic Society had partly underwritten the expedition costs.

19 Robyn Davidson, *Tracks*, pp. 105–6. The six quotations that follow are from pp. 202, 102, 107–8, 190, 191–2 and 97 respectively.

20 For example, Davidson's expectation of finding solitude there is rudely shattered, firstly by the recurrent visits of Rick, the photographer for the *National Geographic* article and later by the invasive hordes of tourists and media representatives. Her cherished hope of achieving close rapport with Aborigines evaporates when she finds she is expected to pay for spontaneously joining in the women's dance: 'I felt it as a symbolic defeat. A final summing up of how I could never enter their reality, would always be a whitefella tourist on the outside looking in.' (p. 148)

21 *Tracks*, pp. 216–17. Although this ecstatic passage is immediately converted into dramatic irony by the sudden death of Davidson's dog from a poison bait, the overriding impressions are of self-empowerment on the one hand, and, on the other, a simultaneous losing of the self in a cosmic net.

22 Davidson was also well aware that the elements of danger and isolation were minimal compared with those of the early expeditions into the unknown. She had maps, a radio (although it turned out not to work!), water drops, periodic visits from the *National Geographic* photographer, a flight back to Alice Springs to seek veterinary advice about the camels, the company of an Aboriginal elder, Eddie, for some 350 km, lengthy stops at cattle stations and, towards the end of her trip, the crass incursions on her privacy of curious tourists and reporters. The two quotations that follow are from pp. 231 and 232 respectively.

23 In 1973 C. Warren Bonython and Charles McCubbin trekked some 560 km across the Simpson Desert, pulling their aluminium cart of provisions, 'The Comalco Camel', for 460 km. The record of their 32-day journey is told in Bonython, *Walking the Simpson Desert*. While their journey was an inspiration for Denis Bartell, they did not fulfil the essential pre-requisite of solitude.

24 Giles, *Australia Twice Traversed*, book IV, ch. 1, p. 255.

25 Quoted in Barry Hill, *The Rock*, p. 270. The two quotations that follow are from Hill, pp. 270 and 167–9 respectively. Hill records in detail the reasons why the second request was refused.

26 *ibid.*, pp. 167–9.

27 Kevin Roberts, 'I do not climb the Rock', *Red Centre Journal* (1992), 40. Quoted in R. Kimber, personal communication, p. 43. For many of the references and ideas in this chapter I am greatly indebted to Richard Kimber's article, 'Australian Rangelands in Contemporary Literature', *Rangelands Journal* 16:2 (1994), 311–20, and to subsequent discussion with him.

28 Kathleen Phillips, 'The Road through the Desert: Oz Video Clips' in Shiel and Spearritt, *Lie of the Land*, p. 16.

29 For a comprehensive discussion of Morgan's fiction posing as fact and the way it has been marketed to a gullible public, see Gareth Griffiths, 'Mixed Up Messages'.

30 Marlo Morgan, *Mutant Message*, p. 148.

31 Pascoe, *Fox*, p. 154.

32 *ibid.*, p. 160. Among tribes of the Mallee districts the constellation Lyra traditionally represented the spirit of Neilloan, the Mallee fowl, which taught them how to find its eggs, an important source of food in October. When Lyra set with the Sun, the eggs were ready to seek. See Roslynn D. Haynes, 'Dreaming'.

33 Eliade, 'Sacred Space'.

34 Tuan, *Topophilia*, p.146.

35 Collis, *Soul Stone*. The six quotations that follow are from pp. 296, 363–4. 415, 391, 104 and 282 respectively.

36 Tacey, *Edge of the Sacred*, p. 8.

37 In the US, too, indigenous cultures are endowed with a reputation for moral superiority over the greed and materialism of Western culture.

38 Les Murray, 'The Inverse Transports' in *Collected Poems*, pp. 313–14.

39 Charlesworth, '2000 A.D.', p. 287.

Chapter 15

1 Geoffrey Bardon, quoted in Judith Ryan, *Mythscapes*, p. 31.

2 John Wolseley, quoted in Hawley, *Encounters*, p. 146.

3 See Philip Jones, 'Perceptions of Aboriginal Art: A History', in Sutton, *Dreamings*, p. 165.

4 Willis, *Illusions*, p. 152.

5 Preston, 'Indigenous Art of Australia', 34.

6 Warlukurlangu Artists, *Kuruwarri: Yuendumu Doors* (Canberra: Australian Institute of Aboriginal Studies, 1987), p. 3.

7 See, for example, Christopher Anderson and Françoise Dussart, 'Dreamings in Acrylic: Western Desert Art', in Sutton, *Dreamings*, pp. 121–2.

8 Montgomery, 'Australia', 3.

9 Willis, *Illusions*, p. 118.

10 *Mount Allen Land Claim*, Report no. 19 (Canberra: Australian Government Publishing Service, 1985), p. 4. I am indebted for this information to Judith Ryan, *Mythscapes*, p. 72.

11 Quoted in Elke Wiesmann and David Jagger, 'Desert Hearts on Canvas', *Weekend Australian* (28–29 June 1997), 'Weekend Review' 12.

12 D.J. Mulvaney, 'Visions of Environment: An Afterview', in *Australian Environment*, p. 113.

13 Geoffrey Bardon, quoted in Judith Ryan, *Mythscapes*, pp. 31–2.

Epilogue

1 George Seddon, *Landprints*, p. 247.

2 Ken Barratt, 'Burke and Wills' in Elliott, *Jindyworobaks*, p. 177.

Adams, Brian. *Sidney Nolan: Such is Life*. Melbourne: Hutchinson, 1987.

Adams, Robert Martin. *Nil: Episodes in the Literary Conquest of Void during the Nineteenth Century*. New York: Oxford University Press, 1966.

Albinski, Nan Bowman. 'A Survey of Australian Utopian and Dystopian Fiction', *Australian Literary Studies* 13:1 (1987), 15–28.

Allen, C. Holdsworth. 'How Long', *Bulletin* (18 April 1903), 3.

Allen, H.C. *Bush and Backwoods: A Comparison of the Frontier in Australia and the United States*. Michigan: Michigan State University Press, 1959.

Allen, John L. 'Lands of Myth, Waters of Wonder: The Place of Imagination in the History of Geographical Exploration', in David Lowenthal and Martyn J. Bowden (eds), *Geographies of the Mind: Essays in Historical Geography*, pp. 41–61. New York: Oxford University Press, 1976.

Allen, Louis A. *Time Before Morning*. Adelaide: Rigby, 1975.

Allen, Margaret. 'Catherine Martin, Writer: Her Life and Ideas', *Australian Literary Studies* 13:2 (1987), 184–97.

Allen, Mary Cecil. 'Notes on Central Australia', *Meanjin* 9:3 (1950), 191–2.

Allenby, Jeni. 'Arabesque: The Mythology of Orientalism; Where Exactly is the Orient?', *Artonview* 4 (1995–96), 51–8.

Amadio, Nadine and Richard Kimber. *Wildbird Dreaming: Aboriginal Art from the Central Deserts of Australia*. Melbourne: Greenhouse Publications, 1988.

Anderson, B. *Imagined Communities: Reflections on the Origin and Spread of Nationalism*. London: Verso, 1983.

Angas, George French. *Savage Life and Scenes in Australia and New Zealand: Being an Artist's Impressions of Countries and People at the Antipodes*, 2 vols. London: Smith, Elder & Co., 1847. Adelaide: Libraries Board of South Australia, 1969.

——. *South Australia Illustrated*. London: M'Lean, 1847.

Anon. '"Oo-a-deen": or, The Mysteries of the Interior Unveiled' (1847), republished in V. Ikin (ed.), *Australian Science Fiction*. St Lucia, Qld: University of Queensland Press, 1982, pp. 7–27.

Appleyard, Ron, Barbara Fargher, and Ron Radford. *S.T. Gill, The South Australian Years, 1839–1852*. Adelaide: Art Gallery of South Australia, 1986.

Ashcroft, Bill. *The Gimbals of Unease: The Poetry of Francis Webb*. Nedlands, WA: Centre for Studies in Australian Literature, 1996.

Astbury, Leigh. 'Marketing the Last Frontier', *Studio International* 199 (December–February, 1986–87), 3–7.

Astley, Thea. *An Item from the Late News*. Ringwood, Vic.: Penguin, 1982.

Auhl, Ian and Denis Marfleet. *Journey to Lake Frome, 1843: Paintings and Sketches by Edward Charles Frome and James Henderson*. Adelaide: Blackwood, 1977.

Aurousseau, Marcel. 'The Identity of Voss', *Meanjin* 17:1 (1958), 85–7.

——. *The Letters of F.W. Ludwig Leichhardt*. Cambridge: Cambridge University Press, 1968.

Bachelard, Gaston. *The Poetics of Space*, transl. Maria Jolas. Boston: Beacon Press, 1969.

Ballyn, Susan, D. MacDermott, and K. Firth (eds). *Australia's Changing Landscapes*. Proceedings of the Second EASA Conference (October, 1993). Barcelona: Universitat de Barcelona, 1995.

Bardon, Geoffrey. *Aboriginal Art of the Western Desert.* Adelaide: Rigby, 1979.
———. *Papunya Tula: Art of the Western Desert.* Ringwood, Vic.: McPhee Gribble/Penguin, 1991.
Bates, Daisy. *The Passing of the Aborigines: A Lifetime Spent Among the Natives of Australia* [1938]. 2nd edn. Melbourne: Heinemann and London: John Murray, 1966.
Beadell, Len. *Too Long in the Bush* [1965]. Adelaide: Rigby, 1985.
Beale, Edgar. *Sturt, the Chipped Idol: A Study of Charles Sturt, Explorer.* Sydney: Sydney University Press, 1979.
Bean, C.E.W. *On the Wool Track* [1910]. Sydney: Angus & Robertson, 1963.
———. *The Dreadnought of the Darling.* London: Rivers, 1911.
Beckler, Hermann. *A Journey to Cooper's Creek,* transl. Stephen Jeffries and Michael Kertesz, ed. Stephen Jeffries. Melbourne: Melbourne University Press & State Library of Victoria, 1993.
Bell, Pamela. 'Jon Molvig', *Art and Australia* 8:2 (1970), 122.
Benko, Nancy. *Art and Artists of South Australia.* Adelaide: Hyde Park Publishers, 1969.
———. *The Art of David Boyd.* Adelaide: Lidums, 1973.
Bennett, Bruce. 'Concepts of "the West" in Canadian and Australian Literary Studies', *Westerly* 29:2 (1984), 75–84.
Bergin, Tom. *In the Steps of Burke & Wills.* Sydney: Griffin Press Ltd/ABC, 1981.
Berndt, Catherine and Ronald. 'Aboriginal Australia: Literature in an Oral Tradition' in A. Paolucci (ed.), *Review of National Literatures,* pp. 39–63. New York: Griffon House Publications, 1982, vol. II.
Berndt, Ronald M. 'Territoriality and the Problem of Demarcating Socio-cultural Space' in Nicolas Peterson (ed.), *Tribes and Boundaries in Australia.* Canberra: Australian Institute of Aboriginal Studies, Humanities Press, 1976.
Berndt, Ronald M. and Catherine H. *The Speaking Land: Myth and Story in Aboriginal Australia.* Ringwood, Vic.: Penguin Books, 1989.
Berry, Francis. 'Eyre Remembers: An Extract', in J. Daalder and M. Fryar (eds), *Aspects of Australian Culture,* pp. 15–20. Adelaide: Abel Tasman Press, 1982.
Beston, John B. 'An Interview with Randolph Stow', *World Literature Written in English* 14 (April 1975), 221–30.
Bird, Delys. 'Women in the Wilderness: Gender, Landscape and Eliza Brown's Letters and Journal', *Westerly* 36:4 (1991), 33–8.
Birkett, Dea. *Spinsters Abroad: Victorian Lady Explorers.* Oxford: Blackwell, 1989.
Blackburn, Julia. *Daisy Bates in the Desert.* London: Secker & Warburg, 1994.
Blackman, Barbara. 'The Antipodean Affair', *Art and Australia* 5:4 (1968), 607–16.
Blainey, Geoffrey. *Triumph of the Nomads: A History of Ancient Australia* [1975]. Sydney: Macmillan, 1994.
Blight, John. 'Leichhardt as Voss', *Literature in Northern Queensland* 6:3 (1978), 31–2.
Bodi, Leslie. 'Antipodean Inversion and Australian Reality: On the Image of Australia in German Literature', in W. Veit (ed.), *Captain James Cook: Image and Impact,* vol. II, pp. 76–94. Melbourne: Hawthorn Press, 1972.
Bohls, Elizabeth A. *Women Travel Writers and the Language of Aesthetics, 1716–1818.* Cambridge: Cambridge University Press, 1995.
Bolton, A.T. (ed.). *Walkabout's Australia: An Anthology of Articles and Photographs from Walkabout Magazine.* Sydney: Ure Smith, 1964.
Bolton, G. 'The Historian as Artist and Interpreter of the Environment' in G. Seddon and M. Davis (eds), *Man and Landscape in Australia: Towards an Ecological Vision,* pp. 113–24. Canberra: Australian Government Publishing Service, 1976.
Bonyhady, Tim. *Images in Opposition: Australian Landscape Painting 1801–1890* [1985]. Melbourne: Oxford University Press, 1991.
———. *Burke and Wills: From Melbourne to Myth.* Sydney: David Ell Press, 1991.
Bonython, C. Warren. *Walking the Flinders Ranges.* Adelaide: Rigby, 1971.
———. *Walking the Simpson Desert.* Adelaide: Rigby, 1980.

Borlase, Nancy. 'The Lost Antipodean: Jon Molvig', *Quadrant* 28:6 (1984), 82–3.

Bowden, K.M. *Samuel Thomas Gill, Artist*. Maryborough, Victoria: Hedges & Bell, 1971.

Boyd, David. *Retrospective 1957–1982*. Sydney: Wagner Art Gallery, 1983.

Brack, John. *Four Contemporary Australian Landscape Painters*. Melbourne: Oxford University Press, 1968.

Brady, Edwin J. *Australia Unlimited*, vol. II. Melbourne: George Robertson, 1918.

Brady, Veronica. 'The Novelist and the New World: Patrick White's *Voss*', *Texas Studies in Literature and Language* 21:2 (1979), 169–85.

Branagan, David, and Elaine Lim. 'J.W. Gregory, Traveller in the Dead Heart', *Historical Records of Australian Science* 6:1 (1984), 71–84.

Brantlinger, Patrick. 'Victorians and Africans: The Genealogy of the Myth of the Dark Continent', *Critical Inquiry* 12:1 (1985), 166–203.

——. *Rule of Darkness: British Literature and Imperialism, 1830–1914*. Ithaca and London: Cornell University Press, 1988.

Brauer, Fay and Candice Bruce (eds). *Australian Journal of Art: Colonizing the Country* 12, (1994–95). Special issue in memoriam: Ian Burn.

Breeden, Stanley. *Uluru: Looking After Uluru–Kata Tjuta – The Anangu Way*. Sydney: Simon & Schuster, 1994.

Brock, Daniel George. *To the Desert with Sturt: A Diary of the 1844 Expedition*, ed. K. Peake-Jones. Adelaide: Royal Geographical Society of Australasia, South Australian Branch, 1988.

Brown, Cavan. 'The Language of the Landscape', *Faith and Freedom* 1:2 (1992), 30–35.

——. *Pilgrim Through This Barren Land*. Sydney: Albatross Books, 1991.

Bruce, Candice. 'A Landscape of Longing', *Australian Journal of Art*, 12 (1994–95).

Brydon, Diana. 'Landscape and Authenticity: The Development of National Literatures in Canada and Australia', *Dalhousie Review* 61:2 (1987), 2778–90.

——. 'The Myths that Write Us: Decolonising the Mind', *Commonwealth* 10:1 (1987), 1–14.

Bunce, Daniel. *Travels with Dr Leichhardt* [1859]. Melbourne: Oxford University Press, 1979.

Bunkse, Edmunds V. 'Humboldt and an Aesthetic Tradition in Geography', *The Geographical Review* 71:2 (1981), 127–46.

Burn, Ian. 'Beating About the Bush: The Landscapes of the Heidelberg School', in A. Bradley and T. Smith (eds), *Australian Art and Architecture: Essays Presented to Bernard Smith*, pp. 83–98. Melbourne: Oxford University Press, 1980.

——. *National Life and Landscapes: Australian Painting 1900–1940*. Sydney: Bay Books, 1990.

Burrows, J.F. '"Voss" and the Explorers', *AUMLA* 26 (November 1966), 234–40.

Campbell, David. 'Strzelecki', in *Collected Poems*, ed. L. Kramer, p. 199. Sydney: Angus & Robertson, 1989.

Campbell, Robert. 'Sir Hans Heysen', *Art and Australia* 6:4 (1969), 290–96.

Cantrell, Leon (ed.). *The 1890s: Stories, Verses, and Essays* [1977]. St Lucia, Qld: University of Queensland Press, 1991.

Carnegie, David W. *Spinifex and Sand: A Narrative of Five Years' Pioneering and Exploration in Western Australia*. London: Arthur Pearson, 1898.

Carr, D.J. (ed.). *Sydney Parkinson, Artist of Cook's Endeavour Voyage*. Canberra: British Museum [Natural History], 1983.

Carroll, Alison. *The Centre: Works on Paper by Contemporary Australian Artists*. Adelaide: Art Gallery of South Australia, 1984.

Carter, David. 'Modernity and Belatedness in Australian Cultural Discourse', *Southerly* 54:4 (1994–95), 6–18.

Carter, Paul. 'Reassessing Russell Drysdale', *Art and Australia* 25:1 (1987), 58–64.

——. *The Road to Botany Bay: An Essay in Spatial History*. London and Boston: Faber & Faber, 1987.

——. *Living in a New Country*. London: Faber, 1992.

Caruana, Wally. *Windows on the Dreaming: Aboriginal Paintings in the Australian National Gallery*. Sydney: Australian National Gallery & Ellsyd Press, 1989.

——. *Aboriginal Art*. London and New York: Thames & Hudson, 1993.

Catalano, Gary. 'A Passionate Nearness: The Art of John Olsen, John Wolseley and Marion Hardman', *Quadrant* 26 (July 1982), 49–55.

——. 'Some Versions of Identity: Russell Drysdale, Jon Molvig, Joy Hester', *Meanjin* 43:3 (1984), 429–40.

——. 'The Source of Things: An Interview with John Wolseley', *Art Monthly Australia* 76 (December 1994), 18–21.

Charlesworth, Max. '2000 A.D.: *Terra Australis* and the Holy Spirit' in Helen Daniel (ed.), *Millennium: Time-Pieces by Australian Writers*. Ringwood, Vic.: Penguin Books, 1991.

Charlesworth, Max, Howard Morphy, Diane Bell, and Kenneth Maddock (eds). *Religion in Aboriginal Australia: An Anthology* [1984]. St Lucia, Qld: University of Queensland Press, 1992.

Chatwin, Bruce. *The Songlines* [1987]. London: Jonathan Cape, 1988.

Chauvel, Charles and Elsa. *Walkabout*. London: W.H. Allen, 1959.

Chisholm, Alec H. *Strange New World: The Adventures of John Gilbert and Ludwig Leichhardt*. Sydney: Angus & Robertson, 1941.

Christensen, Allan Conrad. *Edward Bulwer Lytton: The Fiction of New Regions*. Athens, Georgia: University of Georgia Press, 1976.

Churcher, Betty. *Molvig: The Lost Antipodean*. Ringwood, Vic.: Allen Lane/Penguin Books, 1984.

Clark, Jane. *Sidney Nolan: Landscapes and Legends. A Retrospective Exhibition: 1937–1987*. Melbourne: National Gallery of Victoria, 1987.

Clark, Kenneth, Colin MacInnes, and Bryan Robertson. *Sidney Nolan*. London: Thames & Hudson, 1961.

Clark, Manning. 'Ludwig Leichhardt's Letters', *Meanjin* 27:4 (1968), 404–8.

——. 'The Quest for an Australian Identity' in *Occasional Writings and Speeches* [1979]. Melbourne: Fontana, 1980.

——. 'Heroes' in S.R. Graubard (ed.), *Australia: The Daedalus Symposium*, pp. 57–84. Sydney: Angus & Robertson, 1985.

Clarke, Marcus. Preface to *Poems of the Late Adam Lindsay Gordon* [1887]. London: Samuel Mullen, 1887.

Clarke, W.B. 'Leichhardt and the Desert', *Sydney Morning Herald* (20 October, 1858), 5.

——. 'On the Search for Leichhardt, and the Australian Desert', *Proceedings of the Royal Geographical Society of London* 3:1–6 (1858–9), 87–91.

Clifford, Jamey. 'Travelling Cultures' in L. Grossberg, C. Nelson, and P.A. Treichler (eds), *Cultural Studies*, pp. 96–116. New York: Routledge, 1992.

Clune, Frank. *Dig: The Burke and Wills Saga* [1937]. Sydney: Angus & Robertson 1991.

——. 'With O'Hara Burke to the Gulf: A Brief Outline of the First Australian Transcontinental Crossing', *Walkabout* 4:5 (1938), 13–19.

——. 'The Man Who Found Leichhardt', in B. Wannan (ed.), *A Treasury of Australian Frontier Tales*, pp. 68–82. Melbourne: Lansdowne Press, 1961.

Clunies-Ross, Bruce. 'The Art of Randolph Stow', *Meridian* 6:1 (May 1987), 47–55.

Collis, Brad. *The Soul Stone*. Rydalmere, NSW: Hodder & Stoughton, 1993.

Conrad, Joseph. *Heart of Darkness* [1902]. Harmondsworth: Penguin Books, 1973.

Cook, Kenneth. *Wake in Fright*. London: Michael Joseph, 1961.

Corkhill, Alan. *Antipodean Encounters: Australia and the German Literary Imagination, 1754–1918*. Berne: Peter Lang, 1990.

Cosgrove, Denis and Stephen Daniels (eds). *The Iconography of Landscape: Essays on the Symbolic Representation, Design and Use of Past Environments*. Cambridge: Cambridge University Press, 1988.

Cotton, Catherine Drummond. *Ludwig Leichhardt and the Great South Land*. Sydney: Angus & Robertson, 1938.

Cowan, Peter. 'E.L. Grant Watson and Western Australia: A Concern for Landscape', *Westerly* 25:1 (1980), 39–58.

——. 'Gold and the Novel', *Westerly* 33:2 (1988), 31–126.

Crandell, Gina. *Nature Pictorialized: 'The View' in Landscape History*. Baltimore and London: Johns Hopkins University Press, 1992.

Crawford, R.M. 'Australian National Character: Myth and Reality', *Journal of World History* 2:3 (1955), 704–27.

Crocker, A. (ed.). *Papunya: Aboriginal Paintings from the Central Australian Desert*. Sydney: Aboriginal Artists' Agency & Papunya Tula Artists, 1983.

Crumlin, R. and A. Knights (eds). *Aboriginal Art and Spirituality*. Melbourne: Dove, 1991.

Cumpston, J.H.L. *The Inland Sea and the Great River: The Story of Australian Exploration*. Sydney: Angus & Robertson, 1965.

——. *Augustus Gregory and the Inland Sea*. Canberra: Roebuck Press, 1972.

Cunningham, Stuart. *Featuring Australia: the Cinema of Charles Chauvel*. Sydney: Allen & Unwin, 1991.

Davidson, J. 'Tasmanian Gothic', *Meanjin* 48:2 (1989), 307–32.

Davidson, Robyn. 'Alone Across the Outback', *National Geographic* 153:5 (May 1978), 581–611.

——. *Tracks* [1980]. St Albans, Herts.: Granada, 1983.

Davis, Jack. *Black Life: Poems*. St Lucia, Qld: University of Queensland Press, 1992.

Dawe, W. Carlton. *The Golden Lake, or The Marvellous History of a Journey through the Great, Lone Land of Australia*. London: A.P. Marsden, 1894.

de Bray, Lys. *The Art of Botanical Ilustration: The Classic Illustrators and their Achievements from 1550 to 1900*. London: The Wellfleet Press, 1989.

Denholm, David. *The Colonial Australians* [1979]. Ringwood, Vic.: Penguin Books, 1980.

Devaney, John. 'The Lost Explorers', in *Earth Kindred*, pp. 63–5. Melbourne: Frank Wilmot; Coles Library, 1931.

Dixon, Robert. *The Course of Empire: Neo-Classical Culture in New South Wales: 1788–1860*. Melbourne: Oxford University Press, 1986.

——. '"Filling up this Emptiness": Neoclassicism and Colonial Discourse', *Bulletin of the Centre of Tasmanian Historical Studies* 3:2 (1991–92), 11–21.

——. *Writing the Colonial Adventure: Race, Gender and Nation in Anglo–Australian Popular Fiction, 1875–1914*. Cambridge: Cambridge University Press, 1995.

Dixon, R.M.W. and Martin Duwell (eds). *The Honey Ant Men's Love Song and Other Aboriginal Song Poems*. St Lucia, Qld: University of Queensland Press, 1990.

Dixson, Miriam. *The Real Matilda*. Ringwood, Vic.: Penguin Books, 1987.

Dodd, Terri. 'John Coburn: A Man for All Seasons', *Australian Artist* 9:3 (September 1992), 10–16.

Donaldson, Ian (ed.). *Australia and the European Imagination*. Canberra: Humanities Research Centre, ANU, 1982.

Donaldson, Ian and Tamsin Donaldson (eds). *Seeing the First Australians*. Sydney: Allen & Unwin, 1985.

Donovan, P. 'The Exploration Myth: Exploration in the Northern Territory until the Second World War', *Proceedings of the Royal Geographical Society of Australasia* (SA Branch) 82 (1982), 34–47.

Drewe, Robert. *The Drowner*. Sydney: Macmillan, 1996.

Driscoll, Michael and Brett Whiteley. *Native Rose*. Cammeray, NSW: Richard Griffin, 1986.

Dunae, Patrick A. 'Boys' Literature and the Idea of Empire, 1870–1914', *Victorian Studies* 24 (1980), 105–21.

Dutton, Geoffrey. *Russell Drysdale*. Sydney: Angus & Robertson, 1964.

——. 'Sidney Nolan's Burke and Wills Series', *Art and Australia* 5:2 (1967), 455–9.

——. *Australia's Last Explorer: Ernest Giles*. London: Faber & Faber, 1970.

——. *S.T. Gill's Australia*. Melbourne: Macmillan, 1981.

Eade, J.C. (ed.). *Projecting the Landscape*. Canberra: ANU Humanities Research Centre, 1987.

Eaden, P.R. and F.H. Mares (eds). *Mapped But Not Known: The Australian Landscape of the Imagination; Essays and Poems Presented to Brian Elliott, 1985*. Netley, SA: Wakefield Press, 1986.

Eagle, Mary. *Australian Modern Painting Between the Wars, 1914–1939*. Sydney: Bay Books, 1989.

Eagle, Mary and John Jones. *A Story of Australian Painting*. Sydney: Macmillan, 1994.

Eden, C.H. *Australia's Heroes: A Slight Sketch of the Most Prominent Amongst the Band of Gallant Men*. London: Society for Promoting Christian Knowledge, 1882.

Edmonds, Neale. 'Hermannsburg Mission: The Early Years. Aboriginality, Christianity, Identity and the Politics of History about Aborigines'. Unpublished honours thesis, University of New South Wales, 1991.

Eisler, William and Bernard Smith (eds). *Terra Australis: The Furthest Shore*. Sydney: Beaver Press, 1988.

E.K.S. [A.K. Sylvester]. 'Stanzas' in *Lectures Delivered by Dr. Ludwig Leichhardt, at the Sydney School of Arts*. Sydney: W. Baker, 1846.

Eldershaw, M. Barnard. 'The Man Who Knew the Truth about Leichhardt', *Sydney Mail* (19 January, 1938).

Eliade, Mircea. *The Myth of the Eternal Return* (Bollingen series XLVI). New York: Pantheon Books, 1954.

——. 'Sacred Space and Making the World Sacred', in *The Sacred and the Profane*, pp. 20–65. New York: Harper Torchbooks, 1961.

Elkin, A.P. 'Grey's Northern Kimberley Cave Paintings Re-Found', *Oceania* 19 (1948–49), 1–15.

Elliott, Brian. 'An R.H. Horne Poem on Burke and Wills', *Australian Literary Studies* 1 (December 1963), 126–33.

——. (ed.). *The Jindyworobaks*. St Lucia, Qld: University of Queensland Press, 1979.

Ericksen, Ray. 'Conflict in Vision: Ernest Giles, Explorer and Traveller', *Proceedings of the Royal Geographical Society of Australasia* (SA Branch) 45 (1974), 37–48.

——. *Ernest Giles: Explorer and Traveller, 1835–1897*. Melbourne: Heinemann, 1978.

Etherington, Norman. 'Rider Haggard's Imperial Romances', *Meanjin* 36:2 (1977), 189–99.

Excell, Patricia. ' "Eyre All Alone": Francis Webb as Mythmaker', *Australian Literary Studies* 10 (1981), 101–5.

——. *Dancings of the Sound: A Study of Francis Webb's 'Eyre All Alone'*. (Occasional Paper No. 13, Canberra: English Department, Australian Defence Force Academy, 1989.)

Eyre, Edward John. *Journals of Expeditions of Discovery into Central Australia and Overland from Adelaide to King George's Sound, in the Years 1840–1*, 2 vols. London: T & W. Boone, 1845.

——. *Autobiographical Narrative of Residence and Exploration in Australia, 1832–1839*, ed. J. Waterhouse. London: Caliban Books, 1984.

Farwell, George. *Land of Mirage* [1950]. Adelaide: Rigby, 1960.

Favenc, Ernest. 'Dead in the Bush', *Australian Sketcher* (30 September 1876) republished in Richard D. Jordan and Peter Pierce (eds), *The Poet's Discovery: Nineteenth-Century Australia in Verse*, pp. 195–6. Carlton, Vic.: Melbourne University Press, 1990.

——. 'The Voice of the Desert', *The Cosmos Magazine* (February 1895), 317.

——. *The Secret of the Australian Desert*. London, Glasgow and Dublin: Blackie & Sons, 1896.

——. *Voices of the Desert*. London: Elliot Stock, 1905.

——. 'Into the Stony Desert', in *A Treasury of Australian Frontier Tales*, ed. B. Wannan, pp. 51–8. Melbourne: Lansdowne Press, 1961.

Ferguson, Lee. 'Land and Identity: John Wolseley and Victor Majzner', *Artlink* 15:1 (1995), 40–45.

Finlayson, H.H. *The Red Centre: Man and Beast in the Heart of Australia*. Sydney: Angus & Robertson, 1935.

Finnis, J.L. (ed.), 'Dr. John Harris Browne's Journal of the Sturt Expedition, 1844–1845', *South Australiana* 5:1 (1966), 23–54.

Fitzpatrick, Kathleen (ed.). *Australian Explorers: A Selection from their Writings with an Introduction*. London: Oxford University Press, 1958.

——. 'The Burke and Wills Expedition and the Royal Society of Victoria', *Historical Studies of Australia and New Zealand*, 10:4 (1963), 470–78.

——. 'Ludwig Leichhardt', *The Victorian Historical Magazine* 40:4 (1969), 190–203.

Flynn, Frank. *The Living Heart*. Sydney: F.P. Leonard, 1964.

Forrest, John. *Explorations in Australia*, 3 vols. London: Sampson Low, 1875.

Foucault, Michel. *Power/Knowledge: Selected Interviews and Other Writings 1972–1977*, ed. Colin Gordon. New York: Pantheon, 1980.

Fox, Lady Mary. *Account of an Expedition to the Interior of New Holland*. London: Richard Bentley, 1837.

Frazer, J.G. 'Observations on Central Australian Totemism', *Journal of the Anthropological Institute* 28 (1899), 281–6.

Friedrich, Werner P. (ed.). *Australia in Western Imaginative Prose Writings 1600–1960: An Anthology and a History of Literature*. Chapel Hill: The University of North Carolina Press, 1967.

Frome, E.C. 'Report of the Country to the Eastward of Flinders Range, South Australia', Communicated by Stanley, *Journal of the Royal Geographical Society of Australasia* (SA Branch) 14 (1844), pp. 282–7.

Frost, Alan. 'On Finding "Australia": Mirages, Mythic Images, Historical Circumstances', *Australian Literary Studies* 12:4 (1986), 482–98.

Frost, Cheryl. *The Last Explorer: The Life and Work of Ernest Favenc*. Townsville: James Cook University Press, 1983.

Fuller, Peter. *The Australian Scapegoat: Towards an Antipodean Aesthetic*. Perth: University of Western Australia Press, 1986.

Furphy, Joseph. *Such is Life*. Sydney: Angus & Robertson, 1945.

Garebian, Keith. 'The Desert and the Garden: The Theme of Completeness in *Voss*', *Modern Fiction Studies* 22:4 (1976–77), 557–69.

Gates, Merryn. *Jörg Schmeisser: A Survey of Works 1964–1995*. Canberra: ANU, Canberra School of Art, 1995.

Gibson, Ross. *The Diminishing Paradise: Changing Literary Perceptions of Australia*. Sydney: Angus & Robertson, 1984.

——. 'The Middle Distance', *Art-Network* 19/20 (Winter/Spring, 1986), 29–35.

——. *South of the West: Postcolonialism and the Narrative Construction of Australia*. Bloomington: Indiana University Press, 1992.

Gilbert, Alan. 'The State and Nature in Australia', *Australian Cultural History* 1 (1981), 9–28.

Gilchrist, Maureen. 'Sidney Nolan: The Lanyon Paintings' in M. Gilchrist (ed.), *Nolan at Lanyon*. Canberra: Australian Government Publishing Service, 1976.

Giles, Ernest. *Australia Twice Traversed: The Romance of Exploration; A Narrative Compiled from the Journals of Five Exploring Expeditions Into and Through Central South Australia and Western Australia; From 1872 to 1876*, 2 vols. London: Sampson Low, Marston, Searle & Rivington, 1889.

Gleeson, James. 'Painting in Australia since 1945', *Art and Australia* 1:1 (May 1963), 3–19, 48.

——. *Modern Painters 1931–1970*. Dee Why, NSW: Lansdowne Press, 1971.

Gordon, Adam Lindsay. *The Poetical Works*. London, Melbourne, Toronto: Ward Lock & Co., 1913.

Gosse, W.C. *W.C. Gosse's Explorations: Report and Diary of Mr W.C. Gosse's Central and Western Australian Exploring Expedition 1873*. Adelaide: Government Printer, 1874.

Grandison, Ralph. 'The Relocation of Fifteen Sites Painted by S.T. Gill whilst Accompanying the Horrocks Expedition of 1846', *Proceedings of the Royal Geographical Society of Australasia* (SA Branch) 83 (1983), 12–21.

Green, Dorothy. 'The Daimon and the Fringe-Dweller: The Novels of Grant Watson', *Meanjin* 30 (1971), 277–93.

—— (ed.). *Descent of Spirit: Writings of E.L. Grant Watson*. Sydney: Primavera Press, 1990.

Green, Evan. *Alice to Nowhere*. Sydney: James Fraser, 1984.

Green, Martin. *Dreams of Adventure, Deeds of Empire*. New York: Basic Books, 1979.

329

Greenblatt, Stephen. *Marvelous Possessions: The Wonder of the New World*. Chicago: University of Chicago Press, 1991.

Gregory, Augustus Charles, and Francis Thomas Gregory. *Journals of Australian Explorations*. Brisbane: J.C. Beal, 1884.

Gregory, Derek. *Geographical Imaginations*. Cambridge MA and Oxford: Blackwell, 1994.

Gregory, J.W. *The Dead Heart of Australia: A Journey Around Lake Eyre in the Summer of 1901–1902, With Some Account of the Lake Eyre Basin and the Flowing Wells of Central Australia*. London: John Murray, 1906.

Grey, George. *Journals of Two Expeditions of Discovery in North-West and Western Australia during the Years 1837, 38 and 39*, 2 vols. London: T. & W. Boone, 1841.

Griffith, Michael. 'Francis Webb's Challenge to Mid-Century Mythmaking: The Case of Ludwig Leichhardt', *Australian Literary Studies* 10 (1982), 448–60.

——. *God's Fool: The Life and Poetry of Francis Webb*. Sydney: Angus & Robertson, 1991.

Griffiths, Gareth. 'Mixed Up Messages Down Under: The Marlo Morgan "Hoax" – A Textual Travesty of Aboriginal Culture', *Ulitarra* 9 (1996), 76–85.

Griffiths, Tom. *Hunters and Collectors: The Antiquarian Imagination in Australia*. Cambridge: Cambridge University Press, 1996.

Grishin, Sasha. 'S. T. Gill: Defining a Landscape', *Voices* (Canberra) 2:4 (1992–93), 5–19.

Groom, Arthur. *I Saw a Strange Land: Journeys in Central Australia*. Sydney: Angus & Robertson, 1950.

Gzell, Sylvia. 'Themes and Imagery in *Voss* and *Riders in the Chariot*', *Australian Literary Studies* 1:3 (1964), 180–95.

Haggard, Henry Rider. 'Henry Rider Haggard', *African Review*, 9 (June 1894), 762.

Halloran, Henry. 'Leichhardt', *Empire* (28 April 1853).

Hancock, W.K. *Australia*. London: Ernest Benn, 1930.

Hansson, Karin. 'The Terrible Nostalgia of the Desert Landscapes: Reflections on Patrick White's Australia from a European Point of View', in M. Jurak (ed.), *Australian Papers: Yugoslavia, Europe and Australia*, pp. 255–62. Ljubljana: ZUSGP-TOZD, 1983.

Hardy, Jane, J.V.S. Megaw, and M. Ruth Megaw. *The Heritage of Namatjira*. Port Melbourne, Vic.: Heinemann, 1992.

Harley, J. Brian. 'Maps, Knowledge and Power' in *The Iconography of Landscape: Essays on the Symbolic Representation, Design and Use of Past Environments*, ed. Denis Cosgrove and Stephen Daniels, pp. 277–312. Cambridge: Cambridge University Press, 1988.

——. 'Historical Geography and Cartographic Illusion', *Journal of Historical Geography* 15 (1989), 80–91.

Harney, W.E. ('Bill'). 'West of Alice', in Leonie Kramer (ed.), *My Country: Australian Poetry and Short Stories, Two Hundred Years*, vol. II, pp. 186–7. Sydney: Ure Smith, 1992.

Harris, Max. 'Sturt at Depot Glen' in Geoffrey Dutton and Max Harris (eds), *Ten Years of Australian Art and Letters: The Vital Decade*, pp. 41–2. Melbourne: Sun Books, 1968.

Harrison, Keith. 'Leichhardt in the Desert' in *Points in a Journey and other Poems*, pp. 29–30. London: Macmillan, 1966.

Hart-Smith, William. 'Joshua, Mahomet' in W. Murdoch and A. Mulgan (eds), *A Book of Australian and New Zealand Verse*, p. 361. Melbourne: Oxford University Press, 1955.

Hassall, Anthony J. 'The Poetry of Randolph Stow', *Southerly* 42:3 (1982), 259–76.

——. *Strange Country: A Study of Randolph Stow* [1986]. St Lucia, Qld: University of Queensland Press, 1990.

Hawley, Janet. 'John Olsen: Journey to the Centre of the Art', *Sydney Morning Herald Good Weekend* (31 March 1990), 44–50.

——. *Encounters with Australian Artists*. St Lucia, Qld: University of Queensland Press, 1993.

Haynes, Peter. 'Mandy Martin: From the Sublime to the Industrial', *Art and Australia* 28:2 (1990), 220–27.

Haynes, Roslynn D. 'Shelter from the Holocaust: Thea Astley's *An Item from the Late News*', *Southerly* 48:2 (1988), 138–51.

——. *From Faust to Strangelove: Representations of the Scientist in Western Literature*. Baltimore and London: Johns Hopkins University Press, 1994.

330

——. 'Dreaming the Stars', *Interdisciplinary Science Reviews* 20:3 (1995), 187–97.

——. 'Ambivalent Eulogy: Catherine Martin's "The Explorers"', *Westerly* 41:2 (1996), 29–47.

Healy, J.J. 'Grant Watson and the Aborigine: A Tragic Voice in an Age of Optimism', *Australian Literary Studies* 7:1 (1975), 24–38.

——. *Literature and the Aborigine in Australia 1770–1975*. New York: St Martin's Press, 1978.

——. 'The Lemurian Nineties', *Australian Literary Studies* 8:3 (1978), 307–16.

Heathcote, G.E.A. and R.L. Heathcote. 'German Geographical Literature on Australia 1810–1940: A Preliminary Bibliography and Comment', *The Australian Geographer* 12:2 (1972), 154–76.

Heathcote, R.L. 'Drought in Australia: A Problem of Perception', *The Geographical Review* 59:2 (1969), 175–94.

——. 'The Artist as Geographer: Landscape Painting as a Source for Geographical Research', *Royal Geographical Society of Australasia* 73 (1971–72), 1–21.

——. 'Visions of Australia 1770–1970' in A. Rapoport (ed.), *Australia as Human Setting*, pp. 77–98. Sydney: Angus & Robertson, 1972.

——. 'Images of a Desert? Perceptions of Arid Australia', *Australian Geographical Studies* 25 (1987), 3–25.

Heseltine, H.P. 'Australian Image I: The Literary Heritage', *Meanjin* 21:1 (1962): 35–49.

——. 'The Very Gimbals of Unease: The Poetry of Francis Webb', *Meanjin* 26:3 (1967), 255–74.

——. *Acquainted with the Night: Studies in Classic Australian Fiction*. Townsville: Townsville Foundation for Australian Literary Studies, 1979.

Hewett, Dorothy. 'Silence, Exile and Cunning: the Poetry of Randolph Stow', *Westerly* 2 (June 1988), 59–66.

Heysen, Hans. 'Some Notes on Art', *Art in Australia* Series 3, no. 44 (June 1932), 18–20.

Hiatt, L.R. and Rhys Jones. 'Aboriginal Conceptions of the Workings of Nature', in R.W. Home (ed.), *Australian Science in the Making*, pp. 1–22. Cambridge: Cambridge University Press, 1988.

Hill, Barry. 'Travelling Towards the Other', *Overland* 130 (1993), 8–15.

——. *The Rock: Travelling to Uluru*. Sydney: Allen & Unwin, 1994.

Hill, Ernestine. *The Great Australian Loneliness* [1937]. Sydney: ETT Imprint, 1995.

——. *The Territory*. Sydney: Angus & Robertson, 1951.

Hogan, James Francis. *The Lost Explorer: An Australian Story*. London: Ward & Downey, 1890.

Hollon, W. Eugene. *The Great American Desert: Then and Now*. New York: Oxford University Press, 1966.

Hooton, Joy and Harry Heseltine. *Annals of Australian Literature*, 2nd edn. Melbourne: Oxford University Press, 1992.

Hope, A.D. 'Randolph Stow and the *Tourmaline* Affair' in W.S. Ramson (ed.), *The Australian Experience: Critical Essays on Australian Novels*, pp. 249–68. Canberra: Australian National University Press, 1974.

——. *Collected Poems* [1966]. Sydney: Angus & Robertson, 1984.

Horne, R.H. 'Australian Explorers', *Sydney Morning Herald*, 19 February 1863, republished in Brian Elliott, 'An R.H. Horne Poem on Burke and Wills', *Australian Literary Studies* 1 (December 1963), 126–33.

Horrocks, John Ainsworth. 'John Ainsworth Horrocks' Journal', *Proceedings of the Royal Geographical Society of Australasia* (SA Branch) 8 (1906), 36–47.

Hospital, Janette Turner. *Oyster*. Sydney: Random House, 1996.

Howarth, Patrick. *Play Up and Play the Game: The Heroes of Popular Culture*. London: Eyre Methuen, 1973.

Howells, Coral Ann. 'Disruptive Geographies: or, Mapping the Region of Woman in Contemporary Canadian Women Writing in English', *Journal of Commonwealth Literature* 31:1 (1996), 115–26.

Huggan, Graham. *Territorial Disputes: Maps and Mapping Strategies in Contemporary Canadian and Australian Fiction*. Toronto: University of Toronto Press, 1994.

331

Hughes, Robert. *The Art of Australia*. Ringwood, Vic.: Penguin Books, 1970.

Idriess, Ion. *Lasseter's Last Ride*. Sydney: Angus & Robertson, 1931.

Ikin, Van. 'Introduction: The History of Australian Science Fiction', in V. Ikin (ed.), *Australian Science Fiction*, pp. ix–xii. St Lucia, Qld: University of Queensland Press, 1982.

Indyk, Ivor. 'Pastoral and Priority: The Aboriginal in Australian Pastoral', *New Literary History* 24 (1993), 837–55.

Ingamells, Rex. 'Conditional Culture 1938' in J. Barnes (ed.), *The Writer in Australia: A Collection of Literary Documents 1856 to 1964*, pp. 245–65. Melbourne: Oxford University Press, 1969.

Ironside, Adelaide. 'The Death of Leichhardt', *Australasian* (10 January 1853).

Isaacs, Jennifer. *Aboriginality: Contemporary Aboriginal Paintings and Prints* [1989]. St Lucia, Qld: University of Queensland Press, 1992.

J.K.P. 'Revenge of Charterhouse', *Hermes* 39 (1933), 6–7.

Jackson, Rosemary. *Fantasy: The Literature of Subversion*. London & New York: Routledge, 1988.

Jacobs, Patricia. 'Stories from the Western Desert', *Westerly* 31:3 (1986), 61–79.

Jacobson, Howard. *In the Land of Oz*. Harmondsworth: Penguin Books, 1988.

Jameson, Fredric. *The Political Unconscious: Narrative as a Socially Symbolic Act*. New York: Cornell Univesity Press, 1981.

——. 'Postmodernism, or the Cultural Logic of Late Capitalism', *New Left Review* 146 (1984).

JanMohamed, Abdul R. 'The Economy of Manichean Allegory: The Function of Racial Differences in Colonialist Literature', *Critical Inquiry* 12:1 (1985), 59–87.

Jennings, F. *The Invasion of America. Indians, Colonialism, and the Cant of Conquest*. Williamsburg: Norton, 1976.

Johnston, Dorothy. *Maralinga, My Love*. Ringwood, Vic.: McPhee Gribble/Penguin, 1988.

Johnston, George. 'Gallipoli Paintings', *Art and Australia* 5 (1967), 466–7.

Jones, Dorothy. 'Matters of Geography and Countries of the Mind: *Voss* and *Badlands* Compared', *New Literatures Review* 23 (Summer South 1992), 73–84.

Joppien, Rüdiger. 'The Iconography of the Burke and Wills Expedition in Australian Art', in P. Quartermaine (ed.), *Readings in Australian Arts: Papers from 1976; Exeter Symposium*, pp. 49–61. Exeter: University of Exeter, 1978.

Jordan, Richard D. and Peter Pierce (eds). *The Poet's Discovery: Nineteenth-Century Australia in Verse*. Melbourne: Melbourne University Press, 1990.

Jurgensen, Manfred. 'The Inland Sea', *Poems from Double Shadows Counter Years*, in M. Jurgensen (ed.), *Queensland: Words and All*, p. 283. Brisbane: Phoenix-Outrider, 1993.

Keay, John. *Explorers Extraordinary*. London: John Murray and the British Broadcasting Corporation, 1985.

Kelly, Veronica. 'Explorers and Bushrangers in Nineteenth-century Australian Theatre', in K. Singh (ed.), *The Writer's Sense of Past: Essays on Southeast Asian and Australasian Literature*, pp. 119–32. Singapore: Singapore University Press, 1987.

Kemp, Geoff. 'The Presentation and Allegorical Function of the Explorer Figure in Webb's "Leichhardt in Theatre"', *Australian Literary Studies*, Working Papers III (1979), 17–26.

Kemp, Maud. 'An Interview with Clifton Pugh', *Australian Artist* 2:12 (1986), 16–19.

Kendall, Henry. 'The Fate of the Explorers Burke and Wills', *Empire* (9 December 1861).

——. *Leaves from Australian Forests: The Poetical Works of Henry Kendall* [1869]. Sydney: Lansdowne Press, 1995.

Keneally, Thomas. *Outback*. London: Hodder & Stoughton, 1983.

Kent, D.A. 'The Anzac Book and the Anzac Legend: C.E.W. Bean as Editor and Image-Maker', *Historical Studies* 21:84 (1985), 376–90.

Kimber, Richard G. 'Mosaics You Can Move', *Hemisphere* 21:1 (January, 1977), 2–7, 29–30.

——. *Friendly Country – Friendly People: Desert Lands, Desert Peoples, Desert Art*. Victor Harbor, SA: Ambrose Press, 1990.

——. 'Australian Rangelands in Contemporary Literature', *Rangelands Journal* 16:2 (1994), 311–20

Kingsley, Henry. 'Eyre, the South-Australian Explorer', *Macmillan's Magazine* 12 (May–October 1865), 501–63.

Kinsella, John. *Night Parrots*. Fremantle: Fremantle Arts Centre Press, 1989.

Klepac, Lou. *Russell Drysdale*. Sydney: Bay Books, 1983.

Knight, Stephen. *Continent of Mystery: A Thematic History of Australian Crime Fiction*. Melbourne: Melbourne University Press, 1997.

Knox-Shaw, Peter. *The Explorer in English Fiction*. London: Macmillan Press, 1987.

Kramer, Leonie. 'The Novels of Randolph Stow', *Southerly* 24 (1964), 78–91.

Lambert, Amy. *G.W. Lambert: Thirty Years of an Artist's Life*. Sydney: Society of Artists, 1938.

Langford, Ruby. *Don't Take Your Love to Town*. Ringwood, Vic.: Penguin Books, 1988.

Lansbury, Coral. *Arcady in Australia: The Evocation of Australia in Nineteenth-Century English Literature*. Melbourne: Melbourne University Press, 1970.

Larcombe, E.E. 'The Search for Dr. Leichhardt', *Journal and Proceedings of the Royal Australian Historical Society* 12 (1927), 167–86.

Lawson, Sylvia. *The Archibald Paradox*. Ringwood, Vic.: Allen Lane, 1983.

Layton, Robert. 'Relating to the Country in the Western Desert' in Eric Hirsch and Michael O'Hanlon (eds), *The Anthropology of Landscape: Perspectives on Place and Space*. Oxford: Clarendon, 1995, pp. 210–31.

Leer, Martin. '*Mal du pays*: Symbolic Geography in the Work of Randolph Stow', *Australian Literary Studies* 15:1 (1991), 3–25.

Leichhardt, F.W. Ludwig. *Journal of an Overland Expedition in Australia from Moreton Bay to Port Essington*. London: T. & W. Boone, 1847.

——. *Dr. Ludwig Leichhardt's Letters from Australia: March 23, 1842, to April 3, 1848*. Melbourne: Pan Publishers, n.d.

Leonard, Christopher. 'Art and Memory: John Olsen's Recent Paintings', *Art and Australia* 24:3 (1987), 369–75.

Lever, Susan. 'Aboriginal Subjectivities and Western Conventions: A Reading of *Coonardoo*', *Australian & New Zealand Studies in Canada* 10 (December 1993), 23–9.

Levi-Strauss, Claude. *Totemism*, transl. Rodney Needham. Harmondsworth: Penguin Books, 1973.

Lewin, F. Sesca. 'Australia's Heroes', *Abel Tasman and Other Poems*, pp. 30–33. Adelaide: Scrymgour & Sons, 1889.

Lewis, Reina. *Gendering Orientalism: Race, Femininity and Representation*. London: Routledge, 1996.

Lindsay, David. *Journal of the Elder Scientific Exploring Expedition, 1892*. Adelaide: C.E. Bristow, Government Printer, 1893.

Lindsay, Lionel. 'Heysen's Recent Watercolours', *Art in Australia* 3:24 (June 1928), 43.

Lines, William J. *Taming the Great South Land: A History of the Conquest of Nature in Australia*. Sydney: Allen & Unwin, 1991.

Lloyd, Genevieve. *The Man of Reason: 'Male' and 'Female' in Western Philosophy*. London: Methuen, 1984.

Long, J. (ed.). *Nomadism: John Wolseley. Twelve Years in Australia – Paintings and Drawings*. Melbourne: University of Melbourne, University Gallery, 1988.

Lovegood, John [E.L. Grant Watson]. *The Partners*. London: Victor Gollancz Ltd, 1933.

Lowe, Pat with Jimmy Pike. *Jilji: Life in the Great Sandy Desert*. Broome: Magabala Books, 1990.

Lowenthal, David. 'Perceiving the Australian Environment: A Summary and Commentary' in *Man and Landscape in Australia: Towards an Ecological Vision*, ed. G. Seddon and M. Davis, pp. 357–63. Canberra: Australian Government Publishing Service, 1976.

Lowenthal, David and Martyn J. Bowden (eds). *Geographies of the Mind: Essays in Historical Geography*. New York: Oxford University Press, 1976.

Loxley, Anne. 'A Sydney Artist: Tim Storrier', *Artlink* 14:3 (1994), 23–5.

Loyau, George E. 'Tales in Verse – no. 2: The Desert', in Richard D. Jordan and Peter

Pierce (eds), *The Poet's Discovery: Nineteenth Century Australian Verse*, pp. 373–5. Melbourne: Melbourne University Press, 1990.

Lundgren, Bruce. 'Sturt's Dreaming' in L. Wilson (ed.), *Journeys: A Collection of Poems*, p. 20. Melbourne: Monash University Press, 1990.

Lynn, Elwyn. *Sidney Nolan: Myth and Imagery*. Melbourne: Macmillan, 1967.

——. *Sidney Nolan's Ned Kelly*. Canberra: Australian National Gallery, 1985.

——. *The Art of Robert Juniper*. Seaforth, NSW: Craftsman House, 1986.

Lynn, Elwyn and Sidney Nolan. *Sidney Nolan – Australia*. Sydney and London: Bay Books, 1979.

Macainsh, Noel. *Clifton Pugh*. Melbourne: Georgian House, 1962.

——. 'Doctor Leichhardt on Board' in *Eight by Eight*, p. 63. Brisbane: Jacaranda Press, 1963.

——. *Nietzsche in Australia: A Literary Inquiry into a Nationalistic Ideology*. Townsville: James Cook University of North Queensland, 1975.

Macartney, Frederich T. 'Desert Claypan' in Leonie Kramer (ed.), *My Country: Australian Poetry and Short Stories*, vol. I, p. 580. Sydney: Ure Smith Press, 1992.

MacCormack, Carol, and Marilyn Strathern (eds). *Nature, Culture and Gender*. Cambridge: Cambridge University Press, 1980.

Macdonald, Alexander. *The Lost Explorers: A Story of the Trackless Desert*. London and Glasgow: Blackie & Sons, 1906.

Mackie, Alwynne. 'Painting the Australian Landscape: Hans Heysen', *Art International* 23 (Summer, 1979), 46–51.

Madigan, Cecil T. *Central Australia*. London: Oxford University Press, 1936.

——. *Crossing the Dead Heart* [1946]. Melbourne: Georgian House, 1948.

Madigan, Richard A. *The Australian Painters 1964–1966*. New York: The Corcoran Gallery of Art, 1966.

Marcus, Julie. 'The Journey Out to the Centre. The Cultural Appropriation of Ayers Rock', *Kunapipi* 10 (1988), 254–74.

Marshall, Jock and Russell Drysdale. *Journey Among Men*. London: Hodder & Stoughton, 1962.

Martin, Catherine. *The Explorers and Other Poems*. Melbourne: George Robertson, 1874.

——. *The Incredible Journey* [1923]. London: Pandora Press, 1987.

——. *The Silent Sea* (ed. Rosemary Foxton). Sydney: University of New South Wales Press, 1995.

Martin, Mandy. 'Diary from the Centre: Six Weeks in Alice Springs', *Art Monthly* 45 (November 1991), 13–15.

——. *Reconstructed Narrative: Strzelecki Desert. Homage to Ludwig Becker*. Melbourne: Christine Abrahams Gallery, 1992.

Martin, Mandy and Paul Sinclair. *Tracts: Back O'Bourke*. Canberra: ACT Government Printer, 1997.

Matthews, Brian. 'Australian Colonial Women and their Autobiographies', *Kunapipi* 7:2 (1985), 36–46.

Maver, Igor. 'Mapping the Unknown: Australian Mythical Landscape in Douglas Stewart's "Voyager Poems"' in S. Ballyn, D. MacDermott and K. Firth (eds), *Australia's Changing Landscapes*, pp. 139–44. Barcelona: University of Barcelona, 1995.

McAuley, James. *Selected Poems* [1963]. Sydney: Angus & Robertson, 1967.

McCaughey, Patrick. 'The Artist in Extremis: Arthur Boyd 1972–73', in Anthony Bradley and Terry Smith (eds), *Australian Art and Architecture: Essays Presented to Bernard Smith*, pp. 210–20. Melbourne: Oxford University Press, 1980.

McCubbin, Charles. 'Desert Diary', *Aluminium* 10 (December 1973), 2–10.

McCulloch, Alan. *Artists of the Australian Goldrush*. Melbourne: Lansdowne Press, 1976.

McCulloch, Susan. 'The Printmaker Propelled by Voyages', *Asian Art News* (November/December 1995), 49.

McCullough, Bianca. *Each Man's Wilderness: Reflections by Australian Artists*. Adelaide: Rigby, 1980.

334

McFarlane, Brian. *Words and Images: Australian Novels into Film.* Richmond, Victoria: Heinemann Publishers Australia, 1983.

McGrath, Ann. 'Travels to a Distant Past: The Mythology of the Outback', *Australian Cultural History* 10 (1991), 113–24.

McGrath, Sandra. 'A Remote Eden (John Olsen)', *Art and Australia* 14:2 (1976), 140–51.

McGrath, Sandra and John Olsen. *The Artist and the Desert.* Sydney: Bay Books, 1981.

McLaren, Glen. 'The Development of the Traditions of Scientific Research and Bushmanship in 19th Century Australia, with special reference to the contributions of Ludwig Leichhardt', 2 vols. Unpublished PhD thesis, Curtin University of Technology, 1994.

McLaren, Ian F. 'The Victorian Exploring Expedition and Relieving Expeditions, 1860–61: The Burke and Wills Tragedy', *Victorian Historical Magazine* 29:4 (1959), 211–53.

——. 'William John Wills, 1834–61', *Victorian Historical Magazine* 33:2 (1962), 337–50.

McLean, Ian. 'Dead Heart Black Heart: Aboriginalism and Australian Nationalism', private communication from unpublished PhD thesis.

——. 'White Aborigines: Cultural Imperatives of Australian Colonialism', *Third Text* 22 (Spring, 1993), 17–26.

Megaw, J.V.S. 'Western Desert Acrylic Painting: Artefact or Art?', *Art History* 5:2 (1982), 205–18.

Mellick, Ross (ed.). *Spirit + Place: Art in Australia 1861–1996.* Sydney: Museum of Contemporary Art, 1996.

Melman, Billie. *Women's Orients: English Women and the Middle East.* London: Macmillan, 1992.

Merleau-Ponty, Maurice. *The Phenomenology of Perception*, transl. Colin Smith. London: Routledge & Kegan Paul, 1962.

Millar, Ann. *'I see no end to travelling': Journals of Australian Explorers 1813–1876.* Sydney: Bay Books, 1986.

Minc, Salek. 'Robert Juniper', *Art and Australia* 16:4 (1979), 350–56.

Mitchell, Adrian. 'The Ambivalence of C.E.W. Bean', in Margaret Harris and Elizabeth Webby (eds), *Reconnoitres: Essays in Australian Literature in Honour of G.A. Wilkes*, pp. 103–14. Melbourne: Oxford University Press, 1992.

Mitchell, Thomas Livingstone. *Three Expeditions into the Interior of Eastern Australia, with Descriptions of the Recently Explored Region of Australia Felix, and the Present Colony of New South Wales*, 2 vols. London: T. & W. Boone, 1838.

Mitchell, W.J.T. (ed.). *Landscape and Power.* Chicago: University of Chicago Press, 1994.

Mollison, James. *A Singular Vision: The Art of Fred Williams.* Canberra: Australian National Gallery, 1989.

Mollison, James and Jan Minchin. *Albert Tucker: A Retrospective.* Melbourne: National Gallery of Victoria, 1990.

Montgomery, Jill. 'Australia – The French Discovery of 1983', *Art and Text* 12 & 13 (1983–1984), 3–15.

Moon, Karen. 'Perception and Appraisal of the South Australian Landscape 1836–1850', *Proceedings of the Royal Geographical Society of Australasia* (SA Branch) 70 (1969), 41–64.

Moore, William. *The Story of Australian Art*, 2 vols. Sydney: Angus & Robertson, 1934.

Moorehead, Alan. *Cooper's Creek.* London: Hamish Hamilton, 1963.

Moran, Albert. *Projecting Australia: Government Film Since 1945.* Sydney: Currency Press, 1991.

Morgan, Marlo. *Mutant Message Down Under: A Woman's Journey into Dreamtime Australia.* London: HarperCollins, 1994.

Morgan, Sally. *My Place.* Fremantle: Fremantle Arts Centre Press, 1987.

Morrell, Timothy. 'Antony Hamilton' in Mary Eagle (ed.), *Adelaide Biennial of Australian Art*, pp. 46–7. Adelaide: Art Gallery of South Australia, 1990.

Morrisby, Edwin. 'Jon Molvig: An Australian Painter', *Quadrant* 36 (7–8) (1992): 71–3.

Morton, S.R. and D.J. Mulvaney (eds). *Exploring Central Australia: Society, the Environment and the 1894 Horn Expedition.* Sydney: Surrey Beatty & Sons, 1996.

335

Mountford, Charles P. *Brown Men and Red Sand: Journeyings in Wild Australia* [1948]. Melbourne: Sun Books, 1967.

Mudie, Ian. *The Heroic Journey of John McDouall Stuart.* Sydney: Angus & Robertson, 1968.

——. 'On Reaching the Summit of Horrocks Pass' in *Selected Poems, 1934–1974*, p. 74. Melbourne: Nelson, 1976.

Mulvaney, D.J. *The Prehistory of Australia: Ancient People and Places.* London: Thames & Hudson, 1969.

—— (ed.). *The Humanities and the Australian Environment.* Canberra: Australian Academy of the Humanities, 1991.

Munn, Nancy D. 'Excluded Spaces: The Figure in the Australian Aboriginal Landscape', *Critical Inquiry* 22 (Spring, 1966), 446–65.

Murphy, Bernice. 'Nikolaus Lang' in *Adelaide Biennial of Australian Art*, ed. M. Eagle, pp. 56–7. Adelaide: Art Gallery of South Australia, 1990.

Murray, Les. *Collected Poems.* Melbourne: Heinemann, 1994.

Murray, Neil. *Sing For Me, Countryman.* Rydalmere, NSW: Hodder & Stoughton, 1993.

Murray, Scott. *The New Australian Cinema.* Melbourne: Nelson, 1980.

—— (ed.). *Back of Beyond: Discovering Australian Film and Television.* Sydney: Australian Film Commission and UCLA Film and Television Archive, 1988.

—— (ed.). *Australian Film 1978–1992: A Survey of Theatrical Features.* Melbourne: Oxford University Press, 1993.

Myers, David. *Bleeding Battlers from Ironbark: Australian Myths in Fiction and Film: 1890s–1980s.* Rockhampton: Capricornia Institute, 1987.

Newbolt, Henry. *The Book of the Long Trail.* London: Longmans Green, 1919.

Newland, B.C. 'Edward Charles Frome', *Proceedings of the Royal Geographical Society of Australasia* (SA Branch) 63 (1962), 52–69.

Nolan, Cynthia. *Outback.* London: Methuen & Co., 1962.

Novak, Barbara. *Nature and Culture: American Landscape and Painting 1825–1875.* London: Thames & Hudson, 1980.

Oakley, Barry. 'O'Hara 1861', *Southerly* 20 (1959), 147–56.

O'Brien, Philippa. *Robert Juniper.* Roseville, NSW: Craftsman House, 1992.

O'Connor, Mark. 'Interview in a Desert' [1984], reprinted in *Selected Poems*, p. 65. Sydney: Hale & Iremonger, 1986.

——. 'Aboriginal Literature Becomes a Force', *Kunapipi* 10 (1988), 246–53.

—— (ed.). *Two Centuries of Australian Poetry.* Melbourne: Oxford University Press, 1988.

Oldroyd, David. *Thinking About the Earth: A History of Ideas in Geology.* London: Athlone Press, 1996.

Ong, Walter J. 'Personalism and the Wilderness', *Kenyon Review* 21:1 (1959), 297–304.

Oxley, John. *Journals of Two Expeditions into the Interior of New South Wales 1817–1818.* London: John Murray, 1820.

Page, Geoff. 'Nullarbor, Hay to Balranald', *Quadrant* 38:5 (1994), 77.

Pascoe, Bruce. *Fox.* Ringwood, Vic.: McPhee Gribble/Penguin Books, 1988.

Paterson, A.B. ('Banjo'). 'The Explorers', *The Lone Hand* 7:69 (1913), 179.

——. 'The Lost Leichhardt' in *My Country: Australian Poetry and Short Stories*, ed. Leonie Kramer, vol. I, pp. 286–7. Sydney: Ure Smith Press, 1992.

Pearce, Barry. *Arthur Boyd Retrospective.* Sydney: Art Gallery of New South Wales, 1993.

Pearson, M.N. 'Pilgrims, Travellers, Tourists: The Meanings of Journeys', *Australian Cultural History* 10 (1991), 125–34.

Perry, G. (ed.). *Poetry Australia: Francis Webb (1925–1973).* Commemorative issue. No. 56 (September 1975). Sydney: South Head Press, 1975.

Petersson, Irmtraud. 'Leichhardt and Voss: The Changing Image of a German Explorer' in M. Jurgensen and A. Corkhill (eds), *The German Presence in Queensland, Over the Last 150 Years* (Proceedings of an International Symposium), pp. 313–25. Brisbane: University of Queensland, 1987.

——. 'New "Light" on *Voss*: The Significance of its Title', *World Literature Written in English* 28:2 (1988), 245–59.

336

——. *German Images in Australian Literature from the 1940s to the 1980s*. Frankfurt: Peter Lang, 1990.

Phillips, A.A. 'Australian Image (2): The Literary Heritage Re-Assessed', *Meanjin* 21:2 (1962), 172–80.

——. *The Australian Tradition: Studies in a Colonial Culture*. 2nd edn. Melbourne: Cheshire, 1966.

Pierce, Peter. 'Rider Haggard in Australia', *Meanjin* 36:2 (1977), 200–208.

Pike, Andrew and Ross Cooper. *Australian Film 1900–1977: A Guide to Feature Film Production*. Melbourne: Oxford University Press in association with the Australian Film Institute, 1981.

Pratt, Mary Louise. 'Scratches on the Face of the Country; or, What Mr. Barrow Saw in the Land of the Bushmen', *Critical Inquiry* 12:1 (1985), 138–62.

——. *Imperial Eyes: Travel Writing and Transculturation*. London and New York: Routledge, 1992.

Preston, Margaret. 'The Indigenous Art of Australia', *Art in Australia* 11 (3rd series, March 1925).

Price, A.G. 'The Mystery of Leichhardt: The South Australian Government Expedition of 1938', *Proceedings of the Royal Geographical Society of Australasia* (SA Branch) 39 (1938), 9–48.

Prichard, Katharine Susannah. *Coonardoo*. Sydney: Angus & Robertson, 1982.

Priessnitz, H. 'The "Vossification" of Ludwig Leichhardt' in *From Berlin to the Burdekin: The German Contribution to the Development of Australian Science, Exploration and the Arts*, ed. David Walker and Jürgen Tampke, pp. 196–217. Kensington, NSW: UNSW Press, 1991.

Quartermaine, Peter (ed.). *Readings in Australian Arts: Papers from the 1976 Exeter Symposium*. Exeter: University of Exeter Press, 1978.

——. ' "Speaking to the Eye": Painting, Photography and the Popular Illustrated Press in Australia, 1850–1900' in *Australian Art and Architecture: Essays Presented to Bernard Smith*, ed. A. Bradley and T. Smith, pp. 54–70. Melbourne: Oxford University Press, 1980.

Rabasa, Jose. 'Allegories of the Atlas' in *Europe and its Others*, ed. F. Barker, vol. II, pp. 1–16. Colchester: University of Essex Press, 1985.

Radford, Ron. 'Australia's Forgotten Painters: South Australian Colonial Painting 1836–1880; Part One 1836–1850', *Art and Australia* 24:4 (1987), 519–23.

——. 'Australia's Forgotten Painters: South Australian Colonial Painting 1836–1880; Part Two 1850–1880', *Art and Australia* 25:1 (1987), 92–103.

Ramson, William S. (ed.). *The Australian Experience: Critical Essays on Australian Novels*. Canberra: Australian National University Press, 1974.

Rapoport, Amos (ed.). *Australia as Human Setting*. Sydney: Angus & Robertson, 1972.

Ratcliffe, F. *Flying Fox and Drifting Sand: The Adventures of a Biologist in Australia*. London: Chatto & Windus, 1938.

Rattigan, Neil. *Images of Australia: 100 Films of the New Australian Cinema*. Dallas: Southern Methodist University Press, 1991.

Reed, Bill. *Burke's Company*. Melbourne: Heinemann, 1969.

Reid, Barrett. 'A Landscape of a Painter: the Sidney Nolan Retrospective Exhibition', *Art and Australia* 25:2 (Summer 1987), 179–81.

Relph, Edward. *Rational Landscapes and Humanistic Geography*. Totowa, NJ: Croom Helm; London/Barnes & Noble Books, 1981.

Roberts, Kevin. *Red Centre Journal*. Adelaide: Wakefield Press, 1992.

Roberts, Richard et al. 'Luminescence Dating of Rocks and Past Environments Using Mud-Wasp Nests in Northern Australia', *Nature* 387 (12 June 1997), 696–9.

Robinson, Roland. *Selected Poems*. Sydney: Angus & Robertson, 1989.

Roderick, Colin. 'Outline of Lectures on Patrick White's *Voss*', *Echos du Commonwealth* 3 (1976), 15–27.

——. 'New Light on Leichhardt', *Journal of the Royal Australian History Society* 72:3 (1987), 166–90.

——. *Leichhardt the Dauntless Explorer.* Sydney: Angus & Robertson, 1988.

——. 'The Education of an Explorer: Ludwig Leichhardt' in *From Berlin to the Burdekin: The German Contribution to the Development of Australian Science, Exploration and the Arts*, ed. David Walker and Jürgen Tampke, pp. 22–39. Kensington, NSW: UNSW Press, 1992.

Rose, Deborah Bird. 'Exploring an Aboriginal Land Ethic', *Meanjin* 47:3 (1988), 378–87.

Rose, Gillian. *Feminism and Geography: The Limits of Geographical Knowledge.* Cambridge: Polity Press, 1993.

Rose, Gillian and Miles Ogborn. 'Feminism and Historical Geography', *Journal of Historical Geography* 14 (1988), 405–9.

Rose, Margaret A. 'Alexander von Humboldt and Australian Art and Exploration' in I. Harstorf (ed.), *The German Experience of Australia, 1833–1938*, pp. 106–19. Adelaide: Australian Association of von Humboldt Fellows, 1988.

Ross, Jane. *The Myth of the Digger: The Australian Soldier in Two World Wars.* Sydney: Hale & Iremonger, 1985.

Rossiter, N. 'Narratives of Emergence: Landscape Photography in Late Nineteenth Century Western Australia', *Proceedings of the Association for the Study of Australian Literature* (1994), 20–27.

Ruhen, Olaf. *Naked Under Capricorn* [1958]. Sydney: Angus & Robertson, 1989.

Ryan, Judith. *Mythscapes: Aboriginal Art of the Desert.* Melbourne: National Gallery of Victoria, 1989.

——. *Images of Power: Aboriginal Art of the Kimberley.* Melbourne: National Gallery of Victoria, 1993.

Ryan, Simon. 'A Word with the Natives: Dialogic Encounters in Journals of Australian Exploration', *Australian and New Zealand Studies in Canada* 8 (1992), 71–84.

——. 'Exploring Aesthetics: The Picturesque Appropriation of Land in Journals of Australian Exploration', *Australian Literary Studies* 14:4 (1992), 282–93.

——. 'The Aborigines in Journals of Australian Exploration', *Ariel* 25:3 (1994), 95–112.

——. 'Discovering Myths: The Creation of the Explorer in Journals of Exploration', *Australian–Canadian Studies* 12:2 (1994), 1–13.

——. '"Like a Map at Our Feet": Visually Commanding the Land in Journals of Australian Exploration', *Southern Review* 27:2 (1994), 138–52.

——. 'Voyeurs in Space: The Gendered Scopic Regime of Exploration', *Southerly* 54:1 (1994), 36–49.

——. *The Cartographic Eye.* Cambridge: Cambridge University Press, 1996.

Said, Edward W. *Orientalism: Western Conceptions of the Orient* [1978]. Harmondsworth: Penguin Books, 1991.

——. *Culture and Imperialism.* London: Chatto & Windus, 1993.

Sandison, Alan. *The Wheel of Empire: A Study of the Imperial Idea in Some Late Nineteenth and Early Twentieth-Century Fiction.* London: Macmillan and New York: St Martin's Press, 1967.

Santry, John. 'Tributes: Clifton Pugh', *Art and Australia* 28:4 (1991), 471–508.

Schaffer, Kay. *Women and the Bush: Forces of Desire in the Australian Cultural Tradition* [1988]. Cambridge: Cambridge University Press, 1990.

Schama, Simon. *Landscape and Memory.* London: Fontana, 1996.

Scott, G. Firth. *The Last Lemurian: A Westralian Romance.* London: James Bowden, 1898.

Seddon, George. 'Eurocentrism and Australian Science: Some Examples', *Search* 12:12 (1981–2), 446–50.

——. 'The Nature of Nature', *Westerly* 36:4 (1991), 7–14.

——. 'Journeys Through Landscape', *Westerly* 36:4 (1991), 55–62.

——. *Landprints: Reflections on Place and Landscape.* Cambridge: Cambridge University Press, 1997.

Seddon, George and Mari Davis (eds). *Man and Landscape in Australia: Towards an Ecological Vision.* Canberra: Australian Government Publishing Service, 1976.

Sellick, Robert. 'Burke and Wills and the Colonial Hero: Three Poems', *Australian Literary Studies* 5 (1971), 180–89.
——. *The Epic Confrontation: Australian Exploration and the Centre, 1813–1900; A Literary Study*. Unpublished PhD thesis, University of Adelaide, 1973.
——. 'Francis Webb's "Sturt and the Vultures": A Note on Sources', *Australian Literary Studies* 6 (1974), 310–14.
——. 'The Explorer as Hero: Australian Exploration and the Literary Imagination', *Proceedings of the Royal Geographical Society of Australasia* (SA Branch), 78 (1977), 1–16.
——. 'The Cartography of Exile: Colonial Preoccupations in Recent Australian Fiction', in K. Singh (ed.), *The Writer's Sense of Past: Essays on Southeast Asian and Australasian Literature*, pp. 170–77. Singapore: Singapore University Press, 1987.
Serventy, Vincent. *Desert Walkabout*. Sydney: Collins, 1973.
Shepherd, Mark. *The Simpson Desert*. Sydney: Reed Books, 1992, 1994.
Shepherdson, Gordon. 'Jon Molvig: Self Portrait', *Art and Australia* 20:4 (1983), 514–15.
Shiel, Annette and Peter Spearritt (eds). *The Lie of the Land*. Melbourne: Monash University Press, 1992.
Short, John Rennie. *Imagined Country: Environment, Culture and Society*. London and New York: Routledge, 1991.
Simmons, James C. *Passionate Pilgrims: English Travellers to the World of the Desert Arabs*. New York: W. Morrow & Co., 1987.
Simpson, Colin. *Adam in Ochre: Inside Aboriginal Australia* [1951]. Sydney: Angus & Robertson, 1962, 5th edn.
Slemon, Stephen. 'Monuments of Empire: Allegory/Counter-Discourse/Post-Colonial Writing', *Kunapipi* 9:3 (1987), 1–16.
——. 'Post-Colonial Allegory and the Transformation of History', *Journal of Commonwealth Literature* 23:1 (1988), 157–68.
Smith, Bernard. *European Vision and the South Pacific* [1960]. Melbourne: Oxford University Press, 1989.
——. *Australian Painting 1788 –1970*. Melbourne: Oxford University Press, 1971.
Soja, Edward W. *Postmodern Geographies: The Reassertion of Space in Critical Social Theory* [1989]. London: Verso, 1993.
Soper, Kate. *What is Nature? Culture, Politics and the Non-Human*. Oxford: Blackwell, 1995.
Southall, Ivan. *Journey into Mystery: A Story of the Explorers Burke and Wills*. Melbourne: Lansdowne Press, 1961.
Spate, Virginia. *John Olsen*. Melbourne: Georgian House, 1963.
Spence, Lewis. *The Problem of Lemuria*. London: Rider & Co., 1933.
Spencer, W.B. *Report on the Work of the Horn Scientific Expedition to Central Australia*, 4 vols. Melbourne and London: Melville, Mullen & Slade, 1896.
Spencer, W.B. and F.J. Gillen. *The Arunta*. London: Macmillan, 1927.
Splatt, William. *Australian Landscape Painting*. Harmondsworth: Viking–Penguin, 1989.
Spurr, David. *The Rhetoric of Empire: Colonial Discourse in Journalism, Travel Writing and Imperial Administration*. Durham and London: Duke University Press, 1993.
Stafford, Barbara Maria. *Voyage into Substance: Art, Science, Nature and the Illustrated Travel Account, 1760–1840*. Boston: Massachusetts Institute of Technology Press, 1984.
Stanner, W.E.H. *On Aboriginal Religion*. Sydney: Oceania Monographs, 1963.
——. *White Man Got No Dreaming: Essays 1938–1973*. Canberra: Australian National University Press, 1979.
Stanton, J.E. *Painting the Country: Contemporary Aboriginal Art*. Perth: University of Western Australia Press, 1989.
Stanton, Jenny. *The Australian Geographic Book of the Red Centre*. Terrey Hills, NSW: Australian Geographic, 1995.
Stewart, Douglas. *Voyager Poems*. Brisbane: Jacaranda Press, 1960.
——. 'The Birdsville Track' in *Selected Poems*, pp. 129–40. Sydney: Angus & Robertson, 1973.

Stivens, Dal. 'Landscape in Australian Literature', *Westerly* 3 (1964), 46–9.

——. *A Horse of Air.* Sydney: Angus & Robertson, 1970.

Stokes, John Lort. *Discoveries in Australia With an Account of the Coast and Rivers Explored and Surveyed during the Voyage of H.M.S. Beagle in the Years 1837–1843*, 2 vols. London: T. & W. Boone, 1846.

Stow, Randolph. 'Raw Material: Some ideas for a new, epic art in an Australian setting', *Westerly* 2 (1961), 3–5.

——. *A Counterfeit Silence: Selected Poems.* Sydney: Angus & Robertson, 1969.

——. *Midnite: The Story of a Wild Colonial Boy.* Ringwood, Vic.: Penguin Books, 1969.

——. *Tourmaline* [1963]. Sydney: Angus & Robertson, 1983.

——. *To the Islands.* Sydney: Angus & Robertson, 1985.

Strehlow, T.G.H. 'Personal Monototemism in a Polytotemic Community' in *Festschrift für Ad. E. Jensen*, ed. E. Harborland, pp. 723–53. Munich: Renner, 1964.

——. *Central Australian Religion, Special Studies in Religions*, 2. Bedford Park, SA: Australian Association for the Study of Religions, 1978.

Stuart, John McDouall. *Exploration of the Interior: Diary of J.M. Stuart from March 2 to September 3, 1860.* Adelaide: SA Government Printer, 1860.

——. *Explorations in Australia: The Journals of John McDouall Stuart, During the Years 1858, 1859, 1860, 1861, & 1862; When He Fixed The Centre of The Continent and Successfully Crossed It From Sea To Sea*, ed. William Hardman. 2nd edn. London: Saunders, Otley & Co., 1865.

Sturt, Charles. *Two Expeditions into the Interior of Southern Australia, during the Years 1828, 1829, 1830, and 1831*, 2 vols. London: Smith Elder & Co., 1833.

——. *Narrative of an Expedition into Central Australia: Performed Under the Authority of Her Majesty's Government, During the Years 1844, 5, and 6; Together with a Notice of the Province of South Australia in 1847*, 2 vols. London: T. & W. Boone, 1849.

——. *Journal of the Central Australian Expedition, 1844–5*, ed. J. Waterhouse. London: Caliban Books, 1984.

Sutton, Peter (ed.). *Dreamings: The Art of Aboriginal Australia.* New York: Viking/The Asia Society Galleries, 1988.

Sweet, I.P. and I.H. Crick. *Uluru & Kata Tjuta: A Geographical History.* Canberra: Australian Geological Survey Organisation; Government Printing Services, 1992.

Tacey, David J. *Patrick White: Fiction and the Unconscious.* Melbourne: Oxford University Press, 1988.

——. *The Edge of the Sacred.* Blackburn, Vic.: HarperCollins, 1995.

Taylor, Andrew. *Reading Australian Poetry.* St Lucia, Qld: University of Queensland Press, 1987.

Taylor, Griffith. 'The Physiographic Control of Australian Exploration', *The Geographic Journal* 53 (1919), 172–92.

Taylor, Ken. *A Secret Australia: Selected and New Poems.* Melbourne: Rigmarole Books, 1977.

Thiele, Colin. *Heysen of Hahndorf.* Adelaide: Rigby, 1968.

Thomas, Margaret. 'Death in the Bush' in D.B.W. Sladen (ed.), *A Century of Australian Song*, p. 500. London: Walter Scott Publishing Co., 1888.

Thomas, Sue. 'Interracial Encounters in Katharine Susannah Prichard's *Coonardoo*', *World Literature Written in English* 27:2 (1987), 234–44.

Thompson, Christina. 'Romance Australia: Love in Australian Literature of Exploration', *Australian Literary Studies* 13:2 (1987), 161–72.

Thomson, Alistair. ' "Steadfast until Death"? C.E.W. Bean and the Representation of Australian Military Manhood', *Australian Historical Studies* 23:93 (1989), 462–78.

Tietkens, W.H. *Journal of the Central Australian Exploring and Prospecting Association's Expedition, 1889, under command of William Henry Tietkens.* Adelaide: C.E. Bristow, 1891.

Tiffin, Helen. '*Tourmaline* and the *Tao Teh Ching*: Randolph Stow's *Tourmaline*' in K.G. Hamilton (ed.), *Studies in the Australian Novel*, pp. 84–120. St Lucia, Qld: Queensland University Press, 1978.

——. 'Post-Colonial Literatures and Counter-Discourse', *Kunapipi* 9:3 (1987), 17–34.

Tinamin, George. 'One Land, One Law, One People', from *Spirit Song: A Collection of Aboriginal Poetry*, compiled by Lorraine Mafi-Williams , p. 4. Norwood, SA: Omnibus, 1993.

Tipping, Marjorie. 'The Artist as Historian', *Victorian Historical Magazine* 42:4 (1971), 679–87.

——. *Ludwig Becker: Artist and Naturalist with the Burke and Wills Expedition*. Parkville, Vic.: Melbourne University Press, 1979.

Tooley, R.V. 'The History of Australian Cartography' in *The Mapping of Australia*, ed. R.V. Tooley, pp. vii–vix. London: Holland Press Cartographica, 1979.

Tregenza, John. *George French Angas*. Art Gallery Board of SA, 1980.

——. 'The Visual Dimension of Colonial History', *Art and Australia* 19:1 (1981), 91–6.

Tuan, Yi-Fu. *Topophilia: A Study of Environmental Perception, Attitudes, and Values*. Englewood Cliffs, NJ: Prentice-Hall, 1974.

——. 'Desert and Ice: Ambivalent Aesthetics' in *Landscape, Natural Beauty and the Arts*, ed. Salim Kemal and Ivan Gaskell, pp. 143–57. Cambridge: Cambridge University Press, 1993.

Tulloch, John. *Legends of the Screen: The Narrative Film in Australia, 1919–29*. Sydney: Currency Press, 1981.

Turnbull, Henry. *Leichhardt's Second Journey: A First-Hand Account*. Sydney: Halstead Press, 1983.

Turner, Graeme. *National Fictions: Literature, Film, and the Construction of Australian Narrative*. Sydney: Allen & Unwin, 1986.

Uhl, Christopher. *Tucker*. Melbourne: Lansdowne; Australian Art Library, 1969.

Vernon, John. *The Garden and the Map: Schizophrenia in Twentieth-Century Literature and Culture*. Urbana, Chicago & London: University of Illinois Press, 1973.

von Humboldt, Alexander. *Aspects of Nature in Different Lands and Different Climes with Scientific Elucidations*, transl. Mrs Sabine, 2 vols. London: Longman, Brown, Green & Longmans, 1849.

——. *Cosmos: A Sketch of a Physical Description of the Universe*, transl. E.C. Otté, vol. I. London: Henry G. Bohn, 1849.

Wagstaff, J.M. (ed.). *Landscape and Culture: Geographical and Archaeological Perspectives*. Oxford: Blackwell, 1987.

Walker, David and Jürgen Tampke (eds). *From Berlin to the Burdekin: The German Contribution to the Development of Australian Science, Exploration and the Arts*. Kensington, NSW: UNSW Press, 1991.

Walker, Don D. 'The Western Explorer as a Literary Hero: Jedediah Smith and Ludwig Leichhardt', *Western Humanities Review* 29:3 (1975), 243–59.

Wallace-Crabbe, Robin. 'John Wolseley', *Art and Australia* (December 1978), 137–44.

Walsh, G.L. *Australia's Greatest Rock Art*. Bathurst: E.J. Brill, Robert Brown & Associates, 1988.

Walter, James (ed.). *Australian Studies: A Survey*. Melbourne: Oxford University Press, 1989.

Warburton, Peter Egerton. *Journey Across the Western Interior of Australia*, ed. H.W. Bates. London: Sampson, Low, Marston, Low & Searle, 1875.

——. *Diary of Colonel Warburton's Expedition to Western Australia, 1872–74*. South Australian Parliamentary Paper. Adelaide: SA Government Printer, 1875.

Ward, Russel. *The Australian Legend*. Melbourne: Oxford University Press, 1958.

——. 'The Australian Legend Re-Visited', *Historical Studies* 18:71 (1978), 171–90.

Watson, E.L. Grant. *The Desert Horizon*. London: Jonathan Cape, 1923.

——. *Innocent Desires*. London: Jonathan Cape, 1924.

——. *Daimon*. London: Jonathan Cape, 1925.

——. *The Mainland* [1917]. London: Jonathan Cape, 1931.

——. *The Nun and the Bandit*. London: The Cresset Press Ltd, 1935.

——. *But to What Purpose: The Autobiography of a Contemporary*. London: The Cresset Press, 1946.

Webb, Francis. *Collected Poems* [1952]. Sydney: Angus & Robertson, 1969.

341

Webby, Elizabeth. *Early Australian Poetry: An Annotated Bibliography*. Sydney: Hale & Iremonger, 1982.

Westbrook, Eric. 'Clifton Pugh', *Overland* 83 (April 1981), 62–4.

Weston, Neville. 'Provincialism, Regionalism and Nationalism in Australian and English Painting', in *Readings in Australian Arts: Papers from 1976; Exeter Symposium*, ed. P. Quartermaine, pp. 62–73. Exeter: University of Exeter, 1978.

Westwood, Bryan. 'Tim Storrier, 1981', *Art and Australia* 19:3 (1982), 305–10.

White, Hayden. 'The Discourse of History', *Humanities in Society* 2:1 (1979), 1–15.

White, Patrick. 'The Prodigal Son' in Geoffrey Dutton and Max Harris (eds), *Australian Letters* 1:3 (1958).

——. *Voss*. Harmondsworth: Penguin Books, 1963.

——. *Patrick White Letters*, ed. David Marr. Sydney: Random House, 1994.

White, Richard. *Inventing Australia: Images and Identity 1688–1980*. Sydney: George Allen & Unwin, 1981.

Whitlock, Gillian and Gail Reekie (eds). *Uncertain Beginnings: Debates in Australian Studies*. St Lucia, Qld: University of Queensland Press, 1993.

Wilkes, G.A. (ed.). *Ten Essays on Patrick White, Selected from* Southerly (1964–7). Sydney: Angus & Robertson, 1970.

Williams, George. *Wilderness and Paradise in Christian Thought*. New York: Harper & Bros, 1962.

Williamson, Kirstin. 'The Artist's Eye in the Desert', *The National Times* (November 1–7, 1981), 39.

Willis, Anne-Marie. *Illusions of Identity: The Art of Nation*. Sydney: Hale & Iremonger, 1993.

Wilson, Laura. 'Burke and Wills', *Town and Country Journal* 75 (2037) (17 February 1909), 16.

Wilson, S.C. 'From Shadow Into Light' in *South Australian Women Artists Since Colonisation*, pp. 142–3. Adelaide: Pagel Books, 1988.

Wolseley, John. *Nomadism: Twelve Years in Australia*. Melbourne: Melbourne University Press, 1988.

Wright, John Kirtland. 'Map Makers are Human: Comments on the Subjective in Maps' in *Human Nature in Geography: Fourteen Papers, 1925–1965*, pp. 33–52. Cambridge MA: Harvard University Press, 1966.

Wright, Judith. *Preoccupations in Australian Poetry*. Melbourne: Oxford University Press, 1966.

——. 'Landscape and Dreaming' in Stephen R. Graubard (ed.), *Australia: The Daedalus Symposium*, pp. 29–56. Sydney: Angus & Robertson, 1985.

Young, Jess. 'Recent Journey of Exploration Across the Continent of Australia; Its Deserts, Native Races, and Natural History', *Journal of American Geographic Society of New York* 10 (1878), 116–41.

347